Virtual Serial Port Cookbook

FTDI FT232R USB UART
C# and Visual Basic Express

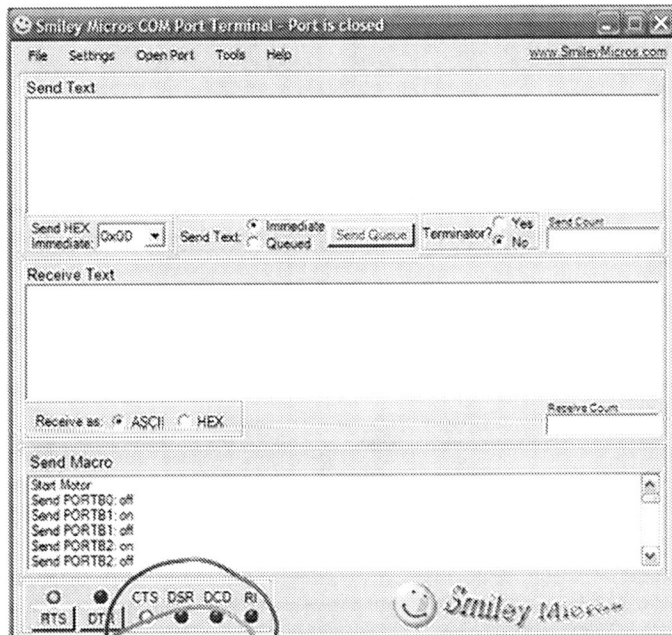

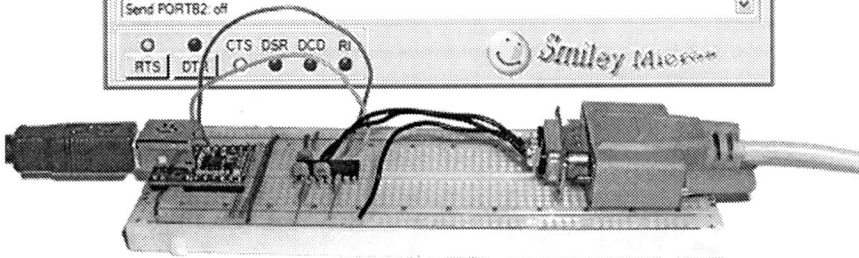

Joe Pardue
SmileyMicros.com

Smiley Micros
5601 Timbercrest Trail
Knoxville, TN 37909
Email: book@SmileyMicros.com
Web: http://www.SmileyMicros.com

ISBN 978-0-9766822-1-9

Chapter 1: Introduction

Why would you be interested in this book?

You'd be interested because you want to use a PC to communicate with a microcontroller, or is you want to use a USB port to do some limited digital I/O.

A microcontroller is usually a small cheap square black lump used to control something. The something could be the ignition timing on your car; the water temperature in your washing machine; the obnoxious tune (that you think is cute) on your cell phone; etc. etc. etc... The word 'ubiquitous' seems almost invented to describe the current uses of microcontrollers: they really are everywhere and the average westerner owns dozens without ever thinking about it.

Most often the microcontroller knows how to do its job and doesn't need any advice from you. If it does deign to accept suggestions, you usually give them via a button (snooze alarm) or touch pad (microwave oven). But some of us, mostly students, hobbyists, and developers, want to spend a lot of time in conversation with a microcontroller. This may be because we want to learn how it works, or get it to follow complex commands that aren't easy to give with buttons, or because we are designing a complex system and we need direct access to the micro's brains while we are trying to figure out why things aren't working like they are supposed to. If you are one of these folks then you might see the benefit of being able to use the vast resources of a PC (if you are using Windows©, perhaps 'half-vast' would be more appropriate?) to carry on a conversation with a microcontroller. This book tries to provide part of the information you can use to do this using the FTDI FT232R USB-UART and Microsoft's free C# and Visual Basic Express .NET programming software.

Caveat Emptor! What this book isn't about:

This book **IS NOT ABOUT USB**; it IS about using the Windows© USB port drivers from FTDI as a virtual PC serial port – without having to know ANYTHING about USB other than which end of the cable to use. All the information given also can be used with a legacy RS232 serial port, if you happen to have one.

In summary: if you are looking for a book about USB – THIS ISN'T IT!

Also, please note that the software is presented in both C# and Visual Basic Express .NET and was written by a guy who learned to program in the dark ages (yes, I have used switches to program a computer) so my programming skills are 'evolved' meaning that I learned as I went along and many of the bad habits I picked up along the way persist. This is another way of saying that I did not get a Computer Science degree (I did get BSEE) and did not learn Object Oriented Programming at the knee of an OOP Guru. I hacked along trying to make a living and learning only what seemed vital to get that next paycheck. So, since C# and Visual Basic Express .NET are object oriented, you may find that my examples don't look exactly like what you'd find in a textbook. It all works, but I'm sure to hear some comments about how I didn't properly instantiate the virtual class inheritance frakenbloogit and I'll just respond – "hey read the introduction of the book – I never claimed to be an OOP Guru, I'm just a poor smuck trying to use the tools to get a job done." Constructive comments are always welcome.

Okay, so what IS the book about?

Coming up with a title for this book was not easy. The book is, on the highest level, about methods for communicating between a PC and a Microcontroller – and at a slightly lower level - using a FTDI FT232R USB UART integrated circuit device to fake a USB connection into imitating a RS232 serial port using a Virtual COM Port AND using C# OR Visual Basic .NET to create graphical user interface software for doing the communicating on the PC-side.

Well now, that's a mouth full and how does one distill all that into a catchy title? Since the book isn't about USB, and it isn't about an old fashioned RS232 style serial port, and it isn't about programming in either C# or Visual Basic, then the book really isn't about this or that but about something in between. Bottom line is that this book is sort of a cookbook for communicating between a PC and a Microcontroller, and has lots and lots of software and hardware examples.

There is a lot of code here in C# and Visual Basic Express that allows you to build Graphical User Interfaces and add Serial Port functions to create communications programs. PC-side Serial Port hardware is based on the FTDI

FT232R USB UART IC for creating a Virtual COM Port. And, not to complicate things, the last part of the book will cover non-serial communication features of the FT232R, such as bit-banged input/output. So what have we got?

Part 1 – Serial Port via USB Made Almost Easy
In the first section you will learn the basics of serial communications using a USB UART bridge. You will further learn to write a simple terminal program in C# and Visual Basic Express .NET.

Part 2 – PC ⇔ Microcontroller Conversations
In the second section you will build on what you have learned and get into more details about GUI programming, using the SerialPort class, and some useful software tools such as XML. You will bring it all together by building a Developer Terminal, which will have most of the bells and whistles that you would want for communicating between a PC and a microcontroller. You will end this section with some neat hardware experiments.

Part 3 – The FTDI FT232R
In the final section you will chuck the serial port paradigm and communicate directly with the FT232R. You will learn how to use the Smiley Micros version of the FTDI D2XX driver, you will do some more hardware experiments bit-banging the BBUSB pins, and finally you will build a software programmer for the FT232R.

What is the Bread Board USB (BBUSB)?

BBUSB

Smiley Micros BBUSB:
- Provides a Virtual COM Port to (imitates legacy PC serial ports)
- FTDI F232R USB UART IC single chip USB solution.
- Provides UART voltage levels of either 5v or 3.3v (not RS232 voltages*)
- Easy to use, royalty-free FTDI drivers for Windows, Linux, and Mac.
  o PC Virtual COM Port drivers for legacy serial communications with microcontroller UARTs.
  o Bit-bang mode using special drivers and software.
- 14 I/O lines for use with RS-232, bit-bang, or special function modes.
- Provides USB Bus power of 5 V or regulated 3.3 V at up to 500 mA.
- Unique serial number for security dongle applications using FTDIChip-ID™.
- Clock generator to drive microcontrollers (6, 12, 24, and 48 MHz).
- LED drivers to show serial traffic.
- Cute as a puppy.
- Available from www.smileymicros.com for a pittance,

*Please note that the BBUSB does not output RS232 voltage levels, instead it outputs UART voltage levels of either 5v or 3.3v, which is a good thing if you are connecting directly to a microcontroller UART. One of the big problems with store bought USB to Serial Port converters is that in order to use them with a microcontroller you have to convert from the RS232 voltages levels to the UART voltage level. However, if you want to imitate a 'real' RS232 Serial Port, including voltages levels, then Smiley Micros provides a USB RS-232 Voltage Level Conversion Kit if you need RS232 voltage levels.

The Breadboard USB (BBUSB) allows you to use your PC to communicate with AND power a breadboard project. You have two choices for communicating: either use the VCP (Virtual COM Port) drivers for serial ports, or use the Smiley Micros version of the FTDI D2XX Direct Drivers from a special Dynamic Link Library (DLL) to directly control access to the USB device and pin I/O. You can also provide your project with either 5 or 3.3V, up to 500mA from the PC USB cable, or you can choose to power the BBUSB and your project from your own power supply.

The BBUSB can be used in any application requiring a drop-in serial communications module, since it has standard .1" by .7" pin spacing. We use gold-plated square header pins that are longer and much more sturdy than usual IC pins or ordinary 'stamp' type board pins making our board ideal for use with breadboards.

Why use C# and Visual Basic .NET ?

One good reason is because they are free. You like free don't you?

Also I decided to present the software in both C# and Visual Basic .NET because there are lots of folks who program in one of the languages and think the other language is the vile realm of Hell-bound heretics. Since the concepts that are being programmed are the same no matter what language is being used (religious wars aside), examples are given in both languages with the C# example given first, followed by the Visual Basic example. Just skip over the language that will damn your immortal soul.

You will notice that Microsoft says that both C# and Visual Basic Express are 'easy to use', 'fun', and 'easy to learn'. Hopefully you've been around long enough to know about Microsoft hype. Though, C# and Visual Basic are all three of those things compared to earlier methods of creating a Graphical User Interface (GUI – pronounced gooey) to communicate with external serial devices. But this is a little like saying a root-canal is 'easy' or 'fun' compared to thumbscrews.

We won't go deep in explaining the fundamentals of how to use C# or Visual Basic, since the Microsoft web site does provide some good materials for getting started. Mostly what you will find in this book is useful source code that you can use as a basis for your projects, or you can just use them as they are and skip learning C# or Visual Basic. That said, if you really want to learn C# or Visual Basic, you'll find that in just a few hours you can learn enough to do useful work (or be dangerous), so if you have the time and inclination don't let my root-canal comment put you off – think of this book as a shot of Novocain and start drilling.

To talk to the microcontroller you will want PC-side software to provide you with a GUI that lets you easily send information to the microcontroller using virtual buttons, checkboxes, and text boxes. The microcontroller's responses can be shown in textboxes, charts, graphs, singing dancing ninja sprites, or whatever your imagination and programming skills can convince the PC to show. You will also need a communication channel between the PC and your microcontroller, which in our case will be a Virtual COM Port using USB, and, of course, you'll want to do this with our BBUSB hardware - though any serial port hardware should work.

You will need one or the other of:

The Free Microsoft C# 2005 Express Edition from:
http://msdn.microsoft.com/vstudio/express/visualcsharp/

The Free Microsoft Visual Basic 2005 Express Edition from:
http://msdn.microsoft.com/vstudio/express/vb

Why the Heck Imitate a PC Serial Port with USB?

In the olden days the PC serial port had a windows software serial port driver and hardware link based on the RS232 electrical specification and used a DB-9 connector and a UART (Universal Asynchronous Receiver Transmitter). It wasn't exactly simple for a novice PC user to hook up a serial link since it required the user to select software interrupts and set hardware jumpers, something you and I, as certifiable geeks, like to do, but something that normal people hate and tend to screw up. These and other complications led to the development of the Plug and Play initiative (more commonly and correctly known as Plug and Pray). One part of all this was to replace the serial port with USB to help simplify things, which it did for the user, but made the developer's life (yours and mine) MUCH more complicated. USB also obsoletes lots of perfectly good serial devices and a couple of decades of knowledge of how to do robust RS232 style serial communications between PCs and external serial devices.

I've read the USB specification, and I'm here to testify (brother amen) that the old ComPort/UART/RS232 was a piece of cake compared to USB. I worked with USB when it first came out and my brain is worse for the wear, but fortunately some genius's thought that they would simplify the life of not just the user but the developer by creating a transitional concept, that is: to have an old fashioned

RS232 style serial port that runs over USB. The FTDI folks call this a Virtual Communications Port (VCP). It allows legacy applications to continue to use the old microcontroller code and the windows serial port software with the USB part all tidily bound up in a black box that the developer doesn't have to open. These transitional devices give us the best of both worlds: the ease of using the serial port and the ubiquity of using USB. The developer has the option of adding RS232 level converts to completely emulate the old way of doing things, or leaving the level converters off and outputting voltage levels directly compatible with a microcontroller's UART.

The FTDI solution to this problem is to dedicate a microcontroller to accept USB data and translate it into UART type data. They also have learned along the way that this 'dedicated' microcontroller can also have some features that aren't really part of either USB or UART. For example the FT232R has pins that can be used to twiddle indicator LEDs, bit-bang I/O, contain a unique serial number (security dongle anyone?), or even provide a clock and power for another microcontroller. All this adds not only to easing the job of communication between the PC and an external serial device it also adds complexity that can at times be quite, well... complex. We'll address some of the complexity in the third section of this book.

Who is this book for?

This book has two primary audiences. The geriatric types (like me) who grew up with serial ports and want to make the transition to USB as painless as possible. And the newbie who just popped into the world of 21st century digital electronics and wants an easy way to learn how to get a PC to communicate with an external device. With such a broad audience, naturally we will frustrate both, so be warned: you'll probably think all this is too simple or too complicated and you'll be right on both counts.

Is this the best approach for a newbie?

There may be a bit of discussion on whether the USB serial port bridge technique is best for the newbie (someone not already familiar with PC <=> Microcontroller communications via RS232) since they could learn to use a PC built-in USB driver, like the Human Interface Driver (HID) and then work directly with USB without the extra layer of complexity the bridge seems to add. I will assert that the extra bridge layer turns the USB into a black box and hides most of the USB complexity while providing a higher layer that, while admittedly somewhat arcane, is nonetheless simpler to use than straight USB. My assertion could be a result of my above mentioned geriatric state of mind, but it also may be due to my own personal frustrations with USB and my perception what I'm presenting here really is easier. I welcome comments on this prejudice of mine.

One major disadvantage of going the pure USB route does need to be mentioned: USB devices require a Vendor ID that costs $1500 renewable every two years. When you use an FTDI device, they let you use their Vendor ID and will give you Product ID that allows Windows© to uniquely identify your device.

And a caution...

This book will have typos, unclear passages, and errors. I will make corrections as they are reported to me and you can find them in the errata section of this book's web page on www.smileymicros.com. You may be the first to find a problem and if you want to be helpful to the community of readers who will use this book, you can report the problem by email to: error@smileymicro.com.

Finally, the purpose of this book is NOT to completely explain either USB or serial ports – for that go to www.lvr.com and buy Jan Axelson's excellent books on the subject.

Chapter 2: BBUSB Quick Start Guide

This chapter will help us get started with the Smiley Micros BBUSB breakout board for the FTDI FT232R USB UART. This board will be used for all the software and hardware experiments in this book.

Layout and Schematic

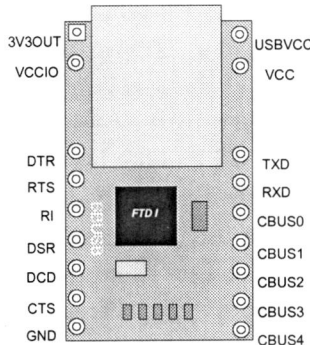

Top view showing pin locations.

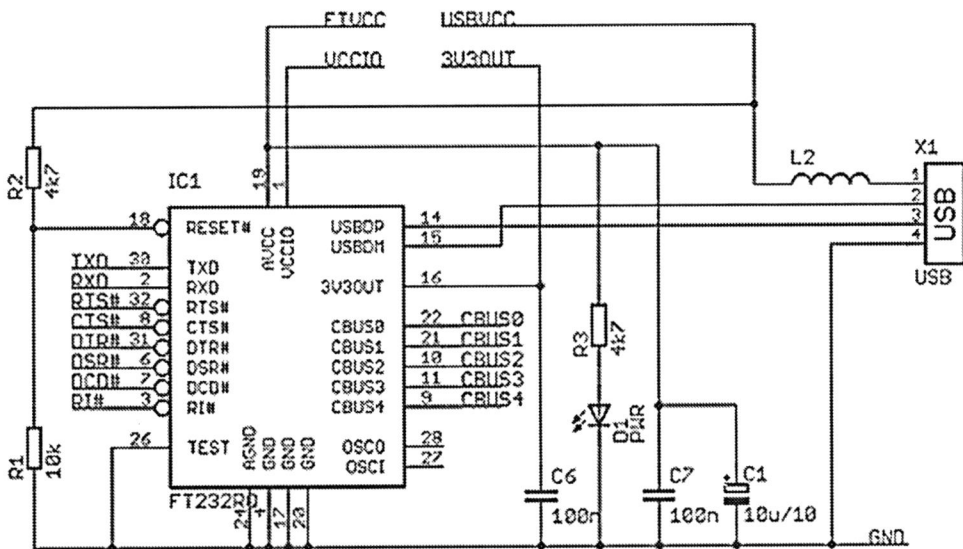

Schematics.

Power

The USB Bus can provide up to 500 mA power to a USB device, but certain rules must be followed. Violating the rules can result in your PC assuming a USB Bus power fault and the PC will then shutdown (no warning, just a black screen and bye-bye to all your unsaved work – this is not an official 'fact' but a personal observation). Save your work frequently when playing with these devices and be prepared to reboot your system.

The USB peripheral tells the USB host how much power it needs in 100mA units up to 500mA. It cannot use more than 100mA while starting up before making a request for more power. And the USB host can deny the peripheral's request for more power. Also, if the USB Host tells the peripheral to go into suspend mode, it must not use more than 500 uA. This can get complex. For instance, a device off a bus-powered hub cannot use more than 100 mA, but you can have hubs with external power that can supply the full 500 mA. For the quick start guide, we will assume that the device is powered either directly from a PC or from an externally powered hub so that we can use up to 500 mA.

Power Wiring:

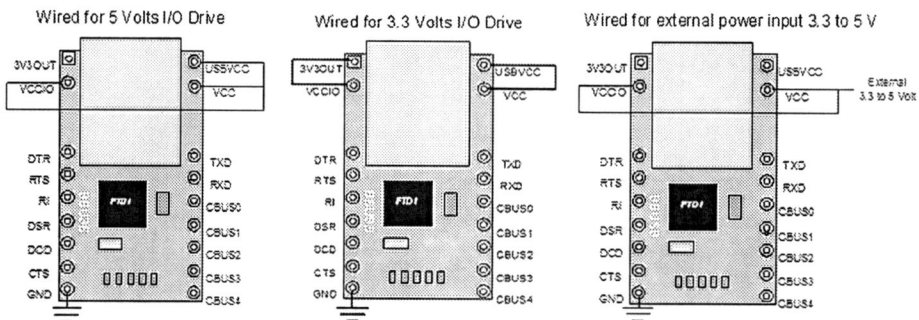

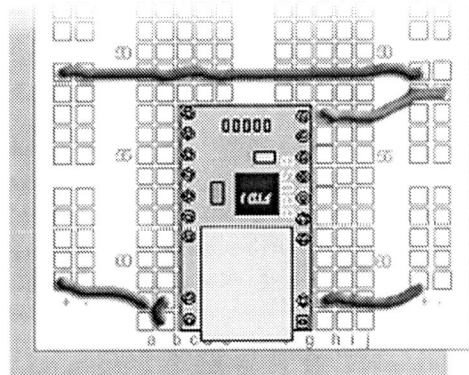

Breadboard Wired for USB Bus 5V

Loop-back Test

Wiring for the loop-back test:

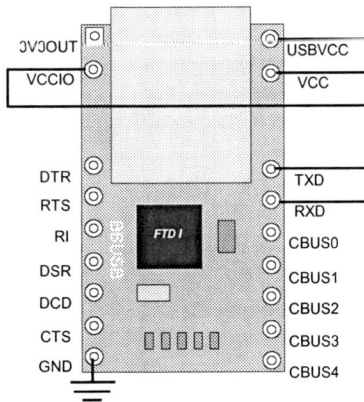

19

- Wire up the BBUSB as in the illustrations above. The capacitor shown isn't really needed for this test.
- Plug a USB cable into your PC and the BBUSB.
- If you are using XP, the following window will appear:

- Click the 'No, not this time' radio button. Actually, I'd prefer a less polite 'Heck NO! Not now not never!!!' option, but it isn't available. Click the 'Next' button and the following window will appear:

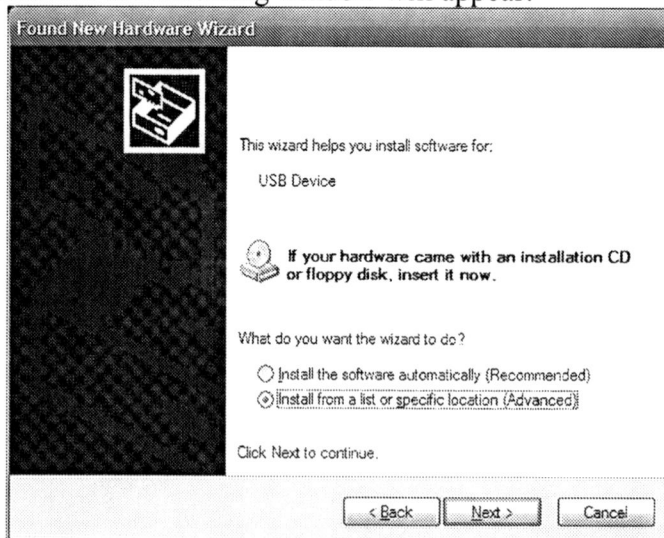

- Select the 'Install from a list or specific location (Advanced) radio button, then click the 'Next' button and the following window will appear:

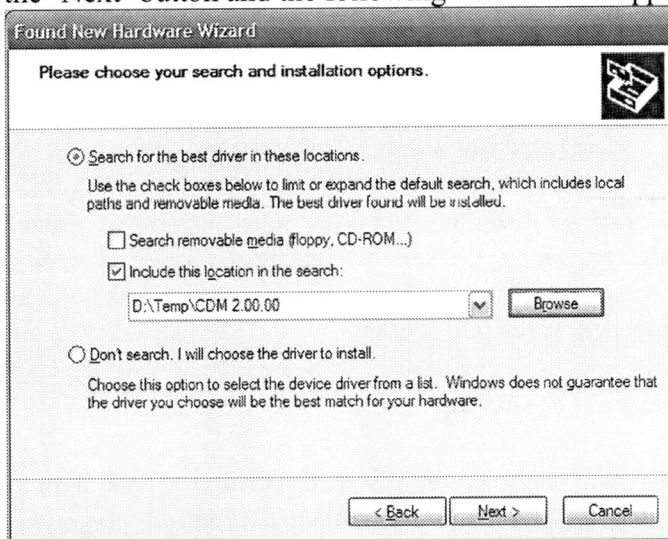

- Click the 'Browse' button and locate the CDM 2.00.00 directory, which contains the FTDI drivers. You can find the FTDI software used in this book in www.smileymicros.com downloads section, or the newest version at www.ftdichip.com. Click the 'Next' button and the following window will appear:

- Click Finish and the following balloon will pop up:

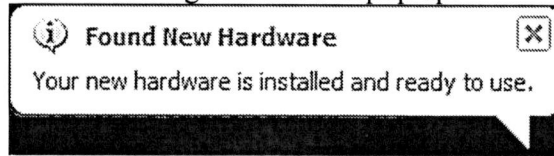

- And be shocked to see that the very first Windows Form in the above sequence pops up again. Rather than waste the space showing all the above forms again, just note that two sets of drivers are installed and this second round will proceed exactly as above.

The Simple Terminal Software:

- You do have .NET Framework 2.0 installed don't you? You will find out as soon as you try to open Simple Terminal (located in www.smileymicros.com downloads section) in the next step. If Simple Terminal opens then you have .NET, if it doesn't then get it at:
  http://msdn.microsoft.com/vstudio/downloads/default.aspx
- Open SimpleTerminalby clicking on SimpleTerm.exe.

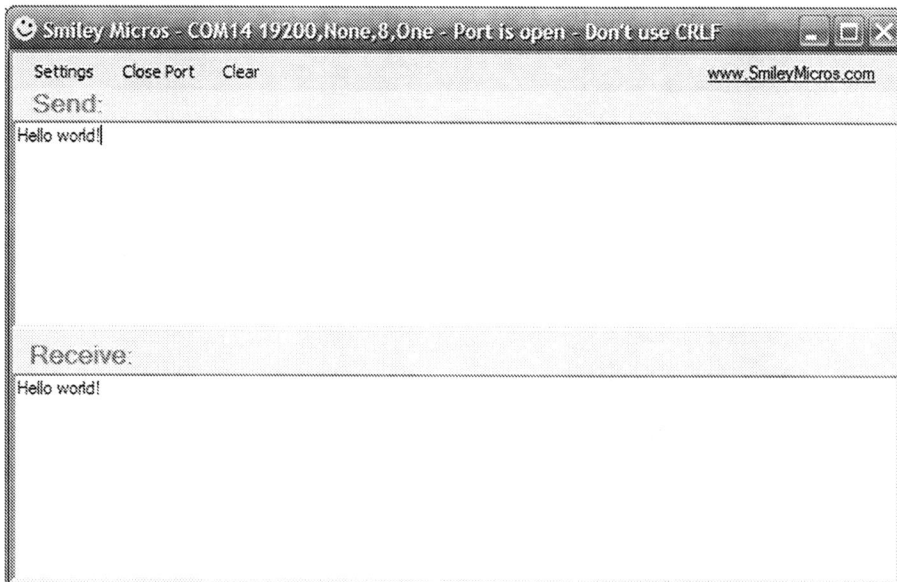

- Click on the Settings menu item
- You should see the Settings form, which will list all your serial port devices. In this case, we select COM10. Your case will probably be different. If you have multiple choices and aren't sure which to choose, unplug your BBUSB, then look at the Settings again to see which one disappeared. Then plug it back in and select that port.

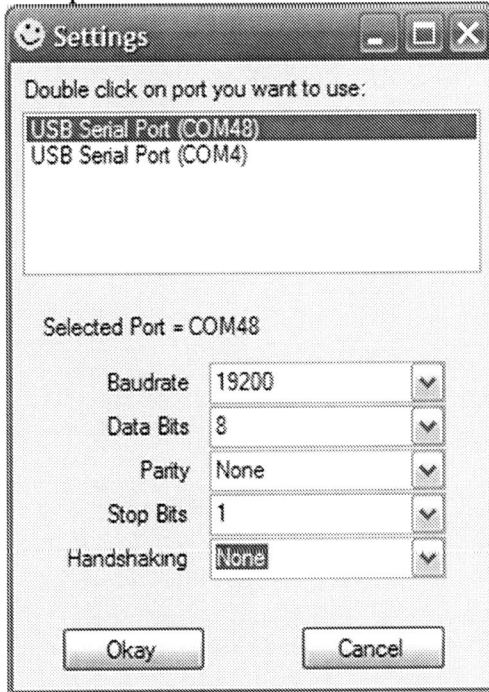

- Click the Okay button.
- Type 'Hello world!" into the Send window and you should see 'Hello world!' appear in the receive window.
- Now you know the hardware and software work.

In this chapter we got started with the Smiley Micros BBUSB (BreadBoard USB). In the next chapter we will get a very brief introduction to the history of serial communications to help us understand were some of the weird terminology came from.

Chapter 2: BBUSB Quick Start Guide

Chapter 3: A VERY Brief History of Serial Communications

Why do we call the communication speed 'Baud rate'? Why does a serial connector have ring indicator pin? Why does a PC keyboard have a 'Ctrl' (control) key? Frankly a lot of the hardware and software terminology for serial communications seems weird when seen out of the context of how we arrived at today's serial communication techniques. This section skims the surface of a large topic primarily to show how some of the terms we will be using came to pass.

Samuel F.B. Morse

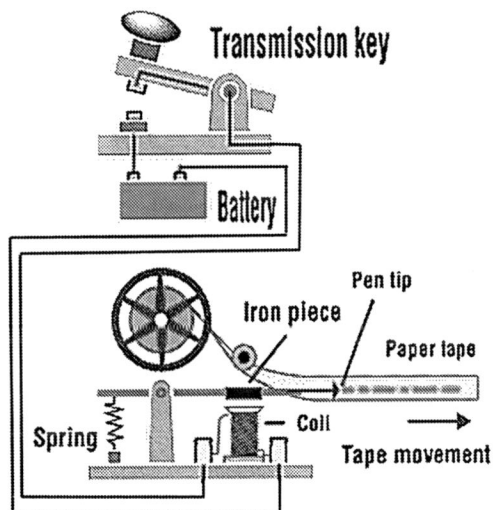

Morse Self Portrait (yes he was an artist) and his Telegraph Machine

Morse patented the Telegraph in 1840. The name comes from the Greek tele = far away and graphos = writing, and true to its name, the original telegraph machine 'wrote' with dots and dashes on paper.

Morse's real invention was not the transmitter or receiver, which were based on devices that were being played with in electric laboratories of the time. His contribution was a binary code that allowed characters to be sent as a serial stream of electric signals. He made the most commonly used characters, such as A, E, and T into the simpler codes and the less commonly used, such as Q, X, and Z into the more complex code.

```
A ● ▬          N ▬ ●          1 ● ▬ ▬ ▬ ▬
B ▬ ● ● ●      O ▬ ▬ ▬        2 ● ● ▬ ▬ ▬
C ▬ ● ▬ ●      P ● ▬ ▬ ●      3 ● ● ● ▬ ▬
D ▬ ● ●        Q ▬ ▬ ● ▬      4 ● ● ● ● ▬
E ●            R ● ▬ ●        5 ● ● ● ● ●
F ● ● ▬ ●      S ● ● ●        6 ▬ ● ● ● ●
G ▬ ▬ ●        T ▬            7 ▬ ▬ ● ● ●
H ● ● ● ●      U ● ● ▬        8 ▬ ▬ ▬ ● ●
I ● ●          V ● ● ● ▬      9 ▬ ▬ ▬ ▬ ●
J ● ▬ ▬ ▬      W ● ▬ ▬        0 ▬ ▬ ▬ ▬ ▬
K ▬ ● ▬        X ▬ ● ● ▬
L ● ▬ ● ●      Y ▬ ● ▬ ▬
M ▬ ▬          Z ▬ ▬ ● ●
```

Emile Baudot

Emile Baudot picture on a French phone card.

In 1874 Emile Baudot invented a 5-bit binary code that used a 5-key transmitter. By using mechanical clockworks the 5-bits were shifted out onto a single wire and used by the receiving station to print a character on paper. 5-bits can uniquely encode 32 characters. Later modifications to Baudot's code changed the code to 26 character codes and 6 control codes. Two of the control codes were used to select either a 26-letter code or a 26-number/punctuation-code table. The remaining 4 control codes were used for mechanical instructions to control the remote printer. With this new code an operator could cause the remote printer to print 52 characters and could also control where on the paper the character was printed.

If you wonder why this matters, look at your computer's keyboard and note the Ctrl key. That is the control key and is used to alter the meaning of the rest of the keyboard in much the same way as was done by Baudot's apparatus which is a direct ancestor of your keyboard. Also, when we transmit something we will use the ASCII code and we will see that we have lots of atavistic printer control codes such as CR (Carriage Return), LF (Line Feed), and BEL (for bell, as in dingaling) [See Appendix 1: ASCII Table] and we might wonder why we need such 'characters' in our attempts to send data between a PC and a microcontroller since neither has a carriage, a roller, or a dingalinger. Now you know.

Baud rate refers to the number of unique symbols that can be transmitted per second –the physical ability of the system to change states each second. There is often some confusion in the use of Bd (Baud) and bps (bits-per-second). The bps refers to the amount of information that can be transmitted each second. If each physical state change represents a bit of information then Bd = bps. And while this often is not the case, in our use where one state change represents one bit of data then we will use them interchangeable.

Teletype Machines

WAC Teletype operators during World War II.

Baudot's invention evolved into the Teletype machine, an electro-mechanical typewriter that could act as both a transmitter and receiver of text messages over long distances.

In early computers a Teletype machine was used to enter characters that were punched into cards or paper tape for loading programs into computers. [During WWII the Colossus computer at Bletchley Park was used to crack encrypted German Teletype messages.] Eventually, direct connections were developed to allow the Teletype to function much like a PC keyboard.

The illustration above shows Dennis Ritchie, inventor of the C programming language standing next to Ken Thompson, inventor of Unix, designing the original Unix operating system at Bell Labs on a PDP-11 using a Teletype machine to 'talk' to the computer.

RS232 and Modems

The Telegraph and Teletype machines used a binary (on or off) signal to transmit and receive data. However, the world was wired not for binary signals, but for telephones that send analog signal (voice - 300 to 3400 Hz). During the 1950's folks figured out how to allow binary signals to be sent over these plain old telephone lines by acoustic frequency MOdulating and DEModulating the signal, thus the name modem.

The RS232 standard was written to allow Teletype machines, which were referred to as DTE (Data Terminal Equipment) to link to a modem, referred to as DCE (Data Communication Equipment) that could then transmit the binary data from a Teletype machine over a phone line to a distant computer. There were several iterations of this standard but by 1969 RS232C became 'the' standard that would eventually be adopted (sort of) by Microsoft for the PC serial port. The 'sort of' is necessary since the PC isn't exactly 100% pure, but close enough that the PC serial port became often known as the RS232 port. The port has 9 pins. Data is transmitted on the TxD pin and received on the RxD pin. Six additional pins are used to control the communications between the PC and the modem. They are the DCD, DSR, DTR, RTS, CTS, and RI, which we'll learn a lot more about later. The serial port was originally intended to be used with modems, but designers found that it could also be used to communicate with other peripheral devices such as mice, drawing pads, oscilloscopes, etc. thus leading to our more generic use for communicating with microcontrollers.

The section has provided a very brief introduction to some of the history that has lead to the arcane terminology we will be using later in the book.

Now you know that we call the communication speed 'Baud rate' after Emile Baudot; that a serial connector has ring indicator pin because the original connector was meant to attach to a modem and use a telephone line which 'rings' when a call comes in; that a PC keyboard has a 'Ctrl' (control) key because it evolved from Baudot's original keyboard; and that any other weird term you come across probably has a historic reason for being used.

In the next three chapters we will learn to create a Simple Terminal for serial port communication using the BBUSB, or any serial port device for that matter.

Chapter 3: A VERY Brief History of Serial Communications

Chapter 4: Simple Terminal - GUI

Source code electronic files for Simple Terminal may be downloaded from the download menu of www.smileymicros.com.

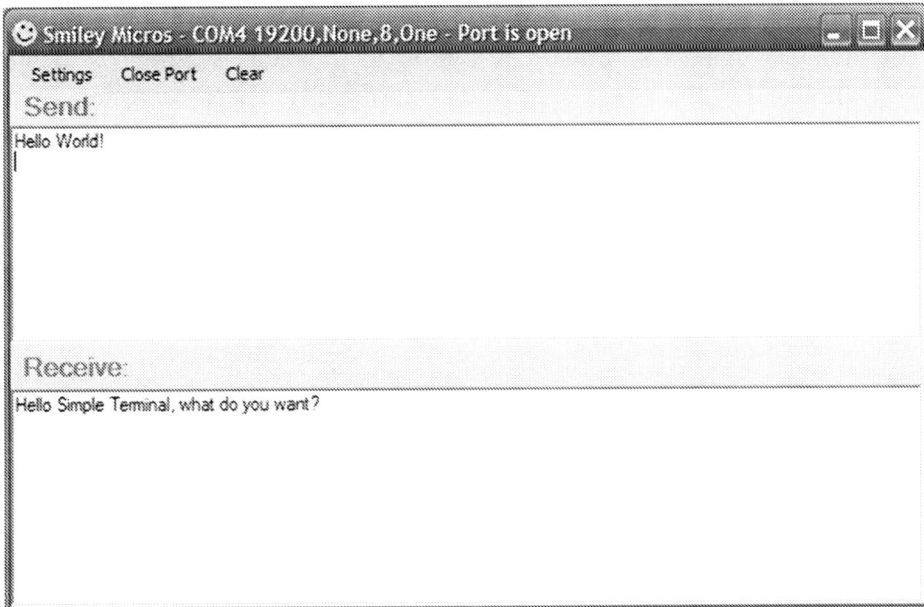

In the next three chapters we will learn enough to create a simple terminal program. By the time we get through the simple terminal software you will likely have forgotten what we are trying to do here. This book isn't just about software, it's also about hardware control and the software is only one element (and King Kong was just one gorilla). If you are new to programming on a PC, this is a significant hurdle to get over, so be prepared to spend a lot of time on this, but try to keep in mind the ultimate goal: We are learning to use tools that will allow us to build GUIs on a PC that we can use to communicate with microcontrollers connected to either a real serial port or a USB Virtual Serial Port. The book will focus intensely on the latter as we go along and the examples are all given using Smiley Micros's BBUSB product.

In this chapter we are going to get into creating GUIs on a PC using C# or Visual Basic Express. If you have already done some PC GUI programming, say in C++, you are gonna think you've died and gone to Heaven, since both C# and Visual Basic Express are sooooo much easier. Either way, the first part of your learning is up to you. We won't go over introductory stuff for C# or Visual Basic Express, since Microsoft, very unlike itself, has provided lots of really good and useful free (FREE!) materials.

If you are entirely new at programming GUIs on Windows then I'd like to suggest that you consider using C#, since it is similar to C which is likely the language you will choose for the other side of the cable: the microcontroller, which I personally prefer for many religious reasons, including having written a book on the subject.

If you already use C, then you probably want to start with C#, remembering that the 'C' in C# really means 'Java', but Microsoft didn't want to pay so, since Java is C-like why not...' (okay, reading the Microminds is a pain, but you get the idea – C# is closer to Java than C, but since Java is a C-like language it really doesn't matter).

If you are already a microcontroller BASIC fan, then you will probably want to use the Visual Basic Express, **BUT** do be prepared for a lot of culture shock.

The IDE shown in many following illustrations will be for C#, but the Visual Basic IDE is virtually identical, so it shouldn't be difficult to transpose the concepts.

I hesitate to put web links in a book because the link will likely go bad before the book does, so be ready to do some searching on your own for similar materials if the stuff I'm recommending and providing links for goes away.

For C# Express:
http://msdn.microsoft.com/vstudio/express/visualcsharp/easytolearn

For Visual Basic Express:
http://msdn.microsoft.com/vstudio/express/vb/easytolearn/

These resources are really great! I already knew how to program in C# and thought I'd skim some of this as a review. Instead I went through all 16 hours of free video and learned a lot (mainly that I didn't know as much as I thought I did). For our purposes, you don't need to view all the lessons, just the introductory materials and the parts on forms, and common controls. This is great stuff and it is free (shock!) What's with all the free stuff from Microsoft; did the Tin Man get a heart? So, to the tune of Wizard of Oz: *We're off to learn C# the wonderful C# of Microsoft... OR We're off to learn Visual Basic the wonderful Visual Basic of Microsoft...* Depending on which you choose. Either way, watch for flying monkeys.

So put a bookmark on this page and go learn some stuff. See you in a day or so…

Time passes… dear reader learns…

Okay, now that you have a good feel for the C# or Visual Basic Express IDE and can build simple forms with textboxes and buttons you are ready to look at the Simple Terminal software source code. Pay careful attention as we go through the steps to create this program. We will go into greater detail for the Simple Terminal program, but other than this and your studies of free Microsoft materials we will assume that you don't need as much hand holding and the subsequent software will have much less detailed explanations.

How is the Simple Terminal source code organized?

We are going to try to think about the software as being made of two conceptually separate parts: the Graphical User Interface, GUI, which we see on the PC screen and conceptually separate the underlying communication code which does the real work we are interested in.

Where to start?

You have two basic options at this point. One, you could just go to the \Software\Chapter4 – Simple Terminal\Simple Term GUI Only directory and open the Simple Terminal source code in C# or Visual Basic Express and start looking at how I coded things. Two, after running the Simple Terminal executable to see how Simple Terminalworks; you could build a similar GUI from scratch while following the cookbook-like instructions in this book and only look at my code when you run into problems. In my opinion the second method is best and it's how I often try to learn new software, but either way will be fine. I usually build the GUI first and test it leaving out all the underlying functionality (except for a messageBoxes) until I'm sure the GUI looks and works properly. I usually test each GUI function by having a messageBox respond to my input. For instance, I'd have the menu 'Settings' button generate a "Settings Button Pressed" message. Later I'd remove the messageBox and add 'real' code.

Build the Graphical User Interface

The Main Form

- Open C# or Visual Basic 2005 Express, they are nearly identical so all the following introduction to the IDE, though in C# Express, works equally well for either.
- From the 'File' menu select 'New Project:

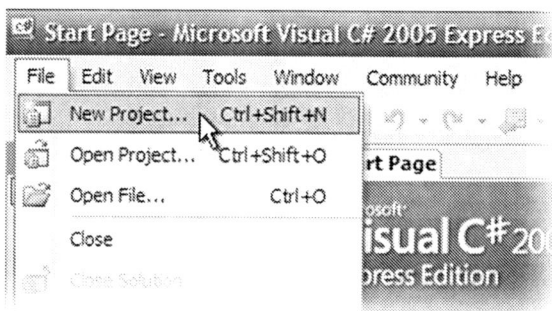

- In the 'New Project' form, highlight Windows Application and change the name to Simple Terminaland click the 'OK' button:

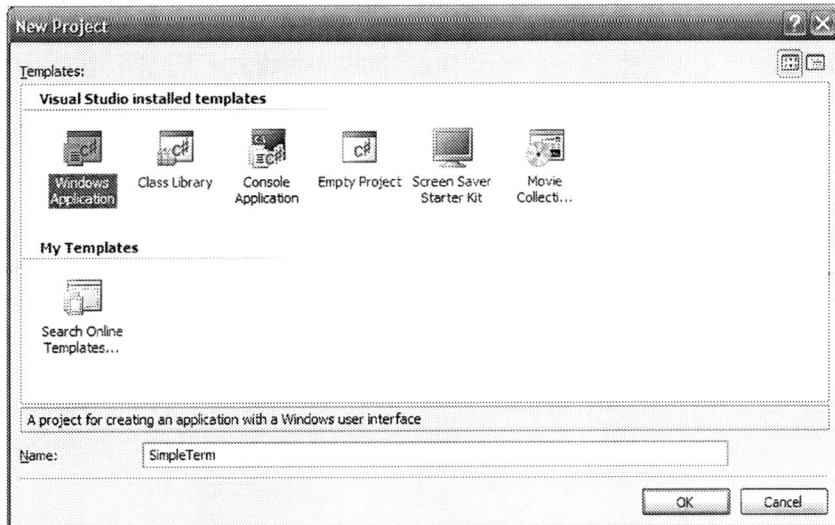

- The IDE should look like:

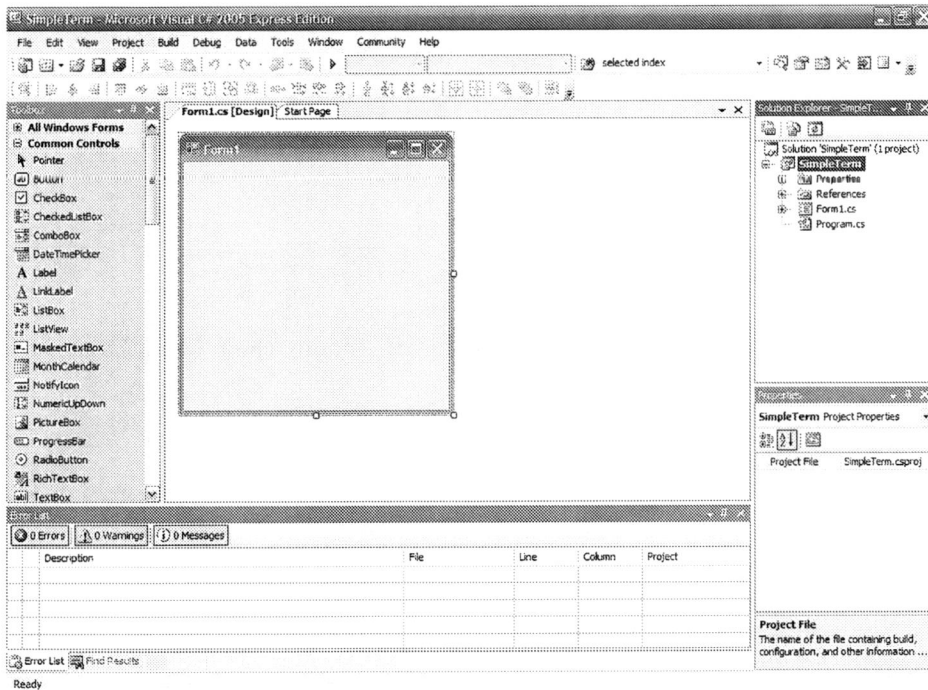

- Take note of the various panels. We will call the central panel the 'Editor Window', the left panel the 'Toolbox', the upper right panel the 'Solutions Explorer', the lower right panel the 'Properties Window'.
- In the Properties Window change the size from 300,300 to 600,380:

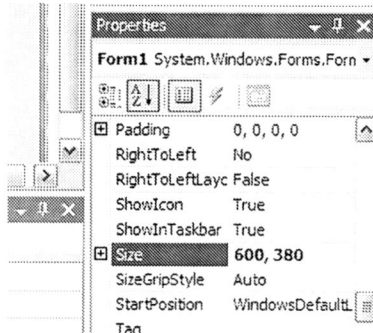

- In the Toolbox click and hold the MenuStrip then drag and drop it on Form1.

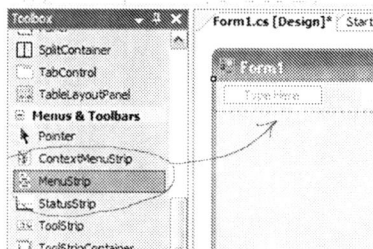

- Note that the specific instance menuStrip1 of the class MenuStrip appears below Form1 in the Edit Window.

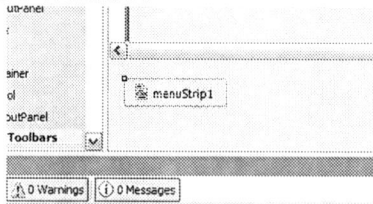

- In the Toolbox click and hold the RichTextBox then drag and drop it on Form1.

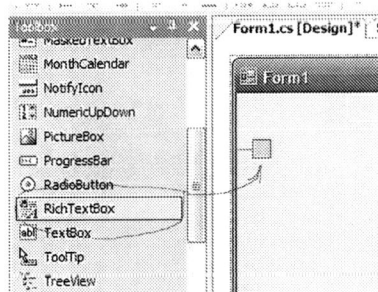

- In the Properties Window change the richTextBox size from 100,96 to 590,136.
- In the Properties Window change the richTextBox location to 0,44.
- You may be wondering where I'm getting these funky dimensions. Well, I just used the cursor to size the items until they looked right, which you can also do, but if you want to get your Simple Terminal to look exactly like mine you'll need to hand-input the dimensions.
- Add another richTextBox (same size), richTextBox2, below the first. Change the location to 0,209.
- From the ToolBox select 'Label' and drag and drop it between the MenuStrip and richTextBox1.
- In the Properties Window change 'Text' from label1 to Send:
- Select a second label and drop it between richTextBox1 and richTextBox2. Change the Text from label2 to Receive:

- BORING! Plain old gray just won't cut it. Let's tart this up a bit.
- Select Form1 and in the Properties Window select BackColor and click the down arrow to show the color menu:

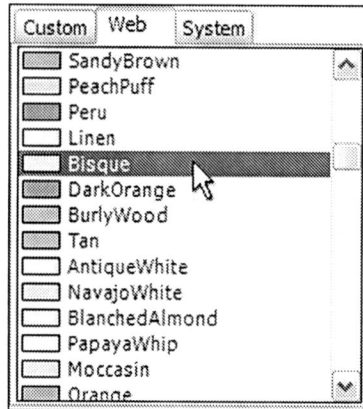

- Select Bisque.
- In the Edit Window select the menuStrip1 and in the Properties Window select 'BackColor' and choose the Web color NavahoWhite.
- Now complain because this book is black and white and I'm talking colors. If you are really doing this on a PC though, you'll see the colors.
- Select label1 and in the Properties Window choose Font. Change Font Style to Bold and Size to 12.

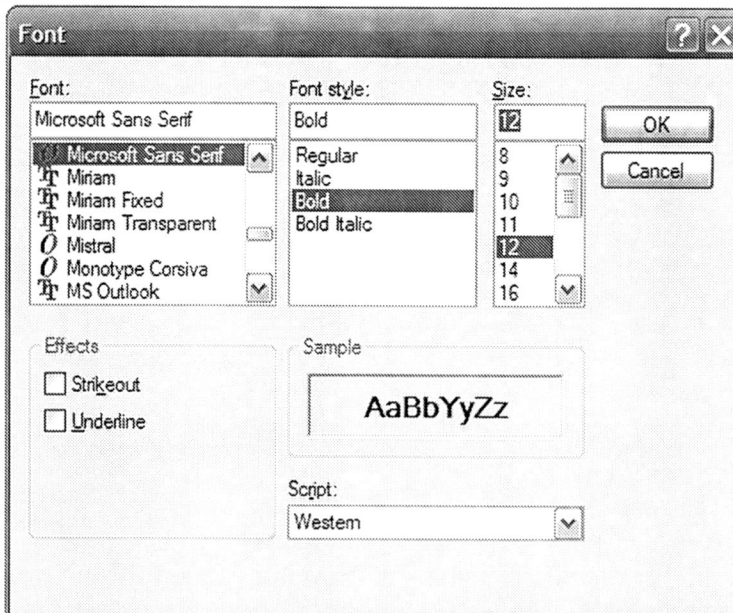

- In the Properties Window for label1 select ForeColor and change to Web DarkGoldenrod.

- Select Form1 and in the Properties Window change text to 'Smiley Micros – Simple Terminal' or some other less commercial name if you prefer.
- Still in the Form1 Properties Window select Icon and then select 'Smiley.ico' (located in the \Software\Graphics\ directory).

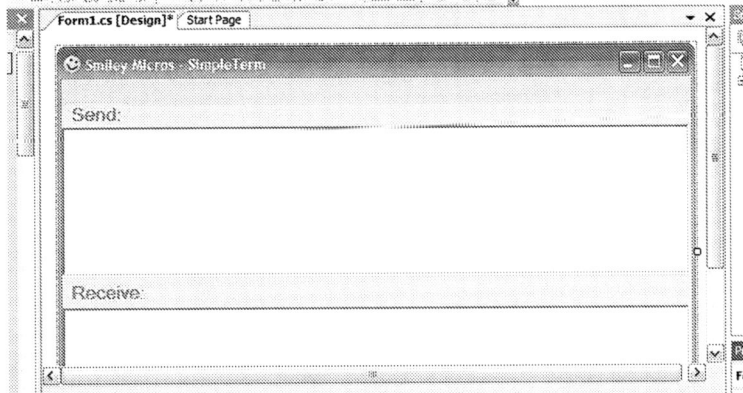

- Now you've just got to admit that a little makeup helps, unless you are looking at the black and white image in the book, in which case, never mind.
- Select the MenuStrip and highlight the 'Type Here' box.

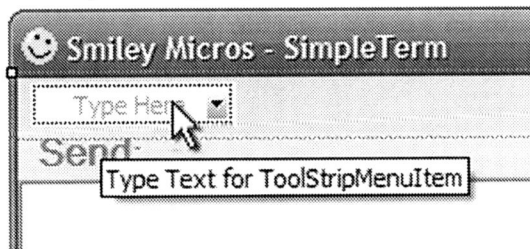

- Type Settings.
- Move your cursor to the next menu position to the right, type Open Port.
- And in the next right type Clear.

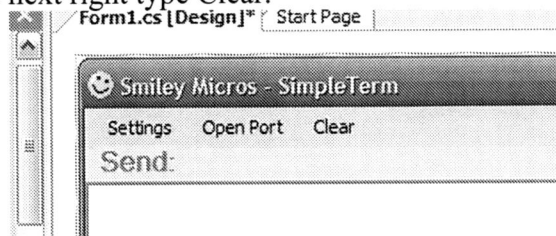

- **NOW SAVE YOUR WORK! (aka Save Your Butt)** – Do this every time you have done enough work that you'd feel bad if you lost it. If you didn't already know this, you will learn it the hard way like the rest of us.
- In the Express IDE menus, select Debug and click Start Debugging.

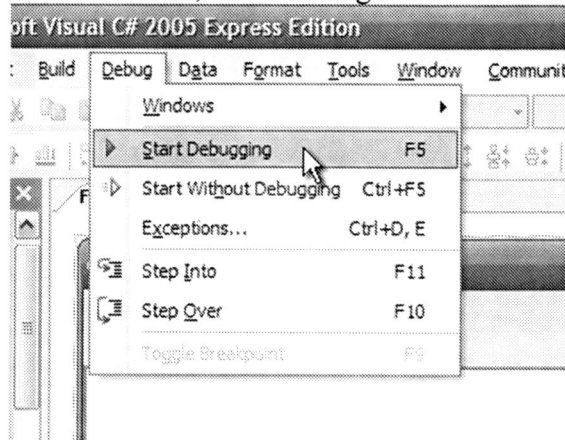

- Whoa, lookit that, you didn't write a word of software and yet you just created a GUI for a serial terminal! Move your mouse over the menu items and notice how they change colors. This is not just pretty, but pretty useless as is. So let's make it useful.
- Click the debug form's close button (the little X in the upper right).

Making the Simple Terminal GUI do something

Add functionality to the menu items
- This is what we see in the C# Edit Window:

```
using System;
using System.Collections.Generic;
using System.ComponentModel;
using System.Data;
using System.Drawing;
using System.Text;
using System.Windows.Forms;

namespace WindowsApplication2
{
    public partial class Form1 : Form
    {
        public Form1()
        {
            InitializeComponent();
```

```
        }
    }
}
```

- In the Visual Basic Edit window you'll see the following:

```
Public Class Form1


End Class
```

- In the IDE double click on the menuStrip1 Settings button.
- In the Edit Window click the 'Form1.cs [Design] tab to view the Design Editor panel. Now click the 'Open Port' menu item.
- Repeat for the 'Clear' menu item.
- In the Form1.cs code window you'll see that the IDE has created three functions that will be run when you click the menu item.
- In C# add the following text to each:

```
private void settingsToolStripMenuItem_Click(object sender, EventArgs e)
{
    MessageBox.Show("Menu item 'Settings'");
}

private void openPortToolStripMenuItem_Click(object sender, EventArgs e)
{
    MessageBox.Show("Menu item 'Open Port'");
}

private void clearToolStripMenuItem_Click(object sender, EventArgs e)
{
    MessageBox.Show("Menu item 'Clear'");
}
```

- In Visual Basic add the following text to each:

```
Public Class Form1

    Private Sub SettingsToolStripMenuItem_Click(ByVal sender As 'wrap'
            System.Object, ByVal e As System.EventArgs) Handle 'wrap'
            SettingsToolStripMenuItem.Click
        MessageBox.Show("Menu item 'Settings'")
    End Sub

    Private Sub OpenPortToolStripMenuItem_Click(ByVal sender As 'wrap'
            System.Object, ByVal e As System.EventArgs) Handles 'wrap'
            OpenPortToolStripMenuItem.Click
        MessageBox.Show("Menu item 'Open Port'")
    End Sub

    Private Sub ClearToolStripMenuItem_Click(ByVal sender A 'wrap'
            System.Object, ByVal e As System.EventArgs) Handles 'wrap'
            ClearToolStripMenuItem.Click
        MessageBox.Show("Menu item 'Clear'")
    End Sub
End Class
```

41

- Note the word *'wrap'*. This means that the prior line of code was too long to display in this book so it was wrapped to the next line for the book only and not wrapped for the actual source code. We will use this as a convention throughout this book. If you enter *'wrap'* in your code, you'll get an error. If you think I'm over-explaining this, you haven't seen my email inbox.
- Run the program in debug mode again (Debug/Start Debugging)
- Click the 'Settings' menu item.

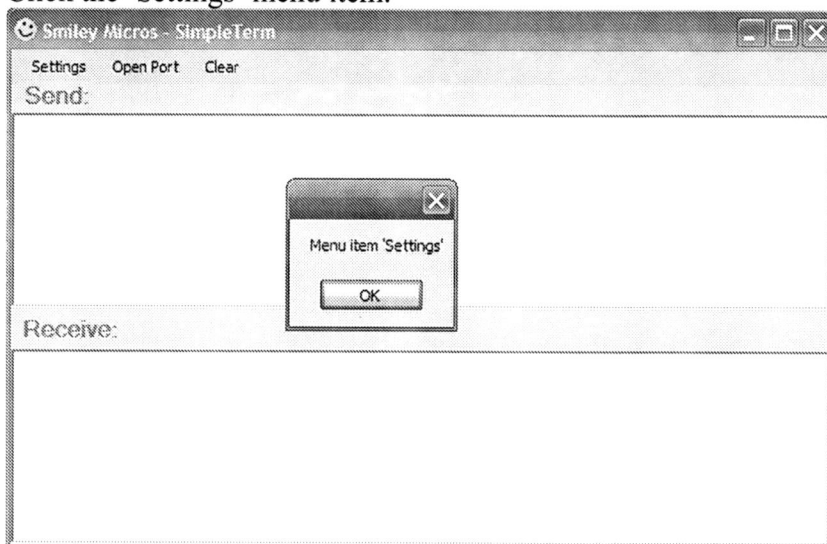

- Likewise test the 'Open Port' and 'Clear' menu items.
- Close the debug form.
- Select Form1.cs and change the Clear menu function to:
- In C# add:

```
private void clearToolStripMenuItem_Click(object sender, EventArgs e)
{
    richTextBox1.Text = "";
    richTextBox2.Text = "";
}
```

- In Visual Basic add:

```
Private Sub ClearToolStripMenuItem_Click(ByVal sender As 'wrap'
    System.Object, ByVal e As System.EventArgs) Handles 'wrap'
    ClearToolStripMenuItem.Click

    RichTextBox1.Text = ""
    RichTextBox2.Text = ""

End Sub
```

- This will cause the text in the rich text boxes to be cleared.
- Run the program in Debug mode and type some text in each richTextBox then click the Clear menu item to see it work.
- The source code is in the \Software\Chapter 4 - Simple Terminal GUI \ directory

In this chapter you went thru the Microsoft tutorials and learned just enough to be dangerous. You built the GUI for a Simple Terminal. In the next chapter you will build a dialog form to get data from the user for selecting a serial port and setting up the UART.

Chapter 4: Simple Terminal - GUI

Chapter 5: Simple Terminal - Getting User Input

In this chapter we will create a dialog form to allow the user to select an available serial port and set the UART parameters needed for the communication link (Baudrate, Data Bits, Parity, Stop Bits, and Handshaking). We have had an introduction to all these parameters in Chapter 3, and we will learn much more about them later, but for now, let's just use them in our settings dialog form.

To create and test the Settings dialog we will use a test form, PortSetTest, to call it. Later, however, we will access this form from the Simple Terminal by clicking the settings menu item. In the GUI code from Chapter 4, clicking the Settings menu item opened a message box, when we add the settings form to Simple Terminal, we will open it from that menu item.

PortSetTest Form   Settings Form

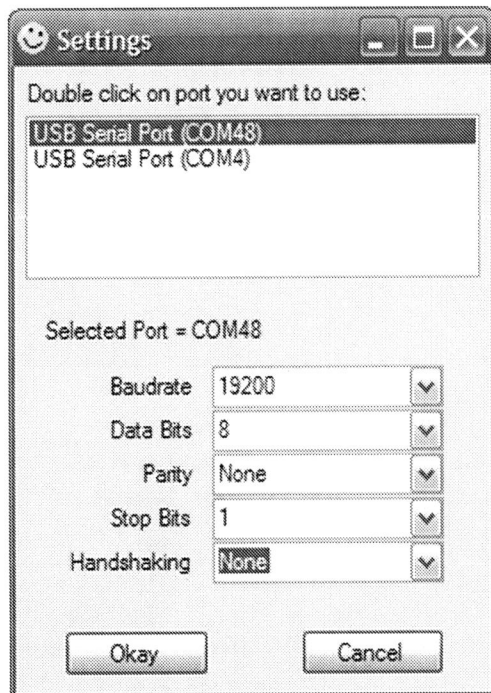

- Open either C# or Visual Basic Express and create a new project named PortSetTest
- Create a form to look like:

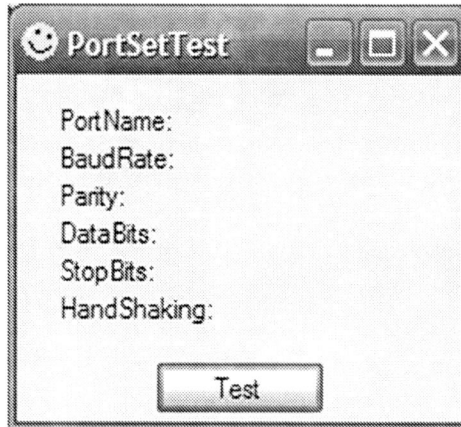

- The text list is made from 6 labels using the text shown.
- In the Solutions Explorer right click 'PortSetTest' and from the drop down menus select Add/NewItem:

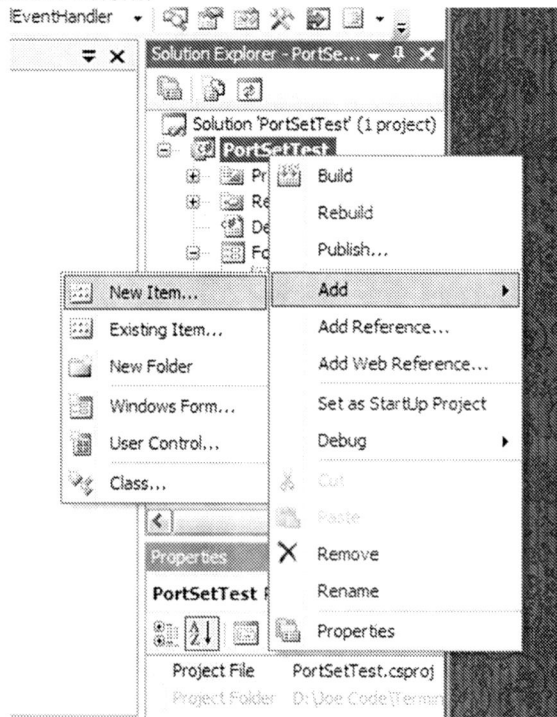

- In the Add New Item form, highlight 'Windows Form', change the name to 'PortSettings.cs' if C# or 'PortSettings.vb' if Visual Basic and click Add.

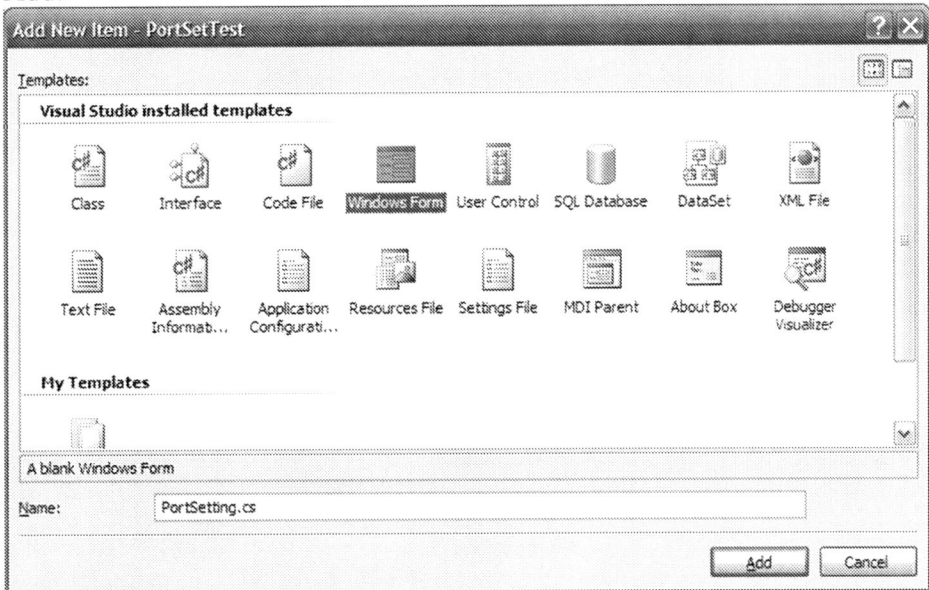

- The blank form will open.
- In the Properties Window select 'FormBorderStyle' and select 'FixedDialog'. This type of form can post a DialogResult message that the calling form, in this case the Simple Terminal form, can process (don't panic, this is all done for you and is simpler than is sounds). We will use the DialogResult to learn if the user clicked the Settings form Okay or Cancel button.
- Now you should be able to do some stuff with out a lot of hand-holding:
  - o Change the form name to 'Setting'
  - o Add the Smiley.ico icon
  - o Change the form color to Bisque
- Add the controls shown below:
  - o The upper white box with listBoxPorts, is a ListBox, which you will name listBoxPorts.
  - o The control with the label 'Baudrate' is a ComboBox, change its name to comboBoxBaud.

47

- Your Settings form should look like:

- Add the DevInfo file to the project:
  - Copy the DevInfo.cs if C# or DevInfo.vb if Visual Basic to the containing the PortSettings project files. You will find this file in \Software\Chapter 5 –Simple Terminal Getting User Input.
  - Refer to the Add/New Item image shown two pages back for the Add/New Item instructions.
  - Open the same menus in the Solution Explorer, but instead of selecting Add/New Item, select Add/Existing Item and select DevInfo.cs if you are using C# or DevInfo.vb if you are using Visual Basic.
  - We will not look at this file until later since it contains some advanced concepts, but we will use it to get the names of the available ports.

- Note that we are intentionally not using the SerialPort GetPortNames function for reasons that will be explained later.
- In C# add to the 'using' list at the top of the program:

```
using DevInfo;
```

- In Visual Basic add to the 'Imports' list at the top of the program:

```
Imports DevInfo
```

- In C# add to the constructor:

```
public PortSettings()
{
    InitializeComponent();

    // Get a list of the Serial port names
    string[] ports = GetPorts();

    int i = 0;
    foreach (string s in ports)
    {
        if (s != "")
        {
            listBoxPorts.Items.Insert(i++, s);
        }
    }

    // Set first Serial port as default
    GetCOM(0);

    // Initialize baudrates in combobox;
    comboBoxBaud.Items.AddRange(new object[] {
                                               "75",
                                               "110",
                                               "134",
                                               "150",
                                               "300",
                                               "600",
                                               "1200",
                                               "1800",
                                               "2400",
                                               "4800",
                                               "7200",
                                               "9600",
                                               "14400",
                                               "19200",
                                               "38400",
                                               "57600",
                                               "115200",
                                               "128000"});
```

```
// Set Handshaking selection
//  We will only use these handshaking types
comboBoxHandshaking.Items.Add("None");
comboBoxHandshaking.Items.Add("RTS/CTS");
comboBoxHandshaking.Items.Add("Xon/Xoff");

// Set Parity types
foreach (string s in Enum.GetNames(typeof(Parity)))
{
    comboBoxParity.Items.Add(s);
}

// Set Databits
// FT232R UART interface supports only 7 or 8 data bits
//comboBoxDataBits.Items.Add("5"); // not supported
//comboBoxDataBits.Items.Add("6"); // not supported
comboBoxDataBits.Items.Add("7");
comboBoxDataBits.Items.Add("8");

// Set Stopbits
// FT232R UART interface supports only 1 or 2 stop bits
//comboBoxStopBits.Items.Add("None"); // not supported
comboBoxStopBits.Items.Add("1");
//comboBoxStopBits.Items.Add("1.5"); // not supported
comboBoxStopBits.Items.Add("2");

comboBoxBaud.Text = "19200";
comboBoxParity.Text = "None";
comboBoxDataBits.Text = "8";
comboBoxStopBits.Text = "1";
comboBoxHandshaking.Text = "None";
}
```

- **In Visual Basic add to the constructor:**

```
Public Sub New()
    InitializeComponent()

    ' Get a list of the Serial port names
    Dim ports As String() = GetPorts()

    Dim i As Integer = 0
    For Each s As String In ports
        If s <> "" Then
            listBoxPorts.Items.Insert(i, s)
            i = i + 1
        End If
    Next s

    ' Set first Serial port as default
    GetCOM(0)

    ' Initialize baudrates in combobox;
    comboBoxBaud.Items.AddRange(New Object() {
                                            "75",
```

```
                                            "110",
                                            "134",
                                            "150",
                                            "300",
                                            "600",
                                            "1200",
                                            "1800",
                                            "2400",
                                            "4800",
                                            "7200",
                                            "9600",
                                            "14400",
                                            "19200",
                                            "38400",
                                            "57600",
                                            "115200",
                                            "128000"});

    ' Set Handshaking selection
    '  We will only use these handshaking types

    comboBoxHandshaking.Items.Add("None")
    comboBoxHandshaking.Items.Add("RTS/CTS")
    comboBoxHandshaking.Items.Add("Xon/Xoff")

    ' Set Parity types
    For Each s As String In System.Enum.GetNames(GetType(Parity))
        comboBoxParity.Items.Add(s)
    Next s

    ' Set Databits
    ' FT232R UART interface supports only 7 or 8 data bits
    'comboBoxDataBits.Items.Add("5"); // not supported
    'comboBoxDataBits.Items.Add("6"); // not supported
    comboBoxDataBits.Items.Add("7")
    comboBoxDataBits.Items.Add("8")

    ' Set Stopbits
    ' FT232R UART interface supports only 1 or 2 stop bits
    'comboBoxStopBits.Items.Add("None"); // not supported
    comboBoxStopBits.Items.Add("1")
    'comboBoxStopBits.Items.Add("1.5"); // not supported
    comboBoxStopBits.Items.Add("2")

    comboBoxBaud.Text = "19200"
    comboBoxParity.Text = "None"
    comboBoxDataBits.Text = "8"
    comboBoxStopBits.Text = "1"
    comboBoxHandshaking.Text = "None"

End Sub
```

- From the Settings Designer form click the Okay button and the Cancel buttons and then in the Settings text editor window add the following DialogResults to the functions:

- In C# add:

```
private void buttonOkay_Click(object sender, EventArgs e)
{
    DialogResult = DialogResult.OK;
}

private void buttonCancel_Click(object sender, EventArgs e)
{
    DialogResult = DialogResult.Cancel;
}
```

- In Visual Basic add:

```
Private Sub buttonOkay_Click(ByVal sender As Object, ByVal e As 'wrap'
                             EventArgs) Handles buttonOkay.Click
    DialogResult = System.Windows.Forms.DialogResult.OK
End Sub

Private Sub buttonCancel_Click(ByVal sender As Object, ByVal e As 'wrap'
                               EventArgs) Handles buttonCancel.Click
    DialogResult = System.Windows.Forms.DialogResult.Cancel
End Sub
```

- These functions close the form and post the DialogResult message for the PortSettingsTest form, which called the Settings form.
- You may have noticed that in the source code shown in the Chapter 5 directory you will see #region and #endregion. The IDE uses #region and #endregion to show or hide code sections. When you click on the + or - to the left #region the code section collapses or expands. We use these to simplify the code visually making it easier to follow the overall code logic. Collapsing the regions looks like:

```
#region Data Assessors
// Assessors for the selected port
// FT232R UART interface supports
//     7 or 8 data bits
//     1 or 2 stop bits
//     odd / even / mark / space / no parity.
// So these will be the only options available

Port Name

Baudrate

Parity

StopBits

DataBits

Handshaking
```

- Create data assessors and index changed functions.

- The index changed functions are created by clicking the 'SelectedIndexChanged' event in the events section (lightning bolt) of the Properties window.
- In C# add:

```csharp
#region Data Assessors
// Data assessors and index changed functions
// FT232R UART interface supports
//       7 or 8 data bits
//       1 or 2 stop bits
//       odd / even / mark / space / no parity.
// So these will be the only options available

#region Port Name
// Assessor for the selected port name
private string SelectedPort = "";
public string selectedPort
{
    get
    {
        return SelectedPort;
    }
    set
    {
        SelectedPort = value;
        labelPort.Text = "Selected Port = " + SelectedPort;
    }
}
#endregion

#region Baudrate
private int SelectedBaudrate;
public int selectedBaudrate
{
    get
    {
        return SelectedBaudrate;
    }
    set
    {
        SelectedBaudrate = value;
        comboBoxBaud.Text = value.ToString();
    }
}

private void comboBoxBaud_SelectedIndexChanged(object sender, EventArgs e)
{
    selectedBaudrate = wrap
                Convert.ToInt32(comboBoxBaud.Items[comboBoxBaud.SelectedIndex]);
}
#endregion

#region Parity
private Parity SelectedParity;// = Parity.None;
public Parity selectedParity
{
```

```
        get
        {
            return SelectedParity;
        }
        set
        {
            SelectedParity = value;
            comboBoxParity.Text = value.ToString();
        }
    }

    private void comboBoxParity_SelectedIndexChanged(object sender, EventArgs e)
    {
        string temp = comboBoxParity.Items[comboBoxParity.SelectedIndex].ToString();

        switch (temp)
        {
            case "Even":
                selectedParity = Parity.Even;
                break;
            case "Mark":
                selectedParity = Parity.Mark;
                break;
            case "None":
                selectedParity = Parity.None;
                break;
            case "Odd":
                selectedParity = Parity.Odd;
                break;
            case "Space":
                selectedParity = Parity.Space;
                break;
            default:
                selectedParity = Parity.None;
                break;
        }
    }
    #endregion

    #region StobBits
    private StopBits SelectedStopBits = StopBits.One;
    public StopBits selectedStopBits
    {
        get
        {
            return SelectedStopBits;
        }
        set
        {
            SelectedStopBits = value;
            comboBoxStopBits.Text = value.ToString();
        }
    }

    private void comboBoxStopBits_SelectedIndexChanged(object sender, EventArgs e)
    {
        string temp = wrap
```

54

```
                comboBoxStopBits.Items[comboBoxStopBits.SelectedIndex].ToString();

    switch (temp)
    {
        case "None":
            selectedStopBits = StopBits.None;
            break;
        case "1":
            selectedStopBits = StopBits.One;
            break;
        //case "1.5": // not supported by FT232R
            //SelectedStopBits = StopBits.OnePointFive;
            //break;
        case "2":
            selectedStopBits = StopBits.Two;
            break;
        default:
            selectedStopBits = StopBits.One;
            break;
    }
}
#endregion

#region DataBits
private int SelectedDataBits = 8;
public int selectedDataBits
{
    get
    {
        return SelectedDataBits;
    }
    set
    {
        SelectedDataBits = value;
        comboBoxDataBits.Text = value.ToString();
    }
}

private void comboBoxDataBits_SelectedIndexChanged(object sender, EventArgs e)
{
    if (comboBoxDataBits.SelectedIndex == 0) selectedDataBits = 7;
    else selectedDataBits = 8;
}
#endregion

#region Handshaking
// We will only use None, Xon/Xoff, or Hardware (which is RTS/CTS)
private Handshake SelectedHandshaking = Handshake.None;
public Handshake selectedHandshaking
{
    get
    {
        return SelectedHandshaking;
    }
    set
    {
        SelectedHandshaking = value;
```

```
                comboBoxHandshaking.Text = value.ToString();
        }
}

private void comboBoxHandshaking_SelectedIndexChanged(object sender, EventArgs e)
{
        if (comboBoxHandshaking.SelectedIndex == 0) selectedHandshaking = wrap
                                                Handshake.None;
        else if (comboBoxHandshaking.SelectedIndex == 1) selectedHandshaking = wrap
                                                Handshake.RequestToSend;
        else if (comboBoxHandshaking.SelectedIndex == 2) wrap
                                        selectedHandshaking = Handshake.XOnXOff;
        else selectedHandshaking = Handshake.None;
}
#endregion
```

- ## In Visual Basic add:

```
#Region "Data Assessors"
' Assessors for the selected port
' FT232R UART interface supports
'       7 or 8 data bits
'       1 or 2 stop bits
'       odd / even / mark / space / no parity.
' So these will be the only options available

#Region "Port Name"
' Assessor for the selected port name
Private SelectedPort_Renamed As String = ""
Public Property selectedPort() As String
    Get
        Return SelectedPort_Renamed
    End Get
    Set(ByVal value As String)
        SelectedPort_Renamed = value
        labelPort.Text = "Selected Port = " & SelectedPort_Renamed
    End Set
End Property
#End Region

#Region "Baudrate"
Private SelectedBaudrate_Renamed As Integer
Public Property selectedBaudrate() As Integer
    Get
        Return SelectedBaudrate_Renamed
    End Get
    Set(ByVal value As Integer)
        SelectedBaudrate_Renamed = value
        comboBoxBaud.Text = value.ToString()
    End Set
End Property

Private Sub comboBoxBaud_SelectedIndexChanged(ByVal sender As Object, ByVal e As
EventArgs) Handles comboBoxBaud.SelectedIndexChanged
    selectedBaudrate = wrap
    Convert.ToInt32(comboBoxBaud.Items(comboBoxBaud.SelectedIndex))
End Sub
#End Region
```

```
#Region "Parity"
Private SelectedParity_Renamed As Parity ' = Parity.None;
Public Property selectedParity() As Parity
    Get
        Return SelectedParity_Renamed
    End Get
    Set(ByVal value As Parity)
        SelectedParity_Renamed = value
        comboBoxParity.Text = value.ToString()
    End Set
End Property

Private Sub comboBoxParity_SelectedIndexChanged(ByVal sender As Object, wrap
ByVal e As EventArgs) Handles comboBoxParity.SelectedIndexChanged
    Dim temp As String = wrap
    comboBoxParity.Items(comboBoxParity.SelectedIndex).ToString()

    Select Case temp
        Case "Even"
            selectedParity = Parity.Even
        Case "Mark"
            selectedParity = Parity.Mark
        Case "None"
            selectedParity = Parity.None
        Case "Odd"
            selectedParity = Parity.Odd
        Case "Space"
            selectedParity = Parity.Space
        Case Else
            selectedParity = Parity.None
    End Select
End Sub
#End Region

#Region "StobBits"
Private SelectedStopBits_Renamed As StopBits = StopBits.One
Public Property selectedStopBits() As StopBits
    Get
        Return SelectedStopBits_Renamed
    End Get
    Set(ByVal value As StopBits)
        SelectedStopBits_Renamed = value
        comboBoxStopBits.Text = value.ToString()
    End Set
End Property

Private Sub comboBoxStopBits_SelectedIndexChanged(ByVal sender As Object, wrap
ByVal e As EventArgs) Handles comboBoxStopBits.SelectedIndexChanged
    Dim temp As String = wrap
    comboBoxStopBits.Items(comboBoxStopBits.SelectedIndex).ToString()

    Select Case temp
        Case "None"
            selectedStopBits = StopBits.None
        Case "1"
            selectedStopBits = StopBits.One
```

```vbnet
                'case "1.5": // not supported by FT232R
                'SelectedStopBits = StopBits.OnePointFive;
                'break;
            Case "2"
                selectedStopBits = StopBits.Two
            Case Else
                selectedStopBits = StopBits.One
        End Select
End Sub
#End Region

#Region "DataBits"
Private SelectedDataBits_Renamed As Integer = 8
Public Property selectedDataBits() As Integer
    Get
        Return SelectedDataBits_Renamed
    End Get
    Set(ByVal value As Integer)
        SelectedDataBits_Renamed = value
        comboBoxDataBits.Text = value.ToString()
    End Set
End Property

Private Sub comboBoxDataBits_SelectedIndexChanged(ByVal sender As Object, wrap
ByVal e As EventArgs) Handles comboBoxDataBits.SelectedIndexChanged
    If comboBoxDataBits.SelectedIndex = 0 Then
        selectedDataBits = 7
    Else
        selectedDataBits = 8
    End If
End Sub
#End Region

#Region "Handshaking"
' We will only use None, Xon/Xoff, or Hardware (which is RTS/CTS)
Private SelectedHandshaking_Renamed As Handshake = Handshake.None
Public Property selectedHandshaking() As Handshake
    Get
        Return SelectedHandshaking_Renamed
    End Get
    Set(ByVal value As Handshake)
        SelectedHandshaking_Renamed = value
        comboBoxHandshaking.Text = value.ToString()
    End Set
End Property

Private Sub comboBoxHandshaking_SelectedIndexChanged(ByVal sender As Object, wrap
 ByVal e As EventArgs) Handles comboBoxHandshaking.SelectedIndexChanged
    If comboBoxHandshaking.SelectedIndex = 0 Then
        selectedHandshaking = Handshake.None
    ElseIf comboBoxHandshaking.SelectedIndex = 1 Then
        selectedHandshaking = Handshake.RequestToSend
    ElseIf comboBoxHandshaking.SelectedIndex = 2 Then
        selectedHandshaking = Handshake.XOnXOff
    Else
        selectedHandshaking = Handshake.None
    End If
```

```
End Sub
#End Region
```

- We will test the Settings dialog by displaying the data in the PortSetTest form.
- Open Form1 (PortSettingsTest) and add the following code.
- In C# add:

```csharp
public partial class Form1 : Form
{
    private string portname = "Not Initialized";
    private string baudrate = "Not Initialized";
    private string parity = "Not Initialized";
    private string stopbits = "Not Initialized";
    private string databits = "Not Initialized";
    private string handshaking = "Not Initialized";

    // Instantiate the PortSettings class
    PortSettings p = new PortSettings();

    public Form1()
    {
        InitializeComponent();
    }

    private void clearSettings()
    {
        portname = "";
        baudrate = "";
        databits = "";
        stopbits = "";
        parity = "";
        handshaking = "";
    }

    private void buttonTest_Click(object sender, EventArgs e)
    {
        if (p.ShowDialog() == DialogResult.Cancel)
        {
            // clear out settings
            clearLabels();
        }
        else
        {
            // set labels to Settings values
            setLabels();
        }
    }

    private void clearLabels()
    {
        labelPortName.Text = "PortName";
        labelBaudRate.Text = "BaudRate";
        labelParity.Text = "Parity";
        labelDataBits.Text = "DataBits";
        labelStopBits.Text = "StopBits";
        labelHandShaking.Text = "HandShaking";
```

```
    }

    private void setLabels()
    {
        labelPortName.Text = "PortName: " + p.selectedPort;
        labelBaudRate.Text = "BaudRate: " + p.selectedBaudrate.ToString();
        labelParity.Text = "Parity: " + p.selectedParity.ToString();
        labelDataBits.Text = "DataBits: " + p.selectedDataBits.ToString();
        labelStopBits.Text = "StopBits: " + p.selectedStopBits.ToString();
        labelHandShaking.Text = "HandShaking: " + wrap
                p.selectedHandshaking.ToString();
    }
}
```

- ## In Visual Basic add:

```
Inherits Form
Private portname As String = "Not Initialized"
Private baudrate As String = "Not Initialized"
Private parity As String = "Not Initialized"
Private stopbits As String = "Not Initialized"
Private databits As String = "Not Initialized"
Private handshaking As String = "Not Initialized"

' Instantiate the PortSettings class
Private p As PortSettings = New PortSettings()

Public Sub New()
    InitializeComponent()
End Sub

Private Sub clearSettings()
    portname = ""
    baudrate = ""
    databits = ""
    stopbits = ""
    parity = ""
    handshaking = ""
End Sub

Private Sub buttonTest_Click(ByVal sender As Object, ByVal wrap
        e As EventArgs) Handles buttonTest.Click
    'MessageBox.Show("Dialog result = " + p.ShowDialog());

    If p.ShowDialog() = DialogResult.Cancel Then
        ' clear out settings
        clearLabels()
    Else
        ' set labels to Settings values
        setLabels()
    End If
End Sub

Private Sub clearLabels()
    labelPortName.Text = "PortName"
    labelBaudRate.Text = "BaudRate"
```

```
        labelParity.Text = "Parity"
        labelDataBits.Text = "DataBits"
        labelStopBits.Text = "StopBits"
        labelHandShaking.Text = "HandShaking"
    End Sub

    Private Sub setLabels()
        labelPortName.Text = "PortName: " & p.selectedPort
        labelBaudRate.Text = "BaudRate: " & p.selectedBaudrate.ToString()
        labelParity.Text = "Parity: " & p.selectedParity.ToString()
        labelDataBits.Text = "DataBits: " & p.selectedDataBits.ToString()
        labelStopBits.Text = "StopBits: " & p.selectedStopBits.ToString()
        labelHandShaking.Text = "HandShaking: " & p.selectedHandshaking.ToString()
    End Sub
End Class
```

- In the IDE click the Debug menu and select the start debugging item. You should see the blank PortSettingsTest form:

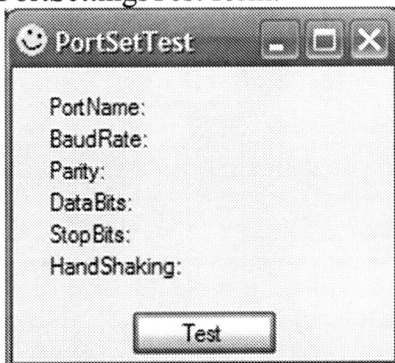

- Click the Test button and you should see the Settings form:

61

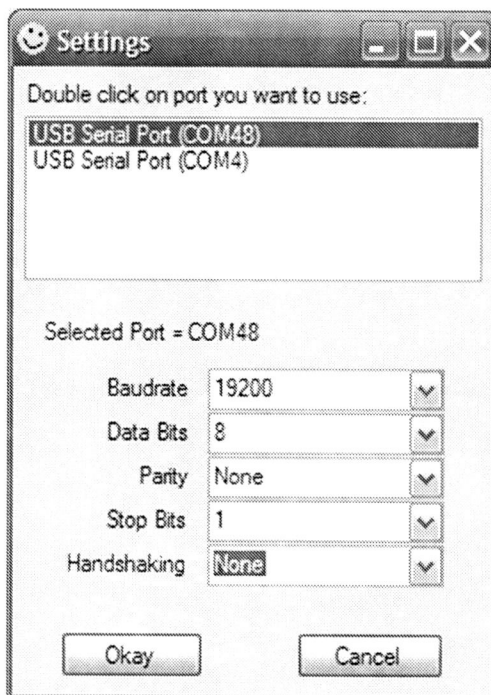

- The actual port names will of course (barring a stunning coincidence) be different from those shown. By highlighting and selecting the items as shown and clicking Okay, the settings will propagate back to the PortSettingTest form as shown:

- The source code is in the directory: \Software\Chapter 5 – Simple Terminal Get User Input

We have covered a lot so far. In the last chapter we created a GUI for our Simple Terminal. Then in this chapter we created and tested a Settings form that we will soon use in our Simple Terminal, and later in our Developer Terminal. You may be a bit tired of this by now, and I have some good news. We will be able to use the Settings object in future projects by simply copying the source code to the new projects directory and using the Add/Existing Item technique shown above to get this object into our code. So the good news is: **we never have to code this again!**

Now you see one of the values of object oriented programming. You can build and test an object, then forget all about how it works and just use it like a black box.

In the next chapter we will add the low level code to make Simple Terminal work.

Chapter 6: Simple Terminal - Using the SerialPort Class

In Chapter 4 we built the Simple Terminal GUI and in Chapter 5 we built a dialog to get settings information from the user. In this chapter we will add the settings dialog and we will add low-level code that will make the whole thing work.

- Create a new directory for your work and add the Port Settings files from the directory: \Software\Chapter 5 – Simple Terminal Getting User Input:
  - In C# from the PortSetTest C# directory copy:
    - o Port Settings.cs
    - o Port Settings.Designer.cs
    - o Port Settings.resz
    - o DevInfo.cs
  - In Visual Basic from the PortSetTest VB directory copy:
    - o Port Settings.vb
    - o Port Settings.Designer.vb
    - o Port Settings.resz
    - o DevInfo.vb
  - Then paste the files into your new directory.
  - Following the Add/Existing Items instructions given earlier, add Port Settings and DevInfo to the project.
- In C# in the 'using' list add:
  ```
  using PortSet;
  ```
- In Visual Basic in the 'Imports' list add:
  ```
  Imports PortSet
  ```

Now that you have added the PortSettings and DevInfo Classes to your Simple Terminal project you are ready to look at the .NET System.IO.Ports library that contains the SerialPort Class and some other goodies that we'll look at as we need to use them. For the Simple Terminal we will be using only the minimum SerialPort methods required for establishing serial communications. Later when we get to the Developer Terminal, we will take a deeper look at System.IO.Ports – what is available and how to use it. Also, I'll do some generic complaining and I'll discuss specifically why I had to write the DevInfo class to supplement the SerialPort class.

- Open the Form1 designer and from the Toolbox drag and drop serialPort1.
- We will set the serial port properties according to the data we enter in the Port Settings class.
- In the Form1 designer double click the 'Settings' menu item to create the click event.
- In C# add:

```
private void settingsToolStripMenuItem_Click(object sender, EventArgs e)
{
    // Make sure the port isn't already open
    if (serialPort1.IsOpen)
    {
        MessageBox.Show("The port must be closed before changing the settings.");
        return;
    }
    else
    {
        // creat an instance of the settings form
        PortSettings settings = new PortSettings();

        if (settings.ShowDialog() == DialogResult.OK)
        {
            if (settings.selectedPort != "")
            {
                // set the serial port to the new settings
                serialPort1.PortName = settings.selectedPort;
                serialPort1.BaudRate = settings.selectedBaudrate;
                serialPort1.DataBits = settings.selectedDataBits;
                serialPort1.Parity = settings.selectedParity;
                serialPort1.StopBits = settings.selectedStopBits;

                // show the new settings in the form text line
                showSettings();
            }
            else
            {
                MessageBox.Show("Error: Settings form returned with wrap
                            no Serial port selected.");
                return; // bail out
            }

        }
        else
        {
            MessageBox.Show("Error: buttonSetup_Click - Settings wrap
                                dialog box did not return Okay.");
            return; // bail out
        }

        // open the port
        try
        {
            serialPort1.Close();
            serialPort1.Open();
```

66

```csharp
            menuStrip1.Items[1].Text = "Close Port";

            showSettings();
        }
        catch (System.Exception ex)
        {
            MessageBox.Show("Error - setupToolStripMenuItem_Click wrap
                            Exception: " + ex);
        }
    }
}

// show the settings in the form text line
private void showSettings()
{
    this.Text = "Smiley Micros - " +
        serialPort1.PortName + " " +
        serialPort1.BaudRate.ToString() + "," +
        serialPort1.Parity + "," +
        serialPort1.DataBits.ToString() + "," +
        serialPort1.StopBits;
    if (serialPort1.IsOpen)
    {
        this.Text += " - Port is open";
    }
    else
    {
        this.Text += " - Port is closed";
    }
}
```

- **In Visual Basic add:**

```vb
Private Sub settingsToolStripMenuItem_Click(ByVal sender As Object, wrap
            ByVal e As EventArgs) Handles settingsToolStripMenuItem.Click
    ' Make sure the port isn't already open
    If serialPort1.IsOpen Then
        MessageBox.Show("The port must be closed before changing the settings.")
        Return
    Else
        ' creat an instance of the settings form
        Dim settings As PortSettings = New PortSettings()

        If settings.ShowDialog() = System.Windows.Forms.DialogResult.OK Then
            If settings.selectedPort <> "" Then
                ' set the serial port to the new settings
                serialPort1.PortName = settings.selectedPort
                serialPort1.BaudRate = settings.selectedBaudrate
                serialPort1.DataBits = settings.selectedDataBits
                serialPort1.Parity = settings.selectedParity
                serialPort1.StopBits = settings.selectedStopBits

                ' show the new settings in the form text line
                showSettings()
            Else
                MessageBox.Show("Error: Settings form returned with no wrap
                                    Serial port selected.")
                Return ' bail out
```

```
                End If

        Else
            MessageBox.Show("Error: buttonSetup_Click - Settings dialog wrap
                                            box did not return Okay.")
            Return ' bail out
        End If

        ' open the port
        Try
            serialPort1.Close()
            serialPort1.Open()
            menuStrip1.Items(1).Text = "Close Port"

            showSettings()
        Catch ex As System.Exception
            MessageBox.Show("Error - setupToolStripMenuItem_Click wrap
                                        Exception:", ex.ToString())
        End Try
    End If
End Sub

' show the settings in the form text line
Private Sub showSettings()
    Me.Text = "Smiley Micros - " wrap
                    & serialPort1.PortName & " " wrap
                    & serialPort1.BaudRate.ToString() & "," wrap
                    & serialPort1.Parity & "," wrap
                    & serialPort1.DataBits.ToString() & "," wrap
                    & serialPort1.StopBits
    If serialPort1.IsOpen Then
        Me.Text &= " - Port is open"
    Else
        Me.Text &= " - Port is closed"
    End If
End Sub
```

- In the form designer click on the 'Open Port' menu item.
- In C# add:

```csharp
private void openPortToolStripMenuItem_Click(object sender, EventArgs e)
{
    try
    {
        if (serialPort1.IsOpen)
        {
            serialPort1.Close();
            openPortToolStripMenuItem.Text = "Open Port";
        }
        else
        {
            serialPort1.Open();
            openPortToolStripMenuItem.Text = "Close Port";
        }

        showSettings();
    }
    catch (System.Exception ex)
```

```
    {
        MessageBox.Show("Error - openPortToolStripMenuItem_Click Exception: wrap
                                                " + ex);
    }
}
```

- In Visual Basic add:

```
' toggle the port state
Private Sub openPortToolStripMenuItem_Click(ByVal sender As Object, wrap
            ByVal e As EventArgs) Handles openPortToolStripMenuItem.Click
    Try
        If serialPort1.IsOpen Then
            serialPort1.Close()
            menuStrip1.Items(1).Text = "Open Port"
        Else
            serialPort1.Open()
            menuStrip1.Items(1).Text = "Close Port"
        End If

        showSettings()
    Catch ex As System.Exception
        MessageBox.Show("Error - openPortToolStripMenuItem_Click wrap
                            Exception: ", ex.ToString())
    End Try
End Sub
```

- In the form designer select the richTextBoxSend component.
- In the properties window click the 'KeyPress' event and to the event handler created -
- In C# add

```
private void richTextBox1_KeyPress(object sender, KeyPressEventArgs e)
{
        sendChar(e.KeyChar);
}

private void sendChar(char c)
{
    char[] data = new Char[1];
    data[0] = c;
    try
    {
        serialPort1.Write(data, 0, 1);
    }
    catch
    {
        MessageBox.Show("Error: sendByte - failed to send.\nIs the port open?");
    }
}
```

- In Visual Basic add:

```
Private Sub richTextBox1_KeyPress(ByVal sender As Object, wrap
            ByVal e As KeyPressEventArgs) Handles richTextBox1.KeyPress
    sendChar(e.KeyChar)
End Sub
```

```
Private Sub sendChar(ByVal c As Char)
    Dim data As Char() = New Char(0) {}
    data(0) = c
    Try
        serialPort1.Write(data, 0, 1)
    Catch
        MessageBox.Show("Error: sendByte - failed to send." wrap
                        & Constants.vbLf & "Is the port open?")
    End Try
End Sub
```

- Our receive functions use a delegate to allow the serial port read thread to write to our receive text box. This is a bit complex, so for the time being just use it as-is and we will see how delegates work later during the discussion of the Developers Terminal.

- In C# add:

```
#region receive functions

// we want to have the serial port thread report back data received, but to
// display that data we must create a delegate function to show the data in the
// richTextBox

// define the delegate
public delegate void SetText();
// define an instance of the delegate
SetText setText;

// create a string that will be loaded with the data received from the port
public string str = "";

// note that this function runs in a separate thread and thus we must use a
// delegate in order
// to display the results in the richTextBox.
private void serialPort1_DataReceived(object sender,
System.IO.Ports.SerialDataReceivedEventArgs e)
{
    // instantiate the delegate to be invoked by this thread
    setText = new SetText(mySetText);

    // load the data into the string
    try
    {
        str = serialPort1.ReadExisting();
    }
    catch (System.Exception ex)
    {
        MessageBox.Show("Error - port_DataReceived Exception: " + ex);
    }

    // invoke the delegate in the MainForm thread
    this.Invoke(setText);
}
```

Chapter 6: Simple Terminal - Using the SerialPort Class

```
// create the instance of the delegate to be used to write the received data to
// the richTextBox
public void mySetText()
{
    // show the text
    richTextBox2.Text += str.ToString();

    moveCaretToEnd();
}

// This rigaramole is needed to keep the last received item displayed
// it kind of flickers and should be fixed
private void richTextBoxReceive_TextChanged(object sender, System.EventArgs e)
{
    moveCaretToEnd();
}

private void moveCaretToEnd()
{
    richTextBox1.SelectionStart = richTextBox1.Text.Length;
    richTextBox1.SelectionLength = 0;
    richTextBox1.ScrollToCaret();
}
#endregion
```

- ### In Visual Basic add:

```
#Region "receive functions"

' we want to have the serial port thread report back data received, but to display
' that data we must create a delegate function to show the data in the richTextBox

' define the delegate
Public Delegate Sub SetText()
' define an instance of the delegate
Private setTextI As SetText

' create a string that will be loaded with the data received from the port
Public str As String = ""

' note that this function runs in a separate thread and thus we must use a
' delegate in order to display the results in the richTextBox.
Private Sub serialPort1_DataReceived(ByVal sender As Object, wrap
        ByVal e As System.IO.Ports.SerialDataReceivedEventArgs) wrap
        Handles serialPort1.DataReceived
    ' instantiate the delegate to be invoked by this thread
    setTextI = New SetText(AddressOf mySetText)

    ' load the data into the string
    Try
        str = serialPort1.ReadExisting()
    Catch ex As System.Exception
        MessageBox.Show("Error - port_DataReceived Exception: ", ex.ToString())
    End Try

    ' invoke the delegate in the MainForm thread
    Me.Invoke(setTextI)
```

71

```
End Sub

' create the instance of the delegate to be used to write the received data
Public Sub mySetText()
    ' show the text
    richTextBox2.Text += str.ToString()

    moveCaretToEnd()
End Sub

' This rigaramole is needed to keep the last received item displayed
' it kind of flickers and should be fixed
Private Sub richTextBoxReceive_TextChanged(ByVal sender As Object, wrap
                    ByVal e As System.EventArgs)
    moveCaretToEnd()
End Sub

Private Sub moveCaretToEnd()
    richTextBox1.SelectionStart = richTextBox1.Text.Length
    richTextBox1.SelectionLength = 0
    richTextBox1.ScrollToCaret()
End Sub

#End Region
```

Testing Simple Terminal

Use the BBUSB setup from the Chapter 2 BBUSB Quick Start Guide to test the Simple Terminal.

Summary of the Last Three Chapters

Man alive, that was a lot of stuff! If you remember, at the start of Chapter 4, I said: "By the time we get through the Simple Terminal software you will likely have forgotten what we are trying to do here." Like I said then, this is not a software book, though it has a lot of software. We are learning to use tools that will allow us to build GUIs on a PC that we can use to communicate with microcontrollers connected to either a real serial port or a USB Virtual COM Port. The book will focus more intensely on the latter as we go along and we will see more hardware examples using Smiley Micros' BBUSB product and the hardware projects kit for the book.

By now you are getting a feel for C# or Visual Basic Express and liking it or hating it (or both). I suspect if you've ever done any GUI programming and serial communications using other programming languages, especially if you've done this with C or C++ and the Windows API or MFC, that you'll think this new way is really great.

What we have done in these chapters:
- Studied the Microsoft website materials to get an introduction to .NET and C# or Visual Basic Express programming.
- Followed my cookbook examples to create a generic serial port GUI.
- Tested the GUI with message boxes before adding 'real' code
- Learned to keep data input separate from underlying code that uses the data.
- Created a Dialog Form for user data input.
- Got accustomed to the idea that objects are things we can use as black boxes without having to know how they work.
- Started using the Serial Port Class, deferring study of it till later – further reinforcing the concept of an object as a useful tool whose details we don't need to understand.
- Created a simple terminal (hmmm… what should we name it?)

All that was fun, right? But now it is time to get serious.

Uh oh…

Chapter 7: Open Method and Catching the Wiley Error

The source code for this and the subsequent chapters can be found at: http://www.smileymicros.com/VCPCBdownloads.html.

In this chapter we will do three things:
- We will learn about the SerialPort Open method.
- We will build our first tool tester – to test the Open method.
- We will use this tool tester to learn some general things about trapping errors.

In the next chapter we will learn to use another error catching tool that is specific to the SerialPort Class, the SerialErrorReceived Event.

Open Method

The Open Method tries to open the serial port and triggers an exception if it fails. An exception is an unusual event such as an error that causes Windows to generate a message that we can catch if this exception occurs while we are in a try/catch block. Let's spend a little time with this and do a small program to let us capture and process the possible failures.

The Open method can generate the following exceptions:
- InvalidOperationException – specified port is open.
- ArgumentOutOfRangeException – ex. Baudrate = -9600
- ArgumentException – port name or file type is invalid.
- IOException – port is in an invalid state.
- UnauthorizedAccessException – port access is denied.

Open Method Tester

Our Open Test form should look like:

Chapter 7: Open Method and Catching the Wiley Error

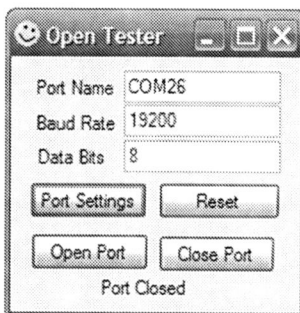

And by now you should be able to jump right in and make the GUI without any help from me – but you should take a closer look at the 'try/catch' technique since we'll discuss it in more detail in a minute.

Let's save some time and reuse the Port Settings and DevInfo classes we learned about a few chapters back, just add them to the Solutions Explorer as before.

Make the Port Settings Button event open the Port Settings form:
- In C# add:

```
// Open the Port Settings form and get the data
private void buttonPortSettings_Click(object sender, EventArgs e)
{
    // creat an instance of the settings form
    PortSettings settings = new PortSettings();

    settings.ShowDialog();

    textBoxPortName.Text = settings.selectedPort;
    textBoxBaudRate.Text = settings.selectedBaudrate.ToString();
    textBoxDataBits.Text = settings.selectedDataBits.ToString();

    setPortSettings();
}
```
- In VB add:

```
' Open the Port Settings form and get the data
Private Sub buttonPortSettings_Click(ByVal sender As Object, ByVal e As EventArgs)
Handles buttonPortSettings.Click
    ' creat an instance of the settings form
    Dim settings As PortSettings = New PortSettings()

    settings.ShowDialog()

    textBoxPortName.Text = settings.selectedPort
    textBoxBaudRate.Text = settings.selectedBaudrate.ToString()
    textBoxDataBits.Text = settings.selectedDataBits.ToString()

    setPortSettings()
```

76

```
End Sub
```

This allows us to get valid Port settings and load them into the Open Tester textboxes. The setPortSettings() function, which we will see in a moment, sets the serial port properties based on the data in the textboxes rather than the data in the settings form. This allows us to intentionally create errors so we can see how to catch them.

Let's write the setPortSettings() function:
- In C# add:
```
// Set the serialPort1 properties
// We use this to test various ways to break the settings input
// process to see what kind of exceptions are generated
private void setPortSettings()
{
    // You must close the port before changeing its settings
    serialPort1.Close();
    labelPortState.Text = "Port Closed";

    try
    {
        serialPort1.PortName = textBoxPortName.Text;
    }
    catch (System.Exception ex)
    {
        MessageBox.Show("Open Tester Port Name Exception: " + ex);
    }

    try
    {
        serialPort1.BaudRate = Convert.ToInt32(textBoxBaudRate.Text);
    }
    catch (System.Exception ex)
    {
        MessageBox.Show("Open Tester Baud Rate Exception: " + ex);
    }

    try
    {
        serialPort1.DataBits = Convert.ToInt32(textBoxDataBits.Text);
    }
    catch (System.Exception ex)
    {
        MessageBox.Show("Open Tester Data Bits Exception: " + ex);
    }
}
```
- In VB add:
```
' Set the serialPort1 properties
' We use this to test various ways to break the settings input
' process to see what kind of exceptions are generated
Private Sub setPortSettings()
    ' You must close the port before changeing its settings
```

```
    serialPort1.Close()
    labelPortState.Text = "Port Closed"

    Try
        serialPort1.PortName = textBoxPortName.Text
    Catch ex As System.Exception
        MessageBox.Show("Open Tester Port Name Exception: " & ex.Message)
    End Try

    Try
        serialPort1.BaudRate = Convert.ToInt32(textBoxBaudRate.Text)
    Catch ex As System.Exception
        MessageBox.Show("Open Tester Baud Rate Exception: " & ex.Message)
    End Try

    Try
        serialPort1.DataBits = Convert.ToInt32(textBoxDataBits.Text)
    Catch ex As System.Exception
        MessageBox.Show("Open Tester Data Bits Exception: " & ex.Message)
    End Try
End Sub
```

Let's add functions so we can mess up and see the exception messages. We want to be able to change the text in the text boxes and have that data sent to the serial port class, so we will use a Reset button.

To the Reset Button event handler -
- In C# add:

```
// Reset the Port Settings - used for placing changes in the
// textboxes into the serialPort1 settings
private void buttonReset_Click(object sender, EventArgs e)
{
    setPortSettings();
}
```

- In VB add:

```
' Reset the Port Settings - used for placing changes in the
' textboxes into the serialPort1 settings
Private Sub buttonReset_Click(ByVal sender As Object, wrap
                        ByVal e As EventArgs) Handles buttonReset.Click
        setPortSettings()
End Sub
```

We want to look for exceptions when opening or closing a port.
To the Open Button event handler –
- In C# add:

```
// Open Port Button
private void buttonOpenPort_Click(object sender, EventArgs e)
{
    try
    {
        serialPort1.Open();
```

78

```csharp
        labelPortState.Text = "Port Open";
    }
    catch (System.Exception ex)
    {
        MessageBox.Show("Open Port Button Exception: " + ex);
    }
}
```

- In VB add:

```vb
' Open Port Button
Private Sub buttonOpenPort_Click(ByVal sender As Object, wrap
            ByVal e As EventArgs) Handles buttonOpenPort.Click
    Try
        serialPort1.Open()
        labelPortState.Text = "Port Open"
    Catch ex As System.Exception
        MessageBox.Show("Open Port Button Exception: " & ex.Message)
    End Try
End Sub
```

To the Close Button event hander -

- In C# add:

```csharp
// Close Port Button
private void buttonClosePort_Click(object sender, EventArgs e)
{
    try
    {
        serialPort1.Close();
        labelPortState.Text = "Port Closed";
    }
    catch (System.Exception ex)
    {
        MessageBox.Show("Close Port Button Exception: " + ex);
    }
}
```

- In VB add:

```vb
' Close Port Button
Private Sub buttonClosePort_Click(ByVal sender As Object, wrap
            ByVal e As EventArgs) Handles buttonClosePort.Click
    Try
        serialPort1.Close()
        labelPortState.Text = "Port Closed"
    Catch ex As System.Exception
        MessageBox.Show("Close Port Button Exception: " & ex.Message)
    End Try
End Sub
```

Catching Errors: The try/catch Technique

We have already used the try/catch technique, but here we will see in a bit more detail how it works and how to get it to provide us with information on what it 'caught' when it fails. For this exercise we will just display system messages so we can see what is happening, but in a real application we would likely call some code that could help use compensate for the failure, or at least give the poor user something more useful (less scary) than the cryptically 'detailed' system messages that we get Windows.

Let's play around and generate some exceptions. Make sure that there is no FTDI device open on COM 1. Run Open Tester and with the textboxes blank click the Open Port button.

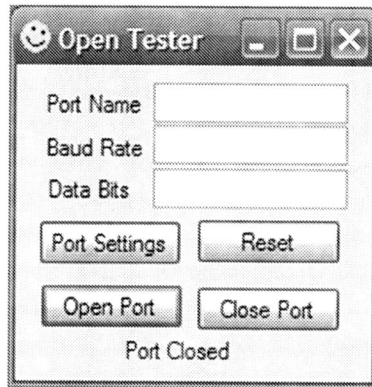

You should see a messageBox with an IOException elaborated:

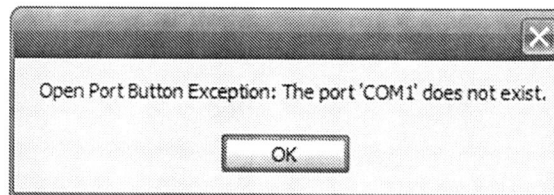

The PortSettings defaulted to COM 1 and since there was no COM1, you get this message.

More tests.

Click the Port Settings Button, and select a valid port then click Open Port. In our example we selected COM 26 – your test will probably select something different. Now open a second instance of the Open Tester and repeat the same process, thus attempting to open a port that is already open. You will receive a messageBox similar to the above except that the first line reads:

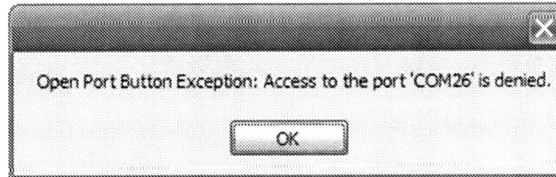

Open Port Button Exception: Access to the port 'COM26' is denied.

OK

Access Denied? Huh? This uninformative message leaves it to you to figure out that the reason access is denied is that COM26 is already open. It could have been a bit more helpful and informative - instead of sounding quite so Gestapo it could have told you more politely, "Sorry sweetie, but COM26 is already open."

Let's change the Data Bits to 3 then click the Reset Button and the Open Port Button and see what happens.

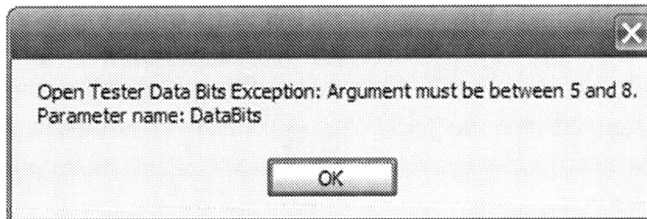

Open Tester Data Bits Exception: Argument must be between 5 and 8.
Parameter name: DataBits

OK

Hey, that is great – an informative message telling you both what happened and how to correct it.

Let's change the Baud Rate to –19200, click Reset and we get:

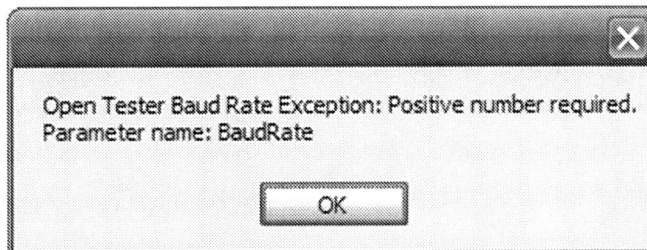

Open Tester Baud Rate Exception: Positive number required.
Parameter name: BaudRate

OK

Amazing, another helpful exception message - see, they aren't all bad.

Let's test the Close() method, but let's be sneaky, we'll open a port then unplug it so it isn't out there anymore, then we click the Close Port Button and we get:

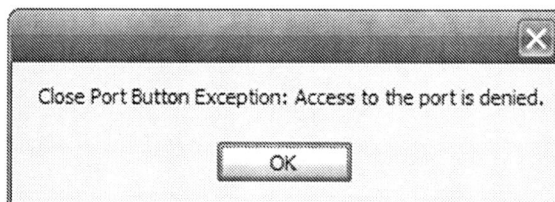

Oh gee, back to the attitude. And, funny that the MSDN Help on the Close() method only mentions that it can generate an InvalidOperationException, which it obviously didn't and for reasons we'll never fathom - more reason to not trust the Help files. And the exception we do get doesn't give any useful information other than it won't close the port, so I guess we'll have to live with that. If you plug the port back in and then re-click the Close Port Button, it closes okay, so at least we know that unplugging and plugging a port back in isn't going to cause a software disaster (in this case anyway). Sometimes it makes sense to forego the System message and put up a message that says something like: "Close Button Error: Is the device still plugged into the port?" As you discover common error conditions you can help your user by providing hints when you catch an exception.

More informative exception messages.

As you develop your software you will come across the uninformative exception messages, but you, as the developer, may know what actually caused them. In the above Open example the problem was that the port was already open. In the Close example the problem was that the port had been unplugged. Knowing this you could add to the catch block of each to provide the user with some hint as to what 'might' be wrong. Always waffle on your suggestion, since it might also be something else.

- To the catch block in the buttonOpenPortClick function –
- In C# add:

```
MessageBox.Show("Open Port Button Exception: " + ex.Message + "\n\nThis error wrap
may be caused if the port is already open.\nMake sure the port is closed wrap
before opening it.");
```

- In VB add:

```
MessageBox.Show("Open Port Button Exception: " & ex.Message & VbCrLf & "This wrap
error may be caused if the port is already open." & VbCrLf & "Make sure the wrap
port is closed before opening it.");
```

Run the tester and open a port, then click open again and you will see:

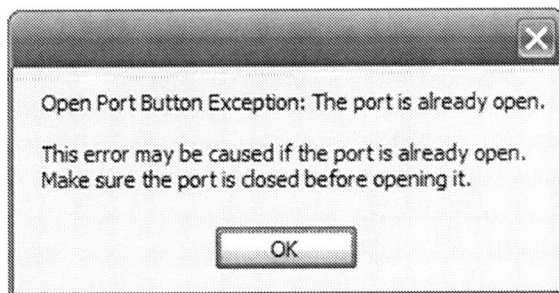

You can provide a list of possibilities if you have several candidates and save your users a lot of confusion and hassles (like sending you irate emails).

This doesn't show us all possible exceptions, play around a bit if you want to see more, but it does give us a good bit of insight into what they are and how to handle them – and how try/catch works.

Windows will generate exceptions that can be difficult to catch. I've observed that if you unplug an open serial port you might or might not get a system message. There are methods for trapping this condition by using a system exception delegate, but that is a bit out of scope for this book, and all it will allow you to do is give a more informative message since once this message is generated your only option is to close the application.

In the next chapter we will learn to use another error catching tool that is specific to the SerialPort Class. Instead of using try/catch we will use the delegate for the SerialErrorReceived Event.

Chapter 7: Open Method and Catching the Wiley Error

Chapter 8: Events and Some UART Bit-Twiddling

Events and delegates are closely related (a delegate is called when an event occurs), but delegates tend to be a bit more confusing, so we will look first at an event the SerialErrorReceived Event and the PinChanged Event, but defer delegates to the SerialDataReceived Event discussion in Chapter 9.

ErrorReceived Event

For the SerialPort Class we have two different kinds of error handling mechanisms. We saw in the last chapter the System errors that are generated by all sorts of events and can be trapped, we hope, using the try/catch technique. The second is the SerialErrorReceived Event. We will create a tester program to help us learn about it.

The SerialErrorReceived Event, is another thing that could have been done better by Microsoft. How? By associating the Error with the event that caused the error and telling the user what precisely caused the error. What happens is, for example, that a PinChanged Event or a DataReceived Event can occur at anytime relative to an ErrorReceived Event. What they say in the Help File is:

PinChanged, DataReceived, and ErrorReceived events may be called out of order, and there may be a slight delay between when the underlying stream reports the error and when code can when the event handler is executed. Only one event handler can execute at a time.

What they mean is that you can get an ErrorReceived Event triggered before you get the DataReceived or the PinChanged Event triggered. Think about it, you can get notice that the error occurred before you get notice that the event occurred. How stupid is that? Oh you'll know it was a pin change or data received that generated the error, just not which specific pin change or byte of data received. So instead of being able to write an error handler that deals with a specific pin or catches the specific byte, you have to deal with this on a more generic level – which virtually forces you to create an extra communication protocol layer that allows you to validate the correctness of an incoming package of data independent of what the SerialPort says and when it says it. Examples of such protocols are

ModBus, CAN, or LIN or something similar that you should probably be using anyway to assure robust communications. We won't be discussing these in this book, but thought you ought to know that you might need them later.

ErrorReceived Event Tester

Let's simplify our life and reuse Simple Terminal for this.
- Copy Simple Terminal to an ErrorReceived Event Tester directory.
- Collapse all the regions in Form1 so the code won't distract you and create a new region: ErrorReceived Test.
- In the design view, select the serialPort1 component and in the Properties window open the Events list and select ErrorReceived.
- In C# add:

```
#region ErrorReceived Event Tester
/*
Error Event Types for the ErrorReceived Event
Frame - The hardware detected a framing error.
Overrun - A character-buffer overrun has occurred. The next character is lost.
RXOver - An input buffer overflow has occurred. There is either no room in the
   input buffer, or a character was received after the end-of-file (EOF) character.
RXParity - The hardware detected a parity error.
TXFull - The application tried to transmit a character, but the output buffer was
   full.
*/
private void serialPort1_ErrorReceived(object sender,
System.IO.Ports.SerialErrorReceivedEventArgs e)
{
    if (e.EventType == System.IO.Ports.SerialError.RXParity)
    {
        MessageBox.Show("ErrorReceived: RXParity.");
    }
    else if (e.EventType == System.IO.Ports.SerialError.TXFull)
    {
        MessageBox.Show("ErrorReceived: TXFull");
    }
    else if (e.EventType == System.IO.Ports.SerialError.RXOver)
    {
        MessageBox.Show("ErrorReceived: RXOver");
    }
    else if (e.EventType == System.IO.Ports.SerialError.Overrun)
    {
        MessageBox.Show("ErrorReceived: Overrun");
    }
    else if (e.EventType == System.IO.Ports.SerialError.Frame)
    {
        MessageBox.Show("ErrorReceived: Frame");
    }
}
```

- In VB add:

```
#Region "ErrorReceived Event Tester"
'
'Error Event Types for the ErrorReceived Event
'Frame - The hardware detected a framing error.
'Overrun - A character-buffer overrun has occurred. The next character is lost.
'RXOver - An input buffer overflow has occurred. There is either no room in the
' input buffer, or a character was received after the end-of-file (EOF) character.
'RXParity - The hardware detected a parity error.
'TXFull - The application tried to transmit a character, but the output buffer was
' full.
'
Private Sub serialPort1_ErrorReceived(ByVal sender As Object, ByVal e As
System.IO.Ports.SerialErrorReceivedEventArgs) Handles serialPort1.ErrorReceived
    If e.EventType = System.IO.Ports.SerialError.RXParity Then
        MessageBox.Show("ErrorReceived: RXParity.")
    ElseIf e.EventType = System.IO.Ports.SerialError.TXFull Then
        MessageBox.Show("ErrorReceived: TXFull")
    ElseIf e.EventType = System.IO.Ports.SerialError.RXOver Then
        MessageBox.Show("ErrorReceived: RXOver")
    ElseIf e.EventType = System.IO.Ports.SerialError.Overrun Then
        MessageBox.Show("ErrorReceived: Overrun")
    ElseIf e.EventType = System.IO.Ports.SerialError.Frame Then
        MessageBox.Show("ErrorReceived: Frame")
    End If
End Sub

#End Region
```

We have chosen to document in the code the types of events that are reported. To test this:
- Open two instances of the ErrorEvent Tester.
- Open a serial port in one using the default settings.
- Open a serial port in the second using a different setting for Parity.
- Send a character from the first to the second and you should see:

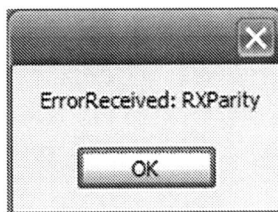

ErrorReceived: RXParity

OK

The remaining ErrorReceived errors would require some special gyrations to test and I'm sure if you feel you need to you can figure it out now that you've got the basics.

PinChanged Event

As we mentioned before, we can't rely on the PinChanged events occurring in any logical order with any other windows event, but we can assume that these signals will be sent out and read in a manner sufficient for their intended purpose – to control a modem communication session. We won't be using them for their intended purpose but to play with for slow and non-real-time binary I/O. This won't prove much of a handicap for monitoring slowly changing binary input from switches or performing binary output on such things as lighting an LED. When we say 'slow' in this context, we mean slow in computer time, not human time. When we send out a signal to turn on a LED it will turn on 'instantly' to us, and when we flick a switch our software will also respond 'instantly' in reference to our poky brain. Developers often refer to these off-brand uses of I/O pins as bit-banging, but we will reserve that term for section three of this book where we will learn to use all the FT232R pins for direct I/O using the FTDI D2XX DLL instead of Microsoft's SerialPort Class.

PinChanged Event Tester

We will create a test program that will allow us to use the modem lines to read switches and light some LEDs.

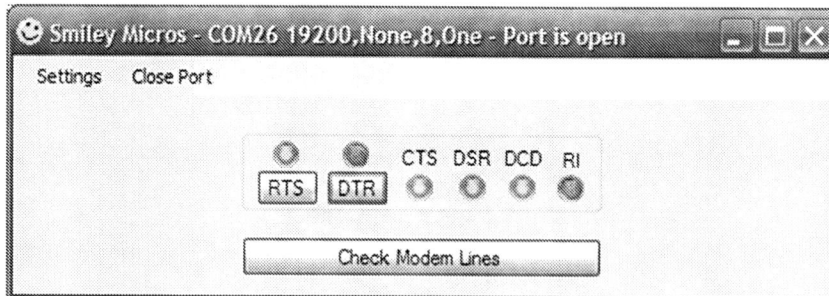

- Copy the Simple Terminal directory to a PinChanged Tester directory.
- Delete the textboxes and related code.
- Add buttons and labels as shown.
- Add six pictureBox components and set their size to 16,16. Name them:

- o pictureBoxRTS
- o pictureBoxDTR
- o pictureBoxCTS
- o pictureBoxDSR
- o pictureBoxDCD
- o pictureBoxRI

- Select an imageList component from the toolbox and drop into the Form1 designer widow.
- In the properties window for imageList1, double click the Collection button and you will see:

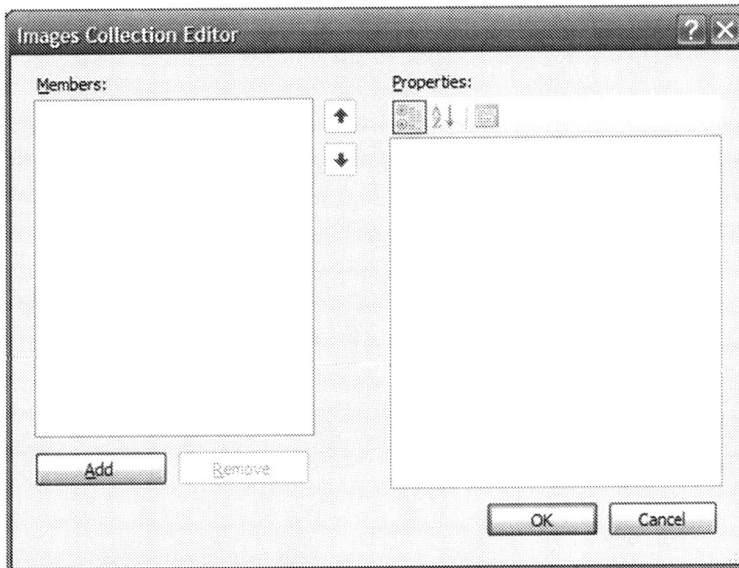

- Click the Add button and select the four LED images that are included in the project directory \Software\Graphics\:

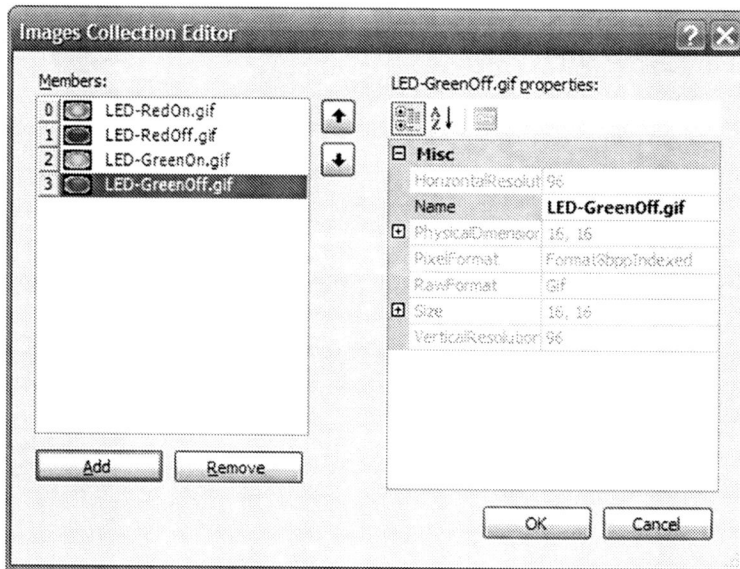

- Make certain that the images are in the order shown so that their index will match the following enumeration.
- At the beginning of the Form1 class above the constructor -
- In C# add:

```
public enum LEDColor { RedOn, RedOff, GreenOn, GreenOff }

private bool RTSState = false;
private bool DTRState = false;
private bool RingIndicator = false;
```

- In VB add;

```
Public Enum LEDColor
    RedOn
    RedOff
    GreenOn
    GreenOff
End Enum

Private RTSState As Boolean = False
Private DTRState As Boolean = False
Private RingIndicator As Boolean = False
```

- To the Form1 constructor –
- In C# add:

```
public Form1()
{
    InitializeComponent();

    pictureBoxRTS.BackgroundImage = imageList1.Images[(int)LEDColor.RedOff];
    pictureBoxDTR.BackgroundImage = imageList1.Images[(int)LEDColor.RedOff];
    pictureBoxCTS.BackgroundImage = imageList1.Images[(int)LEDColor.RedOff];
```

90

```
    pictureBoxDSR.BackgroundImage = imageList1.Images[(int)LEDColor.RedOff];
    pictureBoxDCD.BackgroundImage = imageList1.Images[(int)LEDColor.RedOff];
    pictureBoxRI.BackgroundImage = imageList1.Images[(int)LEDColor.RedOff];
}
```

- **In VB add:**

```
Public Sub New()
    InitializeComponent()

    pictureBoxRTS.BackgroundImage = imageList1.Images(CInt(Fix(LEDColor.RedOff)))
    pictureBoxDTR.BackgroundImage = imageList1.Images(CInt(Fix(LEDColor.RedOff)))
    pictureBoxCTS.BackgroundImage = imageList1.Images(CInt(Fix(LEDColor.RedOff)))
    pictureBoxDSR.BackgroundImage = imageList1.Images(CInt(Fix(LEDColor.RedOff)))
    pictureBoxDCD.BackgroundImage = imageList1.Images(CInt(Fix(LEDColor.RedOff)))
    pictureBoxRI.BackgroundImage = imageList1.Images(CInt(Fix(LEDColor.RedOff)))
End Sub
```

- Refer to the Simple Terminal code and add a Settings and Open Port Menu Items and associate these with the Settings Class as you have done before.

- Open the design view for Form1 and in its Properties/Events window double click the PinChanged event. Add to the resulting serialPort1_PinChanged event handler:

- **In C# add:**

```
// Show the modem states on the virtual LEDs
private          void          serialPort1_PinChanged(object          sender,
System.IO.Ports.SerialPinChangedEventArgs e)
{
    // Toggle RI since we can't determine the state with the SerialPort class
    if (e.EventType == SerialPinChange.Ring) RingIndicator = !RingIndicator;

    showCTS_DSR_CD();
}
```

- **In VB add:**

```
' Show the modem states on the virtual LEDs
Private    Sub    serialPort1_PinChanged(ByVal    sender    As    Object,    ByVal    e    As
System.IO.Ports.SerialPinChangedEventArgs) Handles serialPort1.PinChanged
    ' Toggle RI since we can't determine the state with the SerialPort class
    If e.EventType = SerialPinChange.Ring Then
        RingIndicator = Not RingIndicator
    End If

    showCTS_DSR_CD()
End Sub
```

- Create the showCTS_DSR_CD() function to indicate the input pin states:

- **In C# add:**

```
private void showCTS_DSR_CD()
{
    if (serialPort1.IsOpen)
    {
        if (serialPort1.CtsHolding) this.pictureBoxCTS.BackgroundImage = wrap
                        this.imageList1.Images[(int)LEDColor.GreenOn];
        else this.pictureBoxCTS.BackgroundImage = wrap
                        this.imageList1.Images[(int)LEDColor.RedOn];
```

91

```
        if (serialPort1.DsrHolding) this.pictureBoxDSR.BackgroundImage = wrap
                        this.imageList1.Images[(int)LEDColor.GreenOn];
        else this.pictureBoxDSR.BackgroundImage = wrap
                        this.imageList1.Images[(int)LEDColor.RedOn];

        if (serialPort1.CDHolding) this.pictureBoxDCD.BackgroundImage = wrap
                        this.imageList1.Images[(int)LEDColor.GreenOn];
        else this.pictureBoxDCD.BackgroundImage = wrap
                        this.imageList1.Images[(int)LEDColor.RedOn];

        if (RingIndicator) this.pictureBoxRI.BackgroundImage = wrap
                        this.imageList1.Images[(int)LEDColor.GreenOn];
        else this.pictureBoxRI.BackgroundImage = wrap
                        this.imageList1.Images[(int)LEDColor.RedOn];
    }
    else MessageBox.Show("Error in showCTS_DSR_CD - serailPort1 not open.");
}
```

- **In VB add:**

```
Private Sub showCTS_DSR_CD()
    If serialPort1.IsOpen Then
        If serialPort1.CtsHolding Then
            Me.pictureBoxCTS.BackgroundImage = wrap
                Me.imageList1.Images(CInt(Fix(LEDColor.GreenOn)))
        Else
            Me.pictureBoxCTS.BackgroundImage = wrap
                Me.imageList1.Images(CInt(Fix(LEDColor.RedOn)))
        End If

        If serialPort1.DsrHolding Then
            Me.pictureBoxDSR.BackgroundImage = wrap
                Me.imageList1.Images(CInt(Fix(LEDColor.GreenOn)))
        Else
            Me.pictureBoxDSR.BackgroundImage = wrap
                Me.imageList1.Images(CInt(Fix(LEDColor.RedOn)))
        End If

        If serialPort1.CDHolding Then
            Me.pictureBoxDCD.BackgroundImage = wrap
                Me.imageList1.Images(CInt(Fix(LEDColor.GreenOn)))
        Else
            Me.pictureBoxDCD.BackgroundImage = wrap
                Me.imageList1.Images(CInt(Fix(LEDColor.RedOn)))
        End If

        If RingIndicator Then
            Me.pictureBoxRI.BackgroundImage = wrap
                Me.imageList1.Images(CInt(Fix(LEDColor.GreenOn)))
        Else
            Me.pictureBoxRI.BackgroundImage = wrap
                Me.imageList1.Images(CInt(Fix(LEDColor.RedOn)))
        End If
    Else
        MessageBox.Show("Error in showCTS_DSR_CD - serailPort1 not open.")
    End If
End Sub
```

The modem signal lines are now available for you to use with the SerialPort Class. You can use these lines as intended to control a communication session with a modem, something I will not demonstrate since my modems are all buried in the garage in the 'save for a technical museum' corner (filled with astonishing artifacts once costing a fortune and now not able to give away.)

I will show you how to uses these lines to do some simple binary input and output. You have two output lines: DTR and RTS and four input lines RI, DSR, DCD, and CTS. The original uses of these lines is discussed elsewhere, but for now we will just refer to them by their acronym and not worry about how the naming came to be. We will test these with a BBUSB where we will connect the DTR and RTS output lines to the RI and DSR input lines and then watch the virtual LEDs turn off and on in response to us clicking the DTR and RTS button. Next we will test the outputs with the DCD and CTS input lines. And finally we will hook the outputs up to real LEDs and the inputs up to real switches, since we won't really believe the software if we don't actually light something up and get to play with some switches.

- With a BBUSB properly wired for power on a breadboard, connect the RTS pin to the DSR pin and the DTR pin to the RI pin.
- Click the DTR button and the RI LED will turn green indicating that the RTS line is high, Click the button again and both LEDs should turn red indicating the RTS line is low. Yes, I know the book illustrations are in black and white, but let's just pretend, since if you are writing the code, you'll get to see this in color, unless you are color blind and then, uh...?

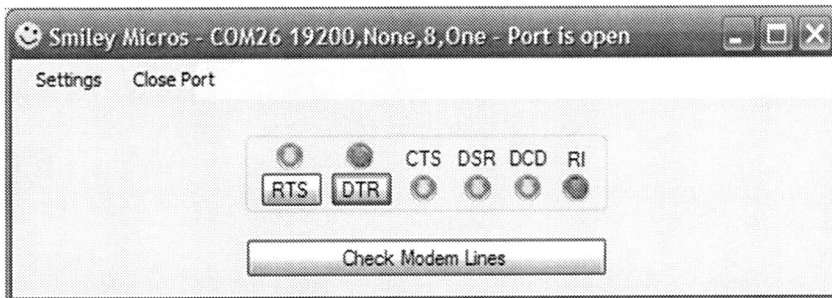

- Now repeat the process with the RTS button and observe DSR button change color.

- You are now officially using your PC software to control external devices and read input from external devices.

Off-Label Use – Reading Switches and Lighting LEDs

Aw, to heck with all those modem lines, who uses old-fashioned phone line modems anymore anyway? But being able to control hardware by reading two on/off voltages or setting four on/off states, well now we are talking some real fun. For this experiment we will check switches for user input, and set LEDs for communicating with a user.

Wire the BBUSB for Some Bit-Twiddling:

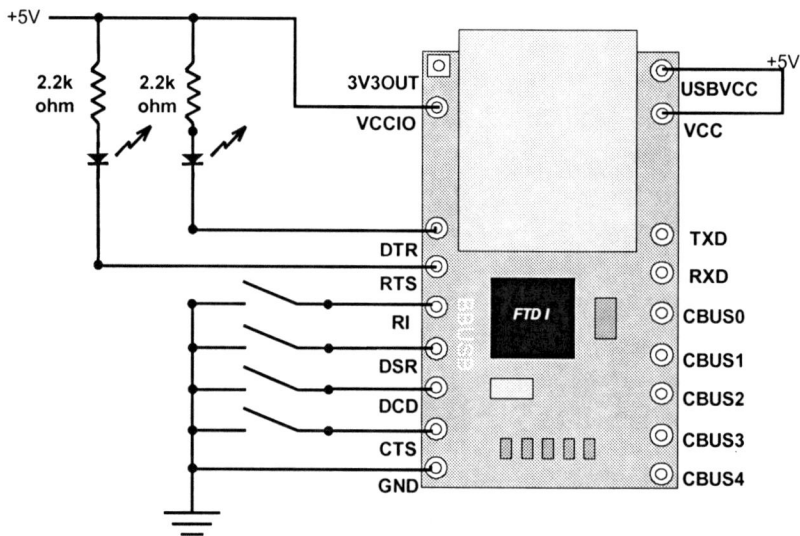

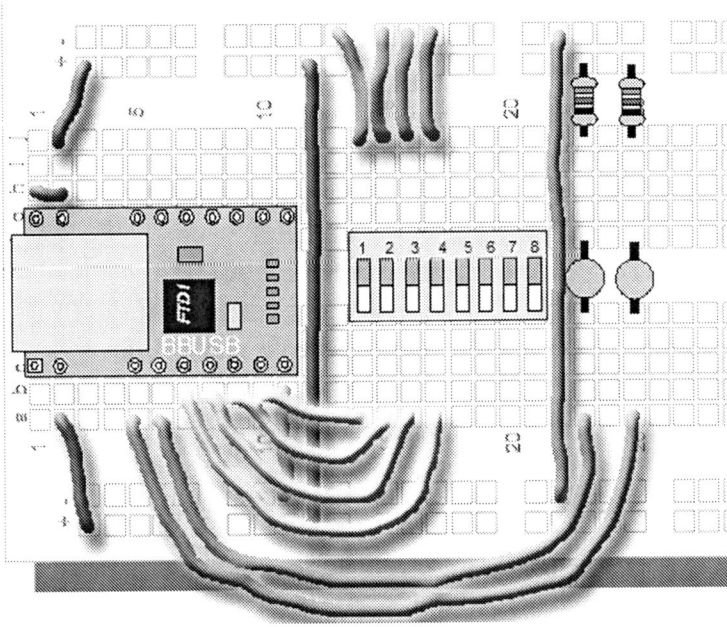

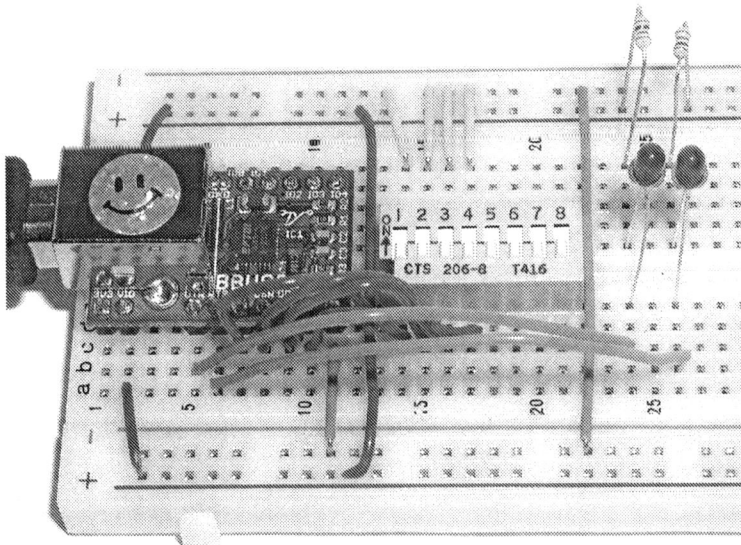

- Before wiring this up, unplug the USB cable. If you accidentally short power to ground your USB may just cut off with a message that it was drawing too much power, or your PC may crash. Guess how I know this.

- Wire the BBUSB for +5V
    - Wire USBVCC to VCC
    - Wire VCC to breadboard +5V
    - Wire VIO to breadboard +5V
    - Wire GND to breadboard GND
- Wire RI, DSR, DCE, and CTS to the off side of the first four switches on the 8-position DIP-switch.
- Connect the ON side of these switches to ground
- Connect DTR and RTS to the short leg (cathode) of the LEDs.
- Connect the LED long leg (anode) to +5V through the 2.2k ohm resistors.
- Open the PinChangedTester and select the BBUSB port.
- Toggle the DTR and RTS buttons and note the LEDs turn on and off.
- Turn the four switches on and off and note the virtual LEDs on the PinChangedTester turn on and off.

How cool is that? Using the methods you just learned are appropriate for a system where you want to have the TxD and RxD to communicate with a microcontroller UART, and you want to use the modem lines for some slow binary input and output. You could potentially use the four binary inputs to monitor external events such as someone breaking a light beam in an entry detection system. You could use the two binary outputs to control two motors with elaborate mechanical levers and gearing so that you could make a manipulator that could grab the USB line and unplug itself – a sort of SuicideBot. Okay, hopefully you can come up with something saner than that. But before you get too excited and spend a lot of time twiddling the modem I/O, just be aware that in the third section of this book we will learn to use the FTDI D2XX DLL which will give us direct control of all 13 of the lines of the BBUSB and use each of them for both input and output.

Now we know how to catch errors and handle events, next we will learn about delegates – a real pain, but a necessary one.

Chapter 9: Delegates and Receiving Data

A word or two (or three) about delegates.

Our programs can have code that runs in different threads. This means that some of our code is running independently of other code. For instance, we may have a GUI with a textBox running and we may also have another tread that is monitoring a port waiting for a byte of data to be received on that port. When that byte is received, we'd like to show it in the textBox thread, but since these are two separate threads we can't have the port monitoring thread put the byte directly into the textBox, we have to provide the port monitoring thread with a delegate function for the textBox that it can call to have the textBox place the character on the screen in the textBox. This is complicated to me, so I will explain it three different ways hoping to make it clearer.

A delegate has a function declaration signature: the return type and parameter list type – and your instance of the delegate must have the same signature. The thread of code that will be using your delegate has no way of knowing how you actually wrote the function you want it to call, so it specifies the signature and assumes you will follow that specification.

Example of a delegate signature:
```
Delegate int SomeDelegate(bool b, string s);
```

This delegate has a signature with a return type of int and takes two parameters: a bool and a string. When you create an instance of this delegate class you will pass a pointer (an address) to your instance to the event function in another thread that you want have use your function.

If you write a function for the event with the same signature:
```
private int SomeFunction(bool bln, string str)
```

You can pass a pointer (the address) of your SomeFunction to the constructor of SomeDelegate when you instantiate it:
```
SomeDelegate sd = new SomeDelegate(SomeFunction);
```

97

Now when the tread that contains the SomeDelegate function calls the delegate, that thread will actually call your SomeFunction.

Yes, this is hard to make clear. If you've already got it, bear with me, if not I'll back up and run over it a few more times. You don't really need to understand delegates to use them cookbook style so you can skip over the next rehash and goto the Serial Data Received Event section.

Rehash

In Chapter 6 we used the DataReceived Event and created a delegate for it when we built the Simple Terminal. I advised:

- Our receive functions use a delegate to allow the serial port read thread to write to our receive text box. This is a bit complex, so for the time being just use it and we will see how it all works later during the discussion of the Developers Terminal.

I used the phrase 'a bit complex' because I was afraid that if I addressed this topic at that point in the discussion, many of my newbie readers would toss the book like a little girl who had just opened a box full or worms, spiders, and frogs (I'm picturing the readers dropping the book, running, screaming, hands flapping, feet stamping) But I figure that by now all the little girls have grown into big strong stomached women and are ready for a challenge. You might not find this challenging, but I sure did, so relax and prepare yourself to open the box.

We have control over when we send text out the serial port, but we have no way of knowing when we will receive text. It's like the telephone; you call at your convenience but you receive calls sometimes when you are naked, wet, and scrubbing something private. Windows won't metaphorically jump out of the tub to answer the phone. Windows attends to the phone when it is darn well ready and relies on an answering machine to take messages. That's why Windows isn't a real-time operating system. For instance, on occasion I'll be typing and notice that the cursor stops even though I'm still typing and after a few seconds all the words I typed suddenly jump on the screen. Windows buffers the keyboard input and usually sends them to Word for display quick enough that it normally appears to be happening in real-time, but sometimes Windows decides that there are other things more important to do than keeping up with my input (like servicing a virus that sends my banking passwords to Nigeria) so it goes off and does those 'more important' things before coming back and catching up with updating the words on the screen.

Oversimplifying things, Windows runs a lot of programs concurrently, each getting a little bit of time, but none getting a large percentage of the available time. Since these programs run intermittently their state is saved before another program snippet is run and when the stopped program gets to run again its prior state is reinstated and since an indeterminate amount of time has passed, the program needs to check for and respond to messages that might have arrived while it was catatonic.

In our case, two programs (or more properly: threads) of interest are running, the GUI that will show characters on PC monitor and the serial port service that is actually getting the characters from the port. The characters can arrive at any time, and several may be in the receive buffer when the GUI awakens. The character receiving function running in one thread has no direct mechanism to put that character on a textBox running in another thread like the GUI thread.

What we do is to delegate the job to a function in the thread containing the textBox so it can accept characters from the SerialDataReceivedEvent and put them in a textBox. Then we invoke that delegate in the thread that is receiving characters from the port. By analogy this is like our GUI Shop sending a guy, the GUI delegate, over to the Receive Shop and having him wait around until a character arrives at which time the Receive Shop guy 'invokes' or yells out, 'Hey, GUI guy, I got a character for you!" which the GUI guy then takes back over to the GUI shop and pastes it in the window. Fortunately, these guys move at GigaHertz speeds. Now of course the analogy is lame and butchers the whole Windows messaging idea, which is more analogous to a post office (including the occasional guy going postal and hosing the place with an assault rifle), but let's leave it.

So our GUI needs to designate a delegate for the textBox that will be used by the SerialPort function to put a character into the textBox.

If you are already familiar with C programming then a delegate is the same as a function pointer. If you aren't already familiar with the concept, it means that the delegate is the address of a function, so you can provide this address to another function and that other function can then call your function when an event occurs.

Let's say that we have a Black-Box Function BBF that is run by windows in response to an event, say the arrival of a byte on a port. The designers of BBF might realize that folks who want to use BBF will want to see that newly arrived byte and use it when it arrives. Since the designers of BBF will have no way of knowing how the user might want to deal with an incoming byte, they provide a mechanism that allows the user to provide BBF with information that BBF can use to call the user function when the event occurs (byte arrives). The BBF designers must provide a contract to the user that says that if you provide me with a function pointer with this specific list of parameters, I'll load the parameters according to our agreement and call your function when the event occurs. This means that a programmer who wants to use BBF can read the documentation and find the 'contract' - the specification - of how the BBF expects the calling function to be written (the function declaration signature), and if the user writes a function to those specs and provides BBF with a delegate (the address of their function) then BBF will call that when the event occurs. Of course if you get the parameter list or return value wrong – who knows what will happen – so be careful and test well.

We are forced to use this mechanism when we want to use the information from an event that will happen in a different thread from the thread in which our main code is running if we want to use that information in a component in the main thread such as a textBox.

Okay, I've tried three times in slightly different ways to explain this – way overkill, but like I said, I had a hard time getting it. We could get really deep in this and try to really fully understand all the aspects of threads, delegates, and invoke but we will get bogged down in minutia that isn't directly related to our goal of having a PC talk to a microcontroller. So, again, I will recommend just try to understand enough to use this code and don't spend time here trying to master it.

SerialDataReceived Event

The SerialDataReceived Event is caused by receiving a character or an Eof (End of file). These events are defined in the SerialData enumeration:
Chars - A character was received and placed in the input buffer.
Eof - The end of file character was received and placed in the input buffer.

You should be able to assign an Eof 'End of file' character and use this to know when a file (or line) has been sent. BUT, I tried to use the Eof event and couldn't get it to work, nor could I find a working example in either MSDN or on the Internet, so I suspect either I am an idiot (likely), or it really doesn't work and Microsoft failed to mention it (also likely). But it is easy to work around it, so we will assume all SerialDataReceived Events are for characters and then allow our code to catch an Eof that we designate and look for if we want to use that method for communicating with files or lines. If you, dear reader, figure out how to use the Eof, please let me know.

We will bypass this embarrassment by using a Boolean to indicate that we are in either character or line mode. And then we will use the character or line send and receive functions based on the flag – NOT on what we are receiving.

Yet Another Caveat:
Note that like in other places the Help File says: *Because the operating system determines whether to raise this event or not, not all parity errors may be reported.* Which translates to, *took another coffee break, so screw you.*

They also repeat what we saw earlier: *PinChanged, DataReceived, and ErrorReceived, events may be called out of order, and there may be a slight delay between when the underlying stream reports the error and when the event handler is executed. Only one event handler can execute at a time.*

Meaning their error detection is more or less useless, so as mentioned earlier, for robust communications you need to use a protocol which deals with the kind of errors that Microsoft was to lazy to deal with.

SerialDataReceived Event Tester

Let's again recycle the Simple Terminal. Copy the file in your Simple Terminal directory to a SerialDataEvent Tester directory and then modify the GUI to look like:

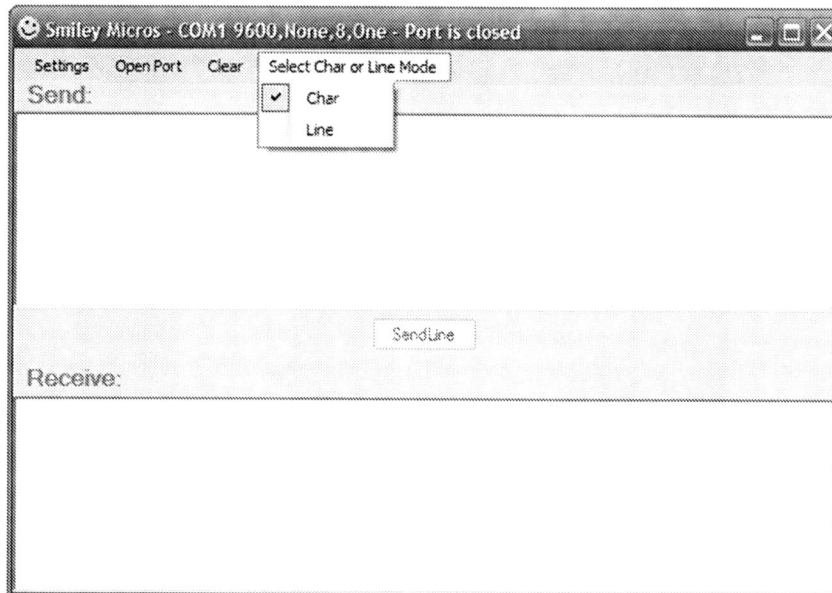

Notice that the SendLine button is disabled and the Char item in the 'Select Char or Line Mode is checked.

In this tester we will provide the serialPort1_DataReceived function with a delegate, setText, that it can invoke to have a character placed in a textBox.

- To the Initialization region –
- In C# add:

```csharp
#region Initialization
// CharMode true use char tranmission and reception
// CharMode false use char tranmission and reception
private bool CharMode = true;

private string SendString = "";

public Form1()
{
```

```
    InitializeComponent();

    // Begin in Char Mode
    charToolStripMenuItem.Checked = true;
    lineToolStripMenuItem.Checked = false;

    // show the settings in the form text line
    showSettings();
}
#endregiOn
```

- **In VB add:**

```
#Region "Initialization"
' CharMode true use char tranmission and reception
' CharMode false use char tranmission and reception
Private CharMode As Boolean = True

Private SendString As String = ""

Public Sub New()
    InitializeComponent()

    ' Begin in Char Mode
    charToolStripMenuItem.Checked = True
    lineToolStripMenuItem.Checked = False

    ' show the settings in the form text line
    showSettings()
End Sub
#End Region
```

- **In the GUI section add code for the SendLine Button and the 'Select Char or Line Mode' menu items -**
- **In C# add:**

```
private void buttonSendLine_Click(object sender, EventArgs e)
{
    try
    {
        serialPort1.WriteLine(SendString);
    }
    catch (System.Exception ex)
    {
        MessageBox.Show("Error - buttonSendLine_Click Exception: " + ex);
    }

    SendString = "";
}

private void charToolStripMenuItem_Click(object sender, EventArgs e)
{
    charToolStripMenuItem.Checked = true;
    lineToolStripMenuItem.Checked = false;
    buttonSendLine.Enabled = false;

    CharMode = true;
```

```
}

private void lineToolStripMenuItem_Click(object sender, EventArgs e)
{
    charToolStripMenuItem.Checked = false;
    lineToolStripMenuItem.Checked = true;
    buttonSendLine.Enabled = true;

    CharMode = false;

}
```
- In VB:
```
Private Sub buttonSendLine_Click(ByVal sender As Object, ByVal e As EventArgs)
Handles buttonSendLine.Click
    Try
        serialPort1.WriteLine(SendString)
    Catch ex As System.Exception
        MessageBox.Show("Error - buttonSendLine_Click Exception: ", ex.ToString())
    End Try

    SendString = ""
End Sub

Private Sub charToolStripMenuItem_Click(ByVal sender As Object, ByVal e As
EventArgs) Handles charToolStripMenuItem.Click
    charToolStripMenuItem.Checked = True
    lineToolStripMenuItem.Checked = False
    buttonSendLine.Enabled = False

    CharMode = True
End Sub

Private Sub lineToolStripMenuItem_Click(ByVal sender As Object, ByVal e As
EventArgs) Handles lineToolStripMenuItem.Click
    charToolStripMenuItem.Checked = False
    lineToolStripMenuItem.Checked = True
    buttonSendLine.Enabled = True

    CharMode = False
End Sub
```
- Here is where we will provide a delegate, setText, to the event handler.
- In the Receive Functions region modify the serialPort1_DataReceived function -
- In C#:
```
private void serialPort1_DataReceived(object sender,
System.IO.Ports.SerialDataReceivedEventArgs e)
{
    // instantiate the delegate to be invoked by this thread
    setText = new SetText(mySetText);

    if (CharMode) // character mode
    {
        // load the data into the string
        try
```

```
        {
            str = serialPort1.ReadExisting();
        }
        catch (System.Exception ex)
        {
            MessageBox.Show("Error - char mode port_DataReceived Exception: wrap
                            " + ex);
        }
    }
    else // line mode
    {
        // load the data into the string
        try
        {
            str = serialPort1.ReadLine();
        }
        catch (System.Exception ex)
        {
            MessageBox.Show("Error - line mode port_DataReceived Exception: wrap
                            " + ex);
        }
    }

    // invoke the delegate in the MainForm thread
    this.Invoke(setText);
}
```

- **In VB:**

```
' note that this function runs in a separate thread and thus we must use a
' delegate in order to display the results in the richTextBox.
Private Sub serialPort1_DataReceived(ByVal sender As Object, ByVal e As
System.IO.Ports.SerialDataReceivedEventArgs) Handles serialPort1.DataReceived
    ' instantiate the delegate to be invoked by this thread
    setTextI = New SetText(AddressOf mySetText)

    If CharMode Then ' character mode
        ' load the data into the string
        Try
            str = serialPort1.ReadExisting()
        Catch ex As System.Exception
            MessageBox.Show("Error - char mode port_DataReceived wrap
                            Exception: ", ex.ToString())
        End Try
    Else ' line mode
        ' load the data into the string
        Try
            str = serialPort1.ReadLine()
        Catch ex As System.Exception
            MessageBox.Show("Error - line mode port_DataReceived wrap
                            Exception: ", ex.ToString())
        End Try
    End If

    ' invoke the delegate in the MainForm thread
    Me.Invoke(setTextI)
End Sub
```

Set up your hardware as shown in Chapter 2: BBUSB Quick Start Guide for the loopback test where you connect the TxD and RxD pins together. Then open the BBUSB in the SerialDataReceivedEvent Tester and test the Menu Select Char or Line Mode items by checking either Char or Line and note that when Char is checked you send one character at a time, but when Line is checked the Send line is not received until the SendLine button is pressed.

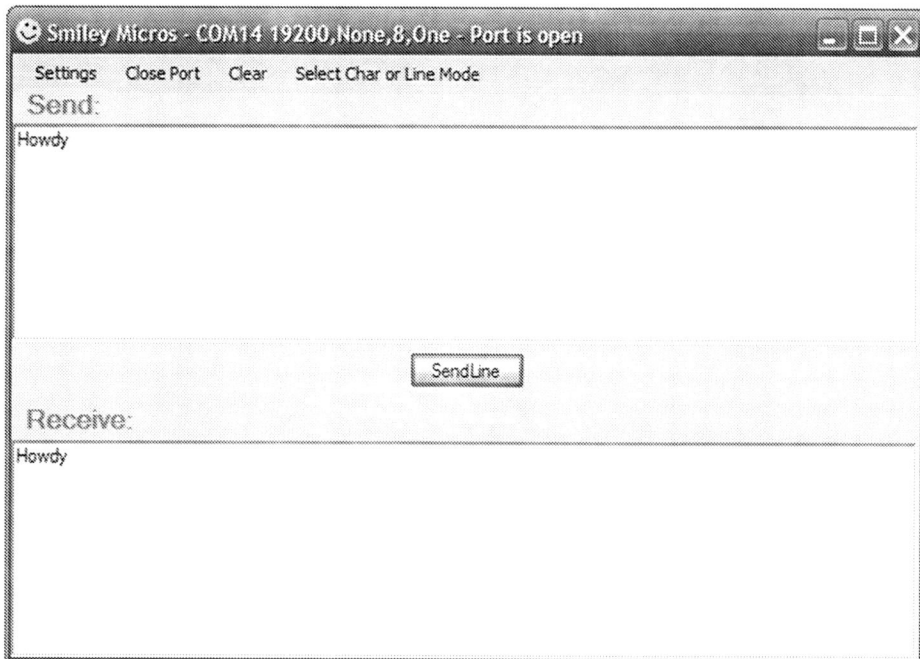

This tester demonstrates the SerialDataReceived Event and some of the methods to read and write characters or lines. We will show details of these methods in the next chapter.

In this chapter we learned more than we ever wanted to know about delegates, but since they are necessary we can at least be happy to know they are behind us. In the next chapter we'll look at something conceptually simpler, serial port reading and writing.

Chapter 10: Reading and Writing

Writing

We have already used both the SerialPort Class Write and WriteLine Methods. The Write method sends one 8-bit byte at a time while the WriteLine method writes a string of 7-bit characters. Try not to get confused about my use of byte and character when reading C# documentation. In C# everything gets put in some sort of Unicode data type, but we are interested in old fashioned data transmission where we would like to send an 8-bit value, which we can do with the Write method, or emulate the old-fashioned 7-bit ASCII code, which we can do by using the WriteLine method. Most developers will find the 8-bit method preferable for our microcontroller communication, but we'll look at the 7-bit method just in case we ever need it.

When we send a line let's try to think of the data transmission as being in a human readable form. Displaying the results of a line transmission is simple since most of the ASCII codes we might be interested in can be displayed. Appendix 1 has the codes.

When we send a byte we are sending an integer from 0 to 255. If a printable character just happens to have one of the byte values then we can look at it, for example the byte with a value of 74 can be shown as the character whose ASCII code is 74: 'J'. But mostly when we send and receive bytes we will look at the actual integer, and we will look at it in Hexadecimal for reasons that make sense when you are interested in knowing the actual bit states of the byte (you might be reading a series of switches each represented by a bit in the byte) but if that didn't make any sense to you then you'll just have to accept for now that we are going to look at bytes in Hex for some mystical reason. Looking at the above example, the character 'J' is coded as decimal 74 which is hexadecimal 0x4A. This will eventually make sense.

Some Write Properties

SerialPort.WriteBufferSize Property

Ignores any value smaller than 2048 – What? Why? And who cares since our professed goal is microcontroller communications, which is unlikey to have a 2048 bytes of RAM to spare, so we can ignore this one.

SerialPort.WriteTimeout Property
The Help File says:
*The following code example demonstrates the use of the **SerialPort** class to allow two users to chat from two separate computers connected by a null modem cable. In this example, the users are prompted for the port settings and a username before chatting. This code example is part of a larger code example provided for the **SerialPort** class.*

Great! Wonderful! We can really use that! But, ummm... guess what? No following code. Tired of me gripping about the Help File? Me too. Man, if I'd paid for this software I'd be really pissed!

So this property is used to set the number of milliseconds before a write timeout occurs. And since they have such a weird mention of but lack of an example, I have to wonder if there is a problem, so I think it would be safer just to skip over this one also.

Reading:

And since I'm in a skip the BS mood, I think we'll simplify our lives a bit and also pass on:

Some Read Properties:
ReadBufferSize Property
ReadTimeout Property
ReceivedBytesThreshold Property

The timeouts might come in handy if you want to write a protocol where you send a byte and need to wait around for a response, but I'm more willing to trust a timer and a flag to handle that situation.

We've used the ReadExisting and ReadLine methods, so let's look at the other read methods.

ReadExisting Method
ReadLine Method
Read Method
        Read Method (Byte[], Int32, Int32)
        Read Method (Char[], Int32, Int32)
ReadByte Method
ReadChar Method
ReadTo Method

ReadTo Method:

The Help File says:
This method reads a string up to the specified value. While the returned string does not include the value, the value is removed from the input buffer.

If it is necessary to switch between reading text and reading binary data from the stream, select a protocol that carefully defines the boundary between text and binary data, such as manually reading bytes and decoding the data.

Note:
Because the SerialPort class buffers data, and the stream contained in the BaseStream property does not, the two might conflict about how many bytes are available to read. The BytesToRead property can indicate that there are bytes to read, but these bytes might not be accessible to the stream contained in the BaseStream property because they have been buffered to the SerialPort class.

I'm seeing:
"select a protocol that carefully defines..."
"the two might conflict about how many bytes are available to read..."

Are these guys nuts?
And I'm trying to stay calm here, but I think I'll just assume like I have for a few other SerialPort tools that the writer is insane and I will pass on using this one.

To top this off I invite the reader to open the Help File and read what it has to say about the ReadByte and ReadChar methods. Okay let's all take a deep breath and repeat: 'I think I'll just stick with the ReadExisting and ReadLine methods since they will do anything I want and don't have the cryptic cautions and warnings.'

Text and Hex Read Write Tester

In the last chapter we showed how to read and write ordinary text, this time let's develop some code for sending and displaying the data in Hex. Let's create a new directory Read Write Tester and copy the LineReadWrite Tester code to it to modify for use here. (Source code in \Software\Chapter 10 – Read and Write\)

- Change the Select Char or Line Mode menu item to:

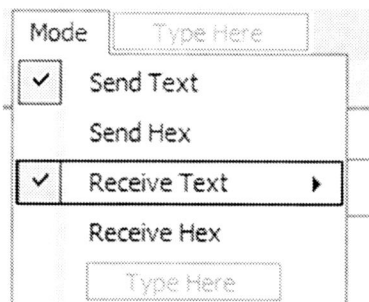

- To the initialization region -
- In C# add:

```csharp
private bool ReceiveHexMode = false;

public Form1()
{
    InitializeComponent();

    // Begin in Text Mode
    receiveTextToolStripMenuItem.Checked = true;
    receiveHexToolStripMenuItem.Checked = false;

    // show the settings in the form text line
    showSettings();
}
```

- In VB add:

```vb
#Region "Initialization"

Private ReceiveHexMode As Boolean = False

Public Sub New()
    InitializeComponent()
```

```
    ' Begin in Text Mode
    receiveTextToolStripMenuItem.Checked = True
    receiveHexToolStripMenuItem.Checked = False

    label2.Text = "Receive Text:"

    ' show the settings in the form text line
    showSettings()
End Sub
```

- **Create click event methods for each of the new menu items.**
- **In C# add:**

```
#region Mode Menu
private void receiveTextToolStripMenuItem_Click(object sender, EventArgs e)
{
    // Receive Text Mode
    receiveTextToolStripMenuItem.Checked = true;
    receiveHexToolStripMenuItem.Checked = false;
    ReceiveHexMode = false;
    label2.Text = "Receive Text:";
}

private void receiveHexToolStripMenuItem_Click(object sender, EventArgs e)
{
    // Receive Hex Mode
    receiveTextToolStripMenuItem.Checked = false;
    receiveHexToolStripMenuItem.Checked = true;
    ReceiveHexMode = true;
    label2.Text = "Receive Hex:";
}
#endregion
```

- **In VB add:**

```
Private Sub receiveTextToolStripMenuItem_Click(ByVal sender As Object, ByVal e As
EventArgs) Handles receiveTextToolStripMenuItem.Click
    ' Receive Text Mode
    receiveTextToolStripMenuItem.Checked = True
    receiveHexToolStripMenuItem.Checked = False
    ReceiveHexMode = False
    label2.Text = "Receive Text:"
End Sub

Private Sub receiveHexToolStripMenuItem_Click(ByVal sender As Object, ByVal e As
EventArgs) Handles receiveHexToolStripMenuItem.Click
    ' Receive Hex Mode
    receiveTextToolStripMenuItem.Checked = False
    receiveHexToolStripMenuItem.Checked = True
    ReceiveHexMode = True
    label2.Text = "Receive Hex:"
End Sub
```

- **Modify mySetText –**
- **In C# add:**

```
// create the instance of the delegate to be used to write the received data to
the richTextBox
```

```
public void mySetText()
{
    if (ReceiveHexMode) // Hex mode
    {
        //MessageBox.Show("ReceiveHexMode");
        foreach (byte b in str)
        {
            if (b > 15)
            {
                richTextBox2.Text += "0x" + b.ToString("X") + ",";
            }
            else richTextBox2.Text += "0x0" + b.ToString("X") + ",";
        }

    }
    else // Text mode
    {
        // show the text
        richTextBox2.Text += str.ToString();

        moveCaretToEnd();
    }
}
```

- **In VB add:**

```
' create the instance of the delegate to be used to write the received data to the
' richTextBox
Public Sub mySetText()
    If ReceiveHexMode Then ' Hex mode

        Dim encoding As New System.Text.ASCIIEncoding()
        encoding.GetBytes(str)

        Dim encodedBytes As Byte() = encoding.GetBytes(str)
        Dim b As Byte
        For Each b In encodedBytes
            If b > 15 Then
                richTextBox2.Text &= "0x" & b.ToString("X") & ","
            Else
                richTextBox2.Text &= "0x0" & b.ToString("X") & ","
            End If
        Next b

    Else ' Text mode
        ' show the text
        richTextBox2.Text += str.ToString()

        moveCaretToEnd()
    End If
End Sub
```

- Test this by opening two instances of the tester program and open two ports. First send 'abc' and a line return to an instance with the mode set to Receive Text. Next change the mode to Receive Hex and again transmit 'abc'. You will see:

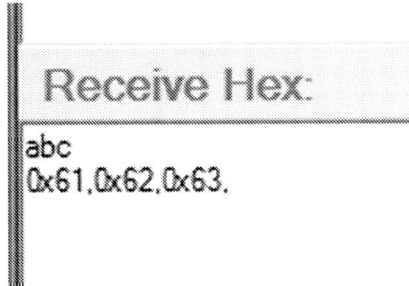

- In the Receive Hex mode you see the value of the ASCII characters a, b, and c expressed in Hex. (see Appendix 1: ASCII Tablet)
- To send Hex data, let's add a comboBox and label to Form1:

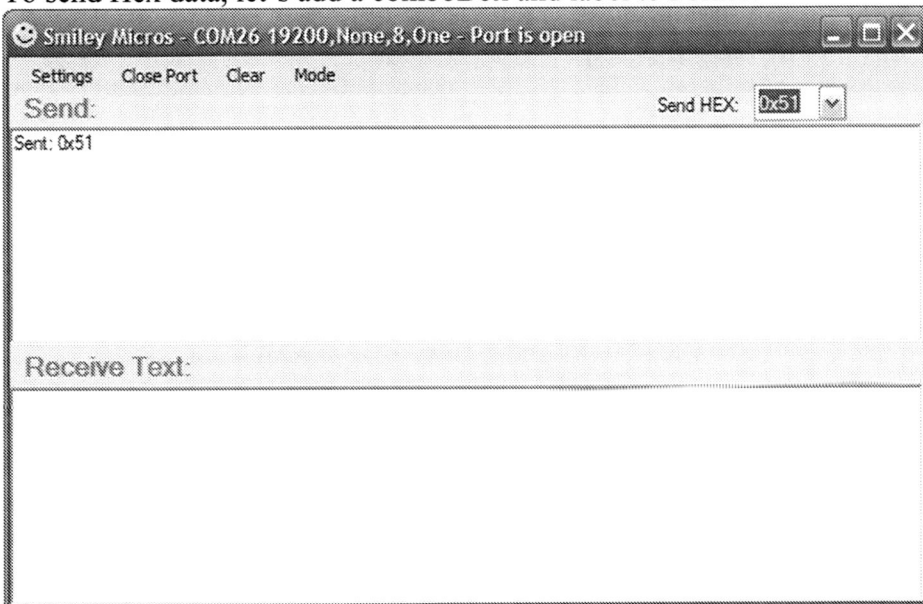

- Select Form1 and add the Load Event and fill the comboBox with Hex 0x00 to 0xFF –
- In C# add:

```
private void Form1_Load(object sender, EventArgs e)
{
    // Load the comboBox with 0x00 to 0xFF
    for (int i = 0; i < 16; i++)
    {
        this.comboBoxSendByte.Items.Add("0x0" + i.ToString("X"));
    }
    for (int i = 16; i < 256; i++)
    {
```

```
        this.comboBoxSendByte.Items.Add("0x" + i.ToString("X"));
    }
}
```

- **In VB add:**

```
Private Sub Form1_Load(ByVal sender As Object, ByVal e As EventArgs) Handles
MyBase.Load
    ' Load the comboBox with 0x00 to 0xFF
    For i As Integer = 0 To 15
        Me.comboBoxSendByte.Items.Add("0x0" & i.ToString("X"))
    Next i
    For i As Integer = 16 To 255
        Me.comboBoxSendByte.Items.Add("0x" & i.ToString("X"))
    Next i
End Sub
```

- **To the comboBox SelectedIndexChanged Event -**

- **In C# add:**

```
private void comboBoxSendByte_SelectedIndexChanged(object sender, EventArgs e)
{
    sendChar((char)comboBoxSendByte.SelectedIndex);
    this.richTextBox1.Text = "Sent: 0x" + wrap
                comboBoxSendByte.SelectedIndex.ToString("X");
}
```

- **In VB add:**

```
Private Sub comboBoxSendByte_SelectedIndexChanged(ByVal sender As Object, wrap
        ByVal e As EventArgs) Handles comboBoxSendByte.SelectedIndexChanged
    sendChar(ChrW(comboBoxSendByte.SelectedIndex))
    Me.richTextBox1.Text = "Sent: 0x" & wrap
                comboBoxSendByte.SelectedIndex.ToString("X")
End Sub
```

- To test this you can send 0x51 and receive it as Hex 0x51 or text 'Q'.

We could write code to interpret Hex formatted text data input in the Send textbox (ex: the actual 4 character for 0x51 – '0','x','5', and '1') and send it out as Hex values, but that would require a lot of effort when there are better (easier) ways.

In the next two chapters we will learn how to make data persistent (like as in saving it to the hard drive) using XML files and we will use this to allow us to use a text editor to write an XML file with Hex data that we can send. This is another section were we will tend to forget what the book is really about which is, umm…

114

Chapter 11: XML - Settings

XML? What the Hell?

Yeah, I kind of wondered that myself when I first started using XML, but I've come to believe that it is essential to have a simple way to store data on the PC in order to use a microcontroller from a PC. There are many such needs, whether you are making a data logger that will download to a PC or you want to keep various sets of initialization parameters for an embedded system and load them depending on variable uses – you will need to save data and XML provides the very great benefit of not only having lots of tools (actually too many), but saving the data in a human readable format. Being able to open a file in Notepad and read and modify it can work wonders in the debugging process. And once you get used to data tags, it all sort of makes good sense.

We will develop a settings facility that will allow us to use Notepad or any other ASCII text editor to create a text file that has various settings parameters that we can use to initialize our PC code or we can send the data to initialize our microcontroller.

In the next chapter will develop a macro facility which will allow us to write sequences of text or Hex data that we will be able to send from our terminal to a microcontroller with a single mouse click, no more repetitive data entry, just enter it once and use it forever.

Cue theme from X-files… "…do you really want to know?…"

My study of using XML revealed that there are so many ways to do this that it is difficult to pick out the best (read easiest) way to accomplish the job at hand. So rather than learning all about the topic, I borrowed some stuff from www.codeproject.com (great place), hacked a bit, and got something that works. I'll try to explain what I came up with, but remember, while this works, it may not be the best way to do this unless you also like easy (and it probably isn't even the easiest, but like the person on the next stool at the bar - drunk and giving you the eye at 2 A.M. - sometimes 'available' is all you really want anyway, and this XML method is available.)

XML is a lot like HTML, and while HTML preceded XML by many years, HTML can be considered a sort of subset of XML. Actually this makes for a long and boring story, so let's just get to the point, if you know HTML you'll find the XML needed for this project to be easy. If you don't know anything about markup languages (XML stands for e<u>X</u>tensible <u>M</u>arkup <u>L</u>anguage), well… very briefly they are text files that contain opening and closing tags like <myTag>some stuff</myTag> which are used to delimit the block of text 'some stuff'. Tags define how the delimited text is to be used by the XML file user. They are much like type declarations, if that helps. So as a user, you'd read the XML file and get the myTag string and use it however you have predefined the type myTag. Let's look at a file we'll call XMLData.xml:

```
<?xml version="1.0" encoding="utf-8"?>
<XMLData xmlns:xsd=http://www.w3.org/2001/XMLSchema wrap
            xmlns:xsi="http://www.w3.org/2001/XMLSchema-instance">

  <COMPort>COM1</COMPort>
  <Baud>19200</Baud>
  <Databits>8</Databits>
  <Parity>None</Parity>
  <Stopbits>1</Stopbits>
  <Handshake>None</Handshake>

</XMLData>
```

The first line provides information specifying the type of xml file. The second line provides the outer delimiter for the <XMLData></XMLData> pair and contains some items that further specify how this xml file should be treated. Just use them as they are – they are too complex to explain here and understanding it wouldn't advance your ability to use XML files one bit.

The next line delimits the serial port name:

```
    <COMPort>COM1</COMPort>
```

And the remaining of the lines provide defaults for the rest of the UART data. The software will interpret some of these lines as strings and some as numbers. How the text between two delimiters is used is entirely up to your software.

XML Settings Tester:

Let's recycle the HexReadWrite Tester by copying it to a XMLSettings Tester directory. We will create a simple XML file containing the Settings data and read that for our default settings. We will also learn to save any changes we make in the settings form to our XML file. Not exactly Flamenco in the moonlight, but it will be useful.

- Copy the contents of the HexReadWrite Tester directory to the XMLSettings Tester directory. NOTE – WE ARE NOT REUSING SIMPLE TERMINAL!
- Using Notepad or some other text editor (if you use Word or any other program that puts hidden formatting code in a file, then be sure to save it as a .txt file) input the text shown on the last page for the XMLData.xml and save it to the \XMLSettings Tester\bin\Debug directory – the directory that contains the executable used when debugging the program.
- We will create two new classes: XMLIO, which we will use to input and output data, and XMLData, which will hold the data itself.
- Below we will present the source code, but if you prefer not to type it all in, you can get the files from the \Software\Chapter 11-12 – XML Settings\ directory and add the XMLData.cs and XMLIO.cs files to your Developer Terminal project.
    - In the Solution Explorer window, right click on the 'Developer Terminal' project, and then select 'Add' and 'Existing Item...'

117

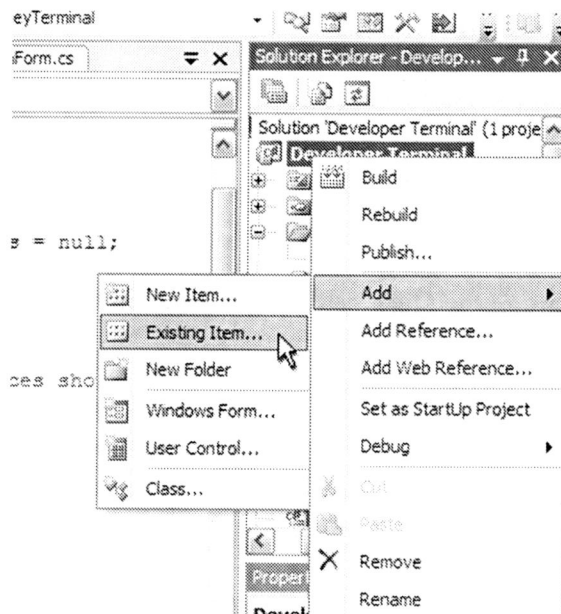

- In the 'Add Existing' dialog box, highlight the files and click the 'Add' button.

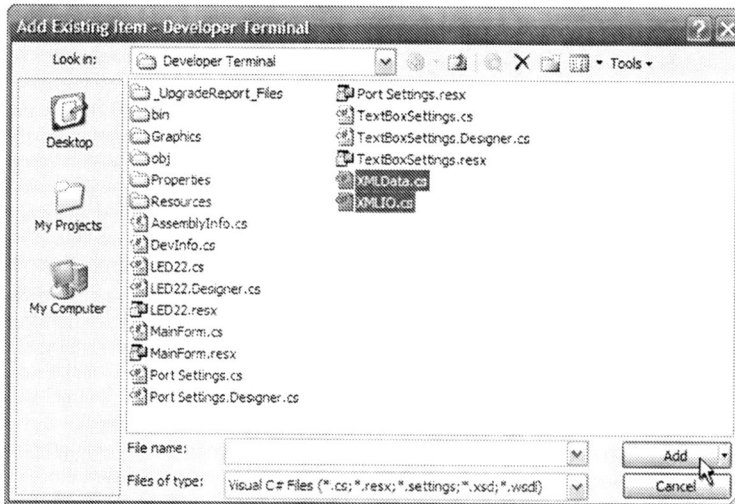

- As mentioned above, much of this was hacked, so just use the following code as-is and only change the filename if you want to use something other than XMLData.xml.

Chapter 11: XML - Settings

- ## In C# create XMLIO.cs:

```
using System;
using System.Windows.Forms;
using System.IO;
using System.Xml.Serialization;

namespace XMLTools
{
      public class XMLIO
      {
            public string appPath; // path to current directory

            public XMLIO()
            {
                  //
                  // TODO: Add constructor logic here
                  //
            }

            public XMLData OpenXMLDataFile()
            {
                  OpenFileDialog openFileDialog = new OpenFileDialog();

                  openFileDialog.Filter = "XML Files (*.xml)|*.xml";
                  openFileDialog.Title = "Open";
                  openFileDialog.DefaultExt = ".xml";

                  if (openFileDialog.ShowDialog() ==
                              wrap System.Windows.Forms.DialogResult.OK)
                  {
                        return XMLRead(openFileDialog.FileName);
                  }
                  else
                  {
                        MessageBox.Show("Error: Couldn't get XML file
                                                    wrap name.");
                        return null;
                  }
            }

            // Use default test button data file name
            public XMLData XMLRead()
            {
                  return XMLRead(appPath + "\\XMLData.xml");
            }

            // Use any test button data file name
            public XMLData XMLRead(string FileName)
            {
                  // Open an instance of the ButtonData class
                  XMLData xMLData = new XMLData();

                  try
                  {
                        // Construct an instance of the XmlSerializer with
                                                    wrap the type
```

119

```
                        // of object that is being deserialized.
                        XmlSerializer mySerializer =
                                new XmlSerializer(typeof(XMLData));
                        // To read the file, create a FileStream object.
                        FileStream myFileStream =
                                new FileStream(FileName, FileMode.Open);
                        // Call the Deserialize method and cast to the
                                                        wrap object type.
                        xMLData = (XMLData)
                                mySerializer.Deserialize(myFileStream);

                        myFileStream.Close();

                }
                catch
                {
                        MessageBox.Show("Error: couldn't read XMLData.xml");
                        return null;
                }

                return xMLData;
        }
    }
}
```

- **In VB create XMLIO.vb:**

```
Imports Microsoft.VisualBasic
Imports System
Imports System.Windows.Forms
Imports System.IO
Imports System.Xml.Serialization

Namespace XMLTools

        Public Class XMLIO
                Public appPath As String ' path to current directory

                Public Sub New()
                        '
                        ' TODO: Add constructor logic here
                        '
                End Sub

                Public Function OpenXMLDataFile() As XMLData
                        Dim openFileDialog As OpenFileDialog = New OpenFileDialog()

                        openFileDialog.Filter = "XML Files (*.xml)|*.xml"
                        openFileDialog.Title = "Open"
                        openFileDialog.DefaultExt = ".xml"

                        If openFileDialog.ShowDialog() = wrap
                                System.Windows.Forms.DialogResult.OK Then
                                Return XMLRead(openFileDialog.FileName)
                        Else
                                MessageBox.Show("Error: Couldn't get XML wrap
                                                        file name.")
```

```vb
                                    Return Nothing
                    End If
            End Function

            ' Use default test button data file name
            Public Function XMLRead() As XMLData
                    Return XMLRead(appPath & "\XMLData.xml")
            End Function

            ' Use any test button data file name
            Public Function XMLRead(ByVal FileName As String) As XMLData
                    ' Open an instance of the ButtonData class
                    Dim xMLData As XMLData = New XMLData()

                    Try
                            ' Construct an instance of the XmlSerializer wrap
                                                    with the type
                            ' of object that is being deserialized.
                            Dim mySerializer As XmlSerializer = New wrap
                                    XmlSerializer(GetType(XMLData))
                            ' To read the file, create a FileStream object.
                            Dim myFileStream As FileStream = New wrap
                                        FileStream(FileName, FileMode.Open)
                            ' Call the Deserialize method and cast to the wrap
                                                        object type.
                            xMLData = CType(mySerializer.Deserialize wrap
                                            (myFileStream),XMLData)

                            myFileStream.Close()

                    Catch
                            MessageBox.Show("Error: couldn't read XMLData.xml")
                            Return Nothing
                    End Try

                    Return xMLData
            End Function
        End Class
End Namespace
```

- Next we will create the XMLData class –
- In C# create XMLData.cs:

```csharp
using System;

namespace XMLTools
{
    public class XMLData
    {
        #region Serial port parameters

        public string COMPort = "Not Initialized";
        public int Baud = 0;
        public int Databits = 0;
        public string Parity = "Not Initialized";
        public string Stopbits = "Not Initialized";
```

121

```
            public string Handshake = "Not Initialized";

            #endregion
    }
```

- In VB create XMLData.vb:

```vb
Imports Microsoft.VisualBasic
Imports System

Namespace XMLTools
        Public Class XMLData
                #Region "Serial port parameters"

                Public COMPort As String = "Not Initialized"
                Public Baud As Integer = 0
                Public Databits As Integer = 0
                Public Parity As String = "Not Initialized"
                Public Stopbits As String = "Not Initialized"
                Public Handshake As String = "Not Initialized"

                #End Region
        End Class
End Namespace
```

- So now you have XMLData.xml in the debug directory, and XMLIO and XMLData in the main directory along with the other class files, let's see how to use them.

- In C# to Form1 in the 'using' list add:

```csharp
using System.IO.Ports;
using XMLTools;
```

- In VB to Form1 in the Imports list add:

```vb
Imports System.IO.Ports

Imports XMLTools
```

- To Form1 above the constructor –

- In C# add:

```csharp
// Create an instance of the settings form
PortSettings portSettings = new PortSettings();

// Create an instance of the TerminalData class
XMLData xMLData = new XMLData();

// Create an instance of the TerminalXMLIO class to read wrap
                        the terminal data
XMLIO dataXMLIO = new XMLIO();
```

- In VB add:

```vb
' Create an instance of the settings form
Private portSettings As PortSettings = New PortSettings()

' Create an instance of the TerminalData class
Private xMLData As XMLData = New XMLData()

' Create an instance of the TerminalXMLIO class to read the terminal data
```

```
Private dataXMLIO As XMLIO = New XMLIO()
```

- To Form1 in the constructor before the ShowSettings call –

- In C# add:

```
// Read the terminal data from TerminalData.xml
dataXMLIO.appPath = System.Environment.CurrentDirectory;
xMLData = dataXMLIO.XMLRead();
```

- In VB add:

```
' Read the terminal data from TerminalData.xml
dataXMLIO.appPath = System.Environment.CurrentDirectory
xMLData = dataXMLIO.XMLRead()
```

- To the Form1_Load event –

- In C# add:

```
// Start the terminal with default settings
serialPort1.PortName = portSettings.selectedPort = xMLData.COMPort;
serialPort1.BaudRate = portSettings.selectedBaudrate = xMLData.Baud;
serialPort1.DataBits = portSettings.selectedDataBits = xMLData.Databits;

string temp = xMLData.Parity;
switch (temp)
{
    case "Even":
        serialPort1.Parity = portSettings.selectedParity = Parity.Even;
        break;
    case "Mark":
        serialPort1.Parity = portSettings.selectedParity = Parity.Mark;
        break;
    case "None":
        serialPort1.Parity = portSettings.selectedParity = Parity.None;
        break;
    case "Odd":
        serialPort1.Parity = portSettings.selectedParity = Parity.Odd;
        break;
    case "Space":
        serialPort1.Parity = portSettings.selectedParity = Parity.Space;
        break;
    default:
        serialPort1.Parity = portSettings.selectedParity = Parity.None;
        break;
}

temp = xMLData.Stopbits;
switch (temp)
{
    case "None":
        serialPort1.StopBits = portSettings.selectedStopBits = StopBits.None;
        break;
    case "1":
        serialPort1.StopBits = portSettings.selectedStopBits = StopBits.One;
        break;
    //case "1.5": // not supported by FT232R
    //serialPort1.StopBits = = StopBits.OnePointFive;
    //break;
    case "2":
        serialPort1.StopBits = portSettings.selectedStopBits = StopBits.Two;
```

```
            break;
        default:
            serialPort1.StopBits = portSettings.selectedStopBits = StopBits.One;
            break;
    }

    temp = xMLData.Handshake;
    switch (temp)
    {
        case "None":
            serialPort1.Handshake = portSettings.selectedHandshaking = wrap
                                                Handshake.None;
            break;
        case "RTS/CTS":
            serialPort1.Handshake = portSettings.selectedHandshaking = wrap
                                                Handshake.RequestToSend;
            break;
        case "Xon/Xoff":
            serialPort1.Handshake = portSettings.selectedHandshaking = wrap
                                                Handshake.XOnXOff;
            break;
        default:
            serialPort1.Handshake = portSettings.selectedHandshaking = wrap
                                                Handshake.None;
            break;
    }

    // show the settings in the form text line
    showSettings();
```

- **In VB add:**

```
' Load the comboBox with 0x00 to 0xFF
For i As Integer = 0 To 15
        Me.comboBoxSendByte.Items.Add("0x0" & i.ToString("X"))
Next i
For i As Integer = 16 To 255
        Me.comboBoxSendByte.Items.Add("0x" & i.ToString("X"))
Next i

' Start the terminal with default settings
portSettings.selectedPort = xMLData.COMPort
serialPort1.PortName = portSettings.selectedPort
portSettings.selectedBaudrate = xMLData.Baud
serialPort1.BaudRate = portSettings.selectedBaudrate
portSettings.selectedDataBits = xMLData.Databits
serialPort1.DataBits = portSettings.selectedDataBits

Dim temp As String = xMLData.Parity
Select Case temp
        Case "Even"
                portSettings.selectedParity = Parity.Even
                serialPort1.Parity = portSettings.selectedParity
        Case "Mark"
                portSettings.selectedParity = Parity.Mark
                serialPort1.Parity = portSettings.selectedParity
        Case "None"
```

```
                portSettings.selectedParity = Parity.None
                serialPort1.Parity = portSettings.selectedParity
        Case "Odd"
                portSettings.selectedParity = Parity.Odd
                serialPort1.Parity = portSettings.selectedParity
        Case "Space"
                portSettings.selectedParity = Parity.Space
                serialPort1.Parity = portSettings.selectedParity
        Case Else
                portSettings.selectedParity = Parity.None
                serialPort1.Parity = portSettings.selectedParity
End Select

temp = xMLData.Stopbits
Select Case temp
        Case "None"
                portSettings.selectedStopBits = StopBits.None
                serialPort1.StopBits = portSettings.selectedStopBits
        Case "1"
                portSettings.selectedStopBits = StopBits.One
                serialPort1.StopBits = portSettings.selectedStopBits
        'case "1.5": // not supported by FT232R
        'serialPort1.StopBits = = StopBits.OnePointFive;
        'break;
        Case "2"
                portSettings.selectedStopBits = StopBits.Two
                serialPort1.StopBits = portSettings.selectedStopBits
        Case Else
                portSettings.selectedStopBits = StopBits.One
                serialPort1.StopBits = portSettings.selectedStopBits
End Select

temp = xMLData.Handshake
Select Case temp
        Case "None"
                portSettings.selectedHandshaking = Handshake.None
                serialPort1.Handshake = portSettings.selectedHandshaking
        Case "RTS/CTS"
                portSettings.selectedHandshaking = Handshake.RequestToSend
                serialPort1.Handshake = portSettings.selectedHandshaking
        Case "Xon/Xoff"
                portSettings.selectedHandshaking = Handshake.XOnXOff
                serialPort1.Handshake = portSettings.selectedHandshaking
        Case Else
                portSettings.selectedHandshaking = Handshake.None
                serialPort1.Handshake = portSettings.selectedHandshaking
End Select

' show the settings in the form text line
showSettings()
```

- You can test this by opening XMLData.xml and changing the 19200 to 9600 then save it as a .xml file (Notepad will try to save it as a .txt file which won't work – you must use the .xml extension for your software to open it). Then

125

run the program and when you open the PortSettings dialog you will see that the Baudrate is set to 9600.

In the next chapter will develop a macro facility which will allow us to write sequences of text or Hex data that we will be able to send from our terminal to a microcontroller with a single mouse click, no more repetitive data entry, just enter it once and use it forever.

Chapter 12: XML - Macros

Macros using XML

We can use our XML tools to add a very useful macros feature to our terminal. Macros are programming 'things' that allow a user to input a lot of data with only a few keystrokes. Macros may be best understood with a couple of examples: A macro may be a single word that a compiler expands into a lot of words. They may be a single keystroke that a word processing program knows to expand to a bunch of words or a formatting instruction. Or, as in our usage, they may be a string of words that we can click on in a window that will cause a terminal to send out a sequence of text or data. This can be very useful when working with microcontrollers since we may have a number of different blocks of data that we want to send to a microcontroller depending on different observed events, the macro gives us the option of sending lots of 'canned' data with a single keystroke.

We will reuse the XMLIO class from the last chapter and modify the XMLData class to use for macros. We will create three XML data types: MacroText, MacroData, and MacroType that will be associated as a unit. The 'Text' will be presented to the user in a comboBox so that the user can mouse click on it to send the data. The 'Data' will not be shown to the user, but will reside in the XML file and constitute the information that will be sent to the microcontroller. The 'Type' will be either ASCII or HEX and will be used by the terminal to know whether to interpret the data as ASCII or Hex before sending it.

For example:

```
<MacroText1>Start Motor</MacroText1>
<MacroData1>CMDstrmtr</MacroData1>
<MacroType1>ASCII</MacroType1>

<MacroText3>Send PORTB1: on</MacroText3>
<MacroData3>0xFE,0x02,0xFF,</MacroData3>
<MacroType3>HEX</MacroType3>
```

I want to take a moment to acknowledge that the software could be written in a more object oriented fashion by creating a Macro Class with the Text, Data, and

Type variables being defined as data for that class so that instead of numbering these macros as I've done, we could create new instances of the class for each macro trio in the XML file. But I ran into problems when attempting that implementation and decided that I really did not want to become an XML guru when I had a working implementation and I couldn't see a lot of gain from the extra elegance. How's that for a cop out? What actually happened was I got stuck and said, " I ain't got time for this poop!" And moved on. As I've mentioned elsewhere, I'm into hardware and the software to me is primarily to support that vice, so I try to minimize the amount of my brain and time I have to devote to the software.

The code for this chapter will be added to the code from the last chapter so use the XMLSettings Tester directory.

- Reopen XMLData.xml in Notepad and add:

```
<?xml version="1.0" encoding="utf-8"?>
<XMLData                          xmlns:xsd="http://www.w3.org/2001/XMLSchema"
xmlns:xsi="http://www.w3.org/2001/XMLSchema-instance">

  <COMPort>COM1</COMPort>
  <Baud>19200</Baud>
  <Databits>8</Databits>
  <Parity>None</Parity>
  <Stopbits>1</Stopbits>
  <Handshake>None</Handshake>

  <TerminalCharacters>0x0A,0x0D,</TerminalCharacters>

  <MacroText1>Start Motor</MacroText1>
  <MacroData1>CMDstrmtr</MacroData1>
  <MacroType1>ASCII</MacroType1>

  <MacroText2>Stop Motor</MacroText2>
  <MacroData2>CMDstpmtr</MacroData2>
  <MacroType2>ASCII</MacroType2>

  <MacroText3>Send PORTB1: on</MacroText3>
  <MacroData3>0xFE,0x02,0xFF,</MacroData3>
  <MacroType3>HEX</MacroType3>

  <MacroText4>Send PORTB1: off</MacroText4>
  <MacroData4>0xFE,0x03,0xFF,</MacroData4>
  <MacroType4>HEX</MacroType4>

  <MacroText5>Send PORTB2: on</MacroText5>
  <MacroData5>0xFE,0x04,0xFF,</MacroData5>
  <MacroType5>HEX</MacroType5>

  <MacroText6>Send PORTB2: off</MacroText6>
```

```
<MacroData6>0xFE,0x05,0xFF,</MacroData6>
<MacroType6>HEX</MacroType6>
```

```
</XMLData>
```

- Modify the XMLData class –
- In C# modify XMLData.cs add:

```csharp
#region Initialize Macros

// Initialize the Macro text
public string MacroText1 = " ";
public string MacroText2 = " ";
public string MacroText3 = " ";
public string MacroText4 = " ";
public string MacroText5 = " ";
public string MacroText6 = " ";

// Initialize the Macro Data
public string MacroData1 = " ";
public string MacroData2 = " ";
public string MacroData3 = " ";
public string MacroData4 = " ";
public string MacroData5 = " ";
public string MacroData6 = " ";

// Initialize the Macro Type
public string MacroType1 = " ";
public string MacroType2 = " ";
public string MacroType3 = " ";
public string MacroType4 = " ";
public string MacroType5 = " ";
public string MacroType6 = " ";

#endregion
```

- In VB modify XMLData.vb add:

```vb
#Region "Initialize Macros"

' Initialize the Macro text
Public MacroText1 As String = " "
Public MacroText2 As String = " "
Public MacroText3 As String = " "
Public MacroText4 As String = " "
Public MacroText5 As String = " "
Public MacroText6 As String = " "

' Initialize the Macro Data
Public MacroData1 As String = " "
Public MacroData2 As String = " "
Public MacroData3 As String = " "
Public MacroData4 As String = " "
Public MacroData5 As String = " "
Public MacroData6 As String = " "

' Initialize the Macro Type
Public MacroType1 As String = " "
Public MacroType2 As String = " "
```

```
Public MacroType3 As String = " "
Public MacroType4 As String = " "
Public MacroType5 As String = " "
Public MacroType6 As String = " "

#End Region
```

- We will store the XML data in arrays. To the declarations section at the head of Form1 –
- In C# add:

```
// Create MacroData arrays
string[] MacroDataText = new string[6];
string[] MacroDataData = new string[6];
string[] MacroDataType = new string[6];
```

- In VB add:

```
' Create MacroData arrays
Private MacroDataText As String() = New String(5){}
Private MacroDataData As String() = New String(5){}
Private MacroDataType As String() = New String(5){}
```

- Create a Send Macros Functions region -
- In C# add:

```
#region Send Macro Functions
// Send Macro Stings
void ListBoxMacrosDoubleClick(object sender, System.EventArgs e)
{
        processMacroClick(MacroDataData[listBoxMacros.SelectedIndex],MacroDataType
[listBoxMacros.SelectedIndex]);
}
private void processMacroClick(string MacroData, string MacroType)
{
        richTextBoxSend.Text = MacroData;
        if(MacroType == "ASCII")
        {
                SendASCIIString(MacroData);
        }
        else if (MacroType == "HEX")
        {
                SendHEXString(MacroData);
        }
        else MessageBox.Show("Error: MacroType: " + MacroType);
}

public void SendASCIIString(string str)
{
    char[] c = str.ToCharArray();

    for (int i = 0; i < c.GetLength(0); i++)
    {
        sendChar(c[i]);
    }
}

// For our purposes, HEX strings must be in the format 0xFF,0xFE,
// including the trailing comma on the last value
```

```
public void SendHEXString(string str)
{
    char[] c = str.ToCharArray();
    byte b = 0;

    if (c.GetLength(0) < 5)
    {
        MessageBox.Show("Error: Hex string incorrect length: " + str + wrap
                        "\nLength = " + c.GetLength(0).ToString());
        return;
    }
    for (int i = 0; i < c.GetLength(0); i += 5)
    {
        // Check array length
        if (i > c.GetLength(0))
        {
            MessageBox.Show("Error: Hex string incorrect length: " wrap
                    + str + "\nLength = " + c.GetLength(0).ToString() wrap
                    + "\ni = " + i.ToString());
            return;
        }
        // Check for remaining length
        if (i + 4 >= c.GetLength(0))
        {
            MessageBox.Show("Error: Hex string: " + str + " problem with length");
            return;
        }
        // Check format trailing comma
        if (c[i + 4] != ',')
        {
            MessageBox.Show("Error: Hex string: " + str + wrap
                                    " lacks a trailing comma.");
            return;
        }
        // Check high nibble range 0 - F
        if ((c[i + 2] >= '0') && (c[i + 2] <= '9') && (c[i + 2] >= 'A') wrap
                                        && (c[i + 2] <= 'F'))
        {
            MessageBox.Show("Error: Hex string first digit: " wrap
                    + c[i + 2].ToString() + " not in range 0 - F");
            return;
        }
        // Check low nibble range 0 - F
        if ((c[i + 3] >= '0') && (c[i + 3] <= '9') && (c[i + 3] >= 'A') wrap
                                        && (c[i + 3] <= 'F'))
        {
            MessageBox.Show("Error: Hex string first digit: " wrap
                    + c[i + 2].ToString() + " not in range 0 - F");
            return;
        }
        if (c[i + 2] <= '9') b = (byte)(c[i + 2] - '0');
        else
        {
            b = (byte)(c[i + 2] - 'A');
            b += 10;
        }
```

```
        b = (byte)(b << 4);

        if (c[i + 3] <= '9') b += (byte)(c[i + 3] - '0');
        else
        {
            b += (byte)(c[i + 3] - 'A');
            b += 10;
        }

        sendChar((char)b);
    }
}

#endregion
```

- **In VB add:**

```
#Region "Send Macro Functions"
' Send Macro Stings
Private Sub listBoxMacros_DoubleClick(ByVal sender As Object, ByVal e As
EventArgs) Handles listBoxMacros.DoubleClick
    processMacroClick(MacroDataData(listBoxMacros.SelectedIndex),
MacroDataType(listBoxMacros.SelectedIndex))
End Sub

Private Sub processMacroClick(ByVal MacroData As String, ByVal MacroType As
String)
    richTextBox1.Text = MacroData
    If MacroType = "ASCII" Then
        SendASCIIString(MacroData)
        'if (UseTermChar) sendTermChar();
    ElseIf MacroType = "HEX" Then
        SendHEXString(MacroData)
        'if (UseTermChar) sendTermChar();
    Else
        MessageBox.Show("Error: MacroType: " & MacroType)
    End If
End Sub

Public Sub SendASCIIString(ByVal str As String)
    Dim c As Char() = str.ToCharArray()

    For i As Integer = 0 To c.GetLength(0) - 1
        sendChar(c(i))
    Next i
End Sub

' For our purposes, HEX strings must be in the format 0xFF,0xFE,
' including the trailing comma on the last value
Public Sub SendHEXString(ByVal str As String)
    Dim c As Char() = str.ToCharArray()
    Dim b As Byte = 0

    If c.GetLength(0) < 5 Then
        MessageBox.Show("Error: Hex string incorrect length: " wrap
        & str & Constants.vbLf & "Length = " & c.GetLength(0).ToString())
        Return
    End If
```

```
    For i As Integer = 0 To c.GetLength(0) - 1 Step 5
        ' Check array length
        If i > c.GetLength(0) Then
            MessageBox.Show("Error: Hex string incorrect length: " wrap
                & str & Constants.vbLf & "Length = " & wrap
                c.GetLength(0).ToString() & Constants.vbLf & "i = " & i.ToString())
            Return
        End If
        ' Check for remaining length
        If i + 4 >= c.GetLength(0) Then
            MessageBox.Show("Error: Hex string: " & str & " problem with length")
            Return
        End If
        ' Check format trailing comma
        If c(i + 4) <> ","c Then
            MessageBox.Show("Error: Hex string: " & str & wrap
                                " lacks a trailing comma.")
            Return
        End If
        ' Check high nibble range 0 - F
        If (c(i + 2) >= "0"c) AndAlso (c(i + 2) <= "9"c) AndAlso wrap
                    (c(i + 2) >= "A"c) AndAlso (c(i + 2) <= "F"c) Then
            MessageBox.Show("Error: Hex string first digit: " wrap
                    & c(i + 2).ToString() & " not in range 0 - F")
            Return
        End If
        ' Check low nibble range 0 - F
        If (c(i + 3) >= "0"c) AndAlso (c(i + 3) <= "9"c) AndAlso wrap
                    (c(i + 3) >= "A"c) AndAlso (c(i + 3) <= "F"c) Then
            MessageBox.Show("Error: Hex string first digit: " wrap
                    & c(i + 2).ToString() & " not in range 0 - F")
            Return
        End If
        If c(i + 2) <= "9"c Then
            b = CByte(AscW(c(i + 2)) - AscW("0"c))
        Else
            b = CByte(AscW(c(i + 2)) - AscW("A"c))
            b += CByte(10)
        End If

        b = CByte(b << 4)

        If c(i + 3) <= "9"c Then
            b += CByte(AscW(c(i + 3)) - AscW("0"))
        Else
            b += CByte(AscW(c(i + 3)) - AscW("A"))
            b += CByte(10)
        End If

        sendChar(ChrW(b))
    Next i
End Sub

#End Region
```

- We need a function to get the XML data into our listBox and arrays -
- In C# add:

```
#region Load macro data
void loadXMLData()
{
        listBoxMacros.Items.Add(xMLData.MacroText1);
        listBoxMacros.Items.Add(xMLData.MacroText2);
        listBoxMacros.Items.Add(xMLData.MacroText3);
        listBoxMacros.Items.Add(xMLData.MacroText4);
        listBoxMacros.Items.Add(xMLData.MacroText5);
        listBoxMacros.Items.Add(xMLData.MacroText6);

        MacroDataText[0]  = xMLData.MacroText1;
        MacroDataText[1]  = xMLData.MacroText2;
        MacroDataText[2]  = xMLData.MacroText3;
        MacroDataText[3]  = xMLData.MacroText4;
        MacroDataText[4]  = xMLData.MacroText5;
        MacroDataText[5]  = xMLData.MacroText6;
        MacroDataText[6]  = xMLData.MacroText7;

        MacroDataData[0]  = xMLData.MacroData1;
        MacroDataData[1]  = xMLData.MacroData2;
        MacroDataData[2]  = xMLData.MacroData3;
        MacroDataData[3]  = xMLData.MacroData4;
        MacroDataData[4]  = xMLData.MacroData5;
        MacroDataData[5]  = xMLData.MacroData6;
        MacroDataData[6]  = xMLData.MacroData7;

        MacroDataType[0]  = xMLData.MacroType1;
        MacroDataType[1]  = xMLData.MacroType2;
        MacroDataType[2]  = xMLData.MacroType3;
        MacroDataType[3]  = xMLData.MacroType4;
        MacroDataType[4]  = xMLData.MacroType5;
        MacroDataType[5]  = xMLData.MacroType6;
        MacroDataType[6]  = xMLData.MacroType7;
}

#endregion
```

- **In VB add:**

```
#Region "Load macro data"
Private Sub loadXMLData()
    listBoxMacros.Items.Add(xMLData.MacroText1)
    listBoxMacros.Items.Add(xMLData.MacroText2)
    listBoxMacros.Items.Add(xMLData.MacroText3)
    listBoxMacros.Items.Add(xMLData.MacroText4)
    listBoxMacros.Items.Add(xMLData.MacroText5)
    listBoxMacros.Items.Add(xMLData.MacroText6)

    MacroDataText(0)  = xMLData.MacroText1
    MacroDataText(1)  = xMLData.MacroText2
    MacroDataText(2)  = xMLData.MacroText3
    MacroDataText(3)  = xMLData.MacroText4
    MacroDataText(4)  = xMLData.MacroText5
    MacroDataText(5)  = xMLData.MacroText6

    MacroDataData(0)  = xMLData.MacroData1
    MacroDataData(1)  = xMLData.MacroData2
    MacroDataData(2)  = xMLData.MacroData3
```

```
    MacroDataData(3)  = xMLData.MacroData4
    MacroDataData(4)  = xMLData.MacroData5
    MacroDataData(5)  = xMLData.MacroData6

    MacroDataType(0)  = xMLData.MacroType1
    MacroDataType(1)  = xMLData.MacroType2
    MacroDataType(2)  = xMLData.MacroType3
    MacroDataType(3)  = xMLData.MacroType4
    MacroDataType(4)  = xMLData.MacroType5
    MacroDataType(5)  = xMLData.MacroType6
End Sub

#End Region
```

- Call this from the Form1_Load function –
- In C# add:

```
loadXMLData();
```

- In VB add:

```
loadXMLData();
```

The Developer Terminal program uses a file named XMLData.xml for the UART settings, the termination characters, and the Macros. There are 52 sets of macros and their use was explained earlier.

```
    <MacroText1>Start Motor</MacroText1>
    <MacroData1>CMDstmtr</MacroData1>
    <MacroType1>ASCII</MacroType1>
```

If you want to change any of these, you just open the XMLData.xml file in Notepad and change the text between the delimiters. These files must be in the same directory as the application.

The data in the XMLData.xml file must exactly match the data in the XMLData.cs class. And it isn't easy to get the class and the file to match. When you try it on your own, start with just a couple of data items and test it. A single typo in the XMLData.xml file will cause the program to fail, and it is very hard to find typos in that file.

"…do you really want to know?…"

135

The XML Source Code

In the source shown here we only have 10 generic macros (more than enough to make the point) but in the actual source files we use 52.

XMLData.cs

```csharp
using System;

namespace DeveloperTerminal
{
    public class XMLData
    {
        #region Serial port parameters

        public string COMPort = "Not Initialized";
            public int Baud = 0;
            public int Databits = 0;
        public string Parity = "Not Initialized";
        public string Stopbits = "Not Initialized";
        public string Handshake = "Not Initialized";

        #endregion

        #region Terminal Characters
        public string TerminalCharacters = "";
        #endregion

        #region Initialize Macros

        // Initialize the Macro text
            public string MacroText1 = " ";
            public string MacroText2 = " ";
            public string MacroText3 = " ";
            public string MacroText4 = " ";
            public string MacroText5 = " ";
            public string MacroText6 = " ";
            public string MacroText7 = " ";
            public string MacroText8 = " ";
            public string MacroText9 = " ";
            public string MacroText10 = " ";

            // Initialize the Macro Data
            public string MacroData1 = " ";
            public string MacroData2 = " ";
            public string MacroData3 = " ";
            public string MacroData4 = " ";
            public string MacroData5 = " ";
            public string MacroData6 = " ";
            public string MacroData7 = " ";
            public string MacroData8 = " ";
            public string MacroData9 = " ";
            public string MacroData10 = " ";

            // Initialize the Macro Type
```

```
            public string MacroType1 = " ";
            public string MacroType2 = " ";
            public string MacroType3 = " ";
            public string MacroType4 = " ";
            public string MacroType5 = " ";
            public string MacroType6 = " ";
            public string MacroType7 = " ";
            public string MacroType8 = " ";
            public string MacroType9 = " ";
            public string MacroType10 = " ";


        #endregion
    }
}
```

XMLData.vb

```
Imports Microsoft.VisualBasic
Imports System

Namespace XMLTools
    Public Class XMLData
        #Region "COM port parameters"

        Public COMPort As String = "Not Initialized"
        Public Baud As Integer = 0
        Public Databits As Integer = 0
        Public Parity As String = "Not Initialized"
        Public Stopbits As String = "Not Initialized"
        Public Handshake As String = "Not Initialized"

        #End Region

        #Region "Initialize Macros"

        ' Initialize the Macro text
        Public MacroText1 As String = " "
        Public MacroText2 As String = " "
        Public MacroText3 As String = " "
        Public MacroText4 As String = " "
        Public MacroText5 As String = " "
        Public MacroText6 As String = " "

        ' Initialize the Macro Data
        Public MacroData1 As String = " "
        Public MacroData2 As String = " "
        Public MacroData3 As String = " "
        Public MacroData4 As String = " "
        Public MacroData5 As String = " "
        Public MacroData6 As String = " "

        ' Initialize the Macro Type
        Public MacroType1 As String = " "
        Public MacroType2 As String = " "
        Public MacroType3 As String = " "
        Public MacroType4 As String = " "
        Public MacroType5 As String = " "
```

137

```
                Public MacroType6 As String = " "

                #End Region
        End Class
End Namespace
```

XMLData.xml

```xml
<?xml version="1.0" encoding="utf-8"?>
<XMLData xmlns:xsd="http://www.w3.org/2001/XMLSchema"
xmlns:xsi="http://www.w3.org/2001/XMLSchema-instance">

  <COMPort>COM1</COMPort>
  <Baud>19200</Baud>
  <Databits>8</Databits>
  <Parity>None</Parity>
  <Stopbits>1</Stopbits>
  <Handshake>None</Handshake>

  <TerminalCharacters>0x0A,0x0D,</TerminalCharacters>

  <MacroText1>Start Motor</MacroText1>
  <MacroData1>CMDstrmtr</MacroData1>
  <MacroType1>ASCII</MacroType1>

  <MacroText2>Stop Motor</MacroText2>
  <MacroData2>CMDstpmtr</MacroData2>
  <MacroType2>ASCII</MacroType2>

  <MacroText3>Send PORTB1: on</MacroText3>
  <MacroData3>0xFE,0x02,0xFF,</MacroData3>
  <MacroType3>HEX</MacroType3>

  <MacroText4>Send PORTB1: off</MacroText4>
  <MacroData4>0xFE,0x03,0xFF,</MacroData4>
  <MacroType4>HEX</MacroType4>

  <MacroText5>Send PORTB2: on</MacroText5>
  <MacroData5>0xFE,0x04,0xFF,</MacroData5>
  <MacroType5>HEX</MacroType5>

  <MacroText6>Send PORTB2: off</MacroText6>
  <MacroData6>0xFE,0x05,0xFF,</MacroData6>
  <MacroType6>HEX</MacroType6>

  <MacroText7>Send PORTB3: on</MacroText7>
  <MacroData7>0xFE,0x06,0xFF,</MacroData7>
  <MacroType7>HEX</MacroType7>

  <MacroText8>Send PORTB3: off</MacroText8>
  <MacroData8>0xFE,0x07,0xFF,</MacroData8>
  <MacroType8>HEX</MacroType8>

  <MacroText9>Send PORTB4: on</MacroText9>
  <MacroData9>0xFE,0x08,0xFF,</MacroData9>
  <MacroType9>HEX</MacroType9>

  <MacroText10>Send PORTB4: off</MacroText10>
  <MacroData10>0xFE,0x09,0xFF,</MacroData10>
  <MacroType10>HEX</MacroType10>

</XMLData>
```

Test the code by opening two instances of the XML Settings Tester, attach each to different serial ports and play. Below are examples where the start motor command was sent and the receiver shows in Hex. Clicking the 'Start Motor' in in the Send Macros textBox shows 'CMDstmtr' in the Send box, and in the second instance of the Developer Terminal which receives what is sent, we see the string of hex bytes that were sent.

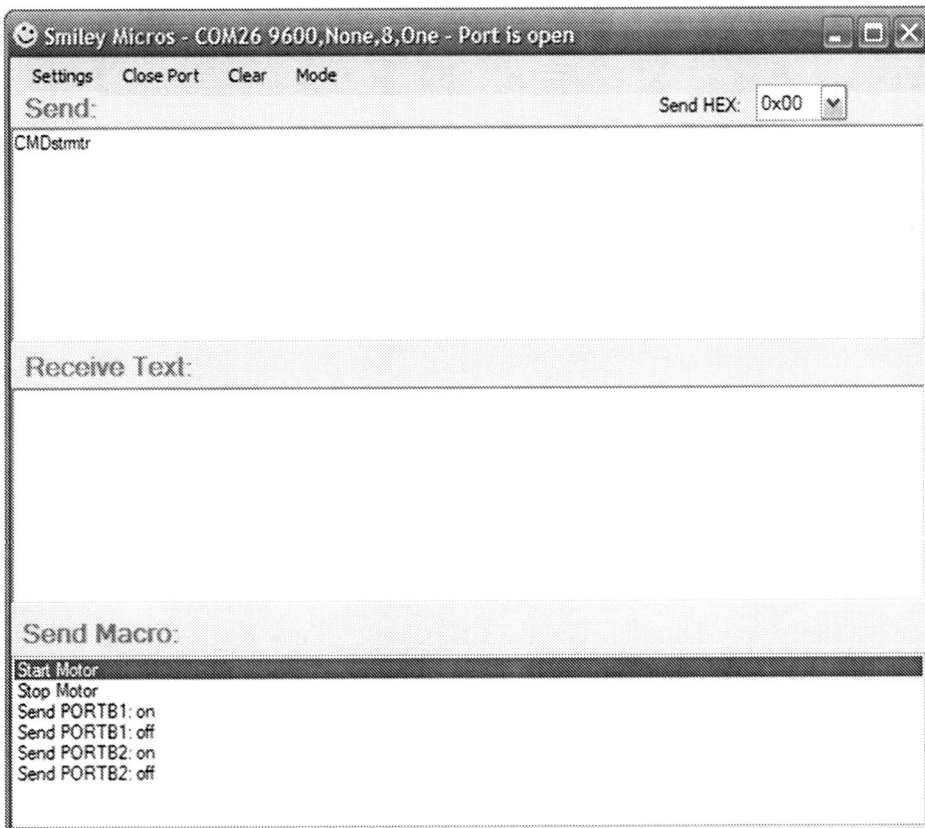

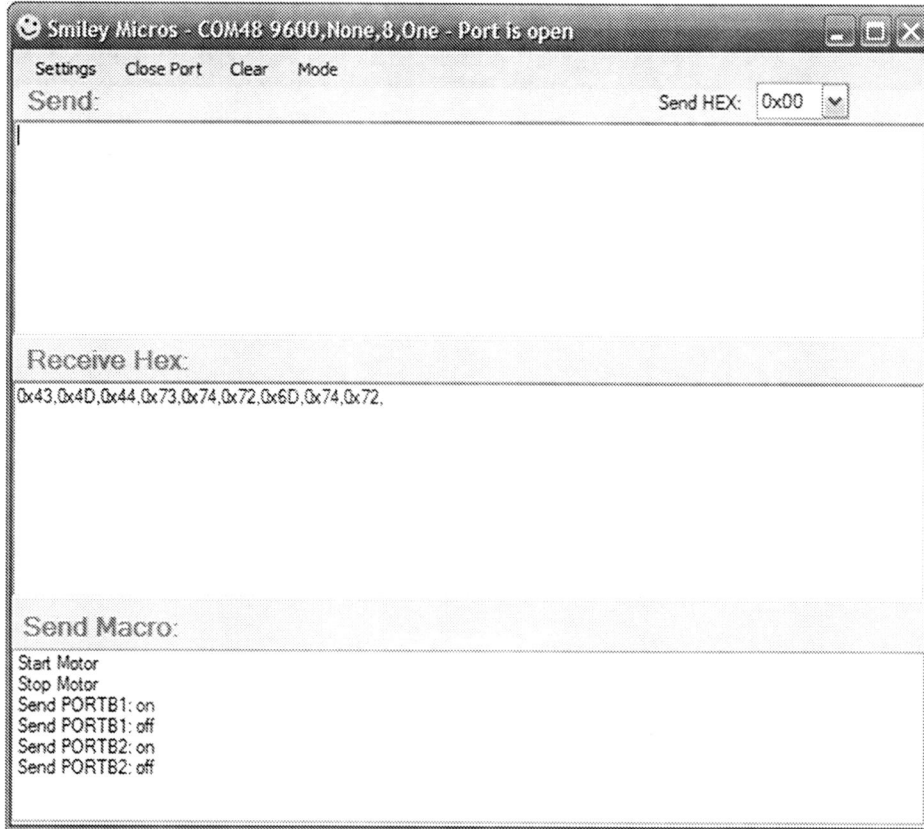

In Chapter 14: Developer Terminal Source Code, we will use XML files to provide data for the Developer Terminal. This will come in handy since it will allow us to have a text file that we can edit with Notepad that can contain any data we might want our program to use, such as baudrate or some string of characters we want to send out periodically – along with the period to send them. Useful stuff.

In the next chapter we will learn to use the Developer Terminal, after learning to use it, we will have a better idea what it does so that we can write the software for it. This may sound a little backwards, but one really should know what a program is supposed to do before writing it, shouldn't one?

Chapter 13: Developer Terminal User Manual

Now that we've learned enough serial communications, C# or VB programming we are ready to create a Developer Terminal with most of the features that a developer might need to communicate between a PC and a microcontroller. I have to assume that by now you don't need the cookbook format for writing this program, so the C# and the VB source code is in the next chapter. By using the code comments and referring to the prior chapters all the software should be understandable.

Using the Developer Terminal

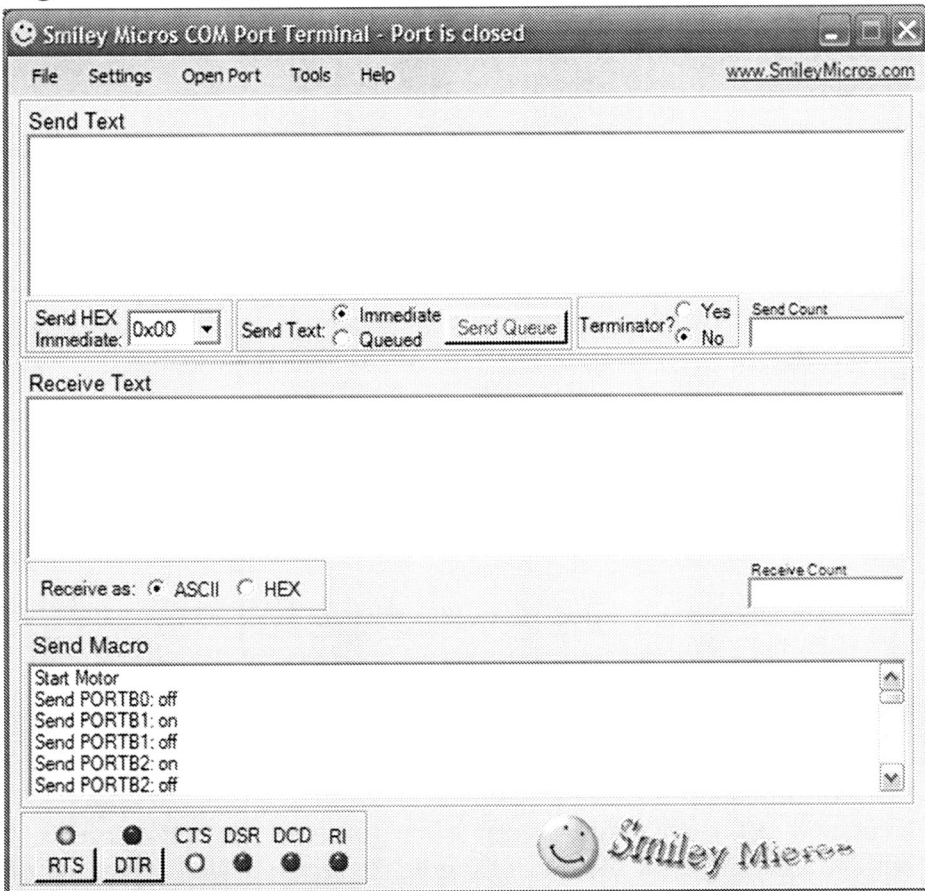

Port Settings

- Click the Setting menu item and click 'Port'

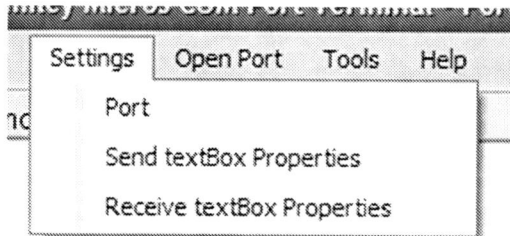

- In the Settings dialog select the device and the UART parameters.

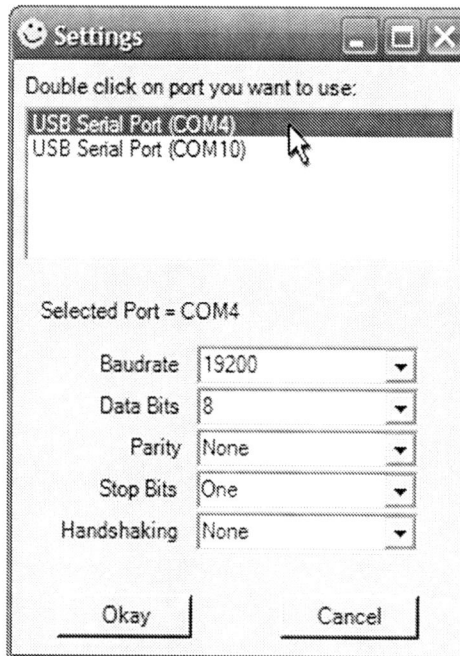

- The terminal is now ready to send and receive data.
- The 'Open Port' menu item has toggled and reads 'Close Port'
    - Click this to close the port
- The default settings that first appear when you open the Settings form come from the XMLData.xml file. For example, the above defaults were set by the following lines:

```
<COMPort>COM1</COMPort>
<Baud>19200</Baud>
<Databits>8</Databits>
<Parity>None</Parity>
<Stopbits>1</Stopbits>
<Handshake>None</Handshake>
```

- You must be very careful if you edit this XML file. Any mistake may prevent the XML file from being opened and no error will be reported. The file must be saved as an ASCII text file with the .xml suffix.

Send Text Features

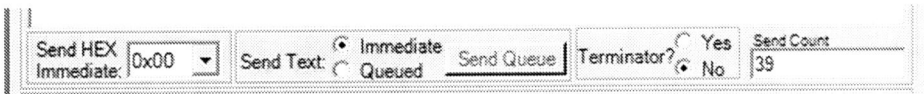

- From the 'Send HEX Immediate' comboBox you can click on the down arrow and then select a hex value from 0x00 to 0xFF to send.
- The 'Send Text' Immediate or Queued area.
    - o Click the 'Immediate' radio button to send each character as they are input into the Send Text box.
    - o Click the 'Queued' radio button to enable the 'Send Queue' button which will allow characters to be queued in the Send Text box and sent as a contiguous sequence when the 'Send Queue' button is pressed.
- The 'Terminator?' box allows you to add a byte or sequence of bytes after each send operation. The defaults are 0x0D,0x0A for "CR+LF" (Carriage Return + Line Feed).
    - o If the 'Send Immediate' is selected, the designated terminator byte(s) will be sent after each byte of input data is sent.
    - o If the 'Send Queued' is selected, the designated terminator byte(s) will be send after the 'Send Queued' button is pressed and the queued data has been sent.
- The terminal byte(s) used are set in the XMLData.xml file, which must be present in the same directory as the Developer Terminal executable.
    - o You can change the terminal byte(s) by editing the TerminalCharacters item.

- o In the following example the bytes representing Carriage Return and Line feed are set as the terminal characters: `<TerminalCharacters>0x0A,0x0D,</TerminalCharacters>`
  - o You must input the data exactly as shown, including the final comma. The XML reader may just skip incorrect data and no error may be generated, so be careful.
- The 'Send Count' box shows the number of characters sent. It is cleared to 0 when the Send Box is cleared

Send textBox Context Menu

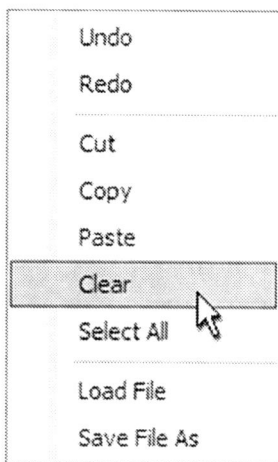

- Move your cursor to the Send textBox or the Receive Text box and click the right mouse button.
- The Edit Context Menu will appear and allow you to perform the editing functions shown.
- PASTING TEXT INTO THE SEND TEXT BOX DOES **_NOT_** CAUSE THAT TEXT TO BE SENT!
  - o It could be done, and if someone wants to add this code, I'd like to see it.

File Menu

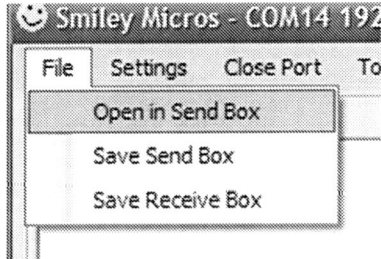

- To test the file sending feature place a loopback wire across the TxD and RxD pins of a BBUSB.
- Open the File Menu and click Open in Send Box.
- The Open Dialog box should default to the same directory containing the Developer Terminal executable, open the file: 'howdy.txt'.
- Click the Send Queued button and the contents of 'howdy.txt' will be sent.

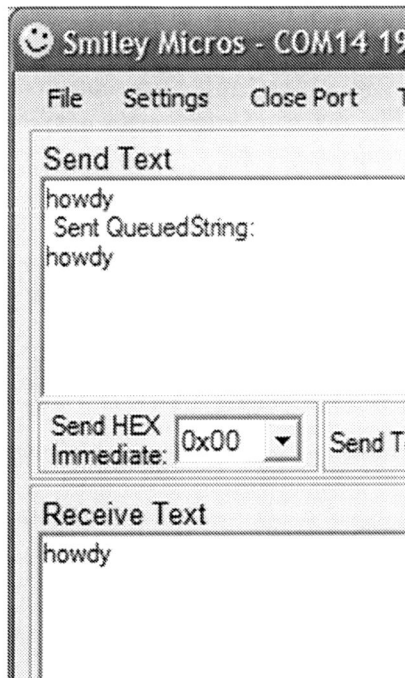

Receive Text Features

- To view received text as ASCII characters, click the ASCII radio button.
    - Non-printable bytes will appear as a box: □.
- To view received text as hexadecimal characters, click the HEX radio button.
- Note that the Receive Context menu has fewer selections since there is no need to edit received data. (Okay... maybe, but if you want that you have the source code so DIY!)

Text Settings

- You can change the font, fore color, and back color settings for each text box. I'm not sure why you'd want to do this, but I added it anyway primarily to show how to do it. The Send Text box below may look cool to some, but the Receive Text box shows how getting crazy can make things unreadable. This, of course looks good in color, and like crap in the printed book as black and white.

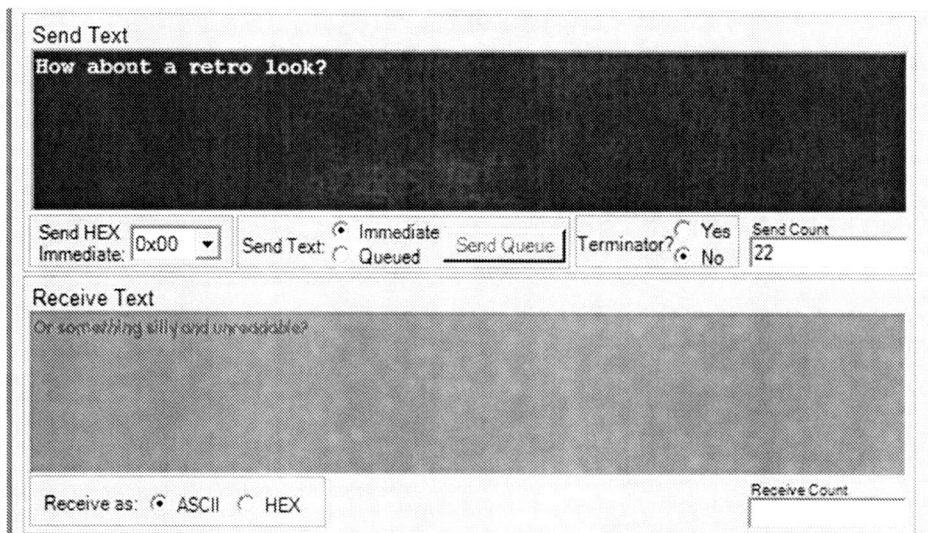

- From the Settings menu select the Send item:

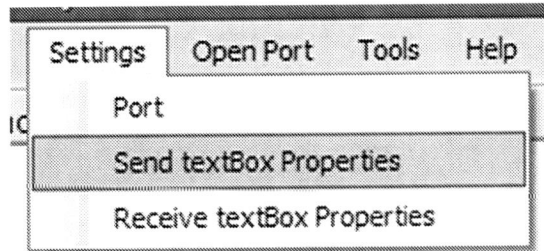

- The Send TextBoxSettings dialog as shown below has three settings: Font, Back Color, and Fore Color.

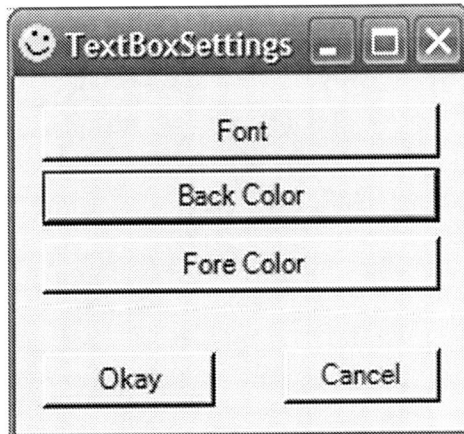

- Click the Font button to open a standard Windows font selection dialog:

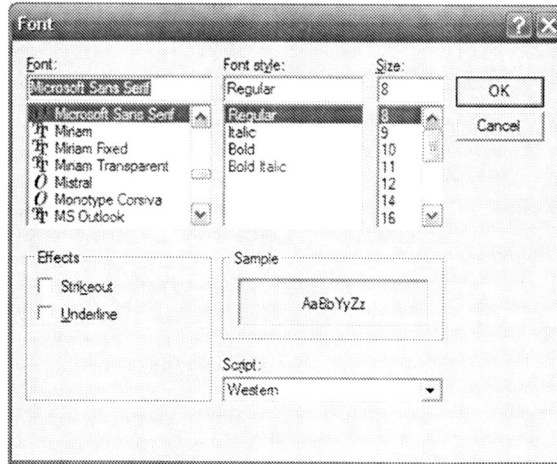

- Click either the Fore Color or the Back Color to open a standard Windows Color selection dialog:

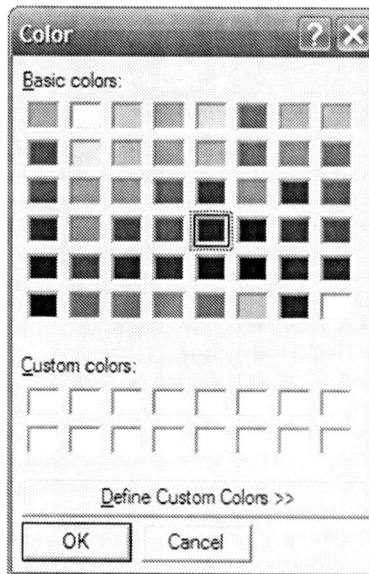

- To change the Receive textBox properties select that item in the Settings Menu and follow the instructions for the Send textBox properties above.

Send Byte Periodically

- You can send a single byte periodically by selecting the byte and the send period from the 'Send byte periodically' menu item in the Tools Menu.

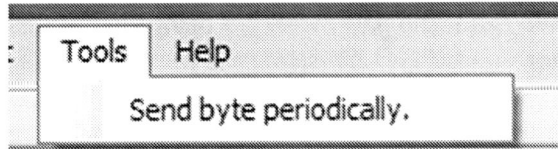

- In the Tools Menu select 'Send byte periodically'.

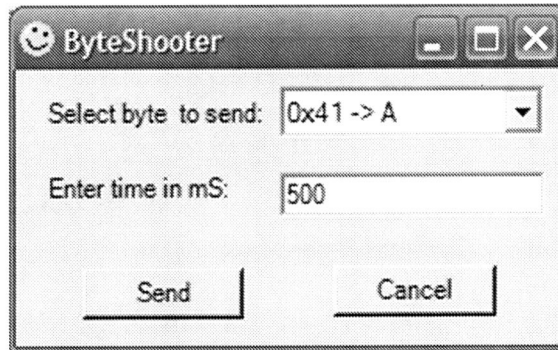

- Select a byte from the send comboBox, which shows both the byte value in Hex and after a '- >' also shows the printable character version of that byte if there is one.
- Select the number of milliseconds between sends.
- In the above dialog, we selected the byte 0x41 to be sent once every 500 milliseconds.
- You can stop sending this byte by selecting the Tools Menu item 'Stop sending bytes!' menu item.

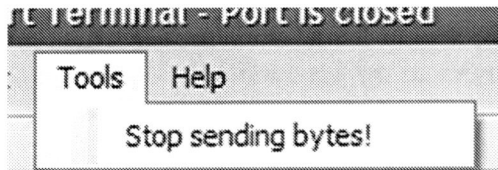

Sending Macros

By convention, strings of text that can be loaded into a terminal and sent as a unit are called macros. The macro feature is based on lines of text entered into an XML file. Each macro has three parameters: a macro name, the macro data, and a macro type. The macro name will be displayed on a line in the Send Macro box. When that name is selected and clicked the associated macro data will be sent. The macro type determines whether the data will be sent as shown in the macro data field or if it will be interpreted as an ASCII representation of a hex value and the hex value will be sent.

For example:

```
<MacroText1>Start Motor</MacroText1>
<MacroData1>CMDstmtr</MacroData1>
<MacroType1>ASCII</MacroType1>
```

Including these lines in XMLData.xml will cause the Developer Terminal to put the string 'Start Motor' in the Send Macro box.

Repeat: You must be very careful if you edit this XML file. Any mistake may prevent the XML file from being opened and no error will be reported. The file must be saved as an ASCII text file with the .xml suffix.

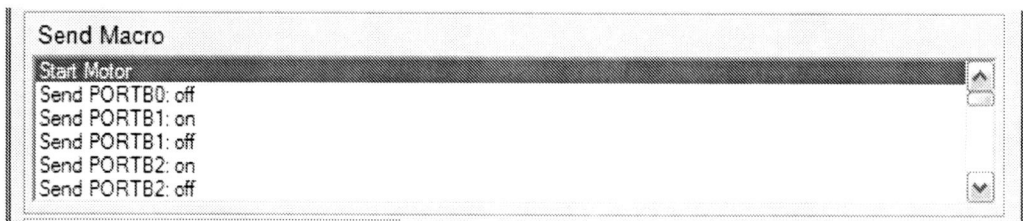

If the user clicks the 'Start Motor' line then the characters 'C', 'M ', 'D ', 's ', 't ', 'm ', 't ', and 'r' will be sent to the microcontroller which in turn could have code that parses this as a command to start a motor.

The second line in the above image shows the results of the following lines:

```
<MacroText2>Send PORTB0: off</MacroText2>
```

150

```
<MacroData2>0xFE,0x01,0xFF,</MacroData2>
<MacroType2>HEX</MacroType2>
```

If the user clicks on the "SendPORTB0" macro, then the terminal will parse the data characters in the string "0xFE,0x00,0xFF," and send the three hex bytes indicated – NOT the 15 characters in the string, as it would if the type was ASCII.

Modem Lines

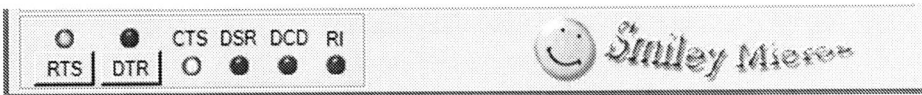

- Toggle the state of the RTS line by clicking the RTS button.
- Toggle the state of the DTR line by clicking the CTS line.
- The states of the CTS, DSR, and DCD lines are indicated by the Virtual LEDs.
- The RI indicates a change of state, not an absolute state due to the SerialPort class function that will only indicate that the RI pin has changed and not its state.

'Ideal' Terminal Specification:

I solicited comments on AvrFreaks.net for what features should be in an 'ideal' developers terminal. I couldn't put in everything suggested, but since I'm providing the source code, anyone needing extended features should be able to add them. I'd like to hear about such additions.

Ideal Terminal Wish List:
- Separate Send and Receive text windows.
    - Clear text button.
- Show received bytes as text or hex.
- Save sent text to file.
- Save received text to file.
- Send an ASCII text file.
- Send a hex data file.
- Send text box accepts data dragged and dropped or pasted from the clipboard.
- Send Hex byte combo box with 0x00 to 0xFF selections.

- Send text immediately or queued option radio buttons.
- Send with terminal character(s) check box.
  - Terminal character(s) read from XML file.
- Count boxes for characters sent and received.
- Select font and backcolor for send text box.
- Select font and backcolor for receive text box.
- Serial port set up dialog.
  - Support serial ports 0 to 255.
  - Serial ports available for selection list box.
  - Combo boxes with standard selectios fo:
    - Baud rate
    - Data bits
    - Parity
    - Stop bits
  - Handshaking:
    - Hardware: RTS/CTS
    - Software: Xon/Xff
    - None
  - Xon and Xoff character selection combo box.
- Open/Close Port button.
- Port status in form text line.
- Macro feature
  - Macros from XML files
    - Show macro name in a text box.
    - Macro text is sent when macro name is double clicked.
    - Macro can send either characters or hex codes.
  - Macro from user input to 3 text boxes
    - Input as text or hex.
    - Timed auto send with repeat mode for macros.
- Help feature to show how to use the terminal.
- Virtual LED state indicators for DCD, DSR, CTS, and RI.
- Radio buttons to set state of DTR and RTS.

Things suggested by AVRFreaks folks, but not included:
- Log and timestamp both sent and received data
- Alarm Mode:

- On specified time or received string match
  - Generate alarm condition.
  - Or, send preset text (macro).
- Option to show received bytes as 'printable' text and if no displayable character is available:
  - Show the hex value.
  - Or we could allow control codes to either be used as control codes or shown as an indicator for the code such as (lf) for 'line feed'.
- Checksum feature for hex macros:
  - Variable source destination width.
  - Positive/Negative/XOR sums.
  - Little/big endian.
- CRC (CCITT) calculation:
  - Append to hex strings.
  - Show for received strings.
- Monitor input to assure that no characters are dropped.
- For inputting hex characters to send, have an auto complete feature that adds a 0x before two hex characters and a comma or space between them.
- User programmable function keys.
- Option to use a single window for input and output like a 'real' terminal.
  - VT100 emulation with full ANSI support.
- "Read a nominated ASCII file and send each line at a nominated time interval."
- Mode to "automatically toggle one of the handshaking lines to control the data direction pin of a half-duplex RS232<->RS485 transceiver."

Since you have the source code you can add any of the omitted features or modify the existing code to your heart's content.

In the next chapter we will see the source code for the Developer Terminal software. This is one big honking long chapter with a lot of code, but you can handle it – you've seen all the bits and pieces already. I assume that by now the dear reader is quite familiar with C# or VB .NET programming so we are going to lighten up on the cookbook instructions and throw you in the deep end while really messing up a metaphor.

Chapter 14: Developer Terminal Source Code

We saw how to use the Developer Terminal in the last chapter, now let's look at the source code. Let's assume that by now you have sufficient skills to build a form with all the components shown in the last chapter. You have also seen how to open a serial port and how to handle XML files and all the other bits and pieces that went into making the Developer Terminal so there really isn't any need to duplicate all that discussion here.

In earlier chapters we built a lot of tools that are needed for a terminal program. Now it is time to assemble these tools into the full Developer Terminal.

Two additional small tools were not discussed: the TextBoxSettings tool which let's you change colors and fonts in the text boxes, and the ByteShooter tool, which allows you to send a byte periodically. Both these tools are simple and by now it should be obvious how to program include them once you look at the code shown below.

Much of this code is redundant with code presented elsewhere for developing the Simple Terminal and developing each of the tool testers shown above. But it seems wise to have all the Developer Terminal code located in one place for easy reference.

PortSettings

PortSettings.cs

```
public partial class PortSettings : Form
{
    #region Initialization

    public PortSettings()
    {
        InitializeComponent();

        // Get a list of the Serial port names
        string[] ports = GetPorts();

        int i = 0;
        foreach (string s in ports)
        {
            if (s != "")
```

155

```
        {
            listBoxPorts.Items.Insert(i++, s);
        }
    }

    // Set first Serial port as default
    GetCOM(0);

    // Initialize baudrates in combobox;
    this.comboBoxBaud.Items.AddRange(new object[] {

                                "75",

                                "110",

                                "134",

                                "150",

                                "300",

                                "600",

                                "1200",

                                "1800",

                                "2400",

                                "4800",

                                "7200",

                                "9600",

                                "14400",

                                "19200",

                                "38400",

                                "57600",

                                "115200",

                                "128000"});

    // Set Handshaking selection
    //   We will only use these handshaking types
    comboBoxHandshaking.Items.Add("None");
    comboBoxHandshaking.Items.Add("RTS/CTS");
    comboBoxHandshaking.Items.Add("Xon/Xoff");

    // Set Parity types
    foreach (string s in Enum.GetNames(typeof(Parity)))
    {
        comboBoxParity.Items.Add(s);
```

```
        }

        // Set Databits
        // FT232R UART interface supports only 7 or 8 data bits
        //comboBoxDataBits.Items.Add("5"); // not supported
        //comboBoxDataBits.Items.Add("6"); // not supported
        comboBoxDataBits.Items.Add("7");
        comboBoxDataBits.Items.Add("8");

        // Set Stopbits
        // FT232R UART interface supports only 1 or 2 stop bits
        //comboBoxStopBits.Items.Add("None"); // not supported
        comboBoxStopBits.Items.Add("1");
        //comboBoxStopBits.Items.Add("1.5"); // not supported
        comboBoxStopBits.Items.Add("2");
    }

#endregion

#region Get Port Name
// We don't use the GetPortNames method of the SerialPort class
// because it doesn't work right the documentation says it reads
// a register key and if that key ain't right then the results
// ain't right. In my test case the key had an orphan port name in it,
// so I reverted to the DeviceInfo class that I'd made earlier before
// the SerialPort stuff came along.
//
// Oh, and DON'T LOOK AT the DeviceInfo class and after you do
// you'll see why I said don't
private static string[] GetPorts()
{
    string[] strArray = DevInfo.DeviceInfo.ParseFriendlyPorts();

    return strArray;
}

// Select the port from the list box
private void listBoxPorts_SelectedIndexChanged(object sender, EventArgs e)
{
    GetCOM(listBoxPorts.SelectedIndex);
}

// Set the selected port and display it in the label
private void GetCOM(int index)
{
    string[] strArray = DevInfo.DeviceInfo.ParsePorts();

    if (strArray[index] != "")
    {
        SelectedPort = strArray[index];
        labelPort.Text = "Selected Port = " + SelectedPort;
    }
}
#endregion

#region Data Assessors
// Assessors for the selected port
```

```csharp
// FT232R UART interface supports
//      7 or 8 data bits
//      1 or 2 stop bits
//      odd / even / mark / space / no parity.
// So these will be the only options available

#region Port Name
// Assessor for the selected port name
private string SelectedPort = "";
public string selectedPort
{
    get
    {
        return SelectedPort;
    }
    set
    {
        SelectedPort = value;
        labelPort.Text = "Selected Port = " + SelectedPort;
    }
}
#endregion

#region Baudrate
private int SelectedBaudrate;
public int selectedBaudrate
{
    get
    {
        return SelectedBaudrate;
    }
    set
    {
        SelectedBaudrate = value;
        comboBoxBaud.Text = value.ToString();
    }
}

private void comboBoxBaud_SelectedIndexChanged(object sender, EventArgs e)
{
    selectedBaudrate = wrap
            Convert.ToInt32(comboBoxBaud.Items[comboBoxBaud.SelectedIndex]);
}
#endregion

#region Parity
private Parity SelectedParity;// = Parity.None;
public Parity selectedParity
{
    get
    {
        return SelectedParity;
    }
    set
    {
        SelectedParity = value;
        comboBoxParity.Text = value.ToString();
```

```
    }
}

private void comboBoxParity_SelectedIndexChanged(object sender, EventArgs e)
{
    string temp = wrap
            comboBoxParity.Items[comboBoxParity.SelectedIndex].ToString();

    switch (temp)
    {
        case "Even":
            selectedParity = Parity.Even;
            break;
        case "Mark":
            selectedParity = Parity.Mark;
            break;
        case "None":
            selectedParity = Parity.None;
            break;
        case "Odd":
            selectedParity = Parity.Odd;
            break;
        case "Space":
            selectedParity = Parity.Space;
            break;
        default:
            selectedParity = Parity.None;
            break;
    }
}
#endregion

#region StobBits
private StopBits SelectedStopBits = StopBits.One;
public StopBits selectedStopBits
{
    get
    {
        return SelectedStopBits;
    }
    set
    {
        SelectedStopBits = value;
        comboBoxStopBits.Text = value.ToString();
    }
}

private void comboBoxStopBits_SelectedIndexChanged(object sender, EventArgs e)
{
    string temp = wrap
            comboBoxStopBits.Items[comboBoxStopBits.SelectedIndex].ToString();

    switch (temp)
    {
        case "None":
            selectedStopBits = StopBits.None;
            break;
```

159

```
        case "1":
            selectedStopBits = StopBits.One;
            break;
        //case "1.5": // not supported by FT232R
        //SelectedStopBits = StopBits.OnePointFive;
        //break;
        case "2":
            selectedStopBits = StopBits.Two;
            break;
        default:
            selectedStopBits = StopBits.One;
            break;
    }
}
#endregion

#region DataBits
private int SelectedDataBits = 8;
public int selectedDataBits
{
    get
    {
        return SelectedDataBits;
    }
    set
    {
        SelectedDataBits = value;
        comboBoxDataBits.Text = value.ToString();
    }
}

private void comboBoxDataBits_SelectedIndexChanged(object sender, EventArgs e)
{
    if (comboBoxDataBits.SelectedIndex == 0) selectedDataBits = 7;
    else selectedDataBits = 8;
}
#endregion

#region Handshaking
// We will only use None, Xon/Xoff, or Hardware (which is RTS/CTS)
private Handshake SelectedHandshaking = Handshake.None;
public Handshake selectedHandshaking
{
    get
    {
        return SelectedHandshaking;
    }
    set
    {
        SelectedHandshaking = value;
        comboBoxHandshaking.Text = value.ToString();
    }
}

private void comboBoxHandshaking_SelectedIndexChanged(object sender, wrap
                                    EventArgs e)
{
```

160

```
        if (comboBoxHandshaking.SelectedIndex == 0) wrap
                                selectedHandshaking = Handshake.None;
        else if (comboBoxHandshaking.SelectedIndex == 1) wrap
                        selectedHandshaking = Handshake.RequestToSend;
        else if (comboBoxHandshaking.SelectedIndex == 2) wrap
                        selectedHandshaking = Handshake.XOnXOff;
        else selectedHandshaking = Handshake.None;
    }
    #endregion

    #region Okay and Cancel buttons
    private void buttonOkay_Click(object sender, EventArgs e)
    {
        DialogResult = DialogResult.OK;
    }

    private void buttonCancel_Click(object sender, EventArgs e)
    {
        DialogResult = DialogResult.Cancel;
    }
    #endregion
    #endregion
}
```

PortSetting.vb

```
Partial Public Class PortSettings
    Inherits Form
#Region "Initialization"
    Public Sub New()
        InitializeComponent()

        ' Get a list of the Serial port names
        Dim ports As String() = GetPorts()

        Dim i As Integer = 0
        For Each s As String In ports
            If s <> "" Then
                listBoxPorts.Items.Insert(i, s)
                i += 1
            End If
        Next s

        ' Set first Serial port as default
        GetCOM(0)

        ' Initialize baudrates in combobox;
        Me.comboBoxBaud.Items.AddRange(New Object() {"75", "110", "134", "150",
"300", "600", "1200", "1800", "2400", "4800", "7200", "9600", "14400", "19200",
"38400", "57600", "115200", "128000"})

        ' Set Handshaking selection
        '  We will only use these handshaking types
        comboBoxHandshaking.Items.Add("None")
        comboBoxHandshaking.Items.Add("RTS/CTS")
        comboBoxHandshaking.Items.Add("Xon/Xoff")
```

161

```vbnet
        ' Set Parity types
        For Each s As String In System.Enum.GetNames(GetType(Parity))
            comboBoxParity.Items.Add(s)
        Next s

        ' Set Databits
        ' FT232R UART interface supports only 7 or 8 data bits
        'comboBoxDataBits.Items.Add("5"); // not supported
        'comboBoxDataBits.Items.Add("6"); // not supported
        comboBoxDataBits.Items.Add("7")
        comboBoxDataBits.Items.Add("8")

        ' Set Stopbits
        ' FT232R UART interface supports only 1 or 2 stop bits
        'comboBoxStopBits.Items.Add("None"); // not supported
        comboBoxStopBits.Items.Add("1")
        'comboBoxStopBits.Items.Add("1.5"); // not supported
        comboBoxStopBits.Items.Add("2")
    End Sub
#End Region

#Region "Get Port Name"
    ' We don't use the GetPortNames method of the SerialPort class
    ' because it doesn't work right the documentation says it reads
    ' a register key and if that key ain't right then the results
    ' ain't right. In my test case the key had an orphan port name in it,
    ' so I reverted to the DeviceInfo class that I'd made earlier before
    ' the SerialPort stuff came along.
    '
    ' Oh, and DON'T LOOK AT the DeviceInfo class and after you do
    ' you'll see why I said don't
    Private Shared Function GetPorts() As String()
        Dim strArray As String() = DevInfo.DeviceInfo.ParseFriendlyPorts()

        Return strArray
    End Function

    ' Select the port from the list box
    Private Sub listBoxPorts_SelectedIndexChanged(ByVal sender As Object, wrap
            ByVal e As EventArgs) Handles listBoxPorts.SelectedIndexChanged
        GetCOM(listBoxPorts.SelectedIndex)
    End Sub

    ' Set the selected port and display it in the label
    Private Sub GetCOM(ByVal index As Integer)
        Dim strArray As String() = DevInfo.DeviceInfo.ParsePorts()

        If strArray(index) <> "" Then
            SelectedPort_Renamed = strArray(index)
            labelPort.Text = "Selected Port = " & SelectedPort_Renamed
        End If
    End Sub
#End Region

#Region "Data Assessors"
    ' Assessors for the selected port
    ' FT232R UART interface supports
```

```vbnet
'       7 or 8 data bits
'       1 or 2 stop bits
'       odd / even / mark / space / no parity.
' So these will be the only options available

#Region "Port Name"
    ' Assessor for the selected port name
    Private SelectedPort_Renamed As String = ""
    Public Property selectedPort() As String
        Get
            Return SelectedPort_Renamed
        End Get
        Set(ByVal value As String)
            SelectedPort_Renamed = value
            labelPort.Text = "Selected Port = " & SelectedPort_Renamed
        End Set
    End Property
#End Region

#Region "Baudrate"
    Private SelectedBaudrate_Renamed As Integer
    Public Property selectedBaudrate() As Integer
        Get
            Return SelectedBaudrate_Renamed
        End Get
        Set(ByVal value As Integer)
            SelectedBaudrate_Renamed = value
            comboBoxBaud.Text = value.ToString()
        End Set
    End Property

    Private Sub comboBoxBaud_SelectedIndexChanged(ByVal sender As Object, wrap
            ByVal e As EventArgs) Handles comboBoxBaud.SelectedIndexChanged
        selectedBaudrate =
Convert.ToInt32(comboBoxBaud.Items(comboBoxBaud.SelectedIndex))
    End Sub
#End Region

#Region "Parity"
    Private SelectedParity_Renamed As Parity ' = Parity.None;
    Public Property selectedParity() As Parity
        Get
            Return SelectedParity_Renamed
        End Get
        Set(ByVal value As Parity)
            SelectedParity_Renamed = value
            comboBoxParity.Text = value.ToString()
        End Set
    End Property

    Private Sub comboBoxParity_SelectedIndexChanged(ByVal sender As Object, wrap
            ByVal e As EventArgs) Handles comboBoxParity.SelectedIndexChanged
        Dim temp As String =
comboBoxParity.Items(comboBoxParity.SelectedIndex).ToString()

        Select Case temp
            Case "Even"
```

```vbnet
                    selectedParity = Parity.Even
            Case "Mark"
                    selectedParity = Parity.Mark
            Case "None"
                    selectedParity = Parity.None
            Case "Odd"
                    selectedParity = Parity.Odd
            Case "Space"
                    selectedParity = Parity.Space
            Case Else
                    selectedParity = Parity.None
        End Select
    End Sub
#End Region

#Region "StobBits"
    Private SelectedStopBits_Renamed As StopBits = StopBits.One
    Public Property selectedStopBits() As StopBits
        Get
            Return SelectedStopBits_Renamed
        End Get
        Set(ByVal value As StopBits)
            SelectedStopBits_Renamed = value
            comboBoxStopBits.Text = value.ToString()
        End Set
    End Property

    Private Sub comboBoxStopBits_SelectedIndexChanged(ByVal sender As wrap
                        Object, ByVal e As EventArgs) Handles wrap
                        comboBoxStopBits.SelectedIndexChanged
        Dim temp As String = wrap
            comboBoxStopBits.Items(comboBoxStopBits.SelectedIndex).ToString()

        Select Case temp
            Case "None"
                selectedStopBits = StopBits.None
            Case "1"
                selectedStopBits = StopBits.One
                'case "1.5": // not supported by FT232R
                'SelectedStopBits = StopBits.OnePointFive;
                'break;
            Case "2"
                selectedStopBits = StopBits.Two
            Case Else
                selectedStopBits = StopBits.One
        End Select
    End Sub
#End Region

#Region "DataBits"
    Private SelectedDataBits_Renamed As Integer = 8
    Public Property selectedDataBits() As Integer
        Get
            Return SelectedDataBits_Renamed
        End Get
        Set(ByVal value As Integer)
            SelectedDataBits_Renamed = value
```

```
                comboBoxDataBits.Text = value.ToString()
        End Set
    End Property

    Private Sub comboBoxDataBits_SelectedIndexChanged(ByVal sender As Object,
ByVal e As EventArgs) Handles comboBoxDataBits.SelectedIndexChanged
        If comboBoxDataBits.SelectedIndex = 0 Then
            selectedDataBits = 7
        Else
            selectedDataBits = 8
        End If
    End Sub
#End Region

#Region "Handshaking"
    ' We will only use None, Xon/Xoff, or Hardware (which is RTS/CTS)
    Private SelectedHandshaking_Renamed As Handshake = Handshake.None
    Public Property selectedHandshaking() As Handshake
        Get
            Return SelectedHandshaking_Renamed
        End Get
        Set(ByVal value As Handshake)
            SelectedHandshaking_Renamed = value
            comboBoxHandshaking.Text = value.ToString()
        End Set
    End Property

    Private Sub comboBoxHandshaking_SelectedIndexChanged(ByVal sender As wrap
                        Object, ByVal e As EventArgs) Handles wrap
                        comboBoxHandshaking.SelectedIndexChanged
        If comboBoxHandshaking.SelectedIndex = 0 Then
            selectedHandshaking = Handshake.None
        ElseIf comboBoxHandshaking.SelectedIndex = 1 Then
            selectedHandshaking = Handshake.RequestToSend
        ElseIf comboBoxHandshaking.SelectedIndex = 2 Then
            selectedHandshaking = Handshake.XOnXOff
        Else
            selectedHandshaking = Handshake.None
        End If
    End Sub
#End Region

#Region "Okay and Cancel buttons"
    Private Sub buttonOkay_Click(ByVal sender As Object, ByVal e As EventArgs)
Handles buttonOkay.Click
        DialogResult = System.Windows.Forms.DialogResult.OK
    End Sub

    Private Sub buttonCancel_Click(ByVal sender As Object, ByVal e As EventArgs)
Handles buttonCancel.Click
        DialogResult = System.Windows.Forms.DialogResult.Cancel
    End Sub
#End Region
#End Region
End Class
```

DevInfo
DevInfo.cs

```
/*'
'This class is necessary because the SerialPort class included with C# Express
'has a method GetPortNames that doesn't work right. The documentation even
'admits it doesn't work right - which isvery unusual for Microsoft - the
'documentation says it reads a register key and if that key ain't right
'then the results ain't right (okay, the don't use 'ain't' but gist is the
'same). In my test case the key had an orphan port name in it, so I reverted
'to the DeviceInfo class that I'd made earlier before the SerialPort .NET
'namespace came along.

'The DevInfo class ignores the registry and looks at the ports to see what
'is there.

'If you are just getting started with C#, you don't want to read this since it
'uses all sorts of hard to follow techniques that violate the spirit of C#
' specifically  and OOP in general. However, it does follow the usual Microsoft
' rule that anythinG that claims to be object oriented must have 'sort of'
'as a prefix.

'This code was derived from the DevInfo.cs module in the Code Project Article:
'.NET - Diving into System Programming - Part 3
'By Vladimir Afanasyev http://www.codeproject.com/csharp/DivingSysProg3.asp

'Joe Pardue added the GetPorts function 7/12/05
'Joe Pardue added the parsePorts function 7/14/05
'Joe Pardue added the parseFriendlyPorts function 7/21/05
'*/

using System;
using System.Text;
using System.Runtime.InteropServices;

namespace DevInfo
{
class DeviceInfo
{
    /// <summary>
    /// The main entry point for the application.
    /// </summary>

    private const int DIGCF_PRESENT = (0x00000002);
    private const int MAX_DEV_LEN = 1000;
    private const int SPDRP_FRIENDLYNAME = (0x0000000C);  // FriendlyName (R/W)
    private const int SPDRP_DEVICEDESC = (0x00000000);    // DeviceDesc (R/W)

    [StructLayout(LayoutKind.Sequential)]
    private class SP_DEVINFO_DATA
    {
        public int cbSize;
        public Guid ClassGuid;
        public int DevInst;    // DEVINST handle
        public ulong Reserved;
    };
```

```
[DllImport("setupapi.dll")]//
private static extern Boolean
  SetupDiClassGuidsFromNameA(string ClassN, ref Guid guids,
    UInt32 ClassNameSize, ref UInt32 ReqSize);

[DllImport("setupapi.dll")]
private static extern IntPtr                    //result HDEVINFO
  SetupDiGetClassDevsA(ref Guid ClassGuid, UInt32 Enumerator,
    IntPtr hwndParent, UInt32 Flags);

[DllImport("setupapi.dll")]
private static extern Boolean
  SetupDiEnumDeviceInfo(IntPtr DeviceInfoSet, UInt32 MemberIndex,
    SP_DEVINFO_DATA DeviceInfoData);

[DllImport("setupapi.dll")]
private static extern Boolean
  SetupDiDestroyDeviceInfoList(IntPtr DeviceInfoSet);

[DllImport("setupapi.dll")]
private static extern Boolean
  SetupDiGetDeviceRegistryPropertyA(
        IntPtr DeviceInfoSet,
        SP_DEVINFO_DATA DeviceInfoData,
        UInt32 Property,
        UInt32 PropertyRegDataType,
        StringBuilder PropertyBuffer,
        UInt32 PropertyBufferSize,
        IntPtr RequiredSize);


public static int EnumerateDevices(UInt32 DeviceIndex, wrap
                  string ClassName, StringBuilder DeviceName)
{
    UInt32 RequiredSize = 0;
    Guid guid = Guid.Empty;
    Guid[] guids = new Guid[1];
    IntPtr NewDeviceInfoSet;
    SP_DEVINFO_DATA DeviceInfoData = new SP_DEVINFO_DATA();

    bool res = SetupDiClassGuidsFromNameA(ClassName, wrap
                  ref guids[0], RequiredSize, ref RequiredSize);
    if (RequiredSize == 0)
    {
        //incorrect class name:
        DeviceName = new StringBuilder("");
        return -2;
    }

    if (!res)
    {
        guids = new Guid[RequiredSize];
        res = SetupDiClassGuidsFromNameA(ClassName, wrap
                  ref guids[0], RequiredSize, ref RequiredSize);
```

```
            if (!res || RequiredSize == 0)
            {
                //incorrect class name:
                DeviceName = new StringBuilder("");
                return -2;
            }
        }

        //get device info set for our device class
        NewDeviceInfoSet = SetupDiGetClassDevsA(ref guids[0], wrap
                                0, IntPtr.Zero, DIGCF_PRESENT);
        if (NewDeviceInfoSet.ToInt32() == -1)
        {
            //device information is unavailable:
            DeviceName = new StringBuilder("");
            return -3;
        }

        DeviceInfoData.cbSize = 28;
        //is devices exist for class
        DeviceInfoData.DevInst = 0;
        DeviceInfoData.ClassGuid = System.Guid.Empty;
        DeviceInfoData.Reserved = 0;

        res = SetupDiEnumDeviceInfo(NewDeviceInfoSet,
                DeviceIndex, DeviceInfoData);
        if (!res)
        {
            //no such device:
            SetupDiDestroyDeviceInfoList(NewDeviceInfoSet);
            DeviceName = new StringBuilder("");
            return -1;
        }


        DeviceName.Capacity = MAX_DEV_LEN;
        if (!SetupDiGetDeviceRegistryPropertyA(NewDeviceInfoSet, DeviceInfoData,
        SPDRP_FRIENDLYNAME, 0, DeviceName, MAX_DEV_LEN, IntPtr.Zero))
        {
            res = SetupDiGetDeviceRegistryPropertyA(NewDeviceInfoSet,
            DeviceInfoData, SPDRP_DEVICEDESC, 0, DeviceName, wrap
                                    MAX_DEV_LEN, IntPtr.Zero);
            if (!res)
            {
                //incorrect device name:
                SetupDiDestroyDeviceInfoList(NewDeviceInfoSet);
                DeviceName = new StringBuilder("");
                return -4;
            }
        }
        return 0;
    }

// Joe Pardue 7/14/05
public static string[] ParsePorts()
{
```

168

```
    string str = GetPorts();

    // Maximum number of possible Serial ports is 256
    // create and intialize array
    string[] strArray = new string[256];
    for (int i = 0; i < 256; i++)
    {
        strArray[i] = "";
    }

    char[] cArray = str.ToCharArray();
    //char[] com = new Char[6];

    int k = 0;
    int j = 0;
    for (int i = 0; i < cArray.Length; i++)
    {
        if (cArray[i] == '(')
        {// JWP 12/20/05 changed 6 to 8 to accomodate up to COM255
            for (j = 0; j < 8; j++)
            {
                if (cArray[i + j] == ')')
                {
                    i += j;
                    k++;
                    break;
                }
                if (cArray[i + j] != '(') strArray[k] += cArray[i + j];
            }// dump an Lpt port
            if (cArray[i - j + 1] == 'L') { strArray[--k] = ""; }
        }
    }
    return strArray;
}

// Joe Pardue 7/21/05 - gets the 'Friendly' port name
public static string[] ParseFriendlyPorts()
{
    string str = GetPorts();

    // Maximum number of possible Serial ports is 256
    // create and intialize array
    string[] strArray = new string[256];
    for (int i = 0; i < 256; i++)
    {
        strArray[i] = "";
    }

    char[] cArray = str.ToCharArray();

    int k = 0;
    for (int i = 0; i < cArray.Length; i++)
    {
        strArray[k] += cArray[i];
        if (cArray[i] == ')')
        {
            // Hack to get rid of LPT string
```

```
                if ((i > 5) && (cArray[i - 4] != 'L'))
                {
                    k++;
                }
                else
                {
                    strArray[k] = "";

                }
                i++;// skip the trailing "\n"
            }
        }
        return strArray;
    }


    // Joe Pardue 7/12/05
    public static string GetPorts()
    {
        StringBuilder devices = new StringBuilder("");
        UInt32 Index = 0;
        int result = 0;

        string str = "";

        while (true)
        {
            //enumerate devices of selected device class
            result = EnumerateDevices(Index++, "Ports", devices);
            if (result != 0) break;
            else str += devices.ToString() + "\n";
        }
        return str;
    }
}
}
```

DevInfo.vb

```
'
'This class is necessary because the SerialPort class included with C# Express
'has a method GetPortNames that doesn't work right. The documentation even
'admits it doesn't work right - which isvery unusual for Microsoft - the
'documentation says it reads a register key and if that key ain't right
'then the results ain't right (okay, the don't use 'ain't' but gist is the
'same). In my test case the key had an orphan port name in it, so I reverted
'to the DeviceInfo class that I'd made earlier before the SerialPort .NET
'namespace came along.

'The DevInfo class ignores the registry and looks at the ports to see what
'is there.

'If you are just getting started with C#, you don't want to read this since it
'uses all sorts of hard to follow techniques that violate the spirit of C#
' specifically  and OOP in general. However, it does follow the usual Microsoft
' rule that anythinG that claims to be object oriented must have 'sort of'
'as a prefix.
```

```
'This code was derived from the DevInfo.cs module in the Code Project Article:
'.NET - Diving into System Programming - Part 3
'By Vladimir Afanasyev http://www.codeproject.com/csharp/DivingSysProg3.asp

'Joe Pardue added the GetPorts function 7/12/05
'Joe Pardue added the parsePorts function 7/14/05
'Joe Pardue added the parseFriendlyPorts function 7/21/05
'

Imports Microsoft.VisualBasic
Imports System
Imports System.Text
Imports System.Runtime.InteropServices

Namespace DevInfo

Friend Class DeviceInfo

    Private Const DIGCF_PRESENT As Integer = (&H2)
    Private Const MAX_DEV_LEN As Integer = 1000
    Private Const SPDRP_FRIENDLYNAME As Integer = (&HC) ' FriendlyName (R/W)
    Private Const SPDRP_DEVICEDESC As Integer = (&H0) ' DeviceDesc (R/W)

    <StructLayout(LayoutKind.Sequential)> _
    Private Class SP_DEVINFO_DATA
        Public cbSize As Integer
        Public ClassGuid As Guid
        Public DevInst As Integer ' DEVINST handle
        Public Reserved As ULong
    End Class

    <DllImport("setupapi.dll")> _
    Private Shared Function SetupDiClassGuidsFromNameA(ByVal ClassN As String,
ByRef guids As Guid, ByVal ClassNameSize As UInt32, ByRef ReqSize As UInt32) As
Boolean
    End Function

    <DllImport("setupapi.dll")> _
    Private Shared Function SetupDiGetClassDevsA(ByRef ClassGuid As Guid, ByVal
Enumerator As UInt32, ByVal hwndParent As IntPtr, ByVal Flags As UInt32) As IntPtr
    End Function

    <DllImport("setupapi.dll")> _
    Private Shared Function SetupDiEnumDeviceInfo(ByVal DeviceInfoSet As IntPtr,
ByVal MemberIndex As UInt32, ByVal DeviceInfoData As SP_DEVINFO_DATA) As Boolean
    End Function

    <DllImport("setupapi.dll")> _
    Private Shared Function SetupDiDestroyDeviceInfoList(ByVal DeviceInfoSet As
IntPtr) As Boolean
    End Function

    <DllImport("setupapi.dll")> _
    Private Shared Function SetupDiGetDeviceRegistryPropertyA(ByVal DeviceInfoSet
As IntPtr, ByVal DeviceInfoData As SP_DEVINFO_DATA, ByVal Propert As UInt32, ByVal
```

171

```vb
PropertyRegDataType As UInt32, ByVal PropertyBuffer As StringBuilder, ByVal
PropertyBufferSize As UInt32, ByVal RequiredSize As IntPtr) As Boolean
    End Function


    Public Shared Function EnumerateDevices(ByVal DeviceIndex As UInt32, wrap
        ByVal ClassName As String, ByVal DeviceName As StringBuilder) As Integer
        Dim RequiredSize As UInt32 = 0
        Dim guid As Guid = Guid.Empty
        Dim guids As Guid() = New Guid(0) {}
        Dim NewDeviceInfoSet As IntPtr
        Dim DeviceInfoData As SP_DEVINFO_DATA = New SP_DEVINFO_DATA()


        Dim res As Boolean = SetupDiClassGuidsFromNameA(ClassName, wrap
                                    guids(0), RequiredSize, RequiredSize)
        If RequiredSize = 0 Then
            'incorrect class name:
            DeviceName = New StringBuilder("")
            Return -2
        End If

        If (Not res) Then
            guids = New Guid(System.Convert.ToInt32(RequiredSize) - 1) {}
            res = SetupDiClassGuidsFromNameA(ClassName, guids(0), wrap
                                    RequiredSize, RequiredSize)

            If (Not res) OrElse RequiredSize = 0 Then
                'incorrect class name:
                DeviceName = New StringBuilder("")
                Return -2
            End If
        End If

        'get device info set for our device class
        NewDeviceInfoSet = SetupDiGetClassDevsA(guids(0), 0, wrap
                                    IntPtr.Zero, DIGCF_PRESENT)
        If NewDeviceInfoSet.ToInt32() = -1 Then
            'device information is unavailable:
            DeviceName = New StringBuilder("")
            Return -3
        End If

        DeviceInfoData.cbSize = 28
        'is devices exist for class
        DeviceInfoData.DevInst = 0
        DeviceInfoData.ClassGuid = System.Guid.Empty
        DeviceInfoData.Reserved = 0

        res = SetupDiEnumDeviceInfo(NewDeviceInfoSet, DeviceIndex, DeviceInfoData)
        If (Not res) Then
            'no such device:
            SetupDiDestroyDeviceInfoList(NewDeviceInfoSet)
            DeviceName = New StringBuilder("")
            Return -1
        End If
```

```
        DeviceName.Capacity - MAX_DEV_LEN
        If (Not SetupDiGetDeviceRegistryPropertyA(NewDeviceInfoSet, wrap
                DeviceInfoData, SPDRP_FRIENDLYNAME, 0, DeviceName, wrap
                            MAX_DEV_LEN, IntPtr.Zero)) Then
            res = SetupDiGetDeviceRegistryPropertyA wrap
                    (NewDeviceInfoSet, DeviceInfoData, wrap
                    SPDRP_DEVICEDESC, 0, DeviceName, MAX_DEV_LEN, IntPtr.Zero)
            If (Not res) Then
                'incorrect device name:
                SetupDiDestroyDeviceInfoList(NewDeviceInfoSet)
                DeviceName = New StringBuilder("")
                Return -4
            End If
        End If
        Return 0
    End Function

    ' Joe Pardue 7/14/05
    Public Shared Function ParsePorts() As String()
        Dim str As String = GetPorts()

        ' Maximum number of possible Serial ports is 256
        ' create and intialize array
        Dim strArray As String() = New String(255) {}
        For i As Integer = 0 To 255
            strArray(i) = ""
        Next i

        Dim cArray As Char() = str.ToCharArray()

        Dim k As Integer = 0
        Dim j As Integer = 0
        For i As Integer = 0 To cArray.Length - 1
            If cArray(i) = "("c Then
                ' JWP 12/20/05 changed 6 to 8 to accomodate up to COM255
                For j = 0 To 7
                    If cArray(i + j) = ")"c Then
                        i += j
                        k += 1
                        Exit For
                    End If
                    If cArray(i + j) <> "("c Then
                        strArray(k) += cArray(i + j)
                    End If
                Next j
                If cArray(i - j + 1) = "L"c Then ' dump an Lpt port
                    k -= 1
                    strArray(k) = ""
                End If
            End If
        Next i
        Return strArray
    End Function

    ' Joe Pardue 7/21/05 - gets the 'Friendly' port name
    Public Shared Function ParseFriendlyPorts() As String()
        Dim str As String = GetPorts()
```

```vb
        ' Maximum number of possible Serial ports is 256
        ' create and intialize array
        Dim strArray As String() = New String(255) {}
        For i As Integer = 0 To 255
            strArray(i) = ""
        Next i

        Dim cArray As Char() = str.ToCharArray()

        Dim k As Integer = 0
        For i As Integer = 0 To cArray.Length - 1
            strArray(k) += cArray(i)
            If cArray(i) = ")"c Then
                ' Hack to get rid of LPT string
                If (i > 5) AndAlso (cArray(i - 4) <> "L"c) Then
                    k += 1
                Else
                    strArray(k) = ""

                End If
                i += 1 ' skip the trailing Constants.vbLf
            End If
        Next i

        Return strArray
    End Function


    ' Joe Pardue 7/12/05
    Public Shared Function GetPorts() As String
        Dim devices As StringBuilder = New StringBuilder("")
        Dim Index As UInt32 = 0
        Dim result As Integer = 0

        Dim str As String = ""

        Do
            result = DevInfo.DeviceInfo.EnumerateDevices(Index, "Ports", devices)
            Index += CUInt(1)
            If result <> 0 Then
                Exit Do
            Else
                str &= devices.ToString() & Constants.vbLf
            End If
        Loop
        Return str
    End Function
End Class
End Namespace
```

XMLData

XMLData.cs

```csharp
using System;
```

Chapter 14: Developer Terminal Source Code

```
namespace DeveloperTerminal
{
        public class XMLData
    {
        #region Serial port parameters

        public string COMPort = "Not Initialized";
                public int Baud = 0;
                public int Databits = 0;
        public string Parity = "Not Initialized";
        public string Stopbits = "Not Initialized";
        public string Handshake = "Not Initialized";

        #endregion

        #region Terminal Characters

        public string TerminalCharacters = "";

        #endregion

        #region Send Bytes Periodically

        public int SendByte = 0;
        public int SendPeriod = 0;

        #endregion

        #region Initialize Macros

        // Initialize the Macro text
                public string MacroText1 = "  ";
                public string MacroText2 = "  ";
                public string MacroText3 = "  ";
                public string MacroText4 = "  ";
                public string MacroText5 = "  ";
                public string MacroText6 = "  ";
                public string MacroText7 = "  ";
                public string MacroText8 = "  ";
                public string MacroText9 = "  ";
                public string MacroText10 = "  ";
                public string MacroText11 = "  ";
                public string MacroText12 = "  ";
                public string MacroText13 = "  ";
                public string MacroText14 = "  ";
                public string MacroText15 = "  ";
                public string MacroText16 = "  ";
                public string MacroText17 = "  ";
                public string MacroText18 = "  ";
                public string MacroText19 = "  ";
                public string MacroText20 = "  ";
                public string MacroText21 = "  ";
                public string MacroText22 = "  ";
                public string MacroText23 = "  ";
                public string MacroText24 = "  ";
                public string MacroText25 = "  ";
                public string MacroText26 = "  ";
```

```
public string MacroText27 = " ";
public string MacroText28 = " ";
public string MacroText29 = " ";
public string MacroText30 = " ";
public string MacroText31 = " ";
public string MacroText32 = " ";
public string MacroText33 = " ";
public string MacroText34 = " ";
public string MacroText35 = " ";
public string MacroText36 = " ";
public string MacroText37 = " ";
public string MacroText38 = " ";
public string MacroText39 = " ";
public string MacroText40 = " ";
public string MacroText41 = " ";
public string MacroText42 = " ";
public string MacroText43 = " ";
public string MacroText44 = " ";
public string MacroText45 = " ";
public string MacroText46 = " ";
public string MacroText47 = " ";
public string MacroText48 = " ";
public string MacroText49 = " ";
public string MacroText50 = " ";
public string MacroText51 = " ";
public string MacroText52 = " ";

// Initialize the Macro Data
public string MacroData1 = " ";
public string MacroData2 = " ";
public string MacroData3 = " ";
public string MacroData4 = " ";
public string MacroData5 = " ";
public string MacroData6 = " ";
public string MacroData7 = " ";
public string MacroData8 = " ";

public string MacroData9 = " ";
public string MacroData10 = " ";
public string MacroData11 = " ";
public string MacroData12 = " ";
public string MacroData13 = " ";
public string MacroData14 = " ";
public string MacroData15 = " ";
public string MacroData16 = " ";
public string MacroData17 = " ";
public string MacroData18 = " ";
public string MacroData19 = " ";
public string MacroData20 = " ";
public string MacroData21 = " ";
public string MacroData22 = " ";
public string MacroData23 = " ";
public string MacroData24 = " ";
public string MacroData25 = " ";
public string MacroData26 = " ";
public string MacroData27 = " ";
public string MacroData28 = " ";
```

```
public string MacroData29 = " ";
public string MacroData30 = " ";
public string MacroData31 = " ";
public string MacroData32 = " ";
public string MacroData33 = " ";
public string MacroData34 = " ";
public string MacroData35 = " ";
public string MacroData36 = " ";
public string MacroData37 = " ";
public string MacroData38 = " ";
public string MacroData39 = " ";
public string MacroData40 = " ";
public string MacroData41 = " ";
public string MacroData42 = " ";
public string MacroData43 = " ";
public string MacroData44 = " ";
public string MacroData45 = " ";
public string MacroData46 = " ";
public string MacroData47 = " ";
public string MacroData48 = " ";
public string MacroData49 = " ";
public string MacroData50 = " ";
public string MacroData51 = " ";
public string MacroData52 = " ";

// Initialize the Macro Type
public string MacroType1 = " ";
public string MacroType2 = " ";
public string MacroType3 = " ";
public string MacroType4 = " ";
public string MacroType5 = " ";
public string MacroType6 = " ";
public string MacroType7 = " ";
public string MacroType8 = " ";
public string MacroType9 = " ";
public string MacroType10 = " ";
public string MacroType11 = " ";
public string MacroType12 = " ";
public string MacroType13 = " ";
public string MacroType14 = " ";
public string MacroType15 = " ";
public string MacroType16 = " ";
public string MacroType17 = " ";
public string MacroType18 = " ";
public string MacroType19 = " ";
public string MacroType20 = " ";
public string MacroType21 = " ";
public string MacroType22 = " ";
public string MacroType23 = " ";
public string MacroType24 = " ";
public string MacroType25 = " ";
public string MacroType26 = " ";
public string MacroType27 = " ";
public string MacroType28 = " ";
public string MacroType29 = " ";
public string MacroType30 = " ";
public string MacroType31 = " ";
```

```
                  public string MacroType32 = " ";
                  public string MacroType33 = " ";
                  public string MacroType34 = " ";
                  public string MacroType35 = " ";
                  public string MacroType36 = " ";
                  public string MacroType37 = " ";
                  public string MacroType38 = " ";
                  public string MacroType39 = " ";
                  public string MacroType40 = " ";
                  public string MacroType41 = " ";
                  public string MacroType42 = " ";
                  public string MacroType43 = " ";
                  public string MacroType44 = " ";
                  public string MacroType45 = " ";
                  public string MacroType46 = " ";
                  public string MacroType47 = " ";
                  public string MacroType48 = " ";
                  public string MacroType49 = " ";
                  public string MacroType50 = " ";
                  public string MacroType51 = " ";
                  public string MacroType52 = " ";

          #endregion
      }
}
```

XMLData.vb

```
Imports Microsoft.VisualBasic
Imports System

Namespace DeveloperTerminal
        Public Class XMLData
#Region "Serial port parameters"

        Public COMPort As String = "Not Initialized"
        Public Baud As Integer = 0
        Public Databits As Integer = 0
        Public Parity As String = "Not Initialized"
        Public Stopbits As String = "Not Initialized"
        Public Handshake As String = "Not Initialized"

#End Region

#Region "Terminal Characters"
        Public TerminalCharacters As String = ""
#End Region

#Region "Send Bytes Periodically"

        Public SendByte As Integer = 0
        Public SendPeriod As Integer = 0

#End Region

#Region "Initialize Macros"
```

178

```
' Initialize the Macro text
Public MacroText1 As String = " "
Public MacroText2 As String = " "
Public MacroText3 As String = " "
Public MacroText4 As String = " "
Public MacroText5 As String = " "
Public MacroText6 As String = " "
Public MacroText7 As String = " "
Public MacroText8 As String = " "
Public MacroText9 As String = " "
Public MacroText10 As String = " "
Public MacroText11 As String = " "
Public MacroText12 As String = " "
Public MacroText13 As String = " "
Public MacroText14 As String = " "
Public MacroText15 As String = " "
Public MacroText16 As String = " "
Public MacroText17 As String = " "
Public MacroText18 As String = " "
Public MacroText19 As String = " "
Public MacroText20 As String = " "
Public MacroText21 As String = " "
Public MacroText22 As String = " "
Public MacroText23 As String = " "
Public MacroText24 As String = " "
Public MacroText25 As String = " "
Public MacroText26 As String = " "
Public MacroText27 As String = " "
Public MacroText28 As String = " "
Public MacroText29 As String = " "
Public MacroText30 As String = " "
Public MacroText31 As String = " "
Public MacroText32 As String = " "
Public MacroText33 As String = " "
Public MacroText34 As String = " "
Public MacroText35 As String = " "
Public MacroText36 As String = " "
Public MacroText37 As String = " "
Public MacroText38 As String = " "
Public MacroText39 As String = " "
Public MacroText40 As String = " "
Public MacroText41 As String = " "
Public MacroText42 As String = " "
Public MacroText43 As String = " "
Public MacroText44 As String = " "
Public MacroText45 As String = " "
Public MacroText46 As String = " "
Public MacroText47 As String = " "
Public MacroText48 As String = " "
Public MacroText49 As String = " "
Public MacroText50 As String = " "
Public MacroText51 As String = " "
Public MacroText52 As String = " "

' Initialize the Macro Data
Public MacroData1 As String = " "
```

```
Public MacroData2 As String = " "
Public MacroData3 As String = " "
Public MacroData4 As String = " "
Public MacroData5 As String = " "
Public MacroData6 As String = " "
Public MacroData7 As String = " "
Public MacroData8 As String = " "

Public MacroData9 As String = " "
Public MacroData10 As String = " "
Public MacroData11 As String = " "
Public MacroData12 As String = " "
Public MacroData13 As String = " "
Public MacroData14 As String = " "
Public MacroData15 As String = " "
Public MacroData16 As String = " "
Public MacroData17 As String = " "
Public MacroData18 As String = " "
Public MacroData19 As String = " "
Public MacroData20 As String = " "
Public MacroData21 As String = " "
Public MacroData22 As String = " "
Public MacroData23 As String = " "
Public MacroData24 As String = " "
Public MacroData25 As String = " "
Public MacroData26 As String = " "
Public MacroData27 As String = " "
Public MacroData28 As String = " "
Public MacroData29 As String = " "
Public MacroData30 As String = " "
Public MacroData31 As String = " "
Public MacroData32 As String = " "
Public MacroData33 As String = " "
Public MacroData34 As String = " "
Public MacroData35 As String = " "
Public MacroData36 As String = " "
Public MacroData37 As String = " "
Public MacroData38 As String = " "
Public MacroData39 As String = " "
Public MacroData40 As String = " "
Public MacroData41 As String = " "
Public MacroData42 As String = " "
Public MacroData43 As String = " "
Public MacroData44 As String = " "
Public MacroData45 As String = " "
Public MacroData46 As String = " "
Public MacroData47 As String = " "
Public MacroData48 As String = " "
Public MacroData49 As String = " "
Public MacroData50 As String = " "
Public MacroData51 As String = " "
Public MacroData52 As String = " "

' Initialize the Macro Type
Public MacroType1 As String = " "
Public MacroType2 As String = " "
Public MacroType3 As String = " "
```

180

```
        Public MacroType4 As String = " "
        Public MacroType5 As String = " "
        Public MacroType6 As String = " "
        Public MacroType7 As String = " "
        Public MacroType8 As String = " "
        Public MacroType9 As String = " "
        Public MacroType10 As String = " "
        Public MacroType11 As String = " "
        Public MacroType12 As String = " "
        Public MacroType13 As String = " "
        Public MacroType14 As String = " "
        Public MacroType15 As String = " "
        Public MacroType16 As String = " "
        Public MacroType17 As String = " "
        Public MacroType18 As String = " "
        Public MacroType19 As String = " "
        Public MacroType20 As String = " "
        Public MacroType21 As String = " "
        Public MacroType22 As String = " "
        Public MacroType23 As String = " "
        Public MacroType24 As String = " "
        Public MacroType25 As String = " "
        Public MacroType26 As String = " "
        Public MacroType27 As String = " "
        Public MacroType28 As String = " "
        Public MacroType29 As String = " "
        Public MacroType30 As String = " "
        Public MacroType31 As String = " "
        Public MacroType32 As String = " "
        Public MacroType33 As String = " "
        Public MacroType34 As String = " "
        Public MacroType35 As String = " "
        Public MacroType36 As String = " "
        Public MacroType37 As String = " "
        Public MacroType38 As String = " "
        Public MacroType39 As String = " "
        Public MacroType40 As String = " "
        Public MacroType41 As String = " "
        Public MacroType42 As String = " "
        Public MacroType43 As String = " "
        Public MacroType44 As String = " "
        Public MacroType45 As String = " "
        Public MacroType46 As String = " "
        Public MacroType47 As String = " "
        Public MacroType48 As String = " "
        Public MacroType49 As String = " "
        Public MacroType50 As String = " "
        Public MacroType51 As String = " "
        Public MacroType52 As String = " "

#End Region
        End Class
End Namespace
```

XMLIO

XMLIO.cs

```csharp
using System;
using System.Windows.Forms;
using System.IO;
using System.Xml.Serialization;

namespace DeveloperTerminal
{
public class XMLIO
{
        public string appPath; // path to current directory

        public XMLIO()
        {
                //
                // TODO: Add constructor logic here
                //
        }

        public XMLData OpenXMLDataFile()
        {
                OpenFileDialog openFileDialog = new OpenFileDialog();

                openFileDialog.Filter = "XML Files (*.xml)|*.xml";
                openFileDialog.Title = "Open";
                openFileDialog.DefaultExt = ".xml";

                if (openFileDialog.ShowDialog() == wrap
                        System.Windows.Forms.DialogResult.OK)
                {
                        return XMLRead(openFileDialog.FileName);
                }
                else
                {
                        MessageBox.Show("Error: Couldn't get XML file name.");
                        return null;
                }
        }

        // Use default test button data file name
        public XMLData XMLRead()
        {
                return XMLRead(appPath + "\\XMLData.xml");
        }

        // Use any test button data file name
        public XMLData XMLRead(string FileName)
        {
                // Open an instance of the ButtonData class
                XMLData xMLData = new XMLData();

                try
                {
                        // Construct an instance of the XmlSerializer with the type
```

```
                            // of object that is being deserialized.
                            XmlSerializer mySerializer =
                                    new XmlSerializer(typeof(XMLData));
                            // To read the file, create a FileStream object.
                            FileStream myFileStream =
                                    new FileStream(FileName, FileMode.Open);
                            // Call the Deserialize method and cast to the object type.
                            xMLData = (XMLData)
                                    mySerializer.Deserialize(myFileStream);

                            myFileStream.Close();

                    }
                    catch
                    {
                            MessageBox.Show("Error: couldn't read XMLData.xml");
                            return null;
                    }

                    return xMLData;
            }
    }
}
```

XMLIO.vb

```vb
Imports Microsoft.VisualBasic
Imports System
Imports System.Windows.Forms
Imports System.IO
Imports System.Xml.Serialization

Namespace DeveloperTerminal
Public Class XMLIO
    Public appPath As String ' path to current directory

    Public Sub New()
        '
        ' TODO: Add constructor logic here
        '
    End Sub

    Public Function OpenXMLDataFile() As XMLData
        Dim openFileDialog As OpenFileDialog = New OpenFileDialog()

        openFileDialog.Filter = "XML Files (*.xml)|*.xml"
        openFileDialog.Title = "Open"
        openFileDialog.DefaultExt = ".xml"

        If openFileDialog.ShowDialog() = System.Windows.Forms.DialogResult.OK Then
            Return XMLRead(openFileDialog.FileName)
        Else
            MessageBox.Show("Error: Couldn't get XML file name.")
            Return Nothing
        End If
    End Function
```

183

```vb
' Use default test button data file name
Public Function XMLRead() As XMLData
    Return XMLRead(appPath & "\XMLData.xml")
End Function

' Use any test button data file name
Public Function XMLRead(ByVal FileName As String) As XMLData
    ' Open an instance of the ButtonData class
    Dim xMLData As XMLData = New XMLData()

    Try
        ' Construct an instance of the XmlSerializer with the type
        ' of object that is being deserialized.
    Dim mySerializer As XmlSerializer = New wrap
                                    XmlSerializer(GetType(XMLData))
        ' To read the file, create a FileStream object.
        Dim myFileStream As FileStream = New FileStream wrap
                                (FileName, FileMode.Open)
        ' Call the Deserialize method and cast to the object type.
        xMLData = CType(mySerializer.Deserialize(myFileStream), XMLData)

        myFileStream.Close()

    Catch
        MessageBox.Show("Error: couldn't read XMLData.xml")
        Return Nothing
    End Try

    Return xMLData
End Function
End Class
End Namespace
```

LED22

LED22.cs

```csharp
using System;
using System.Collections.Generic;
using System.ComponentModel;
using System.Drawing;
using System.Data;
using System.Text;
using System.Windows.Forms;

namespace LED
{
    public partial class LED22 : UserControl
    {
        public enum LEDColor { RedOn, RedOff, YellowOn, YellowOff, wrap
                    OrangeOn, OrangeOff, GreenOn, GreenOff, BlueOn, BlueOff }

        public LED22()
        {
```

```
        InitializeComponent();

        this.BackgroundImage = imageList1.Images[(int)LEDColor.RedOn];

        setImage((int)LEDColor.RedOn);
    }

    private int Image = (int)LEDColor.RedOn;
    public int image
    {
        get
        {
            return Image;
        }
        set
        {
            Image = value;
            setImage(Image);
        }
    }

    private void setImage(int num)
    {
        if (num <= (int)LEDColor.BlueOff)
        {
            //MessageBox.Show("Set backgroung image to: " + num.ToString());
            this.BackgroundImage = imageList1.Images[num];
        }
        else MessageBox.Show("Error: LED control, setImage - wrap
                                        num > LEDColor.BlueOff.");
    }

    }
}
```

LED22.vb

```
Imports Microsoft.VisualBasic
Imports System
Imports System.Collections.Generic
Imports System.ComponentModel
Imports System.Drawing
Imports System.Data
Imports System.Text
Imports System.Windows.Forms

Namespace LED
        Public Partial Class LED22
                Inherits UserControl
                Public Enum LEDColor
                        RedOn
                        RedOff
                        YellowOn
                        YellowOff
                        OrangeOn
                        OrangeOff
                        GreenOn
```

185

```
                        GreenOff
                        BlueOn
                        BlueOff
                End Enum

                Public Sub New()
                        InitializeComponent()

                        Me.BackgroundImage = wrap
                                imageList1.Images(CInt(Fix(LEDColor.RedOn)))

                        setImage(CInt(Fix(LEDColor.RedOn)))
                End Sub

                Private Image_Renamed As Integer = CInt(Fix(LEDColor.RedOn))
                Public Property image() As Integer
                        Get
                                Return Image_Renamed
                        End Get
                        Set(ByVal value As Integer)
                                Image_Renamed = value
                                setImage(Image_Renamed)
                        End Set
                End Property

                Private Sub setImage(ByVal num As Integer)
                        If num <= CInt(Fix(LEDColor.BlueOff)) Then
                                'MessageBox.Show("Set backgroung image to: wrap
                                                " + num.ToString());
                                Me.BackgroundImage = imageList1.Images(num)
                        Else
                                MessageBox.Show("Error: LED control, wrap
                                                setImage - num > LEDColor.BlueOff.")
                        End If
                End Sub

        End Class
End Namespace
```

TextBoxSettings

TextBoxSettings.cs

```
using System;
using System.Collections.Generic;
using System.ComponentModel;
using System.Data;
using System.Drawing;
using System.Text;
using System.Windows.Forms;

namespace DeveloperTerminal
{
    public partial class TextBoxSettings : Form
    {
```

```csharp
#region Initialization
public TextBoxSettings()
{
    InitializeComponent();
}
#endregion

#region Assessors
private Color BackColr = Color.White;
public Color backColor
{
    get
    {
        return BackColr;
    }
}

private Color ForeColr = Color.Black;
public Color foreColor
{
    get
    {
        return ForeColr;
    }
}

private Font Fnt = null;
public Font font
{
    get
    {
        return Fnt;
    }
}
#endregion

#region Components
private void buttonFont_Click(object sender, EventArgs e)
{
    fontDialog1.ShowDialog();
    Fnt = fontDialog1.Font;
}

private void buttonForeColor_Click(object sender, EventArgs e)
{
    colorDialog1.ShowDialog();
    ForeColr = colorDialog1.Color;
}

private void buttonBackColor_Click(object sender, EventArgs e)
{
    colorDialog1.ShowDialog();
    BackColr = colorDialog1.Color;
}

private void buttonOkay_Click(object sender, EventArgs e)
{
```

```csharp
        DialogResult = DialogResult.OK;
    }

    private void buttonCancel_Click(object sender, EventArgs e)
    {
        DialogResult = DialogResult.Cancel;
    }
    #endregion
    }
}
```

TextBoxSettings.vb

```vb
Imports Microsoft.VisualBasic
Imports System
Imports System.Collections.Generic
Imports System.ComponentModel
Imports System.Data
Imports System.Drawing
Imports System.Text
Imports System.Windows.Forms

Namespace DeveloperTerminal
    Public Partial Class TextBoxSettings
        Inherits Form
        #Region "Initialization"
        Public Sub New()
            InitializeComponent()
        End Sub
        #End Region

        #Region "Assessors"
        Private BackColr As Color = Color.White
Public ReadOnly Property backClr() As Color
    Get
        Return BackColr
    End Get
End Property

        Private ForeColr As Color = Color.Black
Public ReadOnly Property foreClr() As Color
    Get
        Return ForeColr
    End Get
End Property

Private Ft As Font = Nothing
Public ReadOnly Property fnt() As Font
    Get
        Return Ft
    End Get
End Property
        #End Region

        #Region "Components"
        Private Sub buttonFont_Click(ByVal sender As Object, wrap
            ByVal e As EventArgs) Handles buttonFont.Click
```

188

```
                              fontDialog1.ShowDialog()
            FL = fontDialog1.Font
                End Sub

                Private Sub buttonForeColor_Click(ByVal sender As Object, wrap
                            ByVal e As EventArgs) Handles buttonForeColor.Click
                    colorDialog1.ShowDialog()
                    ForeColr = colorDialog1.Color
                End Sub

                Private Sub buttonBackColor_Click(ByVal sender As Object, wrap
                            ByVal e As EventArgs) Handles buttonBackColor.Click
                    colorDialog1.ShowDialog()
                    BackColr = colorDialog1.Color
                End Sub

                Private Sub buttonOkay_Click(ByVal sender As Object, wrap
                            ByVal e As EventArgs) Handles buttonOkay.Click
                    DialogResult = System.Windows.Forms.DialogResult.OK
                End Sub

        Private Sub buttonCancel_Click(ByVal sender As Object, wrap
                            ByVal e As EventArgs) Handles buttonCancel.Click
            DialogResult = DialogResult.Cancel
        End Sub
#End Region
    End Class
End Namespace
```

ByteShooter

ByteShooter.cs

```
using System;
using System.Collections.Generic;
using System.ComponentModel;
using System.Data;
using System.Drawing;
using System.Text;
using System.Windows.Forms;

namespace DeveloperTerminal
{
    public partial class ByteShooter : Form
    {
        #region initialization
        private int Interval = 100;

        public ByteShooter()
        {
            InitializeComponent();
        }

        private void ByteShooter_Load(object sender, EventArgs e)
        {
            char c;
            // Load the comboBox with 0x00 to 0xFF
```

189

```
    for (int i = 0; i < 16; i++)
    {
        c = (char)i;
        this.comboBoxSendByte.Items.Add("0x0" + i.ToString("X") wrap
                                    + " -> " + c.ToString());
    }
    for (int i = 16; i < 256; i++)
    {
        c = (char)i;
        this.comboBoxSendByte.Items.Add("0x" + i.ToString("X") wrap
                                    + " -> " + c.ToString());
    }

    this.comboBoxSendByte.SelectedIndex = index;
}
#endregion

#region Data Assessors
public int interval
{
    get
    {
        return Interval;
    }
    set
    {
        this.textBox1.Text = value.ToString();
    }
}

private byte ByteToSend = 0;
public byte byteToSend
{
    get
    {
        return ByteToSend;
    }
    set
    {
        this.comboBoxSendByte.Text = value.ToString("X");
    }
}

private byte Index = 0;
public byte index
{
    get
    {
        return Index;
    }
    set
    {
        Index = value;
    }
}

#endregion
```

```
#region Components
private void textBox1_TextChanged(object sender, EventArgs e)
{
    try
    {
        Interval = Convert.ToInt32(textBox1.Text);
        timer1.Interval = Interval;
    }
    catch
    {
        timer1.Enabled = false;
        MessageBox.Show("Error with interval");
    }
}

private void comboBoxSendByte_SelectedIndexChanged(wrap
                                object sender, EventArgs e)
{
    ByteToSend = (byte)comboBoxSendByte.SelectedIndex;
}

private void buttonSend_Click(object sender, EventArgs e)
{
    this.DialogResult = DialogResult.OK;
}

private void buttonCancel_Click(object sender, EventArgs e)
{
    this.DialogResult = DialogResult.Cancel;
}
#endregion

    }
}
```

ByteShooter.vb

```
Imports Microsoft.VisualBasic
Imports System
Imports System.Collections.Generic
Imports System.ComponentModel
Imports System.Data
Imports System.Drawing
Imports System.Text
Imports System.Windows.Forms

Namespace DeveloperTerminal
        Public Partial Class ByteShooter
                Inherits Form
                #Region "initialization"
                Private Interval_Renamed As Integer = 100

                Public Sub New()
                        InitializeComponent()
                End Sub
```

191

```
        Private Sub ByteShooter_Load(ByVal sender As Object, wrap
                ByVal e As EventArgs) Handles MyBase.Load
            Dim c As Char
            ' Load the comboBox with 0x00 to 0xFF
            For i As Integer = 0 To 15
                c = ChrW(i)
                Me.comboBoxSendByte.Items.Add("0x0" & wrap
                        i.ToString("X") & " -> " & c.ToString())
            Next i
            For i As Integer = 16 To 255
                c = ChrW(i)
                Me.comboBoxSendByte.Items.Add("0x" & wrap
                        i.ToString("X") & " -> " & c.ToString())
            Next i
        End Sub
        #End Region

        #Region "Data Assessors"
Public Property interval() As Integer
    Get
        Return Interval_Renamed
    End Get
    Set(ByVal value As Integer)
        Me.textBox1.Text = value.ToString()
    End Set
End Property

        Private ByteToSend_Renamed As Byte = 0
Public Property byteToSend() As Byte
    Get
        Return ByteToSend_Renamed
    End Get
    Set(ByVal value As Byte)
        Me.comboBoxSendByte.Text = value.ToString("X")
    End Set
End Property

Private Index_Renamed As Byte = 0
Public Property index() As Byte
    Get
        Return Index_Renamed
    End Get
    Set(ByVal value As Byte)
        Index_Renamed = value
    End Set
End Property

        #End Region

        #Region "Components"
        Private Sub textBox1_TextChanged(ByVal sender As Object, wrap
            ByVal e As EventArgs) Handles textBox1.TextChanged
            Try
                Interval_Renamed = Convert.ToInt32(textBox1.Text)
                timer1.Interval = Interval_Renamed
            Catch
                timer1.Enabled = False
```

192

```
                            MessageBox.Show("Error with interval")
                End Try
        End Sub

        Private Sub comboBoxSendByte_SelectedIndexChanged(ByVal wrap
                    sender As Object, ByVal e As EventArgs) Handles wrap
                    comboBoxSendByte.SelectedIndexChanged
            ByteToSend_Renamed = CByte(comboBoxSendByte.SelectedIndex)
        End Sub

        Private Sub buttonSend_Click(ByVal sender As Object, wrap
                    ByVal e As EventArgs) Handles buttonSend.Click
            Me.DialogResult = System.Windows.Forms.DialogResult.OK
        End Sub

        Private Sub buttonCancel_Click(ByVal sender As Object, wrap
                    ByVal e As EventArgs) Handles buttonCancel.Click
            Me.DialogResult = DialogResult.Cancel
        End Sub
        #End Region

    End Class
End Namespace
```

MainForm

We will not show the code in the regions named "C# Express added Definitions" or the "Window Form Designer generated code" – if you write this code from scratch, all that will be in a separate class and since it is generated for you, no need to write it yourself.

MainForm.cs

```
//
// Smiley Terminal evolved over time and like many a creature of evolution,
// you might find some atavistic artifacts. As my Grandpappy, the hog
// farmer, used to say: "That's about as useful as tits an a boar." Well,
// I'm going to guess that you'll find some artifacts in this code that
// are even less useful.
//
// Don't you just love the legalistic bullshit that is usually inserted at
// this point? I've rewritten some standard boilerplate stuff to say what
// I think we really mean:
//   This work is entirely by Joe Pardue (except for the major portions he
//   stole and forgot to attribute). Copyright by Joe Pardue 4/26/07. and all
//   rights are reserved - any theft of this intellectual property will
//   result in a challenge to an arm wrestling contest
//
//   This software is not warrented in any way what-so-ever. It WILL screw
//   something up and will kill someone after doing serious property
//   damage. You've been warned. If you sic a lawyer on me, just remember:
//   I'm old, grouchy, have little to lose, and support the Second Amendment.
//
// Ah, yes I feel much better now.
```

Chapter 14: Developer Terminal Source Code

```
//
// Please send any bug reports, comments, or concerns to joe@smileymicros.com
//
// 7/6/06 - Version 0.0 moved up to C# 2005 Express
// 3/14/07 - Revision 0.1 got back to it and added a bunch of stuff.
// 4/26/07 - Revision 0.2 God only knows what I did, but it is different.
// 4/28/07 - Revision 0.3 changes marked by comment: // JWP 4/28/07

// BETA - THIS IS THE BETA RELEASE AND WILL HAVE PROBLEMS THAT I MISSED AND YOU WON'T
// BETA - SINCE MICROSOFT RELEASES CODE FOR THE BUYER TO DEBUG, I THOUGHT 'HELL, WHY NOT'
// BETA - PLEASE SEND COMMENTS AND CORRECTIONS TO joe@smileymicros.com

using System;
using System.Drawing;
using System.Collections;
using System.ComponentModel;
using System.Windows.Forms;
using System.Data;
using System.IO;
using System.IO.Ports;

using LED;

namespace DeveloperTerminal
{
        public class MainForm : System.Windows.Forms.Form
    {


#region Initialization
/* If you build Developer Terminal from scratch using the Express edition
 * you will see some differences in the intializaion section. This is because
 * most of this code was written in earlier versions and imported into Express.
 * The code will work the same thought.*/

#region Startup definitions

// Create an instance of the settings form
PortSettings portSettings = new PortSettings();

// Booleans to toggle the modem lines
private bool RTSToggle = true;
private bool DTRToggle = true;

// Keep count of sent and received bytes
private int SendCount = 0;
private int ReceiveCount = 0;

// Immediate or Queued state for sending data
private bool SendImmediate = true;
private string QueuedString = "";

// Send with terminal characters
private bool UseTermChar = false;

// Receive as ASCII or Hex state
private bool ReceiveASCII = true;
```

Chapter 14: Developer Terminal Source Code

```csharp
// Create an instance of the TerminalData class
XMLData xMLData = new XMLData();

// Create an instance of the TerminalXMLIO class to read the terminal data
XMLIO dataXMLIO = new XMLIO();

// Create MacroData arrays
string[] MacroDataText = new string[52];
string[] MacroDataData = new string[52];
string[] MacroDataType = new string[52];

// Boolean for the port open state
public bool PortOpen = false;
private ToolStripMenuItem toolsToolStripMenuItem;
private ToolStripMenuItem sendCharToolStripMenuItem;
private Timer timerSendByte;
private ToolStripMenuItem fileToolStripMenuItem;
private ToolStripMenuItem openInSendBoxToolStripMenuItem;
private ToolStripMenuItem saveSendBoxToolStripMenuItem;
private ToolStripMenuItem saveReceiveBoxToolStripMenuItem;
private ToolStripMenuItem manualToolStripMenuItem;
private ToolStripMenuItem smileyMicrosToolStripMenuItem;
private ToolStripMenuItem copyToolStripMenuItem1;
private ToolStripMenuItem cutToolStripMenuItem1;
private ToolStripMenuItem deleteToolStripMenuItem1;
private ToolStripMenuItem selectAllToolStripMenuItem1;
private ToolStripSeparator toolStripSeparator4;
private ToolStripMenuItem saveFileAsToolStripMenuItem;
private ContextMenuStrip contextMenuStripReceive;

// Boolean for the Ring Indicator modem state
public bool RingIndicator = false;

#endregion

#region Startup functions

public MainForm()
{
        //
        // Required for Windows Form Designer support
        //
        InitializeComponent();

        // Read the terminal data from TerminalData.xml
        dataXMLIO.appPath = System.Environment.CurrentDirectory;
        xMLData = dataXMLIO.XMLRead();

}

/// <summary>
/// Clean up any resources being used.
/// </summary>
protected override void Dispose( bool disposing )
{
        base.Dispose( disposing );
}
```

Chapter 14: Developer Terminal Source Code

```csharp
/// <summary>
/// The main entry point for the application.
/// </summary>
[STAThread]
static void Main()
{
        Application.Run(new MainForm());
}

private void Form1_Load(object sender, System.EventArgs e)
{
    this.Text = "Smiley Micros Serial port Terminal - Port is closed";
    // Start the terminal with default settings
    serialPort1.PortName = portSettings.selectedPort = xMLData.COMPort;
    serialPort1.BaudRate = portSettings.selectedBaudrate = xMLData.Baud;
    serialPort1.DataBits = portSettings.selectedDataBits = xMLData.Databits;

    string temp = xMLData.Parity;
    switch (temp)
    {
        case "Even":
            serialPort1.Parity = portSettings.selectedParity = Parity.Even;
            break;
        case "Mark":
            serialPort1.Parity = portSettings.selectedParity = Parity.Mark;
            break;
        case "None":
            serialPort1.Parity = portSettings.selectedParity = Parity.None;
            break;
        case "Odd":
            serialPort1.Parity = portSettings.selectedParity = Parity.Odd;
            break;
        case "Space":
            serialPort1.Parity = portSettings.selectedParity = Parity.Space;
            break;
        default:
            serialPort1.Parity = portSettings.selectedParity = Parity.None;
            break;
    }

    temp = xMLData.Stopbits;
    switch (temp)
    {
        case "None":
            serialPort1.StopBits = portSettings.selectedStopBits = StopBits.None;
            break;
        case "1":
            serialPort1.StopBits = portSettings.selectedStopBits = StopBits.One;
            break;
        //case "1.5": // not supported by FT232R
        //serialPort1.StopBits = = StopBits.OnePointFive;
        //break;
        case "2":
            serialPort1.StopBits = portSettings.selectedStopBits = StopBits.Two;
            break;
        default:
```

```
            serialPort1.StopBits = portSettings.selectedStopBits = StopBits.One;
            break;
    }

    temp = xMLData.Handshake;
    switch (temp)
    {
        case "None":
            serialPort1.Handshake = portSettings.selectedHandshaking = wrap
                                            Handshake.None;

            break;
        case "RTS/CTS":
            serialPort1.Handshake = portSettings.selectedHandshaking = wrap
                                            Handshake.RequestToSend;

            break;
        case "Xon/Xoff":
            serialPort1.Handshake = portSettings.selectedHandshaking = wrap
                                            Handshake.XOnXOff;

            break;
        default:
            serialPort1.Handshake = portSettings.selectedHandshaking = wrap
                                            Handshake.None;

            break;
    }

        // Load the comboBox with 0x00 to 0xFF
        for(int i = 0; i < 16; i++)
        {
                this.comboBoxSendByte.Items.Add("0x0" + i.ToString("X"));
        }
        for(int i = 16; i < 256; i++)
        {
                this.comboBoxSendByte.Items.Add("0x" + i.ToString("X"));
        }

        loadXMLData();

    // Set the default LED images
    this.LEDCTS.image = (int)LED.LED22.LEDColor.BlueOn;
    this.LEDDSR.image = (int)LED.LED22.LEDColor.BlueOff;
    this.LEDDCD.image = (int)LED.LED22.LEDColor.BlueOff;
    this.LEDRI.image = (int)LED.LED22.LEDColor.BlueOff;
    this.LEDRTS.image = (int)LED.LED22.LEDColor.RedOn;
    this.LEDDTR.image = (int)LED.LED22.LEDColor.RedOff;

}
#endregion

#endregion

#region GUI

#region Open REALLY GREAT website

// And this is not shameless commercialism. I have NO shame.
// And2 - now you know how to do it.
```

```csharp
private void linkLabelVisitWebSite_LinkClicked(object sender,
System.Windows.Forms.LinkLabelLinkClickedEventArgs e)
{
        System.Diagnostics.Process.Start("www.smileymicros.com");
}

// Open website
private void panel1_MouseClick(object sender, MouseEventArgs e)
{
    System.Diagnostics.Process.Start("www.smileymicros.com");
}

// Show hand cursor and change color to intice click to website
private void panel1_MouseEnter(object sender, EventArgs e)
{
    panel1.Cursor = Cursors.Hand;
    panel1.BackColor = Color.SandyBrown;
}

// Cursor reverts on leaving, but color doesn't so revert it
private void panel1_MouseLeave(object sender, EventArgs e)
{
    panel1.BackColor = Color.Bisque;
}

#endregion

#region Buttons
private void buttonClear_Click(object sender, System.EventArgs e)
{
        richTextBoxReceive.Text = "";
    textBoxSendCount.Text = "";
}

private void buttonClearSend_Click(object sender, EventArgs e)
{
    richTextBoxSend.Text = "";
}

private void buttonSettings_Click(object sender, System.EventArgs e)
{
    PortSettings portSettings = new PortSettings();

    portSettings.ShowDialog();
    if (portSettings.DialogResult == DialogResult.OK)
    {
        serialPort1.PortName = portSettings.selectedPort;
        serialPort1.BaudRate = portSettings.selectedBaudrate;
    }
}

private void buttonSend_Click(object sender, System.EventArgs e)
{
        richTextBoxSend.Text += "\n Sent QueuedString: \n" + QueuedString + "\n";
        SendASCIIString(QueuedString);
        if (UseTermChar) sendTermChar();
        QueuedString = "";
```

```
}

private void buttonOpenClosePort_Click(object sender, System.EventArgs e)
{
        if(PortOpen)
        {
                PortOpen = false;
        serialPort1.Close();
        this.Text = "Smiley Micros Serial port Terminal - Port is closed";
        }
        else
        {
                PortOpen = true;

        try
        {
            serialPort1.Open();
         }
        catch(System.Exception ex)
        {
            MessageBox.Show("Error - buttonOpenClosePort_ClickSystem. wrap
                                            Exception: " + ex);
        }
                showSettings();
        }
}

private void buttonHelp_Click(object sender, System.EventArgs e)
{
        MessageBox.Show("HELP! is coming soon to a computer near you...");
}

void ButtonReloadMacrosClick(object sender, System.EventArgs e)
{
        xMLData = dataXMLIO.XMLRead();
        listBoxMacros.Items.Clear();
        loadXMLData();
}
#endregion

#region Check Box and Radio Buttons

private void radioButtonImmediate_CheckedChanged(object sender, wrap
                                            System.EventArgs e)
{
        if(radioButtonImmediate.Checked == true)
        {
                SendImmediate = true;
                buttonSendQue.Enabled = false;
        }
}

private void radioButtonQueued_CheckedChanged(object sender, System.EventArgs e)
{
        if(radioButtonQueued.Checked == true)
        {
                SendImmediate = false;
```

```csharp
                        buttonSendQue.Enabled = true;
            }
    }

    private void radioButtonASCII_CheckedChanged_1(object sender, System.EventArgs e)
    {
            ReceiveASCII = true;
    }

    private void radioButtonHEX_CheckedChanged_1(object sender, System.EventArgs e)
    {
            ReceiveASCII = false;
    }

    private void radioButtonTermCharYes_CheckedChanged(object sender, EventArgs e)
    {
        if (radioButtonTermCharYes.Checked == true)
        {
            UseTermChar = true;
        }
    }

    private void radioButtonTermCharNo_CheckedChanged(object sender, EventArgs e)
    {
        if (radioButtonTermCharNo.Checked == true)
        {
            UseTermChar = false;
        }
    }

    #endregion

    #endregion

    #region Receive functions
    // We want to ignore the byte receive immediately following a byte sent over
    // an IR 'wire' since it will not just be sent, but received. We will flag this
    // condition with an IRSent bool.
    private bool IRSent = false;

    // we want to have the serial port thread report back data received, but to
    display
    // that data we must create a delegate function to show the data in the
    richTextBox

    // define the delegate
    public delegate void SetText();
    // define an instance of the delegate
    SetText setText;

    // create a string that will be loaded with the data received from the port
    public string str = "";
    // JWP 4/28/07 added public byt for receiving bytes
    public byte byt = 0;

    // note that this function runs in a separate thread and thus we must use a
    delegate in order
```

200

```csharp
// to display the results in the richTextBox.
private void serialPort1_DataReceived(object sender, SerialDataReceivedEventArgs
e)
{
    if (!IRSent) // ignore byte received after an IR byte send
    {
        // instantiate the delegate to be invoked by this thread
        setText = new SetText(mySetText);

        // load the data into the string
        try
        {
            // JWP 4/28/07 added ReceiveASCII and byte reception
            if (ReceiveASCII)
            {
                str = serialPort1.ReadExisting();
            }
            else
            {
                byt = (byte)serialPort1.ReadByte();// .ReadExisting();
            }
        }
        catch (System.Exception ex)
        {
            MessageBox.Show("Error - port_DataReceived Exception: " + ex);
        }

        // invoke the delegate in the MainForm thread
        this.Invoke(setText);
    }
    else IRSent = false;
}

// create the instance of the delegate to be used to write the received wrap
//                                              data to the richTextBox
public void mySetText()
{
    ReceiveCount += str.Length;
    textBoxReceiveCount.Text = ReceiveCount.ToString();

    if (ReceiveASCII)
    {
        richTextBoxReceive.Text += str.ToString();
    }
    else // ReceiveHEX
    {
        // JWP 4/28/07 changed byte display
        /*foreach (byte b in str)
        {
            if (b > 15)
            {
                richTextBoxReceive.Text += "0x" + b.ToString("X") + ",";
            }
            else richTextBoxReceive.Text += "0x0" + b.ToString("X") + ",";
        }*/
        if (byt > 15)
        {
```

201

```
            richTextBoxReceive.Text += "0x" + byt.ToString("X") + ",";
        }
        else richTextBoxReceive.Text += "0x0" + byt.ToString("X") + ",";

    }

}

// This rigaramole is needed to keep the last received item displayed
// it kind of flickers and should be fixed
private void richTextBoxReceive_TextChanged(object sender, System.EventArgs e)
{
    moveCaretToEnd();
}

private void moveCaretToEnd()
{
    richTextBoxReceive.SelectionStart = richTextBoxReceive.Text.Length;
    richTextBoxReceive.SelectionLength = 0;
    richTextBoxReceive.ScrollToCaret();
}

endregion

#region Send Text functions
private void richTextBoxSend_KeyPress(object sender, KeyPressEventArgs e)
{
        if(SendImmediate)
        {
         sendChar(e.KeyChar);
                if(UseTermChar) sendTermChar();
        }
        else
        {
                QueuedString += e.KeyChar;
        }
}

private void sendTermChar()
{
    SendHEXString(xMLData.TerminalCharacters);
}

private void sendChar(char c)
{
    char[] data = new Char[1];
    data[0] = c;
    try
    {
        serialPort1.Write(data, 0, 1);
        SendCount++;
        textBoxSendCount.Text = SendCount.ToString();
        // Show bytes sent by shooter
        if (shoot) richTextBoxSend.Text += c;
    }
    catch
    {
```

```
            MessageBox.Show("Error: sendChar - failed to send.\nIs the port open?");
        }
    }

//JWP 4/28/07 - add sendByte function
private bool sendByte(byte b)
{
    byte[] data = new byte[1];
    data[0] = b;
    try
    {
        serialPort1.Write(data, 0, 1);
        SendCount++;
        textBoxSendCount.Text = SendCount.ToString();
        // Show bytes sent by shooter
        //JWP 4/28/07 added show with 0x or 0x0
        if (shoot)
        {
            if (byt > 15)
            {
                richTextBoxSend.Text += "0x" + b.ToString("X") + ",";
            }
            else richTextBoxSend.Text += "0x0" + b.ToString("X") + ",";
        }
    }
    catch
    {
        return false;
    }
    return true;
}

// Send single hex bytes immediately
private void comboBoxSendByte_SelectedIndexChanged(object sender,
                                                   System.EventArgs e)
{
    //JWP 4/28/07 - changed from sendChar to sendByte
    //sendChar((char)comboBoxSendByte.SelectedIndex);
    sendByte((byte)comboBoxSendByte.SelectedIndex);
    this.richTextBoxSend.Text = "Sent: 0x" +
                        comboBoxSendByte.SelectedIndex.ToString("X");
}



#endregion

#region Send Macro Functions
// Send Macro Stings
void ListBoxMacrosDoubleClick(object sender, System.EventArgs e)
{
        processMacroClick(MacroDataData[listBoxMacros.SelectedIndex],
                                   MacroDataType[listBoxMacros.SelectedIndex]);
}
private void processMacroClick(string MacroData, string MacroType)
{
        richTextBoxSend.Text = MacroData;
```

203

```
        if(MacroType == "ASCII")
        {
                SendASCIIString(MacroData);
         if (UseTermChar) sendTermChar();
        }
        else if (MacroType == "HEX")
        {
                SendHEXString(MacroData);
         if (UseTermChar) sendTermChar();
        }
        else MessageBox.Show("Error: MacroType: " + MacroType);
}

public void SendASCIIString(string str)
{
    char[] c = str.ToCharArray();

    for (int i = 0; i < c.GetLength(0); i++)
    {
        sendChar(c[i]);
    }
}

// For our purposes, HEX strings must be in the format 0xFF,0xFE,
// including the trailing comma on the last value
public void SendHEXString(string str)
{
    char[] c = str.ToCharArray();
    byte b = 0;

    if (c.GetLength(0) < 5)
    {
        MessageBox.Show("Error: Hex string incorrect length: " + str + wrap
                                "\nLength = " + c.GetLength(0).ToString());
        return;
    }
    for (int i = 0; i < c.GetLength(0); i += 5)
    {
        // Check array length
        if (i > c.GetLength(0))
        {
            MessageBox.Show("Error: Hex string incorrect length: " + wrap
                    str + "\nLength = " + c.GetLength(0).ToString() + wrap
                    "\ni = " + i.ToString());
            return;
        }
        // Check for remaining length
        if (i + 4 >= c.GetLength(0))
        {
            MessageBox.Show("Error: Hex string: " + str + " problem with length");
            return;
        }
        // Check format trailing comma
        if (c[i + 4] != ',')
        {
            MessageBox.Show("Error: Hex string: " + str + wrap
                                " lacks a trailing comma.");
```

204

```
            return;
    }
    // Check high nibble range 0 - F
    if ((c[i + 2] >= '0') && (c[i + 2] <= '9') && (c[i + 2] >= 'A') wrap
                                                 && (c[i + 2] <= 'F'))
    {
        MessageBox.Show("Error: Hex string first digit: " + wrap
                        c[i + 2].ToString() + " not in range 0 - F");
        return;
    }
    // Check low nibble range 0 - F
    if ((c[i + 3] >= '0') && (c[i + 3] <= '9') && wrap
                            (c[i + 3] >= 'A') && (c[i + 3] <= 'F'))
    {
        MessageBox.Show("Error: Hex string first digit: " wrap
                        + c[i + 2].ToString() + " not in range 0 - F");
        return;
    }
    if (c[i + 2] <= '9') b = (byte)(c[i + 2] - '0');
    else
    {
        b = (byte)(c[i + 2] - 'A');
        b += 10;
    }

    b = (byte)(b << 4);

    if (c[i + 3] <= '9') b += (byte)(c[i + 3] - '0');
    else
    {
        b += (byte)(c[i + 3] - 'A');
        b += 10;
    }

    sendChar((char)b);
    }
}

#endregion

#region Load macro data
void loadXMLData()
{
        listBoxMacros.Items.Add(xMLData.MacroText1);
        listBoxMacros.Items.Add(xMLData.MacroText2);
        listBoxMacros.Items.Add(xMLData.MacroText3);
        listBoxMacros.Items.Add(xMLData.MacroText4);
        listBoxMacros.Items.Add(xMLData.MacroText5);
        listBoxMacros.Items.Add(xMLData.MacroText6);
        listBoxMacros.Items.Add(xMLData.MacroText7);
        listBoxMacros.Items.Add(xMLData.MacroText8);
        listBoxMacros.Items.Add(xMLData.MacroText9);
        listBoxMacros.Items.Add(xMLData.MacroText10);
        listBoxMacros.Items.Add(xMLData.MacroText11);
        listBoxMacros.Items.Add(xMLData.MacroText12);
        listBoxMacros.Items.Add(xMLData.MacroText13);
        listBoxMacros.Items.Add(xMLData.MacroText14);
```

```
listBoxMacros.Items.Add(xMLData.MacroText15);
listBoxMacros.Items.Add(xMLData.MacroText16);
listBoxMacros.Items.Add(xMLData.MacroText17);
listBoxMacros.Items.Add(xMLData.MacroText18);
listBoxMacros.Items.Add(xMLData.MacroText19);
listBoxMacros.Items.Add(xMLData.MacroText20);
listBoxMacros.Items.Add(xMLData.MacroText21);
listBoxMacros.Items.Add(xMLData.MacroText22);
listBoxMacros.Items.Add(xMLData.MacroText23);
listBoxMacros.Items.Add(xMLData.MacroText24);
listBoxMacros.Items.Add(xMLData.MacroText25);
listBoxMacros.Items.Add(xMLData.MacroText26);
listBoxMacros.Items.Add(xMLData.MacroText27);
listBoxMacros.Items.Add(xMLData.MacroText28);
listBoxMacros.Items.Add(xMLData.MacroText29);
listBoxMacros.Items.Add(xMLData.MacroText30);
listBoxMacros.Items.Add(xMLData.MacroText31);
listBoxMacros.Items.Add(xMLData.MacroText32);
listBoxMacros.Items.Add(xMLData.MacroText33);
listBoxMacros.Items.Add(xMLData.MacroText34);
listBoxMacros.Items.Add(xMLData.MacroText35);
listBoxMacros.Items.Add(xMLData.MacroText36);
listBoxMacros.Items.Add(xMLData.MacroText37);
listBoxMacros.Items.Add(xMLData.MacroText38);
listBoxMacros.Items.Add(xMLData.MacroText39);
listBoxMacros.Items.Add(xMLData.MacroText40);
listBoxMacros.Items.Add(xMLData.MacroText41);
listBoxMacros.Items.Add(xMLData.MacroText42);
listBoxMacros.Items.Add(xMLData.MacroText43);
listBoxMacros.Items.Add(xMLData.MacroText44);
listBoxMacros.Items.Add(xMLData.MacroText45);
listBoxMacros.Items.Add(xMLData.MacroText46);
listBoxMacros.Items.Add(xMLData.MacroText47);
listBoxMacros.Items.Add(xMLData.MacroText48);
listBoxMacros.Items.Add(xMLData.MacroText49);
listBoxMacros.Items.Add(xMLData.MacroText50);
listBoxMacros.Items.Add(xMLData.MacroText51);
listBoxMacros.Items.Add(xMLData.MacroText52);

MacroDataText[0]  = xMLData.MacroText1;
MacroDataText[1]  = xMLData.MacroText2;
MacroDataText[2]  = xMLData.MacroText3;
MacroDataText[3]  = xMLData.MacroText4;
MacroDataText[4]  = xMLData.MacroText5;
MacroDataText[5]  = xMLData.MacroText6;
MacroDataText[6]  = xMLData.MacroText7;
MacroDataText[7]  = xMLData.MacroText8;
MacroDataText[8]  = xMLData.MacroText9;
MacroDataText[9]  = xMLData.MacroText10;
MacroDataText[10] = xMLData.MacroText11;
MacroDataText[11] = xMLData.MacroText12;
MacroDataText[12] = xMLData.MacroText13;
MacroDataText[13] = xMLData.MacroText14;
MacroDataText[14] = xMLData.MacroText15;
MacroDataText[15] = xMLData.MacroText16;
MacroDataText[16] = xMLData.MacroText17;
MacroDataText[17] = xMLData.MacroText18;
```

```
MacroDataText[18]  = xMLData.MacroText19;
MacroDataText[19]  = xMLData.MacroText20;
MacroDataText[20]  = xMLData.MacroText21;
MacroDataText[21]  = xMLData.MacroText22;
MacroDataText[22]  = xMLData.MacroText23;
MacroDataText[23]  = xMLData.MacroText24;
MacroDataText[24]  = xMLData.MacroText25;
MacroDataText[25]  = xMLData.MacroText26;
MacroDataText[26]  = xMLData.MacroText27;
MacroDataText[27]  = xMLData.MacroText28;
MacroDataText[28]  = xMLData.MacroText29;
MacroDataText[29]  = xMLData.MacroText30;
MacroDataText[30]  = xMLData.MacroText31;
MacroDataText[31]  = xMLData.MacroText32;
MacroDataText[32]  = xMLData.MacroText33;
MacroDataText[33]  = xMLData.MacroText34;
MacroDataText[34]  = xMLData.MacroText35;
MacroDataText[35]  = xMLData.MacroText36;
MacroDataText[36]  = xMLData.MacroText37;
MacroDataText[37]  = xMLData.MacroText38;
MacroDataText[38]  = xMLData.MacroText39;
MacroDataText[39]  = xMLData.MacroText40;
MacroDataText[40]  = xMLData.MacroText41;
MacroDataText[41]  = xMLData.MacroText42;
MacroDataText[42]  = xMLData.MacroText43;
MacroDataText[43]  = xMLData.MacroText44;
MacroDataText[44]  = xMLData.MacroText45;
MacroDataText[45]  = xMLData.MacroText46;
MacroDataText[46]  = xMLData.MacroText47;
MacroDataText[47]  = xMLData.MacroText48;
MacroDataText[48]  = xMLData.MacroText49;
MacroDataText[49]  = xMLData.MacroText50;
MacroDataText[50]  = xMLData.MacroText51;
MacroDataText[51]  = xMLData.MacroText52;

MacroDataData[0]  = xMLData.MacroData1;
MacroDataData[1]  = xMLData.MacroData2;
MacroDataData[2]  = xMLData.MacroData3;
MacroDataData[3]  = xMLData.MacroData4;
MacroDataData[4]  = xMLData.MacroData5;
MacroDataData[5]  = xMLData.MacroData6;
MacroDataData[6]  = xMLData.MacroData7;
MacroDataData[7]  = xMLData.MacroData8;
MacroDataData[8]  = xMLData.MacroData9;
MacroDataData[9]  = xMLData.MacroData10;
MacroDataData[10]  = xMLData.MacroData11;
MacroDataData[11]  = xMLData.MacroData12;
MacroDataData[12]  = xMLData.MacroData13;
MacroDataData[13]  = xMLData.MacroData14;
MacroDataData[14]  = xMLData.MacroData15;
MacroDataData[15]  = xMLData.MacroData16;
MacroDataData[16]  = xMLData.MacroData17;
MacroDataData[17]  = xMLData.MacroData18;
MacroDataData[18]  = xMLData.MacroData19;
MacroDataData[19]  = xMLData.MacroData20;
MacroDataData[20]  = xMLData.MacroData21;
MacroDataData[21]  = xMLData.MacroData22;
```

```
MacroDataData[22] = xMLData.MacroData23;
MacroDataData[23] = xMLData.MacroData24;
MacroDataData[24] = xMLData.MacroData25;
MacroDataData[25] = xMLData.MacroData26;
MacroDataData[26] = xMLData.MacroData27;
MacroDataData[27] = xMLData.MacroData28;
MacroDataData[28] = xMLData.MacroData29;
MacroDataData[29] = xMLData.MacroData30;
MacroDataData[30] = xMLData.MacroData31;
MacroDataData[31] = xMLData.MacroData32;
MacroDataData[32] = xMLData.MacroData33;
MacroDataData[33] = xMLData.MacroData34;
MacroDataData[34] = xMLData.MacroData35;
MacroDataData[35] = xMLData.MacroData36;
MacroDataData[36] = xMLData.MacroData37;
MacroDataData[37] = xMLData.MacroData38;
MacroDataData[38] = xMLData.MacroData39;
MacroDataData[39] = xMLData.MacroData40;
MacroDataData[40] = xMLData.MacroData41;
MacroDataData[41] = xMLData.MacroData42;
MacroDataData[42] = xMLData.MacroData43;
MacroDataData[43] = xMLData.MacroData44;
MacroDataData[44] = xMLData.MacroData45;
MacroDataData[45] = xMLData.MacroData46;
MacroDataData[46] = xMLData.MacroData47;
MacroDataData[47] = xMLData.MacroData48;
MacroDataData[48] = xMLData.MacroData49;
MacroDataData[49] = xMLData.MacroData50;
MacroDataData[50] = xMLData.MacroData51;
MacroDataData[51] = xMLData.MacroData52;

MacroDataType[0]  = xMLData.MacroType1;
MacroDataType[1]  = xMLData.MacroType2;
MacroDataType[2]  = xMLData.MacroType3;
MacroDataType[3]  = xMLData.MacroType4;
MacroDataType[4]  = xMLData.MacroType5;
MacroDataType[5]  = xMLData.MacroType6;
MacroDataType[6]  = xMLData.MacroType7;
MacroDataType[7]  = xMLData.MacroType8;
MacroDataType[8]  = xMLData.MacroType9;
MacroDataType[9]  = xMLData.MacroType10;
MacroDataType[10] = xMLData.MacroType11;
MacroDataType[11] = xMLData.MacroType12;
MacroDataType[12] = xMLData.MacroType13;
MacroDataType[13] = xMLData.MacroType14;
MacroDataType[14] = xMLData.MacroType15;
MacroDataType[15] = xMLData.MacroType16;
MacroDataType[16] = xMLData.MacroType17;
MacroDataType[17] = xMLData.MacroType18;
MacroDataType[18] = xMLData.MacroType19;
MacroDataType[19] = xMLData.MacroType20;
MacroDataType[20] = xMLData.MacroType21;
MacroDataType[21] = xMLData.MacroType22;
MacroDataType[22] = xMLData.MacroType23;
MacroDataType[23] = xMLData.MacroType24;
MacroDataType[24] = xMLData.MacroType25;
MacroDataType[25] = xMLData.MacroType26;
```

```
        MacroDataType[26] = xMLData.MacroType27;
        MacroDataType[27] = xMLData.MacroType28;
        MacroDataType[28] = xMLData.MacroType29;
        MacroDataType[29] = xMLData.MacroType30;
        MacroDataType[30] = xMLData.MacroType31;
        MacroDataType[31] = xMLData.MacroType32;
        MacroDataType[32] = xMLData.MacroType33;
        MacroDataType[33] = xMLData.MacroType34;
        MacroDataType[34] = xMLData.MacroType35;
        MacroDataType[35] = xMLData.MacroType36;
        MacroDataType[36] = xMLData.MacroType37;
        MacroDataType[37] = xMLData.MacroType38;
        MacroDataType[38] = xMLData.MacroType39;
        MacroDataType[39] = xMLData.MacroType40;
        MacroDataType[40] = xMLData.MacroType41;
        MacroDataType[41] = xMLData.MacroType42;
        MacroDataType[42] = xMLData.MacroType43;
        MacroDataType[43] = xMLData.MacroType44;
        MacroDataType[44] = xMLData.MacroType45;
        MacroDataType[45] = xMLData.MacroType46;
        MacroDataType[46] = xMLData.MacroType47;
        MacroDataType[47] = xMLData.MacroType48;
        MacroDataType[48] = xMLData.MacroType49;
        MacroDataType[49] = xMLData.MacroType50;
        MacroDataType[50] = xMLData.MacroType51;
        MacroDataType[51] = xMLData.MacroType52;
}

#endregion

#region Send Textbox Context menus
private void richTextBoxSend_MouseDown(object sender, MouseEventArgs e)
{
    if (e.Button == MouseButtons.Right)
    {
        contextMenuStripSend.Show(MousePosition);
    }
}

private void copyToolStripMenuItem_Click(object sender, EventArgs e)
{
    richTextBoxSend.Copy();
}

private void cutToolStripMenuItem_Click(object sender, EventArgs e)
{
    richTextBoxSend.Cut();
}


private void deleteToolStripMenuItem_Click(object sender, EventArgs e)
{
    richTextBoxSend.Clear();
    textBoxSendCount.Text = "0";
    SendCount = 0;
}
```

```
private void selectAllToolStripMenuItem_Click(object sender, EventArgs e)
{
    richTextBoxSend.SelectAll();
}

private void undoToolStripMenuItem_Click(object sender, EventArgs e)
{
    richTextBoxSend.Undo();
}

private void redoToolStripMenuItem_Click(object sender, EventArgs e)
{
    richTextBoxSend.Redo();
}

private void saveAsToolStripMenuItem_Click(object sender, EventArgs e)
{
    saveSendBox();
}

private void pasteToolStripMenuItem_Click(object sender, EventArgs e)
{
    richTextBoxSend.Paste();
    setToQueued();
}

// use for paste and load
private void setToQueued()
{
    // set to send queued
    radioButtonQueued.Checked = true;
    SendImmediate = false;
    buttonSendQue.Enabled = true;
    QueuedString = richTextBoxSend.Text;
}

// Context menu item
private void loadFileToolStripMenuItem_Click(object sender, EventArgs e)
{
    openInSendBox();
}
// File menu item
private void openInSendBoxToolStripMenuItem_Click_1(object sender, EventArgs e)
{
    openInSendBox();
}

private void saveSendBoxToolStripMenuItem_Click(object sender, EventArgs e)
{
    saveSendBox();
}

private void saveSendBoxToolStripMenuItem_Click_1(object sender, EventArgs e)
{
    saveSendBox();
}
```

```
private void openInSendBox()
{
    string filename = "";
    if (openFileDialog1.ShowDialog() == DialogResult.OK)
    {
        filename = openFileDialog1.FileName;
        if (filename != "")
        {
            richTextBoxSend.LoadFile(filename, RichTextBoxStreamType.PlainText);
            setToQueued();
        }
    }
    else
    {
        MessageBox.Show("Error loading file.");
    }
}

private void saveSendBox()
{
    string filename = "";
    if (saveFileDialog1.ShowDialog() == DialogResult.OK)
    {
        filename = saveFileDialog1.FileName;
        if (filename != "") richTextBoxSend.SaveFile(filename,
RichTextBoxStreamType.PlainText);
    }
}

#endregion

#region Receive Textbox Context menus

private void richTextBoxReceive_MouseDown(object sender, MouseEventArgs e)
{
    if (e.Button == MouseButtons.Right)
    {
        contextMenuStripReceive.Show(MousePosition);
    }
}

private void copyToolStripMenuItem1_Click(object sender, EventArgs e)
{
    richTextBoxReceive.Copy();
}

private void cutToolStripMenuItem1_Click(object sender, EventArgs e)
{
    richTextBoxReceive.Cut();
}

private void selectAllToolStripMenuItem1_Click(object sender, EventArgs e)
{
    richTextBoxReceive.SelectAll();
}

private void deleteToolStripMenuItem1_Click(object sender, EventArgs e)
```

```
{
    richTextBoxReceive.Clear();
}

private void saveFileAsToolStripMenuItem_Click(object sender, EventArgs e)
{
    saveReceiveBox();
}

private void saveReceiveBoxToolStripMenuItem_Click(object sender, EventArgs e)
{
    saveReceiveBox();
}

private void saveReceiveBoxToolStripMenuItem_Click_1(object sender, EventArgs e)
{
    saveReceiveBox();
}

private void saveReceiveBox()
{
    string filename = "";
    if (saveFileDialog1.ShowDialog() == DialogResult.OK)
    {
        filename = saveFileDialog1.FileName;
        if (filename != "") richTextBoxReceive.SaveFile(filename,
RichTextBoxStreamType.PlainText);
    }
}

#endregion

#region Send & Receive richTextBox settings
private void sendToolStripMenuItem_Click(object sender, EventArgs e)
{
    TextBoxSettings send = new TextBoxSettings();

    if (send.ShowDialog() == DialogResult.OK)
    {
        richTextBoxSend.BackColor = send.backColor;
        richTextBoxSend.ForeColor = send.foreColor;
        if(send.font != null) richTextBoxSend.Font = send.font;
    }
    else
    {
        MessageBox.Show("Send richTextBox settings canceled.");
    }

}

private void receiveToolStripMenuItem_Click(object sender, EventArgs e)
{
    TextBoxSettings receive = new TextBoxSettings();

    if (receive.ShowDialog() == DialogResult.OK)
    {
        richTextBoxReceive.BackColor = receive.backColor;
```

```
            richTextBoxReceive.ForeColor = receive.foreColor;
            if (receive.tont != null) richTextBoxReceive.Font = receive.font;
        }
        else
        {
            MessageBox.Show("Receive richTextBox settings canceled.");
        }
    }

    #endregion

    #region Serial port settings
    private void portToolStripMenuItem_Click(object sender, EventArgs e)
    {
        // Make sure the port isn't already open
        if (serialPort1.IsOpen)
        {
            MessageBox.Show("The port must be closed before changing the settings.");
            return;
        }
        else
        {
            if (portSettings.ShowDialog() == DialogResult.OK)
            {
                if (portSettings.selectedPort != "")
                {
                    // set the serial port to the new settings
                    serialPort1.PortName = portSettings.selectedPort;
                    serialPort1.BaudRate = portSettings.selectedBaudrate;
                    serialPort1.DataBits = portSettings.selectedDataBits;
                    serialPort1.Parity = portSettings.selectedParity;
                    serialPort1.StopBits = portSettings.selectedStopBits;

                    // Show the new settings in the form text line
                    showSettings();
                }
                else
                {
                    MessageBox.Show("Error: Settings form returned with wrap
                                          no Serial port selected.");
                    return; // bail out
                }
            }
            else
            {
                MessageBox.Show("Error: buttonSetup_Click - Settings wrap
                                      dialog box did not return Okay.");
                return; // bail out
            }

            // Open the port
            openPort();

            // Show the modem line states
            showCTS_DSR_CD();
        }
    }
```

213

```
// show the settings in the form text line
private void showSettings()
{
    this.Text = "Smiley Micros - " +
        portSettings.selectedPort + " " +
        portSettings.selectedBaudrate.ToString() + "," +
        portSettings.selectedParity + "," +
        portSettings.selectedDataBits.ToString() + "," +
        portSettings.selectedStopBits + " - " +
        portSettings.selectedHandshaking;
    if (serialPort1.IsOpen)
    {
        this.Text += " - Port is open";
    }
    else
    {
        this.Text += " - Port is closed";
    }
}

private void openPortToolStripMenuItem_Click(object sender, EventArgs e)
{
    openPort();
}

private void openPort()
{
    try
    {
        if (serialPort1.IsOpen)
        {
            serialPort1.Close();
            openPortToolStripMenuItem.Text = "Open Port";
        }
        else
        {
            serialPort1.Open();
            openPortToolStripMenuItem.Text = "Close Port";
        }

        showSettings();
    }
    catch (System.Exception ex)
    {
        MessageBox.Show("Error - openPortToolStripMenuItem_Click wrap
                                             Exception: " + ex);
    }
}
#endregion

#region Modem lines
private void showCTS_DSR_CD()
{
    if (serialPort1.IsOpen)
    {
        if (serialPort1.CtsHolding) this.LEDCTS.image = wrap
```

214

```
                                              (int)LED.LED22.LEDColor.BlueOn;
        else this.LEDCTS.image = (int)LED.LED22.LEDColor.BlueOff;

        if (serialPort1.DsrHolding) this.LEDDSR.image = wrap
                                              (int)LED.LED22.LEDColor.BlueOn;
        else this.LEDDSR.image = (int)LED.LED22.LEDColor.BlueOff;

        if (serialPort1.CDHolding) this.LEDDCD.image = wrap
                                              (int)LED.LED22.LEDColor.BlueOn;
        else this.LEDDCD.image = (int)LED.LED22.LEDColor.BlueOff;

        if (RingIndicator) this.LEDRI.image = (int)LED.LED22.LEDColor.BlueOn;
        else this.LEDRI.image = (int)LED.LED22.LEDColor.BlueOff;
    }
}

// Toggle RTS state
private void buttonRTS_Click(object sender, EventArgs e)
{
    if (RTSToggle)
    {
        serialPort1.RtsEnable = true;
        LEDRTS.image = (int)LED.LED22.LEDColor.RedOn;
    }
    else
    {
        serialPort1.RtsEnable = false;
        LEDRTS.image = (int)LED.LED22.LEDColor.RedOff;
    }
    RTSToggle = !RTSToggle;
}

// Toggle DTR state
private void buttonDTR_Click(object sender, EventArgs e)
{
    if (DTRToggle)
    {
        serialPort1.DtrEnable = true;
        LEDDTR.image = (int)LED.LED22.LEDColor.RedOn;
    }
    else
    {
        serialPort1.DtrEnable = false;
        LEDDTR.image = (int)LED.LED22.LEDColor.RedOff;
    }
    DTRToggle = !DTRToggle;
}

// Check Modem input line status
private void timerOneSec_Tick(object sender, EventArgs e)
{
    showCTS_DSR_CD();
}

// Show the modem states on the virtual LEDs
private void serialPort1_PinChanged(object sender, SerialPinChangedEventArgs e)
{
```

215

```
    // Toggle RI since we can't determine the state with the SerialPort class
    if(e.EventType == SerialPinChange.Ring) RingIndicator = !RingIndicator;

    showCTS_DSR_CD();
}

#endregion

#region Byte Shooter
// Send a character at regular intervals
private bool shoot = false;
private byte byteToSend = 0;
private void sendCharToolStripMenuItem_Click(object sender, EventArgs e)
{
    if (serialPort1.IsOpen)
    {
        if (!shoot)
        {
            shoot = true;
            sendCharToolStripMenuItem.Text = "Stop sending bytes!";
            ByteShooter shooter = new ByteShooter();

            shooter.index = (byte)xMLData.SendByte;
            shooter.byteToSend = (byte)xMLData.SendByte;
            shooter.interval = xMLData.SendPeriod;

            if (shooter.ShowDialog() == DialogResult.OK)
            {
                byteToSend = shooter.byteToSend;
                timerSendByte.Interval = shooter.interval;
                timerSendByte.Enabled = true;
            }
        }
        else
        {
            timerSendByte.Enabled = false;
            shoot = false;
            sendCharToolStripMenuItem.Text = "Send byte periodically.";
        }
    }
    else MessageBox.Show("A serial port must be open to use the byte shooter.");
}

private void timerSendByte_Tick(object sender, EventArgs e)
{
    //JWP 4/28/07 - changed from sendChar to sendByte
    if (!sendByte(byteToSend))
    {
        timerSendByte.Enabled = false;
        IRSent = false;
        MessageBox.Show("Error: timerSendByte_Tick, sendByte - wrap
                                failed to send.\nIs the port open?");
    }
    else IRSent = true;
}
#endregion
```

```csharp
#region Help

private void manualToolStripMenuItem_Click(object sender, EventArgs e)
{
    System.Diagnostics.Process.Start("Developer Terminal.pdf");
}

private void smileyMicrosToolStripMenuItem_Click(object sender, EventArgs e)
{
    System.Diagnostics.Process.Start("www.smileymicros.com");
}

#endregion
}
}
```

MainForm.vb

```vbnet
'
' Smiley Terminal evolved over time and like many a creature of evolution,
' you might find some atavistic artifacts. As my Grandpappy, the hog
' farmer, used to say: "That's about as useful as tits an a boar." Well,
' I'm going to guess that you'll find some artifacts in this code that
' are even less useful.
'
' Don't you just love the legalistic bullshit that is usually inserted at
' this point? I've rewritten some standard boilerplate stuff to say what
' I think we really mean:
'  This work is entirely by Joe Pardue (except for the major portions he
'  stole and forgot to attribute). Copyright by Joe Pardue 4/26/07. and all
'  rights are reserved - any theft of this intellectual property will
'  result in a challenge to an arm wrestling contest
'
'  This software is not warrented in any way what-so-ever. It WILL screw
'  something up and will kill someone after doing serious property
'  damage. You've been warned. If you sic a lawyer on me, just remember:
'  I'm old, grouchy, have little to lose, and support the Second Amendment?
'
' Ah, yes I feel much better now.
'
' Please send any bug reports, comments, or concerns to joe@smileymicros.com
'
' 7/6/06 - Version 0.0 moved up to C# 2005 Express
' 3/14/07 - Revision 0.1 got back to it and added a bunch of stuff.
' 4/26/07 - Revision 0.2 God only knows what I did, but it is different.
' 4/28/07 - Revision 0.3 changes marked by comment // JWP 4/28/07
'
' BETA - THIS IS THE BETA RELEASE AND WILL HAVE PROBLEMS THAT I MISSED AND YOU WON'T
' BETA - SINCE MICROSOFT RELEASES CODE FOR THE BUYER TO DEBUG, I THOUGHT 'HELL, WHY NOT'
' BETA - PLEASE SEND COMMENTS AND CORRECTIONS TO joe@smileymicros.com


Imports Microsoft.VisualBasic
Imports System
Imports System.Drawing
Imports System.Collections
```

Chapter 14: Developer Terminal Source Code

```
Imports System.ComponentModel
Imports System.Windows.Forms
Imports System.Data
Imports System.IO
Imports System.IO.Ports

Imports LED

Namespace DeveloperTerminal
        Public Class MainForm
Inherits System.Windows.Forms.Form
#Region "Initialization"
' If you build Developer Terminal from scratch using the Express edition
'* you will see some differences in the intializaion section. This is because
'* most of this code was written in earlier versions and imported into Express.
'* The code will work the same thought.


#Region "Startup definitions"

' Create an instance of the settings form
Private portSettings As PortSettings = New PortSettings()

' Booleans to toggle the modem lines
Private RTSToggle As Boolean = True
Private DTRToggle As Boolean = True

' Keep count of sent and received bytes
Private SendCount As Integer = 0
Private ReceiveCount As Integer = 0

' Immediate or Queued state for sending data
Private SendImmediate As Boolean = True
Private QueuedString As String = ""

' Send with terminal characters
Private UseTermChar As Boolean = False

' Receive as ASCII or Hex state
Private ReceiveASCII As Boolean = True

' Create an instance of the TerminalData class
Private xMLData As XMLData = New XMLData()

' Create an instance of the TerminalXMLIO class to read the terminal data
Private dataXMLIO As XMLIO = New XMLIO()

' Create MacroData arrays
Private MacroDataText As String() = New String(51) {}
Private MacroDataData As String() = New String(51) {}
Private MacroDataType As String() = New String(51) {}

' Boolean for the port open state
Public PortOpen As Boolean = False
Private toolsToolStripMenuItem As ToolStripMenuItem
Private WithEvents sendCharToolStripMenuItem As ToolStripMenuItem
Private WithEvents timerSendByte As Timer
Private fileToolStripMenuItem As ToolStripMenuItem
```

218

```
Private WithEvents openInSendBoxToolStripMenuItem As ToolStripMenuItem
Private WithEvents saveSendBoxToolStripMenuItem As ToolStripMenuItem
Private WithEvents saveReceiveBoxToolStripMenuItem As ToolStripMenuItem
Private WithEvents manualToolStripMenuItem As ToolStripMenuItem
Private WithEvents smileyMicrosToolStripMenuItem As ToolStripMenuItem
Private WithEvents copyToolStripMenuItem1 As ToolStripMenuItem
Private WithEvents cutToolStripMenuItem1 As ToolStripMenuItem
Private WithEvents deleteToolStripMenuItem1 As ToolStripMenuItem
Private WithEvents selectAllToolStripMenuItem1 As ToolStripMenuItem
Private toolStripSeparator4 As ToolStripSeparator
Private WithEvents saveFileAsToolStripMenuItem As ToolStripMenuItem
Private contextMenuStripReceive As ContextMenuStrip

' Boolean for the Ring Indicator modem state
Public RingIndicator As Boolean = False

#End Region

#Region "Startup functions"

Public Sub New()
    '
    ' Required for Windows Form Designer support
    '
    InitializeComponent()

    ' Read the terminal data from TerminalData.xml
    dataXMLIO.appPath = System.Environment.CurrentDirectory
    xMLData = dataXMLIO.XMLRead()

End Sub

''' <summary>
''' Clean up any resources being used.
''' </summary>
Protected Overloads Overrides Sub Dispose(ByVal disposing As Boolean)
    MyBase.Dispose(disposing)
End Sub

''' <summary>
''' The main entry point for the application.
''' </summary>
<STAThread()> _
Shared Sub Main()
    Application.Run(New MainForm())
End Sub

Private Sub Form1_Load(ByVal sender As Object, ByVal e As System.EventArgs)
Handles MyBase.Load
    Me.Text = "Smiley Micros Serial port Terminal - Port is closed"
    ' Start the terminal with default settings
    portSettings.selectedPort = xMLData.COMPort
    serialPort1.PortName = portSettings.selectedPort
    portSettings.selectedBaudrate = xMLData.Baud
    serialPort1.BaudRate = portSettings.selectedBaudrate
    portSettings.selectedDataBits = xMLData.Databits
    serialPort1.DataBits = portSettings.selectedDataBits
```

219

```
Dim temp As String = xMLData.Parity
Select Case temp
    Case "Even"
        portSettings.selectedParity = Parity.Even
        serialPort1.Parity = portSettings.selectedParity
    Case "Mark"
        portSettings.selectedParity = Parity.Mark
        serialPort1.Parity = portSettings.selectedParity
    Case "None"
        portSettings.selectedParity = Parity.None
        serialPort1.Parity = portSettings.selectedParity
    Case "Odd"
        portSettings.selectedParity = Parity.Odd
        serialPort1.Parity = portSettings.selectedParity
    Case "Space"
        portSettings.selectedParity = Parity.Space
        serialPort1.Parity = portSettings.selectedParity
    Case Else
        portSettings.selectedParity = Parity.None
        serialPort1.Parity = portSettings.selectedParity
End Select

temp = xMLData.Stopbits
Select Case temp
    Case "None"
        portSettings.selectedStopBits = StopBits.None
        serialPort1.StopBits = portSettings.selectedStopBits
    Case "1"
        portSettings.selectedStopBits = StopBits.One
        serialPort1.StopBits = portSettings.selectedStopBits
        'case "1.5": // not supported by FT232R
        'serialPort1.StopBits = = StopBits.OnePointFive;
        'break;
    Case "2"
        portSettings.selectedStopBits = StopBits.Two
        serialPort1.StopBits = portSettings.selectedStopBits
    Case Else
        portSettings.selectedStopBits = StopBits.One
        serialPort1.StopBits = portSettings.selectedStopBits
End Select

temp = xMLData.Handshake
Select Case temp
    Case "None"
        portSettings.selectedHandshaking = Handshake.None
        serialPort1.Handshake = portSettings.selectedHandshaking
    Case "RTS/CTS"
        portSettings.selectedHandshaking = Handshake.RequestToSend
        serialPort1.Handshake = portSettings.selectedHandshaking
    Case "Xon/Xoff"
        portSettings.selectedHandshaking = Handshake.XOnXOff
        serialPort1.Handshake = portSettings.selectedHandshaking
    Case Else
        portSettings.selectedHandshaking = Handshake.None
        serialPort1.Handshake = portSettings.selectedHandshaking
End Select
```

```vbnet
    ' Load the comboBox with 0x00 to 0xFF
    For i As Integer = 0 To 15
        Me.comboBoxSendByte.Items.Add("0x0" & i.ToString("X"))
    Next i
    For i As Integer = 16 To 255
        Me.comboBoxSendByte.Items.Add("0x" & i.ToString("X"))
    Next i

    loadXMLData()

    ' Set the default LED images
    Me.LEDCTS.image = CInt(Fix(LED.LED22.LEDColor.BlueOn))
    Me.LEDDSR.image = CInt(Fix(LED.LED22.LEDColor.BlueOff))
    Me.LEDDCD.image = CInt(Fix(LED.LED22.LEDColor.BlueOff))
    Me.LEDRI.image = CInt(Fix(LED.LED22.LEDColor.BlueOff))
    Me.LEDRTS.image = CInt(Fix(LED.LED22.LEDColor.RedOn))
    Me.LEDDTR.image = CInt(Fix(LED.LED22.LEDColor.RedOff))

End Sub
#End Region

#End Region

#Region "GUI"

#Region "Open REALLY GREAT website"

' And this is not shameless commercialism. I have NO shame.
' And2 - now you know how to do it.
Private Sub linkLabelVisitWebSite_LinkClicked(ByVal sender As Object, ByVal e As
System.Windows.Forms.LinkLabelLinkClickedEventArgs) Handles
linkLabelVisitWebSite.LinkClicked
    System.Diagnostics.Process.Start("www.smileymicros.com")
End Sub

' Open website
Private Sub panel1_MouseClick(ByVal sender As Object, ByVal e As MouseEventArgs)
Handles panel1.MouseClick
    System.Diagnostics.Process.Start("www.smileymicros.com")
End Sub

' Show hand cursor and change color to intice click to website
Private Sub panel1_MouseEnter(ByVal sender As Object, ByVal e As EventArgs)
Handles panel1.MouseEnter
    panel1.Cursor = Cursors.Hand
    panel1.BackColor = Color.SandyBrown
End Sub

' Cursor reverts on leaving, but color doesn't so revert it
Private Sub panel1_MouseLeave(ByVal sender As Object, ByVal e As EventArgs)
Handles panel1.MouseLeave
    panel1.BackColor = Color.Bisque
End Sub

#End Region
```

```vb
#Region "Buttons   "
Private Sub buttonClear_Click(ByVal sender As Object, ByVal e As System.EventArgs)
    richTextBoxReceive.Text = ""
    textBoxSendCount.Text = ""
End Sub

Private Sub buttonClearSend_Click(ByVal sender As Object, ByVal e As EventArgs)
    richTextBoxSend.Text = ""
End Sub

Private Sub buttonSettings_Click(ByVal sender As Object, ByVal e As
System.EventArgs)
    Dim portSettings As PortSettings = New PortSettings()

    portSettings.ShowDialog()
    If portSettings.DialogResult = System.Windows.Forms.DialogResult.OK Then
        serialPort1.PortName = portSettings.selectedPort
        serialPort1.BaudRate = portSettings.selectedBaudrate
    End If
End Sub

Private Sub buttonSend_Click(ByVal sender As Object, ByVal e As System.EventArgs)
Handles buttonSendQue.Click
    richTextBoxSend.Text += Constants.vbLf & " Sent QueuedString: " &
Constants.vbLf & QueuedString & Constants.vbLf
    SendASCIIString(QueuedString)
    If UseTermChar Then
        sendTermChar()
    End If
    QueuedString = ""
End Sub

Private Sub buttonOpenClosePort_Click(ByVal sender As Object, ByVal e As
System.EventArgs)
    If PortOpen Then
        PortOpen = False
        serialPort1.Close()
        Me.Text = "Smiley Micros Serial port Terminal - Port is closed"
    Else
        PortOpen = True

        Try
            serialPort1.Open()
        Catch ex As System.Exception
            MessageBox.Show("Error - buttonOpenClosePort_ClickSystem. wrap
                                        Exception: ", ex.Message)
        End Try
        showSettings()
    End If
End Sub

Private Sub buttonHelp_Click(ByVal sender As Object, ByVal e As System.EventArgs)
    MessageBox.Show("HELP! is coming soon to a computer near you...")
End Sub

Private Sub ButtonReloadMacrosClick(ByVal sender As Object, wrap
                                        ByVal e As System.EventArgs)
```

```
        xMLData = dataXMLIO.XMLRead()
        listBoxMacros.Items.Clear()
        loadXMLData()
End Sub
#End Region

#Region "Check Box and Radio Buttons"

Private Sub radioButtonImmediate_CheckedChanged(ByVal sender As Object, wrap
        ByVal e As System.EventArgs) Handles radioButtonImmediate.CheckedChanged
    If radioButtonImmediate.Checked = True Then
        SendImmediate = True
        buttonSendQue.Enabled = False
    End If
End Sub

Private Sub radioButtonQueued_CheckedChanged(ByVal sender As Object, wrap
        ByVal e As System.EventArgs) Handles radioButtonQueued.CheckedChanged
    If radioButtonQueued.Checked = True Then
        SendImmediate = False
        buttonSendQue.Enabled = True
    End If
End Sub

Private Sub radioButtonASCII_CheckedChanged_1(ByVal sender As Object, wrap
        ByVal e As System.EventArgs) Handles radioButtonASCII.CheckedChanged
    ReceiveASCII = True
End Sub

Private Sub radioButtonHEX_CheckedChanged_1(ByVal sender As Object, wrap
        ByVal e As System.EventArgs) Handles radioButtonHEX.CheckedChanged
    ReceiveASCII = False
End Sub

Private Sub radioButtonTermCharYes_CheckedChanged(ByVal sender As Object, wrap
        ByVal e As EventArgs) Handles radioButtonTermCharYes.CheckedChanged
    If radioButtonTermCharYes.Checked = True Then
        UseTermChar = True
    End If
End Sub

Private Sub radioButtonTermCharNo_CheckedChanged(ByVal sender As Object, wrap
            ByVal e As EventArgs) Handles radioButtonTermCharNo.CheckedChanged
    If radioButtonTermCharNo.Checked = True Then
        UseTermChar = False
    End If
End Sub

#End Region

#End Region

#Region "Receive functions"
' We want to ignore the byte receive immediately following a byte sent over
' an IR 'wire' since it will not just be sent, but received. We will flag this
' condition with an IRSent bool.
Private IRSent As Boolean = False
```

Chapter 14: Developer Terminal Source Code

```vbnet
' we want to have the serial port thread report back data received, but to display
' that data we must create a delegate function to show the data in the richTextBox

' define the delegate
Public Delegate Sub SetText()
' define an instance of the delegate
Private setTextI As SetText

' create a string that will be loaded with the data received from the port
Public str As String = ""
' JWP 4/28/07 added public byt for receiving bytes
Public byt As Byte = 0

' note that this function runs in a separate thread and thus we must use a
delegate in order
' to display the results in the richTextBox.
Private Sub serialPort1_DataReceived(ByVal sender As Object, ByVal e As
SerialDataReceivedEventArgs) Handles serialPort1.DataReceived
    If (Not IRSent) Then ' ignore byte received after an IR byte send
        ' instantiate the delegate to be invoked by this thread
        setTextI = New SetText(AddressOf mySetText)

        ' load the data into the string
        Try
            ' JWP 4/28/07 added ReceiveASCII and byte reception
            If ReceiveASCII Then
                str = serialPort1.ReadExisting()
            Else
                byt = CByte(serialPort1.ReadByte()) '.ReadExisting();
            End If
        Catch ex As System.Exception
            MessageBox.Show("Error - port_DataReceived Exception: ", ex.Message)
        End Try

        ' invoke the delegate in the MainForm thread
        Me.Invoke(setTextI)
    Else
        IRSent = False
    End If

End Sub

' create the instance of the delegate to be used to write the received data to the
richTextBox
Public Sub mySetText()
    ReceiveCount += str.Length
    textBoxReceiveCount.Text = ReceiveCount.ToString()

    If ReceiveASCII Then
        richTextBoxReceive.Text += str.ToString()
    Else ' ReceiveHEX
        ' JWP 4/28/07 changed byte display
        If byt > 15 Then
            richTextBoxReceive.Text &= "0x" & byt.ToString("X") & ","
        Else
            richTextBoxReceive.Text &= "0x0" & byt.ToString("X") & ","
```

```vbnet
            End If

        End If

End Sub

' This rigaramole is needed to keep the last received item displayed
' it kind of flickers and should be fixed
Private Sub richTextBoxReceive_TextChanged(ByVal sender As Object, ByVal e As
System.EventArgs) Handles richTextBoxReceive.TextChanged
    moveCaretToEnd()
End Sub

Private Sub moveCaretToEnd()
    richTextBoxReceive.SelectionStart = richTextBoxReceive.Text.Length
    richTextBoxReceive.SelectionLength = 0
    richTextBoxReceive.ScrollToCaret()
End Sub

#End Region

#Region "Send Text functions"
Private Sub richTextBoxSend_KeyPress(ByVal sender As Object, ByVal e As
KeyPressEventArgs) Handles richTextBoxSend.KeyPress
    If SendImmediate Then
        sendChar(e.KeyChar)
        If UseTermChar Then
            sendTermChar()
        End If
    Else
        QueuedString &= e.KeyChar
    End If
End Sub

Private Sub sendTermChar()
    SendHEXString(xMLData.TerminalCharacters)
End Sub

Private Sub sendChar(ByVal c As Char)
    Dim data As Char() = New Char(0) {}
    data(0) = c
    Try
        serialPort1.Write(data, 0, 1)
        SendCount += 1
        textBoxSendCount.Text = SendCount.ToString()
        ' Show bytes sent by shooter
        If shoot Then
            richTextBoxSend.Text += c
        End If
    Catch
        MessageBox.Show("Error: sendChar - failed to send." & wrap
                                Constants.vbLf & "Is the port open?")
    End Try
End Sub

'JWP 4/28/07 - add sendByte function
Private Function sendByte(ByVal b As Byte) As Boolean
```

```
    Dim data As Byte() = New Byte(0) {}
    data(0) = b
    Try
        serialPort1.Write(data, 0, 1)
        SendCount += 1
        textBoxSendCount.Text = SendCount.ToString()
        ' Show bytes sent by shooter
        'JWP 4/28/07 added show with 0x or 0x0
        If shoot Then
            If byt > 15 Then
                richTextBoxSend.Text &= "0x" & b.ToString("X") & ","
            Else
                richTextBoxSend.Text &= "0x0" & b.ToString("X") & ","
            End If
        End If
    Catch
        Return False
    End Try
    Return True
End Function

' Send single hex bytes immediately
Private Sub comboBoxSendByte_SelectedIndexChanged(ByVal sender As Object, ByVal e
As System.EventArgs) Handles comboBoxSendByte.SelectedIndexChanged
    'JWP 4/28/07 - changed from sendChar to sendByte
    'sendChar((char)comboBoxSendByte.SelectedIndex);
    sendByte(Convert.ToByte(comboBoxSendByte.SelectedIndex))
    Me.richTextBoxSend.Text = "Sent: 0x" &
comboBoxSendByte.SelectedIndex.ToString("X")
End Sub



#End Region

#Region "Send Macro Functions"
' Send Macro Stings
Private Sub ListBoxMacrosDoubleClick(ByVal sender As Object, ByVal e As
System.EventArgs) Handles listBoxMacros.DoubleClick
    processMacroClick(MacroDataData(listBoxMacros.SelectedIndex),
MacroDataType(listBoxMacros.SelectedIndex))
End Sub
Private Sub processMacroClick(ByVal MacroData As String, ByVal MacroType As
String)
    richTextBoxSend.Text = MacroData
    If MacroType = "ASCII" Then
        SendASCIIString(MacroData)
        If UseTermChar Then
            sendTermChar()
        End If
    ElseIf MacroType = "HEX" Then
        SendHEXString(MacroData)
        If UseTermChar Then
            sendTermChar()
        End If
    Else
        MessageBox.Show("Error: MacroType: " & MacroType)
```

```vb
    End If
End Sub

Public Sub SendASCIIString(ByVal str As String)
    Dim c As Char() = str.ToCharArray()

    For i As Integer = 0 To c.GetLength(0) - 1
        sendChar(c(i))
    Next i
End Sub

' For our purposes, HEX strings must be in the format 0xFF,0xFE,
' including the trailing comma on the last value
Public Sub SendHEXString(ByVal str As String)
    Dim c As Char() = str.ToCharArray()
    Dim b As Byte = 0

    If c.GetLength(0) < 5 Then
        MessageBox.Show("Error: Hex string incorrect length: " & wrap
                str & Constants.vbLf & "Length = " & c.GetLength(0).ToString())
        Return
    End If
    For i As Integer = 0 To c.GetLength(0) - 1 Step 5
        ' Check array length
        If i > c.GetLength(0) Then
            MessageBox.Show("Error: Hex string incorrect length: " & wrap
                str & Constants.vbLf & "Length = " & c.GetLength(0).ToString()wrap
                & Constants.vbLf & "i = " & i.ToString())
            Return
        End If
        ' Check for remaining length
        If i + 4 >= c.GetLength(0) Then
            MessageBox.Show("Error: Hex string: " & str & " problem with length")
            Return
        End If
        ' Check format trailing comma
        If c(i + 4) <> ","c Then
            MessageBox.Show("Error: Hex string: " & str & wrap
                                        " lacks a trailing comma.")
            Return
        End If
        ' Check high nibble range 0 - F
        If (c(i + 2) >= "0"c) AndAlso (c(i + 2) <= "9"c) AndAlso (c(i + 2)wrap
                            >= "A"c) AndAlso (c(i + 2) <= "F"c) Then
            MessageBox.Show("Error: Hex string first digit: " wrap
                            & c(i + 2).ToString() & " not in range 0 - F")
            Return
        End If
        ' Check low nibble range 0 - F
        If (c(i + 3) >= "0"c) AndAlso (c(i + 3) <= "9"c) AndAlso wrap
                            (c(i + 3) >= "A"c) AndAlso (c(i + 3) <= "F"c) Then
            MessageBox.Show("Error: Hex string first digit: " & wrap
                                c(i + 2).ToString() & " not in range 0 - F")
            Return
        End If
        If c(i + 2) <= "9"c Then
            b = CByte(AscW(c(i + 2)) - AscW("0"c))
```

227

```vbnet
        Else
            b = CByte(AscW(c(i + 2)) - AscW("A"c))
            b += CByte(10)
        End If

        b = CByte(b << 4)

        If c(i + 3) <= "9"c Then
            b += CByte(AscW(c(i + 3)) - AscW("0"))
        Else
            b += CByte(AscW(c(i + 3)) - AscW("A"))
            b += CByte(10)
        End If

        sendChar(ChrW(b))

    Next i
End Sub

#End Region

#Region "Load macro data"
Private Sub loadXMLData()
    listBoxMacros.Items.Add(xMLData.MacroText1)
    listBoxMacros.Items.Add(xMLData.MacroText2)
    listBoxMacros.Items.Add(xMLData.MacroText3)
    listBoxMacros.Items.Add(xMLData.MacroText4)
    listBoxMacros.Items.Add(xMLData.MacroText5)
    listBoxMacros.Items.Add(xMLData.MacroText6)
    listBoxMacros.Items.Add(xMLData.MacroText7)
    listBoxMacros.Items.Add(xMLData.MacroText8)
    listBoxMacros.Items.Add(xMLData.MacroText9)
    listBoxMacros.Items.Add(xMLData.MacroText10)
    listBoxMacros.Items.Add(xMLData.MacroText11)
    listBoxMacros.Items.Add(xMLData.MacroText12)
    listBoxMacros.Items.Add(xMLData.MacroText13)
    listBoxMacros.Items.Add(xMLData.MacroText14)
    listBoxMacros.Items.Add(xMLData.MacroText15)
    listBoxMacros.Items.Add(xMLData.MacroText16)
    listBoxMacros.Items.Add(xMLData.MacroText17)
    listBoxMacros.Items.Add(xMLData.MacroText18)
    listBoxMacros.Items.Add(xMLData.MacroText19)
    listBoxMacros.Items.Add(xMLData.MacroText20)
    listBoxMacros.Items.Add(xMLData.MacroText21)
    listBoxMacros.Items.Add(xMLData.MacroText22)
    listBoxMacros.Items.Add(xMLData.MacroText23)
    listBoxMacros.Items.Add(xMLData.MacroText24)
    listBoxMacros.Items.Add(xMLData.MacroText25)
    listBoxMacros.Items.Add(xMLData.MacroText26)
    listBoxMacros.Items.Add(xMLData.MacroText27)
    listBoxMacros.Items.Add(xMLData.MacroText28)
    listBoxMacros.Items.Add(xMLData.MacroText29)
    listBoxMacros.Items.Add(xMLData.MacroText30)
    listBoxMacros.Items.Add(xMLData.MacroText31)
    listBoxMacros.Items.Add(xMLData.MacroText32)
    listBoxMacros.Items.Add(xMLData.MacroText33)
    listBoxMacros.Items.Add(xMLData.MacroText34)
```

228

```
listBoxMacros.Items.Add(xMLData.MacroText35)
listBoxMacros.Items.Add(xMLData.MacroText36)
listBoxMacros.Items.Add(xMLData.MacroText37)
listBoxMacros.Items.Add(xMLData.MacroText38)
listBoxMacros.Items.Add(xMLData.MacroText39)
listBoxMacros.Items.Add(xMLData.MacroText40)
listBoxMacros.Items.Add(xMLData.MacroText41)
listBoxMacros.Items.Add(xMLData.MacroText42)
listBoxMacros.Items.Add(xMLData.MacroText43)
listBoxMacros.Items.Add(xMLData.MacroText44)
listBoxMacros.Items.Add(xMLData.MacroText45)
listBoxMacros.Items.Add(xMLData.MacroText46)
listBoxMacros.Items.Add(xMLData.MacroText47)
listBoxMacros.Items.Add(xMLData.MacroText48)
listBoxMacros.Items.Add(xMLData.MacroText49)
listBoxMacros.Items.Add(xMLData.MacroText50)
listBoxMacros.Items.Add(xMLData.MacroText51)
listBoxMacros.Items.Add(xMLData.MacroText52)

MacroDataText(0)  = xMLData.MacroText1
MacroDataText(1)  = xMLData.MacroText2
MacroDataText(2)  = xMLData.MacroText3
MacroDataText(3)  = xMLData.MacroText4
MacroDataText(4)  = xMLData.MacroText5
MacroDataText(5)  = xMLData.MacroText6
MacroDataText(6)  = xMLData.MacroText7
MacroDataText(7)  = xMLData.MacroText8
MacroDataText(8)  = xMLData.MacroText9
MacroDataText(9)  = xMLData.MacroText10
MacroDataText(10) = xMLData.MacroText11
MacroDataText(11) = xMLData.MacroText12
MacroDataText(12) = xMLData.MacroText13
MacroDataText(13) = xMLData.MacroText14
MacroDataText(14) = xMLData.MacroText15
MacroDataText(15) = xMLData.MacroText16
MacroDataText(16) = xMLData.MacroText17
MacroDataText(17) = xMLData.MacroText18
MacroDataText(18) = xMLData.MacroText19
MacroDataText(19) = xMLData.MacroText20
MacroDataText(20) = xMLData.MacroText21
MacroDataText(21) = xMLData.MacroText22
MacroDataText(22) = xMLData.MacroText23
MacroDataText(23) = xMLData.MacroText24
MacroDataText(24) = xMLData.MacroText25
MacroDataText(25) = xMLData.MacroText26
MacroDataText(26) = xMLData.MacroText27
MacroDataText(27) = xMLData.MacroText28
MacroDataText(28) = xMLData.MacroText29
MacroDataText(29) = xMLData.MacroText30
MacroDataText(30) = xMLData.MacroText31
MacroDataText(31) = xMLData.MacroText32
MacroDataText(32) = xMLData.MacroText33
MacroDataText(33) = xMLData.MacroText34
MacroDataText(34) = xMLData.MacroText35
MacroDataText(35) = xMLData.MacroText36
MacroDataText(36) = xMLData.MacroText37
MacroDataText(37) = xMLData.MacroText38
```

```
MacroDataText(38)  = xMLData.MacroText39
MacroDataText(39)  = xMLData.MacroText40
MacroDataText(40)  = xMLData.MacroText41
MacroDataText(41)  = xMLData.MacroText42
MacroDataText(42)  = xMLData.MacroText43
MacroDataText(43)  = xMLData.MacroText44
MacroDataText(44)  = xMLData.MacroText45
MacroDataText(45)  = xMLData.MacroText46
MacroDataText(46)  = xMLData.MacroText47
MacroDataText(47)  = xMLData.MacroText48
MacroDataText(48)  = xMLData.MacroText49
MacroDataText(49)  = xMLData.MacroText50
MacroDataText(50)  = xMLData.MacroText51
MacroDataText(51)  = xMLData.MacroText52

MacroDataData(0)  = xMLData.MacroData1
MacroDataData(1)  = xMLData.MacroData2
MacroDataData(2)  = xMLData.MacroData3
MacroDataData(3)  = xMLData.MacroData4
MacroDataData(4)  = xMLData.MacroData5
MacroDataData(5)  = xMLData.MacroData6
MacroDataData(6)  = xMLData.MacroData7
MacroDataData(7)  = xMLData.MacroData8
MacroDataData(8)  = xMLData.MacroData9
MacroDataData(9)  = xMLData.MacroData10
MacroDataData(10) = xMLData.MacroData11
MacroDataData(11) = xMLData.MacroData12
MacroDataData(12) = xMLData.MacroData13
MacroDataData(13) = xMLData.MacroData14
MacroDataData(14) = xMLData.MacroData15
MacroDataData(15) = xMLData.MacroData16
MacroDataData(16) = xMLData.MacroData17
MacroDataData(17) = xMLData.MacroData18
MacroDataData(18) = xMLData.MacroData19
MacroDataData(19) = xMLData.MacroData20
MacroDataData(20) = xMLData.MacroData21
MacroDataData(21) = xMLData.MacroData22
MacroDataData(22) = xMLData.MacroData23
MacroDataData(23) = xMLData.MacroData24
MacroDataData(24) = xMLData.MacroData25
MacroDataData(25) = xMLData.MacroData26
MacroDataData(26) = xMLData.MacroData27
MacroDataData(27) = xMLData.MacroData28
MacroDataData(28) = xMLData.MacroData29
MacroDataData(29) = xMLData.MacroData30
MacroDataData(30) = xMLData.MacroData31
MacroDataData(31) = xMLData.MacroData32
MacroDataData(32) = xMLData.MacroData33
MacroDataData(33) = xMLData.MacroData34
MacroDataData(34) = xMLData.MacroData35
MacroDataData(35) = xMLData.MacroData36
MacroDataData(36) = xMLData.MacroData37
MacroDataData(37) = xMLData.MacroData38
MacroDataData(38) = xMLData.MacroData39
MacroDataData(39) = xMLData.MacroData40
MacroDataData(40) = xMLData.MacroData41
MacroDataData(41) = xMLData.MacroData42
```

```
MacroDataData(42)  = xMLData.MacroData43
MacroDataData(43)  = xMLData.MacroData44
MacroDataData(44)  = xMLData.MacroData45
MacroDataData(45)  = xMLData.MacroData46
MacroDataData(46)  = xMLData.MacroData47
MacroDataData(47)  = xMLData.MacroData48
MacroDataData(48)  = xMLData.MacroData49
MacroDataData(49)  = xMLData.MacroData50
MacroDataData(50)  = xMLData.MacroData51
MacroDataData(51)  = xMLData.MacroData52

MacroDataType(0)   - xMLData.MacroType1
MacroDataType(1)   = xMLData.MacroType2
MacroDataType(2)   = xMLData.MacroType3
MacroDataType(3)   = xMLData.MacroType4
MacroDataType(4)   = xMLData.MacroType5
MacroDataType(5)   = xMLData.MacroType6
MacroDataType(6)   = xMLData.MacroType7
MacroDataType(7)   = xMLData.MacroType8
MacroDataType(8)   = xMLData.MacroType9
MacroDataType(9)   = xMLData.MacroType10
MacroDataType(10)  = xMLData.MacroType11
MacroDataType(11)  = xMLData.MacroType12
MacroDataType(12)  = xMLData.MacroType13
MacroDataType(13)  = xMLData.MacroType14
MacroDataType(14)  = xMLData.MacroType15
MacroDataType(15)  = xMLData.MacroType16
MacroDataType(16)  = xMLData.MacroType17
MacroDataType(17)  = xMLData.MacroType18
MacroDataType(18)  = xMLData.MacroType19
MacroDataType(19)  = xMLData.MacroType20
MacroDataType(20)  = xMLData.MacroType21
MacroDataType(21)  = xMLData.MacroType22
MacroDataType(22)  = xMLData.MacroType23
MacroDataType(23)  = xMLData.MacroType24
MacroDataType(24)  = xMLData.MacroType25
MacroDataType(25)  = xMLData.MacroType26
MacroDataType(26)  = xMLData.MacroType27
MacroDataType(27)  = xMLData.MacroType28
MacroDataType(28)  = xMLData.MacroType29
MacroDataType(29)  = xMLData.MacroType30
MacroDataType(30)  = xMLData.MacroType31
MacroDataType(31)  = xMLData.MacroType32
MacroDataType(32)  = xMLData.MacroType33
MacroDataType(33)  = xMLData.MacroType34
MacroDataType(34)  = xMLData.MacroType35
MacroDataType(35)  = xMLData.MacroType36
MacroDataType(36)  = xMLData.MacroType37
MacroDataType(37)  = xMLData.MacroType38
MacroDataType(38)  = xMLData.MacroType39
MacroDataType(39)  = xMLData.MacroType40
MacroDataType(40)  = xMLData.MacroType41
MacroDataType(41)  = xMLData.MacroType42
MacroDataType(42)  = xMLData.MacroType43
MacroDataType(43)  = xMLData.MacroType44
MacroDataType(44)  = xMLData.MacroType45
MacroDataType(45)  = xMLData.MacroType46
```

```
        MacroDataType(46) = xMLData.MacroType47
        MacroDataType(47) = xMLData.MacroType48
        MacroDataType(48) = xMLData.MacroType49
        MacroDataType(49) = xMLData.MacroType50
        MacroDataType(50) = xMLData.MacroType51
        MacroDataType(51) = xMLData.MacroType52
End Sub

#End Region

#Region "Send Textbox Context menus "
Private Sub richTextBoxSend_MouseDown(ByVal sender As Object, wrap
            ByVal e As MouseEventArgs) Handles richTextBoxSend.MouseDown
    If e.Button = MouseButtons.Right Then
        contextMenuStripSend.Show(MousePosition)
    End If
End Sub

Private Sub copyToolStripMenuItem_Click(ByVal sender As Object, wrap
                ByVal e As EventArgs) Handles copyToolStripMenuItem.Click
    richTextBoxSend.Copy()
End Sub

Private Sub cutToolStripMenuItem_Click(ByVal sender As Object, wrap
                ByVal e As EventArgs) Handles cutToolStripMenuItem.Click
    richTextBoxSend.Cut()
End Sub


Private Sub deleteToolStripMenuItem_Click(ByVal sender As Object, wrap
                ByVal e As EventArgs) Handles deleteToolStripMenuItem.Click
    richTextBoxSend.Clear()
    textBoxSendCount.Text = "0"
    SendCount = 0
End Sub

Private Sub selectAllToolStripMenuItem_Click(ByVal sender As Object, wrap
            ByVal e As EventArgs) Handles selectAllToolStripMenuItem.Click
    richTextBoxSend.SelectAll()
End Sub

Private Sub undoToolStripMenuItem_Click(ByVal sender As Object, wrap
                ByVal e As EventArgs) Handles undoToolStripMenuItem.Click
    richTextBoxSend.Undo()
End Sub

Private Sub redoToolStripMenuItem_Click(ByVal sender As Object, wrap
                ByVal e As EventArgs) Handles redoToolStripMenuItem.Click
    richTextBoxSend.Redo()
End Sub

Private Sub saveAsToolStripMenuItem_Click(ByVal sender As Object, wrap
            ByVal e As EventArgs) Handles saveAsToolStripMenuItem.Click
    saveSendBox()
End Sub

Private Sub pasteToolStripMenuItem_Click(ByVal sender As Object, wrap
```

```vbnet
                    ByVal e As EventArgs) Handles pasteToolStripMenuItem.Click
        richTextBoxSend.Paste()
        setToQueued()
    End Sub

    ' use for paste and load
    Private Sub setToQueued()
        ' set to send queued
        radioButtonQueued.Checked = True
        SendImmediate = False
        buttonSendQue.Enabled = True
        QueuedString = richTextBoxSend.Text
    End Sub

    ' Context menu item
    Private Sub loadFileToolStripMenuItem_Click(ByVal sender As Object, wrap
                    ByVal e As EventArgs) Handles loadFileToolStripMenuItem.Click
        openInSendBox()
    End Sub
    ' File menu item
    Private Sub openInSendBoxToolStripMenuItem_Click_1(ByVal sender As Object, wrap
                    ByVal e As EventArgs) Handles openInSendBoxToolStripMenuItem.Click
        openInSendBox()
    End Sub

    Private Sub saveSendBoxToolStripMenuItem_Click(ByVal sender As Object, wrap
                    ByVal e As EventArgs)
        saveSendBox()
    End Sub

    Private Sub saveSendBoxToolStripMenuItem_Click_1(ByVal sender As Object, wrap
                    ByVal e As EventArgs) Handles saveSendBoxToolStripMenuItem.Click
        saveSendBox()
    End Sub

    Private Sub openInSendBox()
        Dim filename As String = ""
        If openFileDialog1.ShowDialog() = System.Windows.Forms.DialogResult.OK Then
            filename = openFileDialog1.FileName
            If filename <> "" Then
                richTextBoxSend.LoadFile(filename, RichTextBoxStreamType.PlainText)
                setToQueued()
            End If
        Else
            MessageBox.Show("Error loading file.")
        End If
    End Sub

    Private Sub saveSendBox()
        Dim filename As String = ""
        If saveFileDialog1.ShowDialog() = System.Windows.Forms.DialogResult.OK Then
            filename = saveFileDialog1.FileName
            If filename <> "" Then
                richTextBoxSend.SaveFile(filename, RichTextBoxStreamType.PlainText)
            End If
        End If
    End Sub
```

```
#End Region

#Region "Receive Textbox Context menus"

Private Sub richTextBoxReceive_MouseDown(ByVal sender As Object, wrap
            ByVal e As MouseEventArgs) Handles richTextBoxReceive.MouseDown
    If e.Button = MouseButtons.Right Then
        contextMenuStripReceive.Show(MousePosition)
    End If
End Sub

Private Sub copyToolStripMenuItem1_Click(ByVal sender As Object, wrap
            ByVal e As EventArgs) Handles copyToolStripMenuItem1.Click
    richTextBoxReceive.Copy()
End Sub

Private Sub cutToolStripMenuItem1_Click(ByVal sender As Object, wrap
            ByVal e As EventArgs) Handles cutToolStripMenuItem1.Click
    richTextBoxReceive.Cut()
End Sub

Private Sub selectAllToolStripMenuItem1_Click(ByVal sender As Object, wrap
            ByVal e As EventArgs) Handles selectAllToolStripMenuItem1.Click
    richTextBoxReceive.SelectAll()
End Sub

Private Sub deleteToolStripMenuItem1_Click(ByVal sender As Object, wrap
            ByVal e As EventArgs) Handles deleteToolStripMenuItem1.Click
    richTextBoxReceive.Clear()
End Sub

Private Sub saveFileAsToolStripMenuItem_Click(ByVal sender As Object, wrap
            ByVal e As EventArgs) Handles saveFileAsToolStripMenuItem.Click
    saveReceiveBox()
End Sub

Private Sub saveReceiveBoxToolStripMenuItem_Click(ByVal sender As Object, wrap
            ByVal e As EventArgs)
    saveReceiveBox()
End Sub

Private Sub saveReceiveBoxToolStripMenuItem_Click_1(ByVal sender As Object, wrap
            ByVal e As EventArgs) Handles saveReceiveBoxToolStripMenuItem.Click
    saveReceiveBox()
End Sub

Private Sub saveReceiveBox()
    Dim filename As String = ""
    If saveFileDialog1.ShowDialog() = System.Windows.Forms.DialogResult.OK Then
        filename = saveFileDialog1.FileName
        If filename <> "" Then
            richTextBoxReceive.SaveFile(filename, RichTextBoxStreamType.PlainText)
        End If
    End If
End Sub
```

```
#End Region

#Region "Send & Receive richTextBox settings"
Private Sub sendToolStripMenuItem_Click(ByVal sender As Object, wrap
                    ByVal e As EventArgs) Handles sendToolStripMenuItem.Click
    Dim send As TextBoxSettings = New TextBoxSettings()

    If send.ShowDialog() = System.Windows.Forms.DialogResult.OK Then
        richTextBoxSend.BackColor = send.backClr
        richTextBoxSend.ForeColor = send.foreClr
        If Not send.font Is Nothing Then
            richTextBoxSend.Font = send.fnt
        End If
    Else
        MessageBox.Show("Send richTextBox settings canceled.")
    End If

End Sub

Private Sub receiveToolStripMenuItem_Click(ByVal sender As Object, wrap
            ByVal e As EventArgs) Handles receiveToolStripMenuItem.Click
    Dim receive As TextBoxSettings = New TextBoxSettings()

    If receive.ShowDialog() = System.Windows.Forms.DialogResult.OK Then
        richTextBoxReceive.BackColor = receive.backClr
        richTextBoxReceive.ForeColor = receive.foreClr
        If Not receive.font Is Nothing Then
            richTextBoxReceive.Font = receive.fnt
        End If
    Else
        MessageBox.Show("Receive richTextBox settings canceled.")
    End If
End Sub

#End Region

#Region "Serial port settings"
Private Sub portToolStripMenuItem_Click(ByVal sender As Object, wrap
                    ByVal e As EventArgs) Handles portToolStripMenuItem.Click
    ' Make sure the port isn't already open
    If serialPort1.IsOpen Then
        MessageBox.Show("The port must be closed before changing the settings.")
        Return
    Else
        If portSettings.ShowDialog() = System.Windows.Forms.DialogResult.OK Then
            If portSettings.selectedPort <> "" Then
                ' set the serial port to the new settings
                serialPort1.PortName = portSettings.selectedPort
                serialPort1.BaudRate = portSettings.selectedBaudrate
                serialPort1.DataBits = portSettings.selectedDataBits
                serialPort1.Parity = portSettings.selectedParity
                serialPort1.StopBits = portSettings.selectedStopBits

                ' Show the new settings in the form text line
                showSettings()
            Else
                MessageBox.Show("Error: Settings form returned with no wrap
```

```
                                                        Serial port
                                                selected.")
                    Return ' bail out
                End If
            Else
                MessageBox.Show("Error: buttonSetup_Click - Settings dialog wrap
                                        box did not return Okay.")
                Return ' bail out
            End If

            ' Open the port
            openPort()

            ' Show the modem line states
            showCTS_DSR_CD()
        End If
End Sub

' show the settings in the form text line
Private Sub showSettings()
    Me.Text = "Smiley Micros - " & portSettings.selectedPort & " " & wrap
        portSettings.selectedBaudrate.ToString() & "," & wrap
        portSettings.selectedParity & "," & wrap
        portSettings.selectedDataBits.ToString() & "," & wrap
        portSettings.selectedStopBits & " - " & portSettings.selectedHandshaking
    If serialPort1.IsOpen Then
        Me.Text &= " - Port is open"
    Else
        Me.Text &= " - Port is closed"
    End If
End Sub

Private Sub openPortToolStripMenuItem_Click(ByVal sender As Object, wrap
            ByVal e As EventArgs) Handles openPortToolStripMenuItem.Click
    openPort()
End Sub

Private Sub openPort()
    Try
        If serialPort1.IsOpen Then
            serialPort1.Close()
            openPortToolStripMenuItem.Text = "Open Port"
        Else
            serialPort1.Open()
            openPortToolStripMenuItem.Text = "Close Port"
        End If

        showSettings()
    Catch ex As System.Exception
        MessageBox.Show("Error - openPortToolStripMenuItem_Click wrap
                                Exception: ", ex.Message)
    End Try
End Sub
#End Region

#Region "Modem lines"
Private Sub showCTS_DSR_CD()
```

```
    If serialPort1.IsOpen Then
        If serialPort1.CtsHolding Then
            Me.LEDCTS.image = CInt(Fix(LED.LED22.LEDColor.BlueOn))
        Else
            Me.LEDCTS.image = CInt(Fix(LED.LED22.LEDColor.BlueOff))
        End If

        If serialPort1.DsrHolding Then
            Me.LEDDSR.image = CInt(Fix(LED.LED22.LEDColor.BlueOn))
        Else
            Me.LEDDSR.image = CInt(Fix(LED.LED22.LEDColor.BlueOff))
        End If

        If serialPort1.CDHolding Then
            Me.LEDDCD.image = CInt(Fix(LED.LED22.LEDColor.BlueOn))
        Else
            Me.LEDDCD.image = CInt(Fix(LED.LED22.LEDColor.BlueOff))
        End If

        If RingIndicator Then
            Me.LEDRI.image = CInt(Fix(LED.LED22.LEDColor.BlueOn))
        Else
            Me.LEDRI.image = CInt(Fix(LED.LED22.LEDColor.BlueOff))
        End If
    End If
End Sub

' Toggle RTS state
Private Sub buttonRTS_Click(ByVal sender As Object, ByVal e As EventArgs) Handles
buttonRTS.Click
    If RTSToggle Then
        serialPort1.RtsEnable = True
        LEDRTS.image = CInt(Fix(LED.LED22.LEDColor.RedOn))
    Else
        serialPort1.RtsEnable = False
        LEDRTS.image = CInt(Fix(LED.LED22.LEDColor.RedOff))
    End If
    RTSToggle = Not RTSToggle
End Sub

' Toggle DTR state
Private Sub buttonDTR_Click(ByVal sender As Object, ByVal e As EventArgs) Handles
buttonDTR.Click
    If DTRToggle Then
        serialPort1.DtrEnable = True
        LEDDTR.image = CInt(Fix(LED.LED22.LEDColor.RedOn))
    Else
        serialPort1.DtrEnable = False
        LEDDTR.image = CInt(Fix(LED.LED22.LEDColor.RedOff))
    End If
    DTRToggle = Not DTRToggle
End Sub

' Check Modem input line status
Private Sub timerOneSec_Tick(ByVal sender As Object, ByVal e As EventArgs) Handles
timerModemLines.Tick
    showCTS_DSR_CD()
```

```vb
End Sub

' Show the modem states on the virtual LEDs
Private Sub serialPort1_PinChanged(ByVal sender As Object, ByVal e As
SerialPinChangedEventArgs) Handles serialPort1.PinChanged
    ' Toggle RI since we can't determine the state with the SerialPort class
    If e.EventType = SerialPinChange.Ring Then
        RingIndicator = Not RingIndicator
    End If

    showCTS_DSR_CD()
End Sub

#End Region

#Region "Byte Shooter"
' Send a character at regular intervals
Private shoot As Boolean = False
Private byteToSend As Byte = 0
Private Sub sendCharToolStripMenuItem_Click(ByVal sender As Object, ByVal e As
EventArgs)
    If serialPort1.IsOpen Then
        If (Not shoot) Then
            shoot = True
            sendCharToolStripMenuItem.Text = "Stop sending bytes!"
            Dim shooter As ByteShooter = New ByteShooter()

            shooter.index = CByte(xMLData.SendByte)
            shooter.byteToSend = CByte(xMLData.SendByte)
            shooter.interval = xMLData.SendPeriod

            If shooter.ShowDialog() = System.Windows.Forms.DialogResult.OK Then
                byteToSend = shooter.byteToSend
                timerSendByte.Interval = shooter.interval
                timerSendByte.Enabled = True
            End If
        Else
            timerSendByte.Enabled = False
            shoot = False
            sendCharToolStripMenuItem.Text = "Send byte periodically."
        End If
    Else
        MessageBox.Show("A serial port must be open to use the byte shooter.")
    End If
End Sub
Private Sub timerSendByte_Tick(ByVal sender As Object, ByVal e As EventArgs)
Handles timerSendByte.Tick
    If (sendByte(byteToSend) = False) Then
        timerSendByte.Enabled = False
        IRSent = False
        MessageBox.Show("Error: timerSendByte_Tick, sendByte - wrap
                    failed to send." & Constants.vbLf & "Is the port open?")
    Else
        IRSent = True
    End If
End Sub
#End Region
```

```
#Region "Help"

Private Sub manualToolStripMenuItem_Click(ByVal sender As Object, wrap
            ByVal e As EventArgs) Handles manualToolStripMenuItem.Click
    System.Diagnostics.Process.Start("Developer Terminal.pdf")
End Sub

Private Sub smileyMicrosToolStripMenuItem_Click(ByVal sender As Object, wrap
            ByVal e As EventArgs) Handles smileyMicrosToolStripMenuItem.Click
    System.Diagnostics.Process.Start("www.smileymicros.com")
End Sub

#End Region
```

Well, I suspect that by now you are so sick of source code that you could scream, so scream and get ready for the next chapter which is all hardware experiments.

Chapter 15: Modem Line Hardware Experiments

In Chapter 8 we wrote the PinChangedEvent Tester and demonstrated how to use the BBUSB to read 4 switches and light two LEDs using UART signals. In this chapter we will expand on that and use the hardware more or less as it was intended for RS232 style serial communication.

We will look at:
1. We will connect the RTS/CTS and DTR/DSR lines and show their functions with Developer Terminal button and virtual LEDs.
2. We will look at RS232 voltages by using a MAX232 level converter and create a breadboard version of a USB to RS232 converter cable.
3. We will test this 'converter cable' with Simple Terminal
4. We will use it to communicate from the PC USB to an external device with an RS232 serial connection, the AVR Butterfly.

Demo RTS/CTS and DTR/DSR lines

First let's use the modem line states. We will connect the RTS from one of our devices to the CTS of the other and visa versa. Also we will connect the DTR from one to the DSR of the other. A real modem communication protocol would use these as discussed in the modem section to indicate readiness to send or receive serial data. You could use this for hardware handshaking but here we'll just push some virtual buttons and see the results on virtual LEDs.

We will simply observe that clicking the RTS button on one device causes the Developer Terminal CTS virtual LED to light up on the other and that clicking the DTR button on one device causes the DSR virtual LED to light up on the other.
- Wire BBUSB 1 for +5V
  - Wire USBVCC to VCC
  - Wire VCC to breadboard +5V
  - Wire VIO to breadboard +5V
- Wire BBUSB 2 for +5V
  - Wire USBVCC to VCC
  - Wire VCC to breadboard +5V
  - Wire VIO to breadboard +5V

- Wire the RTS of each device to the CTS of the other.
- Wire the DTR of each device to the DSR of the other.
- The following illustrations show how to wire this experiment. Probably hard to follow in black and white:

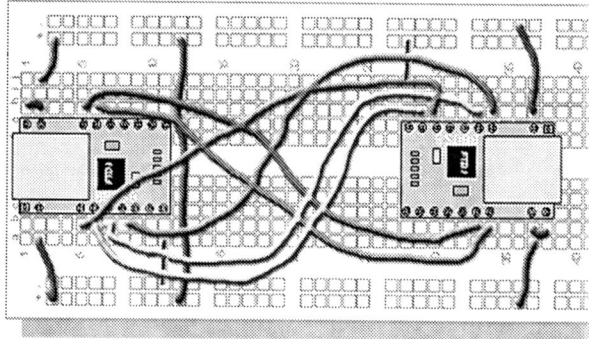

- Possibly a more schematic approach will help?

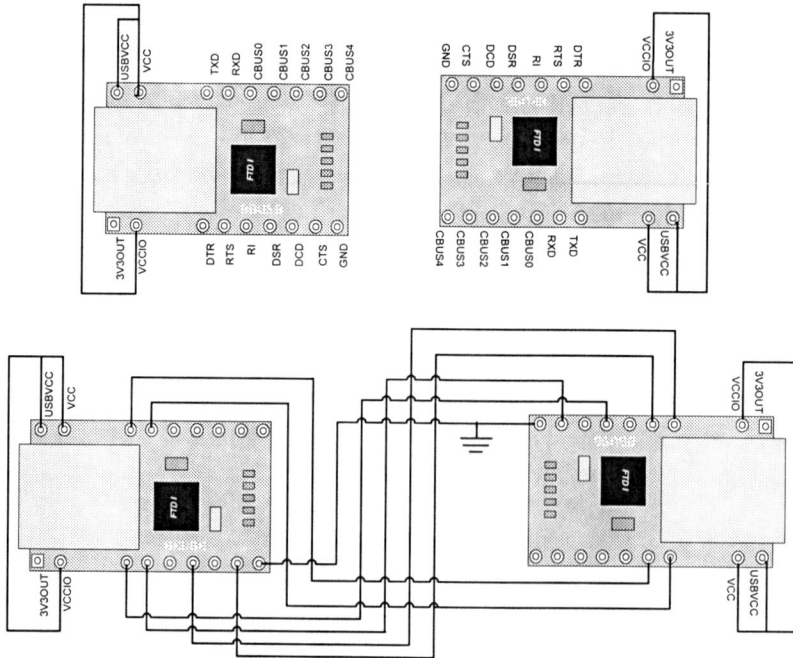

Okay, how about a photo to show the setup I used to do this test. I'm not a neat wirer, but the setup worked.

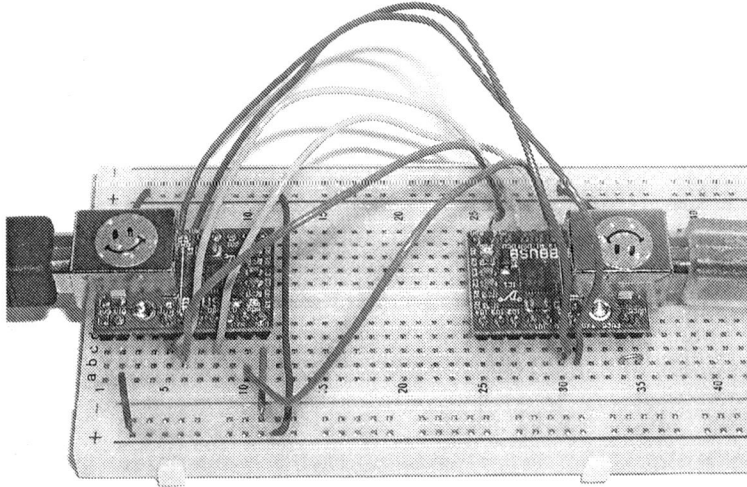

- Open two instances of the Developer Terminal.
- In one, open the serial port for the device on the left, in the other open the serial port for the device on the right.
- Click the RTS button in one and observe the CTS LED light up in the other.

- Click the DTR button in one and observe the DSR LED light up in the other.

USB RS232 Level Conversion

<u>**THIS PROJECT IS VERY HARD TO WIRE PROPERLY AND GET WORKING RIGHT –**</u> <u>**PAY ATTENTION AND EXPECT MISTAKES!**</u> Now let's create a USB to RS232 converter on a breadboard that functions exactly like a pre-made USB to RS232 converter cable. So why would you want to go to the trouble of building one on a breadboard when you can buy one already made for about the same price as rolling your own? Good question and about all I can say is that this way you learn

how that cable works and get the opportunity to use the extra pins on the BBUSB for other projects. You also get the opportunity to make a dozen frustrating mistakes and do a lot of debugging but that's part of the fun isn't it?

The BBUSBRS232 kit (available at www.smileymicros.com) **contains the following items:**

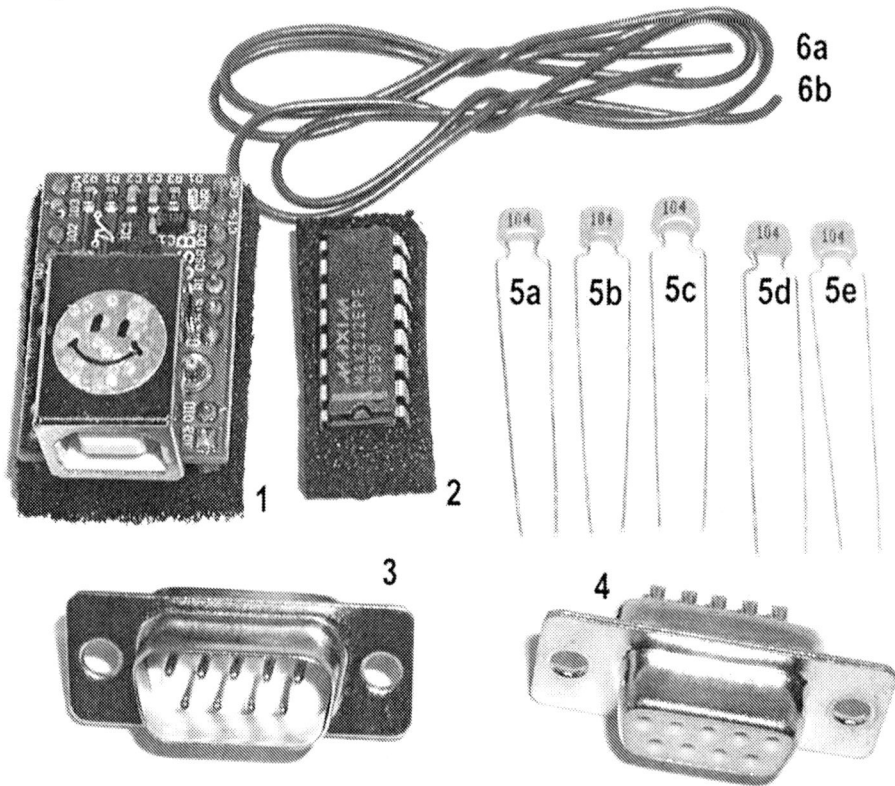

1	BBUSB
2	RS232 converter IC (MAX202 or equivalent)
3	Male DB-9 connector solder cup
4	Female DB-9 connector solder cup
5	5 - 0.1µF Capacitors
6	2 - 9" Wire 22 AWG wire

You will need parts that are NOT part of the kit:

- You will need a breadboard.
- You will need a USB cable.
- If doing the experiment with an older PC, you'll need a RS232 cable.
- You can do this experiment with any RS232 serial device that only requires the Tx, Rx, and SG (Signal Ground) lines, such as an older PC with a RS232 connection or the Smiley Micros Butterfly++ Mini-Kit.
- This experiment is difficult to wire properly, I had to use a scope to find a stupid wiring error, so be careful and patient.
- Solder the wires to the DB9 connector
    - For this experiment we will only use 3 of the 9 pins: Tx, Rx, and SG.
    - Cut 3 3" pieces of 22 AWG wire.
    - Strip about 1/8" insulation from one end and about 1/4" from the other.
    - Solder the 1/8" end to the solder cups for Tx, Rx, and SG on the DB-9 connector.
    - Remember that from the perspective of the PC and the external device the Tx and Rx are switched. This means that you connect the Tx line from the PC to the Rx line of the external device and visa versa.

DB9 Connector Wiring:

Signal	DB-9
DCD	1
Rx	2
Tx	3
DTR	4
SG	5
SR	6
RTS	7
CTS	8
RI	9

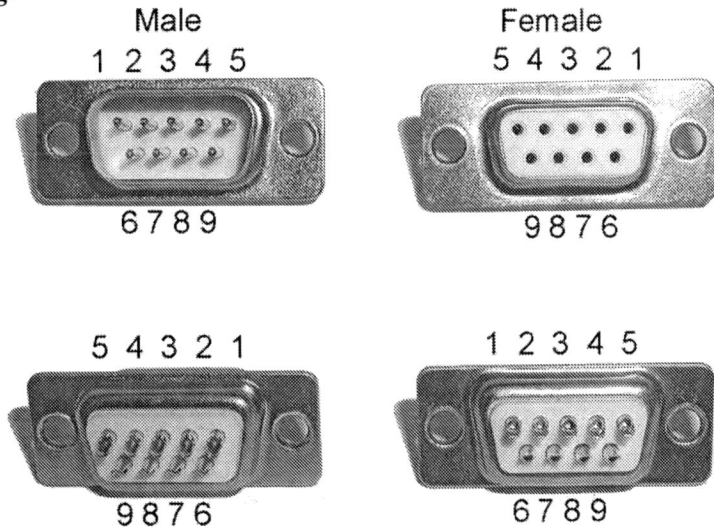

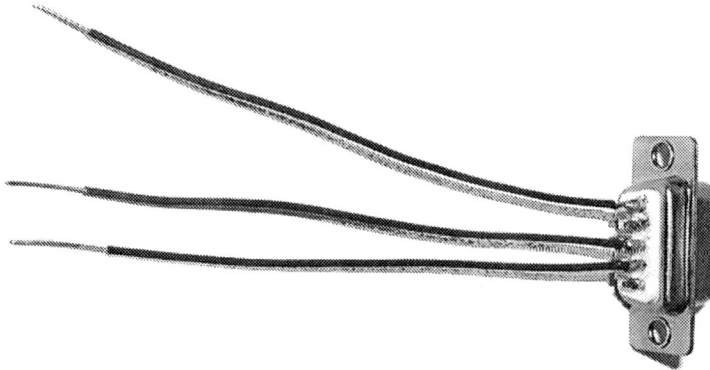

Solder Wires to back of male DB9 connectors

We are using a MAX202 (or equivalent compatible IC), which has two transmitters and two receivers. With this, we can do most common serial communications including having RTS/CTS handshaking. We cannot use the remaining modem lines at the RS232 voltages levels since such chips would add a lot to the cost of the experimenter's kit and add little to the learning.

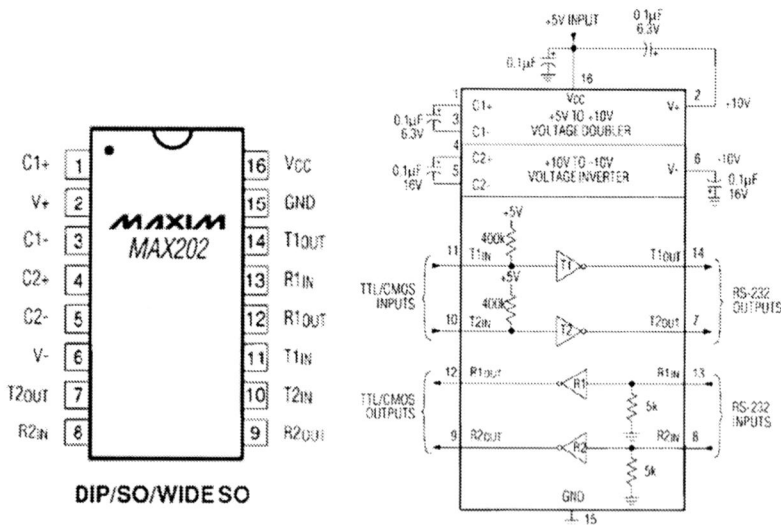

MAX202 wiring and internal schematic are identical for many other equivalent compatible RS232 converter ICs.

- Wire up the MAX202 or equivalent level converter using the illustration shown on the next page.
- Place the BBUSB and the MAX202 or equivalent on the breadboard more or less as shown.
- Wire BBUSB for +5V
  o Wire USBVCC to VCC
  o Wire VCC to breadboard +5V
  o Wire VIO to brcadboard +5V
  o Wire GND to breadboard GND
- Add the 5 0.1μF Caps to the MAX202 or equivalent as shown. Trim legs to get the caps near the board.
  o Cap between +5V and GND, near pins 15 and 16.
  o Cap between +5V and pin 2.
  o Cap between pin 1 and 3.
  o Cap between pin 4 and 5.
  o Cap between pin 6 and GND.
- Wire TxD of BBUSB to pin 11 of the MAX202 or equivalent.
- Wire RxD of BBUSB to pin 12 of the MAX202 or equivalent.
- Wire the DB9 pin 3 (TxD pin) to pin 14 of the MAX202 or equivalent.
- Wire the DB9 pin 2 (RxD pin) to pin 13 of the MAX202 or equivalent.
- Wiring this thing up correctly is harder than it appears, isn't it?

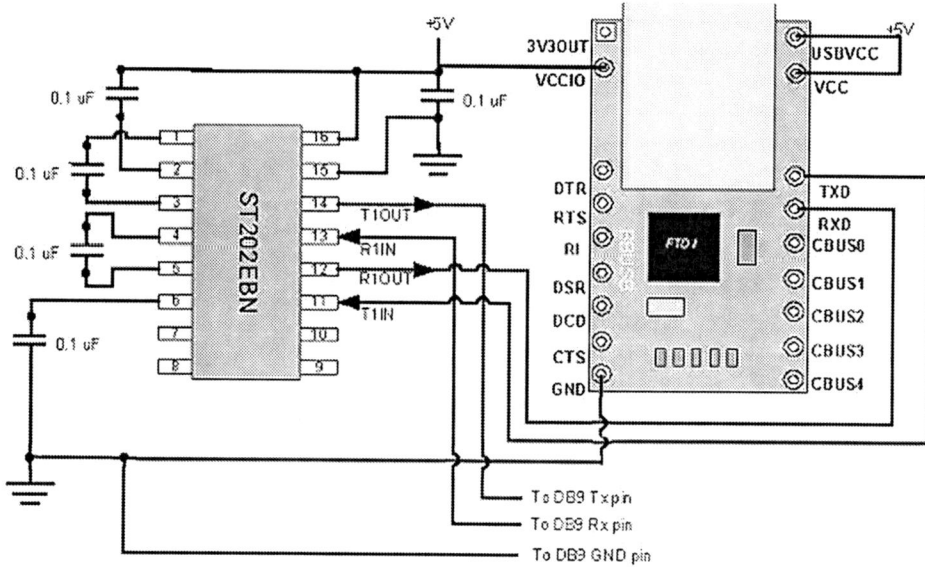

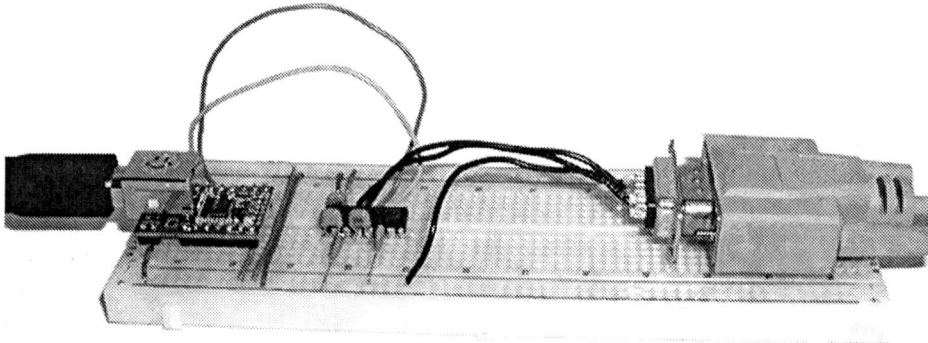

Test with Simple Terminal

Simple Terminal is a simple terminal (duh) written in C# or VB .NET.

- Open Simple Terminal and click on the Settings Menu Item.
- Choose the first serial port.
- Open a second instance of Simple Terminal and follow the above steps, selecting the second serial port. Again, this shows COM4, but yours probably won't.

248

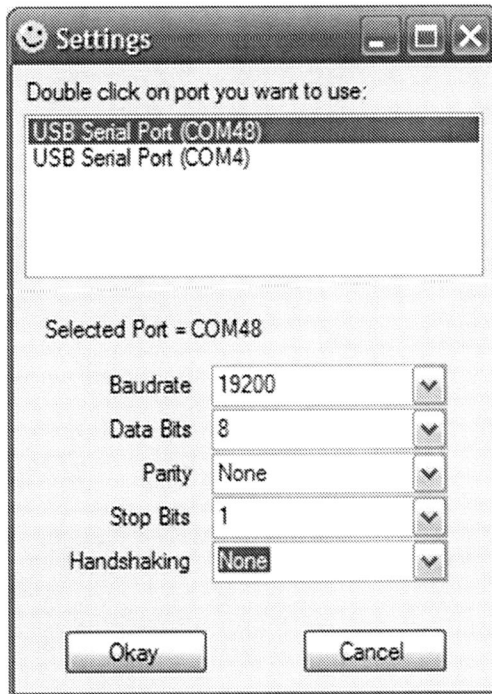

- Type a message in the send box of one terminal and watch it appear in the receive box of the other terminal.

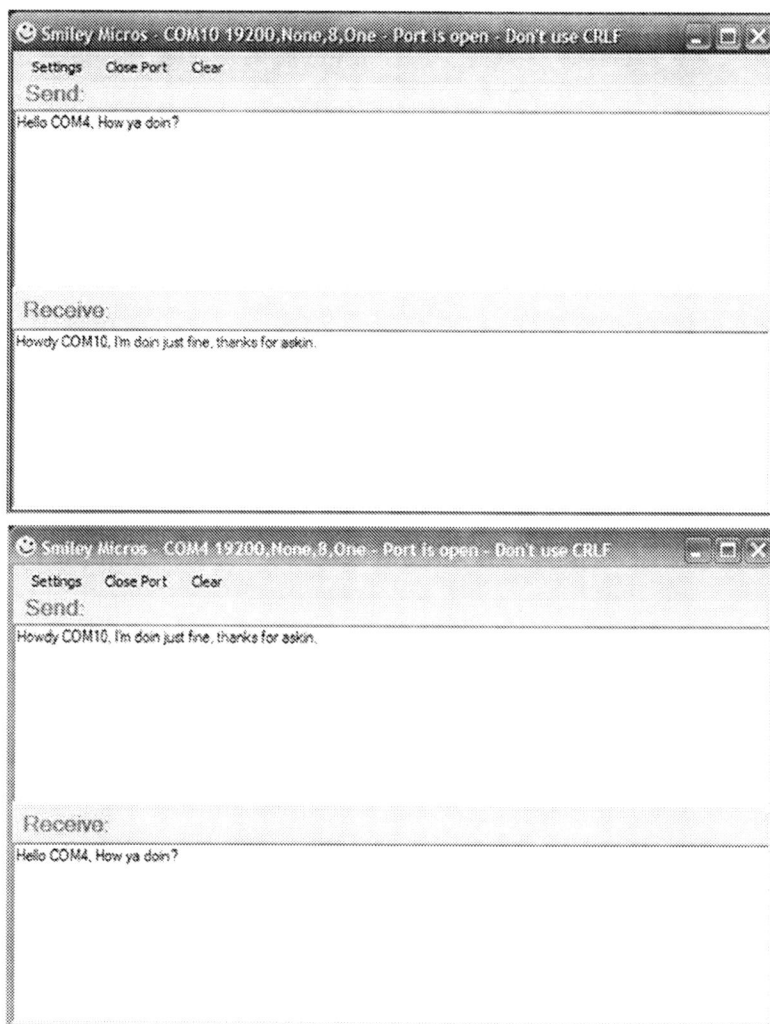

USB Butterfly

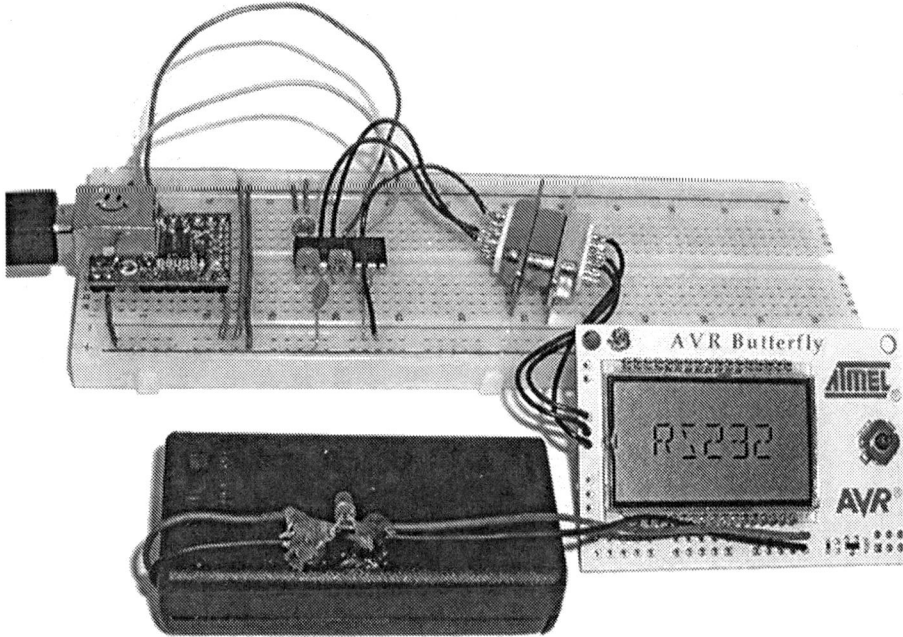

The type of DB9 connector, male or female depends on whether the connection end is on the PC side or the peripheral side. The male is used on the PC side and the female is used on the peripheral side.

- Remove the female DB9 connector form the breadboard
- Following the instructions earlier, make a male DB9 connection with three wire legs to go to the breadboard. Pay attention to the TxD and RxD and remember to ask which is relative to what? It gets confusing.
- Open an instance of Developer Terminal.
- Attach the Butterfly and turn it on with the joystick button pressed to the center. You will see a series of ?????? on the receive panel indicating that the Butterfly is sending okay.
- Turn the Butterfly off and back on.
- Click the joystick upward and the 'AVR BUTTERFLY' message will scroll.
- Click down until you see NAME.
- Click to the right twice to see 'ENTER NAME' scrolling.

251

- Click down to see 'DOWNLOAD'
- Press to the center to see 'WAITING FOR INPUT'.
- In the Send window, enter a name, such as 'RS232'.
- From the Send Hex drop down box select 0x0D then 0x0A to send the Butterfly 'CR+LF' telling it the input is finished.
- Now you should see the name you entered on the Butterfly LCD.
- Lots can go wrong in the way you wire this up, the way you use the Butterfly menu, and the way you use the Developer Terminal. It worked for me, but only after a couple of tries, so be patient.

This brings to an end Part 2 and we are now expert on creating GUIs and using the SerialPort class. In the next part we will stop using the Virtual COM Port drivers and start using the Smiley Micros port of the FTDI D2XX drivers which allows us to talk directly with the FT232R without emulating the legacy serial COM# port paradigm.

Chapter 16: Device Information

Moving on to the FTD2XX.dll

We have finished what we need to use the FT232R as a Virtual COM Port using the FTDIBUS.dll drivers. Now we will learn to use the FTD2XX.dll drivers, which let us bypass the serial port and directly access features on the FT232R chip. We will no longer open a serial port, but will open a FT232R device, so we will first need to learn how to identify what devices are available and how to open them for use with the FTD2XX.dll functions. Technically, we could recreate all the serial functions in FTDIBUS.dll using the FTD2XX.dll, but that would be redundant, so we won't look too deeply at the available serial functions and instead concentrate on the functions that allow us to do things that we can't already do.

It is not really easy or intuitive to use either C# or VB to access DLL (Dynamic Link Library) functions and many of the FTD2XX functions required a bit of hacking to figure out how to use. We will not directly call any of the FTD2XX functions, but instead use the SM_D2XX class to call them using wrappers that are a bit more friendly to C# and VB than direct calls. In many cases a direct call would work just fine, but for consistency we will make all function calls via a wrapper. Since not all the functions are ported, especially the serial functions, the user may want to directly use some functions that I haven't made available. A motivated user can look at the SM_D2XX class and see how various data types were translated into the C# and VB idioms and then use the FTD2XX functions directly, but I do advise waiting till you finish the book, since what is presented here works and doing similar ports for functions not covered could be a trial.

In this chapter we will develop a technique for finding and opening devices. In the next chapter we will learn to read and write the EEPROM. This will be followed by a chapter, which develops a FT232R programmer that duplicates the functions in the FTDI MPROG utility for programming devices, with the added benefit of having the source code available to see how it is done.

Using the SM_D2XX Select and Open Test software

We will develop a module, Select Device, to allow us to select a device using the SM_D2XX class for accessing functions in FTDI's D2XX dynamic link library. We will also write a test program, SM_D2XX Select and Open Test, that will allow us to use the Select Device module to get user information on which device to open.

Using the Select Device Module

First let's look at the program to see how it works.

- Open SelectAndOpenTest.exe from \Software\Chapter 16 – SM_D2XX DLL

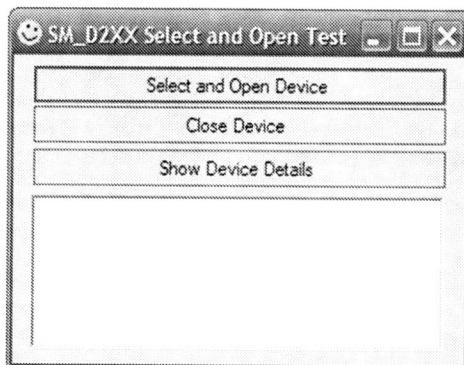

- Click the 'Select and Open device' button to open the Select and Open Device Module that we will be reusing in other programs.

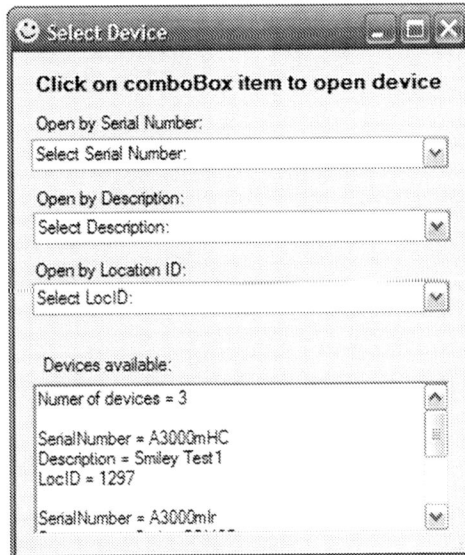

- There were three FT232R devices connected to the computer when this program opened, thus we have 'Number of Devices = 3' and a list of device selection parameters in the 'Devices available' richTextBox.
- We can select any of the devices by clicking the down arrow on any of the three comboBoxes and clicking on one of the three available devices.
- For instance, in the first image below we have selected the 'Open by Serial Number' comboBox and clicked on the 'A3000mlr' device.

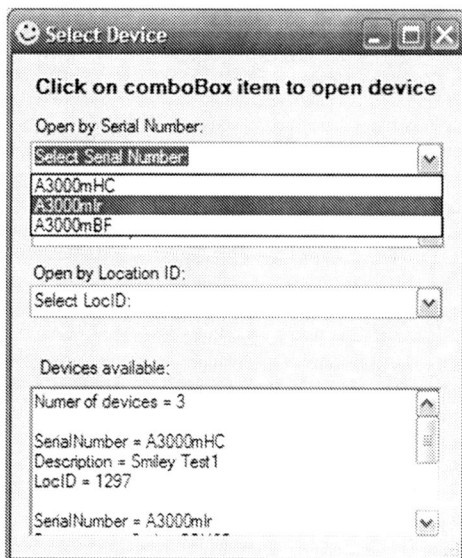

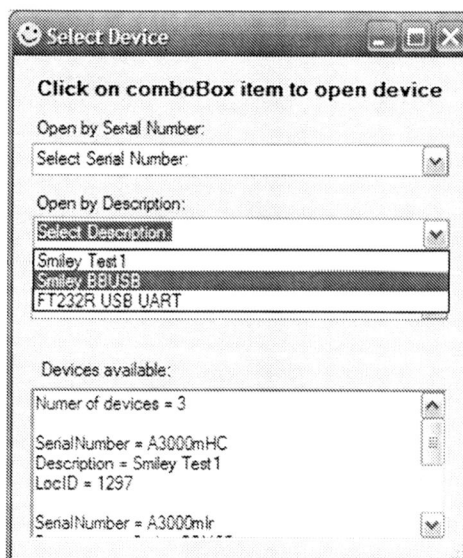

- In the second image above, we select the 'Open by Description' comboBox and clicked on the 'Smiley BBUSB' device.

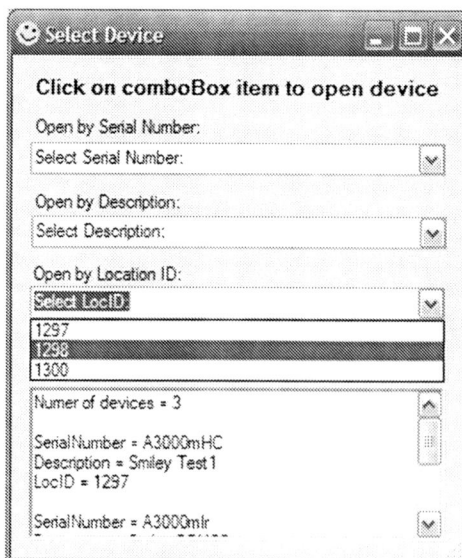

- Finally, in the box above, we select the 'Open by Location ID' comboBox and clicked on the '1298' device.

- Clicking on any of these causes the 'Select and Open Device' form to close. The test form receives the device information needed to open the selected device.
- In the test form we can click the 'Show Device Details' button in the 'SM_D2XX Select and Open Test' form to show the Serial Number and Description of the device opened as shown in the image below.

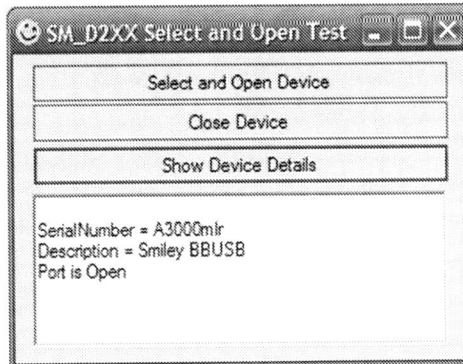

- If we click the 'Close Device' Button, the device is closed and then if we clear the richTextBox and click the 'Show Device Details' we will see the following image showing the device is now closed.

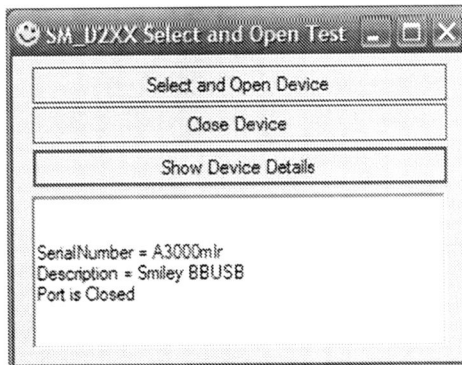

Writing the SM_D2XX Select and Open Test program

Write the Test Program

- Create a Form with the three buttons and richTextBox as shown in the image above.
  - o Name the first button buttonGetDevInfo, and set the text to 'Select and Open Device'.
  - o Name the second button buttonCloseDevice, and set the text to 'Close Device.
  - o Name the third button buttonShowDeviceDetails, and set the text to 'Show Device Details'.
- In C# copy the SM_D2XX.cs from \Software\Chapter 16 – SM_D2XX DLL\Select and Open Test C#
- In VB copy the SM_D2XX.vb from \Software\Chapter 16 – SM_D2XX DLL\Select and Open Test VB
- In the Solutions Explorer Add the SM_D2XX file to the solution.
- Open the Form1 code.
- In C# add:

```csharp
using System;
using System.Collections.Generic;
using System.ComponentModel;
using System.Data;
using System.Drawing;
using System.Text;
using System.Windows.Forms;

using SMD2XX;

namespace SM_D2XX_Test
{
    public partial class Form1 : Form
    {
        #region Initialization

        FT_STATUS ftStatus = 0;
        private UInt32 handle = 0;

        SM_D2XX SM = new SM_D2XX();

        SelectDevice dev = new SelectDevice();

        public Form1()
        {
            InitializeComponent();
        }

        private void Form1_FormClosing(object sender, FormClosingEventArgs e)
        {
```

```
        closeDevice();
    }

#endregion

#region Open device by Serial Number, Description, or Location ID

// open by serial number
private void openBySerialNumber(string SN)
{
    ftStatus = SM.openSerialNumber(SN, ref handle);
    if (ftStatus != FT_STATUS.FT_OK)
    {
        MessageBox.Show("Error: buttonGet_Click failed to open device");
    }
}

// open by description
private void openByDescription(string description)
{
    ftStatus = SM.openDescription(description, ref handle);
    if (ftStatus != FT_STATUS.FT_OK)
    {
        MessageBox.Show("Error: buttonGet_Click failed to open port");
    }
}

// open by location
private void openByLocationID(UInt32 locID)
{
    ftStatus = SM.openLocationID(locID, ref handle);
    if (ftStatus != FT_STATUS.FT_OK)
    {
        MessageBox.Show("Error: buttonGet_Click failed to open port");
    }
}

// Assumes device is open
private void closeDevice()
{
    SM.closeDevice(handle);
}

#endregion

#region Button Events

private void buttonGetDevInfo_Click(object sender, EventArgs e)
{
    dev.ShowDialog();

    switch (dev.OpenBy)
    {
        case (uint)OPENBY.SERIAL_NUMBER: // use OpenEX
            openBySerialNumber(dev.SerialNumber);
            break;
        case (uint)OPENBY.DESCRIPTION: // use OpenEX
```

259

```
                    openByDescription(dev.Description);
                    break;
                case (uint)OPENBY.LOCATIONID: // use OpenEX
                    openByLocationID(dev.LocID);
                    break;
                default:
                    MessageBox.Show("ERROR - OpenBy = " + dev.OpenBy.ToString());
                    break;
            }
        }

        private void buttonShowDeviceDetails_Click(object sender, EventArgs e)
        {
            ftStatus = SM.createDeviceInfoList();
            if (ftStatus != FT_STATUS.FT_OK)
            {
                MessageBox.Show("Error: buttonGetDeviceInfo_Click wrap
                                FT_CreateDeviceInfoList failed.");
                return;
            }

            ftStatus = SM.getDeviceInfoDetail(dev.Index);
            if (ftStatus != FT_STATUS.FT_OK)
            {
                MessageBox.Show("Error: buttonGetDeviceInfo_Click wrap
                                FT_GetDeviceInfoDetail failed.");
                return;
            }

            richTextBox1.Text += "\nSerialNumber = " + SM.SerialNumber;
            richTextBox1.Text += "\nDescription = " + SM.Description;

            if (SM.Flags == 0) richTextBox1.Text += "\nPort is Closed";
            else if (SM.Flags == 1) richTextBox1.Text += "\nPort is Open";
            else richTextBox1.Text += "Error: Flags out of range";

        }

        private void buttonCloseDevice_Click(object sender, EventArgs e)
        {
            closeDevice();
        }

        #endregion
    }
}
```

- **In VB add:**

```
Imports Microsoft.VisualBasic
Imports System
Imports System.Collections.Generic
Imports System.ComponentModel
Imports System.Data
Imports System.Drawing
Imports System.Text
Imports System.Windows.Forms
```

Chapter 16: Device Information

```vbnet
Imports SMD2XX

Namespace SM_D2XX_Test
        Public Partial Class Form1
        Inherits Form
#Region "Initialization"
        Private ftStatus As FT_STATUS = 0
        Private ftHandle As UInt32 = 0

        Private SM As SM_D2XX = New SM_D2XX()

        Private dev As SelectAndOpenDevice = New SelectAndOpenDevice()

        Public Sub New()
            InitializeComponent()
        End Sub
#End Region

#Region "Open device by Serial Number, Description, or Location ID"

        ' open by serial number
        Private Sub openBySerialNumber(ByVal SN As String)
            ftStatus = SM.openSerialNumber(SN, ftHandle)
            If ftStatus <> FT_STATUS.FT_OK Then
                MessageBox.Show("Error: buttonGet_Click failed to open device")
            End If
        End Sub

        ' open by description
        Private Sub openByDescription(ByVal description As String)
            ftStatus = SM.openDescription(description, ftHandle)
            If ftStatus <> FT_STATUS.FT_OK Then
                MessageBox.Show("Error: buttonGet_Click failed to open port")
            End If
        End Sub

        ' open by location
        Private Sub openByLocationID(ByVal locID As UInt32)
            ftStatus = SM.openLocationID(locID, ftHandle)
            If ftStatus <> FT_STATUS.FT_OK Then
                MessageBox.Show("Error: buttonGet_Click failed to open port")
            End If
        End Sub

        ' open by Device Number
        Private Function openByDeviceNumber(ByVal device As UInteger) As FT_STATUS
            ' Open device indicated
            ftStatus = SM.openDevice(device, ftHandle)
            If ftStatus <> FT_STATUS.FT_OK Then
                SM.closeDevice(ftHandle)
                MessageBox.Show("Error: OpenDevice0" & wrap
                                        SM.parseFT_STATUS(ftStatus))
                Return ftStatus
            End If

            Return ftStatus
        End Function
```

261

```
        ' Assumes device is open
        Private Sub closeDevice()
            SM.closeDevice(ftHandle)
        End Sub

#End Region

#Region "Button Events"
        Private Sub buttonGetDevInfo_Click(ByVal sender As Object, wrap
                         ByVal e As EventArgs) Handles buttonGetDevInfo.Click
            closeDevice()

            dev.ShowDialog()

            Select Case dev.OpenBy
                Case CUInt(OPENBY.SERIAL_NUMBER) ' use OpenEX
                    openBySerialNumber(dev.SerialNumber)
                Case CUInt(OPENBY.DESCRIPTION) ' use OpenEX
                    openByDescription(dev.Description)
                Case CUInt(OPENBY.LOCATIONID) ' use OpenEX
                    openByLocationID(dev.LocID)
                Case Else
                    MessageBox.Show("ERROR - OpenBy = " & dev.OpenBy.ToString())
            End Select

        End Sub

        Private Sub Form1_FormClosing(ByVal sender As Object, wrap
                    ByVal e As FormClosingEventArgs) Handles MyBase.FormClosing
            closeDevice()
        End Sub

        Private Sub buttonShowDeviceDetails_Click(ByVal sender As Object, wrap
                    ByVal e As EventArgs) Handles buttonShowDeviceDetails.Click
            ftStatus = SM.createDeviceInfoList()
            If ftStatus <> FT_STATUS.FT_OK Then
                MessageBox.Show("Error: buttonGetDeviceInfo_Click wrap
                                    FT_CreateDeviceInfoList failed.")
                Return
            End If

            ftStatus = SM.getDeviceInfoDetail(dev.Index)
            If ftStatus <> FT_STATUS.FT_OK Then
                MessageBox.Show("Error: buttonGetDeviceInfo_Click wrap
                                    FT_GetDeviceInfoDetail failed.")
                Return
            End If

            richTextBox1.Text += Constants.vbLf & "SerialNumber = " wrap
                                                    & SM.SerialNumber
            richTextBox1.Text += Constants.vbLf & "Description = " wrap
                                                    & SM.Description

            If SM.Flags = 0 Then
                richTextBox1.Text += Constants.vbLf & "Port is Closed"
            ElseIf SM.Flags = 1 Then
```

```
                 richTextBox1.Text += Constants.vbLf & "Port is Open"
            Else
                 richTextBox1.Text &= "Error: Flags out of range"
            End If

        End Sub

        Private Sub buttonCloseDevice_Click(ByVal sender As Object, wrap
                           ByVal e As EventArgs) Handles
                    buttonCloseDevice.Click
            closeDevice()
        End Sub
#End Region
        End Class
End Namespace
```

Select Device Module – Write the Source Code

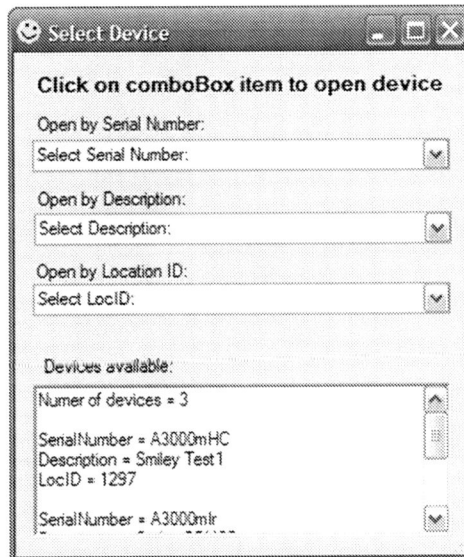

- Create a Form with the three comboBoxes and associated labels, and a richTextBox as shown in the image above.
    - o Name the first comboBoxSerialNumber, and set the label to 'Open by Serial Number'.
    - o Name the second comboBoxDescripton, and set the label to 'Open by Description'.
    - o Name the third comboBoxLocID, and set the label to 'Open by Location ID'.

- Open the Form1 code.
- In C# add:

```csharp
using System;
using System.Collections.Generic;
using System.ComponentModel;
using System.Data;
using System.Drawing;
using System.Text;
using System.Windows.Forms;

using SMD2XX;

namespace SM_D2XX_Test
{

    // 1 opens by serial number using FT_OpenEX
    // 2 opens by description using FT_OpenEX
    // 3 opens by Location Id using FT_OpenEX
    // 4 opens by device number using FT_Open
    public enum OPENBY
    {
        SERIAL_NUMBER = 1,
        DESCRIPTION,
        LOCATIONID,
        DEVICE_NUMBER
    }


    public partial class SelectDevice : Form
    {
        private FT_STATUS ftStatus; // create an instance the FT_STATUS enum

        SM_D2XX SM = new SM_D2XX();

        public SelectDevice()
        {
            InitializeComponent();
        }

        private void SelectAndOpenDevice_Load_1(object sender, EventArgs e)
        {
            ftStatus = SM.createDeviceInfoList();
            if (ftStatus != FT_STATUS.FT_OK)
            {
                MessageBox.Show("Error: buttonGet_Click wrap
                                         FT_CreateDeviceInfoList failed.");
                return;
            }

            comboBoxSerialNumber.Items.Clear();
            comboBoxDescription.Items.Clear();
            comboBoxLocID.Items.Clear();


            richTextBox1.Text = "Numer of devices = " + wrap
                                         SM.NumDevs.ToString() + "\n";
```

```
for (UInt32 n = 0; n < SM.NumDevs; n++)
{
    SM.getDeviceInfoDetail(n);

    serialNumber_p = SM.SerialNumber;
    description_p = SM.Description;
    locID_p = SM.LocID;

    if (ftStatus != FT_STATUS.FT_OK)
    {
        MessageBox.Show("Error: GetDeviceInfoDetail failed.");
        return;
    }
    else
    {
        comboBoxSerialNumber.Items.Add(serialNumber_p);
        comboBoxDescription.Items.Add(description_p);
        comboBoxLocID.Items.Add(locID_p);
        richTextBox1.Text += "\nSerialNumber = " + serialNumber_p;
        richTextBox1.Text += "\nDescription = " + description_p;
        richTextBox1.Text += "\nLocID = " + locID_p.ToString() + "\n";
    }
}
}


#region Properties

private string serialNumber_p = "NOT INITIALIZED";
public string SerialNumber { get { return serialNumber_p; } wrap
                                    set { serialNumber_p = value; } }

private string description_p = "NOT INITIALIZED";
public string Description { get { return description_p; } wrap
                                    set { description_p = value; } }

private UInt32 locID_p;
public UInt32 LocID { get { return locID_p; } set { locID_p = value; } }

private UInt32 index_p;
public UInt32 Index { get { return index_p; } set { index_p = value; } }

private UInt32 openBy_p;
public UInt32 OpenBy { get { return openBy_p; } set { openBy_p = value;} }

#endregion

#region Select Device to Open
private void comboBoxSerialNumber_SelectedIndexChanged(object sender, wrap
                                                        EventArgs e)
{
    openBy_p = (UInt32)OPENBY.SERIAL_NUMBER;
    serialNumber_p = comboBoxSerialNumber.SelectedItem.ToString();
    index_p = (uint)comboBoxSerialNumber.SelectedIndex;
    Close();
}
```

```
        private void comboBoxDescription_SelectedIndexChanged(wrap
                                    object sender, EventArgs e)
        {
            openBy_p = (UInt32)OPENBY.DESCRIPTION;
            description_p = comboBoxDescription.SelectedItem.ToString();
            index_p = (uint)comboBoxDescription.SelectedIndex;
            Close();
        }

        private void comboBoxLocID_SelectedIndexChanged(object sender, wrap
                                    EventArgs e)
        {
            openBy_p = (UInt32)OPENBY.LOCATIONID;
            locID_p = UInt32.Parse(comboBoxLocID.SelectedItem.ToString());
            index_p = (uint)comboBoxLocID.SelectedIndex;
            Close();
        }
        #endregion
    }
}
```

- **In VB add:**

```
Imports Microsoft.VisualBasic
Imports System
Imports System.Collections.Generic
Imports System.ComponentModel
Imports System.Data
Imports System.Drawing
Imports System.Text
Imports System.Windows.Forms

Imports SMD2XX

Namespace SM_D2XX_Test

    ' 1 opens by serial number using FT_OpenEX
    ' 2 opens by description using FT_OpenEX
    ' 3 opens by Location Id using FT_OpenEX
    ' 4 opens by device number using FT_Open
    Public Enum OPEN_BY
        SERIAL_NUMBER = 1
        DESCRIPTION
        LOCATIONID
        DEVICE_NUMBER
    End Enum


    Public Partial Class SelectAndOpenDevice
        Inherits Form
        Private ftStatus As FT_STATUS'create an instance the FT_STATUS enum

        Private SM As SM_D2XX = New SM_D2XX()

        Public Sub New()
            InitializeComponent()
```

266

```
        End Sub

    Private Sub SelectAndOpenDevice_Load_1(ByVal sender As Object, wrap
                        ByVal e As EventArgs) Handles MyBase.Load
            ftStatus = SM.createDeviceInfoList()
            If ftStatus <> FT_STATUS.FT_OK Then
                    MessageBox.Show("Error: buttonGet_Click wrap
                            FT_CreateDeviceInfoList failed.")
                    Return
            End If

            comboBoxSerialNumber.Items.Clear()
            comboBoxDescription.Items.Clear()
            comboBoxLocID.Items.Clear()


richTextBox1.Text = "Numer of devices = " & SM.NumDevs.ToString()wrap
                                            & Constants.vbLf


For n As UInt32 = 0 To SM.NumDevs - CUInt(1)
    SM.getDeviceInfoDetail(n)
    If ftStatus <> FT_STATUS.FT_OK Then
        MessageBox.Show("Error: GetDeviceInfoDetail failed.")
        Return
    Else
        richTextBox1.Text += Constants.vbLf & "SerialNumber = " wrap
                                            & SM.SerialNumber
        comboBoxSerialNumber.Items.Add(SM.SerialNumber)
        richTextBox1.Text += Constants.vbLf & "Description = " wrap
                            & SM.Description
        comboBoxDescription.Items.Add(SM.Description)
        richTextBox1.Text += Constants.vbLf & "LocID = " wrap
                            & SM.LocID.ToString() &
                    Constants.vbLf
        comboBoxLocID.Items.Add(SM.LocID)
    End If
Next n
    End Sub


    #Region "Properties"

    Private serialNumber_p As String = "NOT INITIALIZED"
    Public Property SerialNumber() As String
            Get
                    Return serialNumber_p
            End Get
            Set(ByVal value As String)
                    serialNumber_p = value
            End Set
    End Property

    Private description_p As String = "NOT INITIALIZED"
    Public Property Description() As String
            Get
                    Return description_p
            End Get
```

```
            Set(ByVal value As String)
                    description_p = value
            End Set
    End Property


    Private locID_p As UInt32
    Public Property LocID() As UInt32
            Get
                    Return locID_p
            End Get
            Set(ByVal value As UInt32)
                    locID_p = value
            End Set
    End Property


    Private index_p As UInt32
    Public Property Index() As UInt32
            Get
                    Return index_p
            End Get
            Set(ByVal value As UInt32)
                    index_p = value
            End Set
    End Property


    Private openBy_p As UInt32
    Public Property OpenBy() As UInt32
            Get
                    Return openBy_p
            End Get
            Set(ByVal value As UInt32)
                    openBy_p = value
            End Set
    End Property

    #End Region

    #Region "Select Device to Open"
    Private Sub comboBoxSerialNumber_SelectedIndexChanged( wrap
                ByVal sender As Object, ByVal e As EventArgs) wrap
                Handles comboBoxSerialNumber.SelectedIndexChanged
            openBy_p = CType(OPEN_BY.SERIAL_NUMBER, Integer)
            serialNumber_p = wrap
                    comboBoxSerialNumber.SelectedItem.ToString()
            index_p = CUInt(comboBoxSerialNumber.SelectedIndex)
            Close()
    End Sub

    Private Sub comboBoxDescription_SelectedIndexChanged(wrap
                ByVal sender As Object, ByVal e As EventArgs) wrap
                Handles comboBoxDescription.SelectedIndexChanged
            openBy_p = CUInt(OPEN_BY.DESCRIPTION)
            description_p = comboBoxDescription.SelectedItem.ToString()
            index_p = CUInt(comboBoxDescription.SelectedIndex)
            Close()
    End Sub
```

```
Private Sub comboBoxLocID_SelectedIndexChanged(wrap
        ByVal sender As Object, ByVal e As EventArgs) wrap
        Handles comboBoxLocID.SelectedIndexChanged
    openBy_p = CUInt(OPEN_BY.LOCATIONID)
    locID_p = wrap
        UInt32.Parse(comboBoxLocID.SelectedItem.ToString())
    index_p = CUInt(comboBoxLocID.SelectedIndex)
    Close()
End Sub
#End Region

    End Class
End Namespace
```

In this chapter we learned how to get information on FT232R devices connected to Windows© and open a specific device using the D2XX drivers. In the next chapter we will apply this by opening a device and doing some bit-banged I/O to read switches and turn LEDs on and off.

Chapter 17: Bit-Banging – Hardware Test Code

Let's write a program to write or read the FT232R pins in the bit-bang mode. We can only hope that by now the reader is a bit cookbooked out and willing to throw in a few spices without using a recipe or a measuring spoon, so let's just do some basic explaining and show the code without all the hand-holding. Then we can do some cool experiments.

Because there is so much repetition in the code (we have 12 pins, each doing the same thing so a lot of stuff gets repeated 12 times – and yes, I know this could be coded more compactly by creating and reusing some components, but frankly, the logic is confusing enough without adding extra complexity) we will split off the cool hardware experiments and show them in the next chapter.

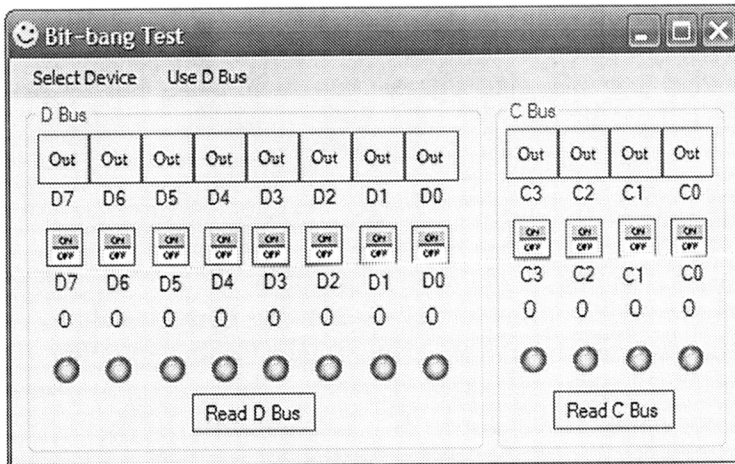

Funky Logic

We can only use one bus at a time for I/O, either the D Bus or the C Bus is selected by clicking the menu item 'Use D Bus' which toggles to 'Use C Bus' and the enables the selected bus group box and disables the other group box.

The actual logic states get funky quick. For the D Bus outputting a 1 causes the pin to go to GND and outputting a 0 causes the pin to go to Vcc. This is inverted logic, and while 'funky' there really is nothing 'logically' wrong with doing this.

Logic represents true or false states, not voltage states, and we can assign any voltage state to either logic state that we like. But just to confuse things, the C Bus logic is not inverted so a logic 0 is GND and a logic 1 is Vcc. We will confuse things even more when we hook up switches and LEDs. For the LEDs we will turn them on by taking the pin from Vcc to GND, so for the D Bus a logic 1 turns them on and for the C Bus a logic 0 turns them on. We will wire the switches so that each pin is taken to the top of a 2.2k-ohm resistor to GND when switched off (meaning the pin will be at Vcc when off and switched directly to GND when the switch is on. But since the D Bus is inverted, then an 'On' taken to GND will show up as a 1, which we will take to mean, yes the switch is on.

Did I say 'funky'? Well, it is quite confusing, but all perfectly logical if you are willing to suspend the idea that Vcc means true and GND means false. Don't think that way, just look at the actual circuit in the next chapter and you'll learn to pay attention to what you have specifically defined as true or false, given the conditions of the specific pin.

I assure you that you will find this all very confusing, but by paying careful attention, you will get it.

The Software

There are 12 I/O pins and 12 columns of components for manipulating the pins. The top row has toggle buttons for setting a pin to input or output. The next row has toggle buttons (with switch-like graphics) for turning an output pin on or off. The next row (all 0 above) will show the state of each output pin, either 0 or 1, or if the pin is set to input it will show 'X'. The bottom row has a set of LEDs that are gray if the pin is output and either bright red or dark red to show the input state after the Read D Bus or Read C Bus button is pressed.

The On and Off button graphics are located in \Software\Graphics\ and should be added to the imageList and used as was shown for the LEDs in the Developer Terminal chapter. The layout is straightforward and the coding is very repetitive since we write nearly identical code for each of the 12 pins.

And just FYI: I made one column work, then used copy/paste for the rest, doing some sequence editing to each copy.

For this project we will need to copy the SMD2XX, SelectDevice, and LED22 files from the last chapter to our directory and add them to out project. Then we will add them to components to our form until it looks like the image shown above and finally we add code.

In C# add:

```
using System;
using System.Collections.Generic;
using System.ComponentModel;
using System.Data;
using System.Drawing;
using System.Text;
using System.Windows.Forms;

using SelectDevice;
using SMD2XX;

namespace BitBangTest
{
    public partial class Form1 : Form
    {
    /*
     * The BBUSB allows access to 12 pins that can be configured individually
     * as either input or output. 8 of these pins are refered to as pins D0 to D7
     * while the remaining 4 are referred to as pins C0 to C3 (CBUS pins).
     * The D0-D7 pins I/O state is set using the setMode function. The CBUS
     * pins must first be set to the I/O mode in EEPROM, then their I/O state
     * can also be set using the setMode function. CBUS4 is not configurable for
     * I/O.
     *
     * Select Pin State
     * Pin I/O states are selected in the topmost row of buttons.
     * Each button is labeled with the corresponding pin name and clicking the
     * button will toggle the pin I/O state and show that state as either an 'I'
     * or 'O'.
     *
     * Toggle Output Pin Logic Level
     * The second row uses buttons with virtual switch images. If the pins I/O
     * state is for output, clicking the button will toggle ON and OFF changing
     * the logic level on the pin. If the pin I/O state is for input, the button
     * will not be clickable and will appear grayed out.
     *
     *
     * Read Input Pin Logic Level
     * Pins with their I/O state set to input will be read and the state will be
     * shown in the bottom row by showing a virtual LED as either OFF or ON image.
     * Pins with their I/O state set to output will show a light gray LED image.
     *
     * Revision History
     * Version 1.0 Joe Pardue 6/3/07
     *
```

```
*/

    #region Intitialization

    FT_STATUS ftStatus = 0;
    private UInt32 handle = 0;

    SM_D2YY SM = new SM_D2YY();

    Select_Device dev = new Select_Device();

    // Constants for logic levels
    private const bool ON = true;
    private const bool OFF = false;

    private byte Input = 0;
    private int Output = 0;
    private byte InputC = 0;
    private int OutputC = 0XF0; // Starts with C pins as output

    private bool UseDBus = true; // If false, use CBUS

    // Constants to indicate pin state
    private const bool State_In = true;
    private const bool State_Out = false;

    // Pin State Variables
    private bool D0_IO_State = State_Out;
    private bool D0_OnOff_State = OFF;

    private bool D1_IO_State = State_Out;
    private bool D1_OnOff_State = OFF;

    private bool D2_IO_State = State_Out;
    private bool D2_OnOff_State = OFF;

    private bool D3_IO_State = State_Out;
    private bool D3_OnOff_State = OFF;

    private bool D4_IO_State = State_Out;
    private bool D4_OnOff_State = OFF;

    private bool D5_IO_State = State_Out;
    private bool D5_OnOff_State = OFF;

    private bool D6_IO_State = State_Out;
    private bool D6_OnOff_State = OFF;

    private bool D7_IO_State = State_Out;
    private bool D7_OnOff_State = OFF;

    private bool C0_IO_State = State_Out;
    private bool C0_OnOff_State = OFF;

    private bool C1_IO_State = State_Out;
    private bool C1_OnOff_State = OFF;
```

```
private bool C2_IO_State = State_Out;
private bool C2_OnOff_State = OFF;

private bool C3_IO_State = State_Out;
private bool C3_OnOff_State = OFF;

public Form1()
{
    InitializeComponent();

    LED0.image = (int)LED.LED22.LEDColor.Disabled;
    buttonSD0.ImageIndex = 0;
    buttonSD0.Show();

    LED1.image = (int)LED.LED22.LEDColor.Disabled;
    buttonSD1.ImageIndex = 0;
    buttonSD1.Show();

    LED2.image = (int)LED.LED22.LEDColor.Disabled;
    buttonSD2.ImageIndex = 0;
    buttonSD2.Show();

    LED3.image = (int)LED.LED22.LEDColor.Disabled;
    buttonSD3.ImageIndex = 0;
    buttonSD3.Show();

    LED4.image = (int)LED.LED22.LEDColor.Disabled;
    buttonSD4.ImageIndex = 0;
    buttonSD4.Show();

    LED5.image = (int)LED.LED22.LEDColor.Disabled;
    buttonSD5.ImageIndex = 0;
    buttonSD5.Show();

    LED6.image = (int)LED.LED22.LEDColor.Disabled;
    buttonSD6.ImageIndex = 0;
    buttonSD6.Show();

    LED7.image = (int)LED.LED22.LEDColor.Disabled;
    buttonSD7.ImageIndex = 0;
    buttonSD7.Show();

    LEDC0.image = (int)LED.LED22.LEDColor.Disabled;
    buttonSC0.ImageIndex = 0;
    buttonSC0.Show();

    LEDC1.image = (int)LED.LED22.LEDColor.Disabled;
    buttonSC1.ImageIndex = 0;
    buttonSC1.Show();

    LEDC2.image = (int)LED.LED22.LEDColor.Disabled;
    buttonSC2.ImageIndex = 0;
    buttonSC2.Show();

    LEDC3.image = (int)LED.LED22.LEDColor.Disabled;
    buttonSC3.ImageIndex = 0;
    buttonSC3.Show();
```

```
        groupBoxDBUS.Enabled = true;
        groupBoxCBUS.Enabled = false;

}
#endregion

#region Menu Items

#region Bus select toggle
private void useDBusToolStripMenuItem_Click(object sender, EventArgs e)
{
    if (UseDBus)
    {
        UseDBus = false; // Use C BUS
        useDBusToolStripMenuItem.Text = "Use C BUS";
        groupBoxDBUS.Enabled = false;
        groupBoxCBUS.Enabled = true;
    }
    else
    {
        UseDBus = true; // Use D BUS
        useDBusToolStripMenuItem.Text = "Use D BUS";
        groupBoxDBUS.Enabled = true;
        groupBoxCBUS.Enabled = false;
    }
}
#endregion

#region Select and Open a Device

private void selectDeviceToolStripMenuItem_Click(object sender, wrap
                                                    EventArgs e)
{
    dev.ShowDialog();

    switch (dev.OpenBy)
    {
        case (uint)OPENBY.SERIAL_NUMBER: // use OpenEX
            openBySerialNumber(dev.SerialNumber);
            break;
        case (uint)OPENBY.DESCRIPTION: // use OpenEX
            openByDescription(dev.Description);
            break;
        case (uint)OPENBY.LOCATIONID: // use OpenEX
            openByLocationID(dev.LocID);
            break;
        default:
            MessageBox.Show("ERROR - OpenBy = " + dev.OpenBy.ToString());
            break;
    }
}

// open by serial number
private void openBySerialNumber(string SN)
{
    ftStatus = SM.openSerialNumber(SN, ref handle);
```

276

```
        if (ftStatus != FT_STATUS.FT_OK)
        {
            MessageBox.Show("Error: buttonGet_Click failed to open device");
        }
    }

    // open by description
    private void openByDescription(string description)
    {
        ftStatus = SM.openDescription(description, ref handle);
        if (ftStatus != FT_STATUS.FT_OK)
        {
            MessageBox.Show("Error: buttonGet_Click failed to open port");
        }
    }

    // open by location
    private void openByLocationID(UInt32 locID)
    {
        ftStatus = SM.openLocationID(locID, ref handle);
        if (ftStatus != FT_STATUS.FT_OK)
        {
            MessageBox.Show("Error: buttonGet_Click failed to open port");
        }
    }

    // Assumes device is open
    private void closeDevice()
    {
        SM.closeDevice(handle);
    }

    #endregion

    #endregion

    #region Set I/O State

    private void buttonD0_Click(object sender, EventArgs e)
    {
        if (D0_IO_State == State_In)
        {
            D0_IO_State = State_Out;
            buttonD0.Text = "Out";
            buttonSD0.Enabled = true;
            LED0.image = (int)LED.LED22.LEDColor.Disabled;
            if (getOutputBit0()) { labelD0.Text = "1"; } else wrap
                                                { labelD0.Text = "0"; }
        }
        else
        {
            D0_IO_State = State_In;
            buttonD0.Text = "In";
            buttonSD0.Enabled = false;
            LED0.image = (int)LED.LED22.LEDColor.RedOff;
            labelD0.Text = "X";
        }
```

277

```
    }
private void buttonD1_Click(object sender, EventArgs e)
{
    if (D1_IO_State == State_In)
    {
        D1_IO_State = State_Out;
        buttonD1.Text = "Out";
        buttonSD1.Enabled = true;
        LED1.image = (int)LED.LED22.LEDColor.Disabled;
        if (getOutputBit1()) { labelD1.Text = "1"; } else wrap
                                        { labelD1.Text = "0"; }
    }
    else
    {
        D1_IO_State = State_In;
        buttonD1.Text = "In";
        buttonSD1.Enabled = false;
        LED1.image = (int)LED.LED22.LEDColor.RedOff;
        labelD1.Text = "X";
    }
}
private void buttonD2_Click(object sender, EventArgs e)
{
    if (D2_IO_State == State_In)
    {
        D2_IO_State = State_Out;
        buttonD2.Text = "Out";
        buttonSD2.Enabled = true;
        LED2.image = (int)LED.LED22.LEDColor.Disabled;
        if (getOutputBit2()) { labelD2.Text = "1"; } else wrap
                                        { labelD2.Text = "0"; }
    }
    else
    {
        D2_IO_State = State_In;
        buttonD2.Text = "In";
        buttonSD2.Enabled = false;
        LED2.image = (int)LED.LED22.LEDColor.RedOff;
        labelD2.Text = "X";
    }
}

private void buttonD3_Click(object sender, EventArgs e)
{
    if (D3_IO_State == State_In)
    {
        D3_IO_State = State_Out;
        buttonD3.Text = "Out";
        buttonSD3.Enabled = true;
        LED3.image = (int)LED.LED22.LEDColor.Disabled;
        if (getOutputBit3()) { labelD3.Text = "1"; } else wrap
                                        { labelD3.Text = "0"; }
    }
    else
    {
        D3_IO_State = State_In;
        buttonD3.Text = "In";
```

```
            buttonSD3.Enabled = false;
            LED3.image = (int)LED.LED22.LEDColor.RedOff;
            labelD3.Text = "X";
        }
    }

    private void buttonD4_Click(object sender, EventArgs e)
    {
        if (D4_IO_State == State_In)
        {
            D4_IO_State = State_Out;
            buttonD4.Text = "Out";
            buttonSD4.Enabled = true;
            LED4.image = (int)LED.LED22.LEDColor.Disabled;
            if (getOutputBit4()) { labelD4.Text = "1"; } else wrap
                                         { labelD4.Text = "0"; }
        }
        else
        {
            D4_IO_State = State_In;
            buttonD4.Text = "In";
            buttonSD4.Enabled = false;
            LED4.image = (int)LED.LED22.LEDColor.RedOff;
            labelD4.Text = "X";
        }
    }

    private void buttonD5_Click(object sender, EventArgs e)
    {
        if (D5_IO_State == State_In)
        {
            D5_IO_State = State_Out;
            buttonD5.Text = "Out";
            buttonSD5.Enabled = true;
            LED5.image = (int)LED.LED22.LEDColor.Disabled;
            if (getOutputBit5()) { labelD5.Text = "1"; } else wrap
                                         { labelD5.Text = "0"; }
        }
        else
        {
            D5_IO_State = State_In;
            buttonD5.Text = "In";
            buttonSD5.Enabled = false;
            LED5.image = (int)LED.LED22.LEDColor.RedOff;
            labelD5.Text = "X";
        }
    }

    private void buttonD6_Click(object sender, EventArgs e)
    {
        if (D6_IO_State == State_In)
        {
            D6_IO_State = State_Out;
            buttonD6.Text = "Out";
            buttonSD6.Enabled = true;
            LED6.image = (int)LED.LED22.LEDColor.Disabled;
            if (getOutputBit6()) { labelD6.Text = "1"; } else wrap
```

```
                                                     { labelD6.Text = "0"; }
        }
        else
        {
            D6_IO_State = State_In;
            buttonD6.Text = "In";
            buttonSD6.Enabled = false;
            LED6.image = (int)LED.LED22.LEDColor.RedOff;
            labelD6.Text = "X";
        }
    }

    private void buttonD7_Click(object sender, EventArgs e)
    {
        if (D7_IO_State == State_In)
        {
            D7_IO_State = State_Out;
            buttonD7.Text = "Out";
            buttonSD7.Enabled = true;
            LED7.image = (int)LED.LED22.LEDColor.Disabled;
            if (getOutputBit1()) { labelD7.Text = "1"; } else wrap
                                                 { labelD7.Text = "0"; }
        }
        else
        {
            D7_IO_State = State_In;
            buttonD7.Text = "In";
            buttonSD7.Enabled = false;
            LED7.image = (int)LED.LED22.LEDColor.RedOff;
            labelD7.Text = "X";
        }
    }

    private void buttonC0_Click(object sender, EventArgs e)
    {
        if (C0_IO_State == State_In)
        {
            C0_IO_State = State_Out;
            buttonC0.Text = "Out";
            buttonSC0.Enabled = true;
            LEDC0.image = (int)LED.LED22.LEDColor.Disabled;
        }
        else
        {
            C0_IO_State = State_In;
            buttonC0.Text = "In";
            buttonSC0.Enabled = false;
            LEDC0.image = (int)LED.LED22.LEDColor.RedOff;
            labelC0.Text = "X";
        }
    }

    private void buttonC1_Click(object sender, EventArgs e)
    {
        if (C1_IO_State == State_In)
        {
            C1_IO_State = State_Out;
```

```
            buttonC1.Text = "Out";
            buttonSC1.Enabled - true;
            LEDC1.image = (int)LED.LED22.LEDColor.Disabled;
        }
        else
        {
            C1_IO_State = State_In;
            buttonC1.Text = "In";
            buttonSC1.Enabled = false;
            LEDC1.image = (int)LED.LED22.LEDColor.RedOff;
            labelC1.Text = "X";
        }
    }

    private void buttonC2_Click(object sender, EventArgs e)
    {
        if (C2_IO_State == State_In)
        {
            C2_IO_State = State_Out;
            buttonC2.Text = "Out";
            buttonSC2.Enabled = true;
            LEDC2.image = (int)LED.LED22.LEDColor.Disabled;
            if (getOutputBitC2()) { labelC2.Text = "1"; } else wrap
                                            { labelC2.Text = "0"; }
        }
        else
        {
            C2_IO_State = State_In;
            buttonC2.Text = "In";
            buttonSC2.Enabled = false;
            LEDC2.image = (int)LED.LED22.LEDColor.RedOff;
            labelC2.Text = "X";
        }
    }

    private void buttonC3_Click(object sender, EventArgs e)
    {
        if (C3_IO_State == State_In)
        {
            C3_IO_State = State_Out;
            buttonC3.Text = "Out";
            buttonSC3.Enabled = true;
            LEDC3.image = (int)LED.LED22.LEDColor.Disabled;
        }
        else
        {
            C3_IO_State = State_In;
            buttonC3.Text = "In";
            buttonSC3.Enabled = false;
            LEDC3.image = (int)LED.LED22.LEDColor.RedOff;
            labelC3.Text = "X";
        }
    }

    #endregion

    #region Toggle Output Logic Levels
```

281

```
private void buttonSD0_Click(object sender, EventArgs e)
{
    if (D0_IO_State == State_Out)
    {
        if (D0_OnOff_State == ON)
        {
            D0_OnOff_State = OFF;
            buttonSD0.ImageIndex = 0;
            labelD0.Text = "0";
            if(Output >= 1 )Output -= 1;
        }
        else
        {
            D0_OnOff_State = ON;
            buttonSD0.ImageIndex = 1;
            labelD0.Text = "1";
            Output += 1;
        }
        bitBangOutD((byte)Output);
    }
}

private void buttonSD1_Click(object sender, EventArgs e)
{
    if (D1_IO_State == State_Out)
    {
        if (D1_OnOff_State == ON)
        {
            D1_OnOff_State = OFF;
            buttonSD1.ImageIndex = 0;
            labelD1.Text = "0";
            if (Output >= 2) Output -= 2;
        }
        else
        {
            D1_OnOff_State = ON;
            buttonSD1.ImageIndex = 1;
            labelD1.Text = "1";
            Output += 2;
        }
        bitBangOutD((byte)Output);
    }
}

private void buttonSD2_Click(object sender, EventArgs e)
{
    if (D2_IO_State == State_Out)
    {
        if (D2_OnOff_State == ON)
        {
            D2_OnOff_State = OFF;
            buttonSD2.ImageIndex = 0;
            labelD2.Text = "0";
            if (Output >= 4) Output -= 4;
        }
        else
```

```
                {
                    D2_OnOff_State = ON;
                    buttonSD2.ImageIndex = 1;
                    labelD2.Text = "1";
                    Output += 4;
                }
                bitBangOutD((byte)Output);
        }
    }
    private void buttonSD3_Click(object sender, EventArgs e)
    {
        if (D3_IO_State == State_Out)
        {
            if (D3_OnOff_State == ON)
            {
                D3_OnOff_State = OFF;
                buttonSD3.ImageIndex = 0;
                labelD3.Text = "0";
                if (Output >= 8) Output -= 8;
            }
            else
            {
                D3_OnOff_State = ON;
                buttonSD3.ImageIndex = 1;
                labelD3.Text = "1";
                Output += 8;
            }
            bitBangOutD((byte)Output);
        }
    }

    private void buttonSD4_Click(object sender, EventArgs e)
    {
        if (D4_IO_State == State_Out)
        {
            if (D4_OnOff_State == ON)
            {
                D4_OnOff_State = OFF;
                buttonSD4.ImageIndex = 0;
                labelD4.Text = "0";
                if (Output >= 16) Output -= 16;
            }
            else
            {
                D4_OnOff_State = ON;
                buttonSD4.ImageIndex = 1;
                labelD4.Text = "1";
                Output += 16;
            }
            bitBangOutD((byte)Output);
        }
    }

    private void buttonSD5_Click(object sender, EventArgs e)
    {
        if (D5_IO_State == State_Out)
        {
```

283

```
                    if (D5_OnOff_State == ON)
                    {
                        D5_OnOff_State = OFF;
                        buttonSD5.ImageIndex = 0;
                        labelD5.Text = "0";
                        if (Output >= 32) Output -= 32;
                    }
                    else
                    {
                        D5_OnOff_State = ON;
                        buttonSD5.ImageIndex = 1;
                        labelD5.Text = "1";
                        Output += 32;
                    }
                    bitBangOutD((byte)Output);
            }
        }


        private void buttonSD6_Click(object sender, EventArgs e)
        {
            if (D6_IO_State == State_Out)
            {
                if (D6_OnOff_State == ON)
                {
                    D6_OnOff_State = OFF;
                    buttonSD6.ImageIndex = 0;
                    labelD6.Text = "0";
                    if (Output >= 64) Output -= 64;
                }
                else
                {
                    D6_OnOff_State = ON;
                    buttonSD6.ImageIndex = 1;
                    labelD6.Text = "1";
                    Output += 64;
                }
                bitBangOutD((byte)Output);
            }
        }


        private void buttonSD7_Click(object sender, EventArgs e)
        {
            if (D7_IO_State == State_Out)
            {
                if (D7_OnOff_State == ON)
                {
                    D7_OnOff_State = OFF;
                    buttonSD7.ImageIndex = 0;
                    labelD7.Text = "0";
                    if (Output >= 128) Output -= 128;
                }
                else
                {
                    D7_OnOff_State = ON;
                    buttonSD7.ImageIndex = 1;
                    labelD7.Text = "1";
                    Output += 128;
```

```
            }
            bitBangOutD((byte)Output);
        }
    }

    private void buttonSC0_Click(object sender, EventArgs e)
    {
        if (C0_IO_State == State_Out)
        {
            if (C0_OnOff_State == ON)
            {
                C0_OnOff_State = OFF;
                buttonSC0.ImageIndex = 0;
                labelC0.Text = "0";
                if (OutputC >= 1) OutputC -= 1;
            }
            else
            {
                C0_OnOff_State = ON;
                buttonSC0.ImageIndex = 1;
                labelC0.Text = "1";
                OutputC += 1;
            }
            bitBangOutC((byte)OutputC);
        }
    }

    private void buttonSC1_Click(object sender, EventArgs e)
    {
        if (C1_IO_State == State_Out)
        {
            if (C1_OnOff_State == ON)
            {
                C1_OnOff_State = OFF;
                buttonSC1.ImageIndex = 0;
                labelC1.Text = "0";
                if (OutputC >= 2) OutputC -= 2;
            }
            else
            {
                C1_OnOff_State = ON;
                buttonSC1.ImageIndex = 1;
                labelC1.Text = "1";
                OutputC += 2;
            }
            bitBangOutC((byte)OutputC);
        }
    }

    private void buttonSC2_Click(object sender, EventArgs e)
    {
        if (C2_IO_State == State_Out)
        {
            if (C2_OnOff_State == ON)
            {
                C2_OnOff_State = OFF;
                buttonSC2.ImageIndex = 0;
```

```csharp
                    labelC2.Text = "0";
                    if (OutputC >= 4) OutputC -= 4;
                }
                else
                {
                    C2_OnOff_State = ON;
                    buttonSC2.ImageIndex = 1;
                    labelC2.Text = "1";
                    OutputC += 4;
                }
                bitBangOutC((byte)OutputC);
            }
        }

        private void buttonSC3_Click(object sender, EventArgs e)
        {
            if (C3_IO_State == State_Out)
            {
                if (C3_OnOff_State == ON)
                {
                    C3_OnOff_State = OFF;
                    buttonSC3.ImageIndex = 0;
                    labelC3.Text = "0";
                    if (OutputC >= 8) OutputC -= 8;
                }
                else
                {
                    C3_OnOff_State = ON;
                    buttonSC3.ImageIndex = 1;
                    labelC3.Text = "1";
                    OutputC += 8;
                }
                bitBangOutC((byte)OutputC);
            }
        }
        #endregion

        #region Get Input Bits

        private bool getInputBit0()
        {
            byte bit0 = (byte)Input;

            bit0 = (byte)(bit0 << 7);
            bit0 = (byte)(bit0 >> 7);

            if (bit0 == 1) return true;
            else return false;
        }
        private bool getInputBit1()
        {
            byte bit1 = (byte)Input;

            bit1 = (byte)(bit1 << 6);
            bit1 = (byte)(bit1 >> 7);

            if (bit1 == 1) return true;
```

```
        else return false;
    }
    private bool getInputBit2()
    {
        byte bit2 = (byte)Input;

        bit2 = (byte)(bit2 << 5);
        bit2 = (byte)(bit2 >> 7);

        if (bit2 == 1) return true;
        else return false;
    }

    private bool getInputBit3()
    {
        byte bit3 = (byte)Input;

        bit3 = (byte)(bit3 << 4);
        bit3 = (byte)(bit3 >> 7);

        if (bit3 == 1) return true;
        else return false;
    }

    private bool getInputBit4()
    {
        byte bit4 = (byte)Input;

        bit4 = (byte)(bit4 << 3);
        bit4 = (byte)(bit4 >> 7);

        if (bit4 == 1) return true;
        else return false;
    }

    private bool getInputBit5()
    {
        byte bit5 = (byte)Input;

        bit5 = (byte)(bit5 << 2);
        bit5 = (byte)(bit5 >> 7);

        if (bit5 == 1) return true;
        else return false;
    }

    private bool getInputBit6()
    {
        byte bit6 = (byte)Input;

        bit6 = (byte)(bit6 << 1);
        bit6 = (byte)(bit6 >> 7);

        if (bit6 == 1) return true;
        else return false;
    }
```

```
private bool getInputBit7()
{
    byte bit7 = (byte)Input;

    bit7 = (byte)(bit7 >> 7);

    if (bit7 == 1) return true;
    else return false;
}

private bool getInputBitC0()
{
    byte bit0 = (byte)InputC;

    bit0 = (byte)(bit0 << 7);
    bit0 = (byte)(bit0 >> 7);

    if (bit0 == 1) return true;
    else return false;
}
private bool getInputBitC1()
{
    byte bit1 = (byte)InputC;

    bit1 = (byte)(bit1 << 6);
    bit1 = (byte)(bit1 >> 7);

    if (bit1 == 1) return true;
    else return false;
}
private bool getInputBitC2()
{
    byte bit2 = (byte)InputC;

    bit2 = (byte)(bit2 << 5);
    bit2 = (byte)(bit2 >> 7);

    if (bit2 == 1) return true;
    else return false;
}

private bool getInputBitC3()
{
    byte bit3 = (byte)InputC;

    bit3 = (byte)(bit3 << 4);
    bit3 = (byte)(bit3 >> 7);

    if (bit3 == 1) return true;
    else return false;
}
#endregion

#region Get Output Bits

private bool getOutputBit0()
{
```

```
        byte bit0 = (byte)Output;

        bit0 = (byte)(bit0 << 7);
        bit0 = (byte)(bit0 >> 7);

        if (bit0 == 1) return true;
        else return false;
    }
    private bool getOutputBit1()
    {
        byte bit1 = (byte)Output;

        bit1 = (byte)(bit1 << 6);
        bit1 = (byte)(bit1 >> 7);

        if (bit1 == 1) return true;
        else return false;
    }
    private bool getOutputBit2()
    {
        byte bit2 = (byte)Output;

        bit2 = (byte)(bit2 << 5);
        bit2 = (byte)(bit2 >> 7);

        if (bit2 == 1) return true;
        else return false;
    }

    private bool getOutputBit3()
    {
        byte bit3 = (byte)Output;

        bit3 = (byte)(bit3 << 4);
        bit3 = (byte)(bit3 >> 7);

        if (bit3 == 1) return true;
        else return false;
    }

    private bool getOutputBit4()
    {
        byte bit4 = (byte)Output;

        bit4 = (byte)(bit4 << 3);
        bit4 = (byte)(bit4 >> 7);

        if (bit4 == 1) return true;
        else return false;
    }

    private bool getOutputBit5()
    {
        byte bit5 = (byte)Output;

        bit5 = (byte)(bit5 << 2);
        bit5 = (byte)(bit5 >> 7);
```

```
        if (bit5 == 1) return true;
        else return false;
    }

    private bool getOutputBit6()
    {
        byte bit6 = (byte)Output;

        bit6 = (byte)(bit6 << 1);
        bit6 = (byte)(bit6 >> 7);

        if (bit6 == 1) return true;
        else return false;
    }

    private bool getOutputBit7()
    {
        byte bit7 = (byte)Output;

        bit7 = (byte)(bit7 >> 7);

        if (bit7 == 1) return true;
        else return false;
    }

    private bool getOutputBitC0()
    {
        byte bit0 = (byte)OutputC;

        bit0 = (byte)(bit0 << 7);
        bit0 = (byte)(bit0 >> 7);

        if (bit0 == 1) return true;
        else return false;
    }
    private bool getOutputBitC1()
    {
        byte bit1 = (byte)OutputC;

        bit1 = (byte)(bit1 << 6);
        bit1 = (byte)(bit1 >> 7);

        if (bit1 == 1) return true;
        else return false;
    }
    private bool getOutputBitC2()
    {
        byte bit2 = (byte)OutputC;

        bit2 = (byte)(bit2 << 5);
        bit2 = (byte)(bit2 >> 7);

        if (bit2 == 1) return true;
        else return false;
    }
```

```csharp
private bool getOutputBitC3()
{
    byte bit3 = (byte)OutputC;

    bit3 = (byte)(bit3 << 4);
    bit3 = (byte)(bit3 >> 7);

    if (bit3 == 1) return true;
    else return false;
}
#endregion

#region Read Bus

private void buttonReadDBus_Click(object sender, EventArgs e)
{
    SM.bitBang_GetBitMode(handle, ref Input);

    if (D0_IO_State == State_In)
    {
        if(getInputBit0()){ LED0.image = (int)LED.LED22.LEDColor.RedOff; }
        else {LED0.image = (int)LED.LED22.LEDColor.RedOn; }
    }

    if (D1_IO_State == State_In)
    {
        if getInputBit1()){ LED1.image = (int)LED.LED22.LEDColor.RedOff; }
        else {   LED1.image = (int)LED.LED22.LEDColor.RedOn; }
    }

    if (D2_IO_State == State_In)
    {
        if(getInputBit2()){ LED2.image = (int)LED.LED22.LEDColor.RedOff; }
        else { LED2.image = (int)LED.LED22.LEDColor.RedOn; }
    }

    if (D3_IO_State == State_In)
    {
        if(getInputBit3()){ LED3.image = (int)LED.LED22.LEDColor.RedOff; }
        else { LED3.image = (int)LED.LED22.LEDColor.RedOn; }
    }

    if (D4_IO_State == State_In)
    {
        if(getInputBit4())LED4.image = (int)LED.LED22.LEDColor.RedOff; }
        else { LED4.image = (int)LED.LED22.LEDColor.RedOn; }
    }

    if (D5_IO_State == State_In)
    {
        if(getInputBit5()){ LED5.image = (int)LED.LED22.LEDColor.RedOff; }
        else { LED5.image = (int)LED.LED22.LEDColor.RedOn; }
    }

    if (D6_IO_State == State_In)
    {
        if(getInputBit6()){ LED6.image = (int)LED.LED22.LEDColor.RedOff; }
```

```
            else { LED6.image = (int)LED.LED22.LEDColor.RedOn; }
        }

        if (D7_IO_State == State_In)
        {
            if(getInputBit7()){ LED7.image = (int)LED.LED22.LEDColor.RedOff; }
            else { LED7.image = (int)LED.LED22.LEDColor.RedOn; }
        }
    }

    private void buttonReadCBus_Click(object sender, EventArgs e)
    {
        // Set CBUS pins to I/O state
        byte temp = 0;

        if (C0_IO_State == State_Out)
        {
            temp += 16;
        }

        if (C1_IO_State == State_Out)
        {
            temp += 32;
        }

        if (C0_IO_State == State_Out)
        {
            temp += 64;
        }

        if (C0_IO_State == State_Out)
        {
            temp += 128;
        }

        // Set to input on CBUS pins
        SM.bitBang_SetBitMode(handle, temp, 0x20);

        // Read the input
        SM.bitBang_GetBitMode(handle, ref InputC);

        if (C0_IO_State == State_In)
        {
            if (getInputBitC0()) { LEDC0.image = wrap
                              (int)LED.LED22.LEDColor.RedOff; }
            else { LEDC0.image = (int)LED.LED22.LEDColor.RedOn; }
        }

        if (C1_IO_State == State_In)
        {
            if (getInputBitC1()) { LEDC1.image = wrap
                              (int)LED.LED22.LEDColor.RedOff; }
            else { LEDC1.image = (int)LED.LED22.LEDColor.RedOn; }
        }

        if (C2_IO_State == State_In)
        {
```

```
            if (getInputBitC2()) { LEDC2.image = wrap
                               (int)LED.LED22.LEDColor.RedOff; }
            else { LEDC2.image = (int)LED.LED22.LEDColor.RedOn; }
        }

        if (C3_IO_State == State_In)
        {
            if (getInputBitC3()) { LEDC3.image = wrap
                               (int)LED.LED22.LEDColor.RedOff; }
            else { LEDC3.image = (int)LED.LED22.LEDColor.RedOn; }
        }
    }

    #endregion

    #region Bit-bang Output

    private void bitBangOutD(byte Out)
    {
        SM.bitBang_SetBitMode(handle, Out, 0x01);
    }

    private void bitBangOutC(byte Out)
    {
        SM.bitBang_SetBitMode(handle, Out, 0x20);
    }

    #endregion

    }
}
```

In VB add:

```
Imports Microsoft.VisualBasic
Imports System
Imports System.Collections.Generic
Imports System.ComponentModel
Imports System.Data
Imports System.Drawing
Imports System.Text
Imports System.Windows.Forms

Imports SelectDevice
Imports SMD2XX

Namespace BitBangTest
Partial Public Class Form1
    Inherits Form
    '
    '* The BBUSB allows access to 12 pins that can be configured individually
    '* as either input or output. 8 of these pins are refered to as pins D0 to D7
    '* while the remaining 4 are referred to as pins C0 to C3 (CBUS pins).
    '* The D0-D7 pins I/O state is set using the setMode function. The CBUS
    '* pins must first be set to the I/O mode in EEPROM, then their I/O state
```

```
'* can also be set using the setMode function. CBUS4 is not configurable for
'* I/O.
'*
'* Select Pin State
'* Pin I/O states are selected in the topmost row of buttons.
'* Each button is labeled with the corresponding pin name and clicking the
'* button will toggle the pin I/O state and show that state as either an 'I'
'* or 'O'.
'*
'* Toggle Output Pin Logic Level
'* The second row uses buttons with virtual switch images. If the pins I/O
'* state is for output, clicking the button will toggle ON and OFF changing
'* the logic level on the pin. If the pin I/O state is for input, the button
'* will not be clickable and will appear grayed out.
'*
'*
'* Read Input Pin Logic Level
'* Pins with their I/O state set to input will be read and the state will be
'* shown in the bottom row by showing a virtual LED as either OFF or ON image.
'* Pins with their I/O state set to output will show a light gray LED image.
'*
'* Revision History
'* Version 1.0 Joe Pardue 6/3/07
'*
'

#Region "Intitialization"

    Private ftStatus As FT_STATUS = 0
    Private ftHandle As UInt32 = 0

    Private SM As SM_D2XX = New SM_D2XX()

    Private dev As Select_Device = New Select_Device()

    ' Constants for logic levels
    Private Const [ON] As Boolean = True
    Private Const [OFF] As Boolean = False

    Private Input As Byte = 0
    Private Output As Integer = 0
    Private InputC As Byte = 0
    Private OutputC As Integer = &HF0 ' Starts with C pins as output

    Private UseDBus As Boolean = True ' If false, use CBUS

    ' Constants to indicate pin state
    Private Const State_In As Boolean = True
    Private Const State_Out As Boolean = False

    ' Pin State Variables
    Private D0_IO_State As Boolean = State_Out
    Private D0_OnOff_State As Boolean = [OFF]

    Private D1_IO_State As Boolean = State_Out
    Private D1_OnOff_State As Boolean = [OFF]
```

294

```
Private D2_IO_State As Boolean = State_Out
Private D2_OnOff_State As Boolean = [OFF]

Private D3_IO_State As Boolean = State_Out
Private D3_OnOff_State As Boolean = [OFF]

Private D4_IO_State As Boolean = State_Out
Private D4_OnOff_State As Boolean = [OFF]

Private D5_IO_State As Boolean = State_Out
Private D5_OnOff_State As Boolean = [OFF]

Private D6_IO_State As Boolean = State_Out
Private D6_OnOff_State As Boolean = [OFF]

Private D7_IO_State As Boolean = State_Out
Private D7_OnOff_State As Boolean = [OFF]

Private C0_IO_State As Boolean = State_Out
Private C0_OnOff_State As Boolean = [OFF]

Private C1_IO_State As Boolean = State_Out
Private C1_OnOff_State As Boolean = [OFF]

Private C2_IO_State As Boolean = State_Out
Private C2_OnOff_State As Boolean = [OFF]

Private C3_IO_State As Boolean = State_Out
Private C3_OnOff_State As Boolean = [OFF]

Public Sub New()
    InitializeComponent()

    LED0.image = CInt(Fix(LED.LED22.LEDColor.Disabled))
    buttonSD0.ImageIndex = 0
    buttonSD0.Show()

    LED1.image = CInt(Fix(LED.LED22.LEDColor.Disabled))
    buttonSD1.ImageIndex = 0
    buttonSD1.Show()

    LED2.image = CInt(Fix(LED.LED22.LEDColor.Disabled))
    buttonSD2.ImageIndex = 0
    buttonSD2.Show()

    LED3.image = CInt(Fix(LED.LED22.LEDColor.Disabled))
    buttonSD3.ImageIndex = 0
    buttonSD3.Show()

    LED4.image = CInt(Fix(LED.LED22.LEDColor.Disabled))
    buttonSD4.ImageIndex = 0
    buttonSD4.Show()

    LED5.image = CInt(Fix(LED.LED22.LEDColor.Disabled))
    buttonSD5.ImageIndex = 0
    buttonSD5.Show()
```

295

```
            LED6.image = CInt(Fix(LED.LED22.LEDColor.Disabled))
            buttonSD6.ImageIndex = 0
            buttonSD6.Show()

            LED7.image = CInt(Fix(LED.LED22.LEDColor.Disabled))
            buttonSD7.ImageIndex = 0
            buttonSD7.Show()

            LEDC0.image = CInt(Fix(LED.LED22.LEDColor.Disabled))
            buttonSC0.ImageIndex = 0
            buttonSC0.Show()

            LEDC1.image = CInt(Fix(LED.LED22.LEDColor.Disabled))
            buttonSC1.ImageIndex = 0
            buttonSC1.Show()

            LEDC2.image = CInt(Fix(LED.LED22.LEDColor.Disabled))
            buttonSC2.ImageIndex = 0
            buttonSC2.Show()

            LEDC3.image = CInt(Fix(LED.LED22.LEDColor.Disabled))
            buttonSC3.ImageIndex = 0
            buttonSC3.Show()

            groupBoxDBUS.Enabled = True
            groupBoxCBUS.Enabled = False

        End Sub
#End Region

#Region "Menu Items"

#Region "Bus select toggle"
    Private Sub useDBusToolStripMenuItem_Click(ByVal sender As Object, wrap
                ByVal e As EventArgs) Handles useDBusToolStripMenuItem.Click
        If UseDBus Then
            UseDBus = False ' Use C BUS
            useDBusToolStripMenuItem.Text = "Use C BUS"
            groupBoxDBUS.Enabled = False
            groupBoxCBUS.Enabled = True
        Else
            UseDBus = True ' Use D BUS
            useDBusToolStripMenuItem.Text = "Use D BUS"
            groupBoxDBUS.Enabled = True
            groupBoxCBUS.Enabled = False
        End If
    End Sub
#End Region

#Region "Select and Open a Device"

    Private Sub selectDeviceToolStripMenuItem_Click(ByVal sender As Object, wrap
                ByVal e As EventArgs) Handles selectDeviceToolStripMenuItem.Click
        dev.ShowDialog()

        Select Case dev.OpenBy
            Case CUInt(OPEN_BY.SERIAL_NUMBER) ' use OpenEX
```

```
            openBySerialNumber(dev.SerialNumber)
        Case CUInt(OPEN_BY.DESCRIPTION) ' use OpenEX
            openByDescription(dev.Description)
        Case CUInt(OPEN_BY.LOCATIONID) ' use OpenEX
            openByLocationID(dev.LocID)
        Case Else
            MessageBox.Show("ERROR - OpenBy = " & dev.OpenBy.ToString())
    End Select
End Sub

' open by serial number
Private Sub openBySerialNumber(ByVal SN As String)
    ftStatus = SM.openSerialNumber(SN, ftHandle)
    If ftStatus <> FT_STATUS.FT_OK Then
        MessageBox.Show("Error: buttonGet_Click failed to open device")
    End If
End Sub

' open by description
Private Sub openByDescription(ByVal description As String)
    ftStatus = SM.openDescription(description, ftHandle)
    If ftStatus <> FT_STATUS.FT_OK Then
        MessageBox.Show("Error: buttonGet_Click failed to open port")
    End If
End Sub

' open by location
Private Sub openByLocationID(ByVal locID As UInt32)
    ftStatus = SM.openLocationID(locID, ftHandle)
    If ftStatus <> FT_STATUS.FT_OK Then
        MessageBox.Show("Error: buttonGet_Click failed to open port")
    End If
End Sub

' Assumes device is open
Private Sub closeDevice()
    SM.closeDevice(ftHandle)
End Sub

#End Region

#End Region

#Region "Set I/O State"

    Private Sub buttonD0_Click(ByVal sender As Object, ByVal e As wrap
                                        EventArgs) Handles buttonD0.Click
        If D0_IO_State = State_In Then
            D0_IO_State = State_Out
            buttonD0.Text = "Out"
            buttonSD0.Enabled = True
            LED0.image = CInt(Fix(LED.LED22.LEDColor.Disabled))
            If getOutputBit0() Then
                labelD0.Text = "1"
            Else
                labelD0.Text = "0"
            End If
```

```
        Else
            D0_IO_State = State_In
            buttonD0.Text = "In"
            buttonSD0.Enabled = False
            LED0.image = CInt(Fix(LED.LED22.LEDColor.RedOff))
            labelD0.Text = "X"
        End If
    End Sub
    Private Sub buttonD1_Click(ByVal sender As Object, ByVal e As wrap
                                    EventArgs) Handles buttonD1.Click
        If D1_IO_State = State_In Then
            D1_IO_State = State_Out
            buttonD1.Text = "Out"
            buttonSD1.Enabled = True
            LED1.image = CInt(Fix(LED.LED22.LEDColor.Disabled))
            If getOutputBit1() Then
                labelD1.Text = "1"
            Else
                labelD1.Text = "0"
            End If
        Else
            D1_IO_State = State_In
            buttonD1.Text = "In"
            buttonSD1.Enabled = False
            LED1.image = CInt(Fix(LED.LED22.LEDColor.RedOff))
            labelD1.Text = "X"
        End If
    End Sub
    Private Sub buttonD2_Click(ByVal sender As Object, ByVal e As wrap
                                    EventArgs) Handles buttonD2.Click
        If D2_IO_State = State_In Then
            D2_IO_State = State_Out
            buttonD2.Text = "Out"
            buttonSD2.Enabled = True
            LED2.image = CInt(Fix(LED.LED22.LEDColor.Disabled))
            If getOutputBit2() Then
                labelD2.Text = "1"
            Else
                labelD2.Text = "0"
            End If
        Else
            D2_IO_State = State_In
            buttonD2.Text = "In"
            buttonSD2.Enabled = False
            LED2.image = CInt(Fix(LED.LED22.LEDColor.RedOff))
            labelD2.Text = "X"
        End If
    End Sub

    Private Sub buttonD3_Click(ByVal sender As Object, ByVal e As wrap
                                    EventArgs) Handles buttonD3.Click
        If D3_IO_State = State_In Then
            D3_IO_State = State_Out
            buttonD3.Text = "Out"
            buttonSD3.Enabled = True
            LED3.image = CInt(Fix(LED.LED22.LEDColor.Disabled))
            If getOutputBit3() Then
```

```
                    labelD3.Text = "1"
            Else
                    labelD3.Text = "0"
            End If
        Else
            D3_IO_State = State_In
            buttonD3.Text = "In"
            buttonSD3.Enabled = False
            LED3.image = CInt(Fix(LED.LED22.LEDColor.RedOff))
            labelD3.Text = "X"
        End If
End Sub

Private Sub buttonD4_Click(ByVal sender As Object, ByVal e As wrap
                                    EventArgs) Handles buttonD4.Click
        If D4_IO_State = State_In Then
            D4_IO_State = State_Out
            buttonD4.Text = "Out"
            buttonSD4.Enabled = True
            LED4.image = CInt(Fix(LED.LED22.LEDColor.Disabled))
            If getOutputBit4() Then
                    labelD4.Text = "1"
            Else
                    labelD4.Text = "0"
            End If
        Else
            D4_IO_State = State_In
            buttonD4.Text = "In"
            buttonSD4.Enabled = False
            LED4.image = CInt(Fix(LED.LED22.LEDColor.RedOff))
            labelD4.Text = "X"
        End If
End Sub

Private Sub buttonD5_Click(ByVal sender As Object, ByVal e As wrap
                                    EventArgs) Handles buttonD5.Click
        If D5_IO_State = State_In Then
            D5_IO_State = State_Out
            buttonD5.Text = "Out"
            buttonSD5.Enabled = True
            LED5.image = CInt(Fix(LED.LED22.LEDColor.Disabled))
            If getOutputBit5() Then
                    labelD5.Text = "1"
            Else
                    labelD5.Text = "0"
            End If
        Else
            D5_IO_State = State_In
            buttonD5.Text = "In"
            buttonSD5.Enabled = False
            LED5.image = CInt(Fix(LED.LED22.LEDColor.RedOff))
            labelD5.Text = "X"
        End If
End Sub

Private Sub buttonD6_Click(ByVal sender As Object, ByVal e As wrap
                                    EventArgs) Handles buttonD6.Click
```

```
    If D6_IO_State = State_In Then
        D6_IO_State = State_Out
        buttonD6.Text = "Out"
        buttonSD6.Enabled = True
        LED6.image = CInt(Fix(LED.LED22.LEDColor.Disabled))
        If getOutputBit6() Then
            labelD6.Text = "1"
        Else
            labelD6.Text = "0"
        End If
    Else
        D6_IO_State = State_In
        buttonD6.Text = "In"
        buttonSD6.Enabled = False
        LED6.image = CInt(Fix(LED.LED22.LEDColor.RedOff))
        labelD6.Text = "X"
    End If
End Sub

Private Sub buttonD7_Click(ByVal sender As Object, ByVal e As wrap
                                EventArgs) Handles buttonD7.Click
    If D7_IO_State = State_In Then
        D7_IO_State = State_Out
        buttonD7.Text = "Out"
        buttonSD7.Enabled = True
        LED7.image = CInt(Fix(LED.LED22.LEDColor.Disabled))
        If getOutputBit1() Then
            labelD7.Text = "1"
        Else
            labelD7.Text = "0"
        End If
    Else
        D7_IO_State = State_In
        buttonD7.Text = "In"
        buttonSD7.Enabled = False
        LED7.image = CInt(Fix(LED.LED22.LEDColor.RedOff))
        labelD7.Text = "X"
    End If
End Sub

Private Sub buttonC0_Click(ByVal sender As Object, ByVal e As wrap
                                EventArgs) Handles buttonC0.Click
    If C0_IO_State = State_In Then
        C0_IO_State = State_Out
        buttonC0.Text = "Out"
        buttonSC0.Enabled = True
        LEDC0.image = CInt(Fix(LED.LED22.LEDColor.Disabled))
    Else
        C0_IO_State = State_In
        buttonC0.Text = "In"
        buttonSC0.Enabled = False
        LEDC0.image = CInt(Fix(LED.LED22.LEDColor.RedOff))
        labelC0.Text = "X"
    End If
End Sub

Private Sub buttonC1_Click(ByVal sender As Object, ByVal e As wrap
```

```vbnet
                                                EventArgs) Handles buttonC1.Click
        If C1_IO_State = State_In Then
            C1_IO_State = State_Out
            buttonC1.Text = "Out"
            buttonSC1.Enabled = True
            LEDC1.image = CInt(Fix(LED.LED22.LEDColor.Disabled))
        Else
            C1_IO_State = State_In
            buttonC1.Text = "In"
            buttonSC1.Enabled = False
            LEDC1.image = CInt(Fix(LED.LED22.LEDColor.RedOff))
            labelC1.Text = "X"
        End If
    End Sub

    Private Sub buttonC2_Click(ByVal sender As Object, ByVal e As wrap
                                    EventArgs) Handles buttonC2.Click
        If C2_IO_State = State_In Then
            C2_IO_State = State_Out
            buttonC2.Text = "Out"
            buttonSC2.Enabled = True
            LEDC2.image = CInt(Fix(LED.LED22.LEDColor.Disabled))
            If getOutputBitC2() Then
                labelC2.Text = "1"
            Else
                labelC2.Text = "0"
            End If
        Else
            C2_IO_State = State_In
            buttonC2.Text = "In"
            buttonSC2.Enabled = False
            LEDC2.image = CInt(Fix(LED.LED22.LEDColor.RedOff))
            labelC2.Text = "X"
        End If
    End Sub

    Private Sub buttonC3_Click(ByVal sender As Object, ByVal e As wrap
                                    EventArgs) Handles buttonC3.Click
        If C3_IO_State = State_In Then
            C3_IO_State = State_Out
            buttonC3.Text = "Out"
            buttonSC3.Enabled = True
            LEDC3.image = CInt(Fix(LED.LED22.LEDColor.Disabled))
        Else
            C3_IO_State = State_In
            buttonC3.Text = "In"
            buttonSC3.Enabled = False
            LEDC3.image = CInt(Fix(LED.LED22.LEDColor.RedOff))
            labelC3.Text = "X"
        End If
    End Sub

#End Region

#Region "Toggle Output Logic Levels"

    Private Sub buttonSD0_Click(ByVal sender As Object, ByVal e As wrap
```

```
                                                EventArgs) Handles buttonSD0.Click
        If D0_IO_State = State_Out Then
            If D0_OnOff_State = [ON] Then
                D0_OnOff_State = [OFF]
                buttonSD0.ImageIndex = 0
                labelD0.Text = "0"
                If Output >= 1 Then
                    Output -= 1
                End If
            Else
                D0_OnOff_State = [ON]
                buttonSD0.ImageIndex = 1
                labelD0.Text = "1"
                Output += 1
            End If
            bitBangOutD(CByte(Output))
        End If
End Sub

    Private Sub buttonSD1_Click(ByVal sender As Object, ByVal e As wrap
                                                EventArgs) Handles buttonSD1.Click
        If D1_IO_State = State_Out Then
            If D1_OnOff_State = [ON] Then
                D1_OnOff_State = [OFF]
                buttonSD1.ImageIndex = 0
                labelD1.Text = "0"
                If Output >= 2 Then
                    Output -= 2
                End If
            Else
                D1_OnOff_State = [ON]
                buttonSD1.ImageIndex = 1
                labelD1.Text = "1"
                Output += 2
            End If
            bitBangOutD(CByte(Output))
        End If
End Sub

    Private Sub buttonSD2_Click(ByVal sender As Object, ByVal e As wrap
                                                EventArgs) Handles buttonSD2.Click
        If D2_IO_State = State_Out Then
            If D2_OnOff_State = [ON] Then
                D2_OnOff_State = [OFF]
                buttonSD2.ImageIndex = 0
                labelD2.Text = "0"
                If Output >= 4 Then
                    Output -= 4
                End If
            Else
                D2_OnOff_State = [ON]
                buttonSD2.ImageIndex = 1
                labelD2.Text = "1"
                Output += 4
            End If
            bitBangOutD(CByte(Output))
        End If
```

```
        End Sub
        Private Sub buttonSD3_Click(ByVal sender As Object, ByVal e As wrap
                                                EventArgs) Handles buttonSD3.Click

            If D3_IO_State = State_Out Then
                If D3_OnOff_State = [ON] Then
                    D3_OnOff_State = [OFF]
                    buttonSD3.ImageIndex = 0
                    labelD3.Text = "0"
                    If Output >= 8 Then
                        Output -= 8
                    End If
                Else
                    D3_OnOff_State = [ON]
                    buttonSD3.ImageIndex = 1
                    labelD3.Text = "1"
                    Output += 8
                End If
                bitBangOutD(CByte(Output))
            End If
        End Sub

        Private Sub buttonSD4_Click(ByVal sender As Object, ByVal e As wrap
                                                EventArgs) Handles buttonSD4.Click

            If D4_IO_State = State_Out Then
                If D4_OnOff_State = [ON] Then
                    D4_OnOff_State = [OFF]
                    buttonSD4.ImageIndex = 0
                    labelD4.Text = "0"
                    If Output >= 16 Then
                        Output -= 16
                    End If
                Else
                    D4_OnOff_State = [ON]
                    buttonSD4.ImageIndex = 1
                    labelD4.Text = "1"
                    Output += 16
                End If
                bitBangOutD(CByte(Output))
            End If
        End Sub

        Private Sub buttonSD5_Click(ByVal sender As Object, ByVal e As EventArgs)
Handles buttonSD5.Click
            If D5_IO_State = State_Out Then
                If D5_OnOff_State = [ON] Then
                    D5_OnOff_State = [OFF]
                    buttonSD5.ImageIndex = 0
                    labelD5.Text = "0"
                    If Output >= 32 Then
                        Output -= 32
                    End If
                Else
                    D5_OnOff_State = [ON]
                    buttonSD5.ImageIndex = 1
                    labelD5.Text = "1"
                    Output += 32
                End If
```

```
        bitBangOutD(CByte(Output))
    End If
End Sub

Private Sub buttonSD6_Click(ByVal sender As Object, ByVal e As wrap
                               EventArgs) Handles buttonSD6.Click
    If D6_IO_State = State_Out Then
        If D6_OnOff_State = [ON] Then
            D6_OnOff_State = [OFF]
            buttonSD6.ImageIndex = 0
            labelD6.Text = "0"
            If Output >= 64 Then
                Output -= 64
            End If
        Else
            D6_OnOff_State = [ON]
            buttonSD6.ImageIndex = 1
            labelD6.Text = "1"
            Output += 64
        End If
        bitBangOutD(CByte(Output))
    End If
End Sub

Private Sub buttonSD7_Click(ByVal sender As Object, ByVal e As wrap
                               EventArgs) Handles buttonSD7.Click
    If D7_IO_State = State_Out Then
        If D7_OnOff_State = [ON] Then
            D7_OnOff_State = [OFF]
            buttonSD7.ImageIndex = 0
            labelD7.Text = "0"
            If Output >= 128 Then
                Output -= 128
            End If
        Else
            D7_OnOff_State = [ON]
            buttonSD7.ImageIndex = 1
            labelD7.Text = "1"
            Output += 128
        End If
        bitBangOutD(CByte(Output))
    End If
End Sub

Private Sub buttonSC0_Click(ByVal sender As Object, ByVal e As wrap
                               EventArgs) Handles buttonSC0.Click
    If C0_IO_State = State_Out Then
        If C0_OnOff_State = [ON] Then
            C0_OnOff_State = [OFF]
            buttonSC0.ImageIndex = 0
            labelC0.Text = "0"
            If OutputC >= 1 Then
                OutputC -= 1
            End If
        Else
            C0_OnOff_State = [ON]
            buttonSC0.ImageIndex = 1
```

304

```
            labelC0.Text = "1"
            OutputC += 1
        End If
        bitBangOutC(CByte(OutputC))
    End If
End Sub

Private Sub buttonSC1_Click(ByVal sender As Object, ByVal e As wrap
                                    EventArgs) Handles buttonSC1.Click

    If C1_IO_State = State_Out Then
        If C1_OnOff_State = [ON] Then
            C1_OnOff_State = [OFF]
            buttonSC1.ImageIndex = 0
            labelC1.Text = "0"
            If OutputC >= 2 Then
                OutputC -= 2
            End If
        Else
            C1_OnOff_State = [ON]
            buttonSC1.ImageIndex = 1
            labelC1.Text = "1"
            OutputC += 2
        End If
        bitBangOutC(CByte(OutputC))
    End If
End Sub

Private Sub buttonSC2_Click(ByVal sender As Object, ByVal e As wrap
                                    EventArgs) Handles buttonSC2.Click

    If C2_IO_State = State_Out Then
        If C2_OnOff_State = [ON] Then
            C2_OnOff_State = [OFF]
            buttonSC2.ImageIndex = 0
            labelC2.Text = "0"
            If OutputC >= 4 Then
                OutputC -= 4
            End If
        Else
            C2_OnOff_State = [ON]
            buttonSC2.ImageIndex = 1
            labelC2.Text = "1"
            OutputC += 4
        End If
        bitBangOutC(CByte(OutputC))
    End If
End Sub

Private Sub buttonSC3_Click(ByVal sender As Object, ByVal e As wrap
                                    EventArgs) Handles buttonSC3.Click

    If C3_IO_State = State_Out Then
        If C3_OnOff_State = [ON] Then
            C3_OnOff_State = [OFF]
            buttonSC3.ImageIndex = 0
            labelC3.Text = "0"
            If OutputC >= 8 Then
                OutputC -= 8
            End If
```

```
                Else
                    C3_OnOff_State = [ON]
                    buttonSC3.ImageIndex = 1
                    labelC3.Text = "1"
                    OutputC += 8
                End If
                bitBangOutC(CByte(OutputC))
            End If
        End Sub
#End Region

#Region "Get Input Bits"

    Private Function getInputBit0() As Boolean
        Dim bit0 As Byte = CByte(Input)

        bit0 = CByte(bit0 << 7)
        bit0 = CByte(bit0 >> 7)

        If bit0 = 1 Then
            Return True
        Else
            Return False
        End If
    End Function
    Private Function getInputBit1() As Boolean
        Dim bit1 As Byte = CByte(Input)

        bit1 = CByte(bit1 << 6)
        bit1 = CByte(bit1 >> 7)

        If bit1 = 1 Then
            Return True
        Else
            Return False
        End If
    End Function
    Private Function getInputBit2() As Boolean
        Dim bit2 As Byte = CByte(Input)

        bit2 = CByte(bit2 << 5)
        bit2 = CByte(bit2 >> 7)

        If bit2 = 1 Then
            Return True
        Else
            Return False
        End If
    End Function

    Private Function getInputBit3() As Boolean
        Dim bit3 As Byte = CByte(Input)

        bit3 = CByte(bit3 << 4)
        bit3 = CByte(bit3 >> 7)

        If bit3 = 1 Then
```

```
            Return True
        Else
            Return False
        End If
End Function

Private Function getInputBit4() As Boolean
        Dim bit4 As Byte = CByte(Input)

        bit4 = CByte(bit4 << 3)
        bit4 = CByte(bit4 >> 7)

        If bit4 = 1 Then
            Return True
        Else
            Return False
        End If
End Function

Private Function getInputBit5() As Boolean
        Dim bit5 As Byte = CByte(Input)

        bit5 = CByte(bit5 << 2)
        bit5 = CByte(bit5 >> 7)

        If bit5 = 1 Then
            Return True
        Else
            Return False
        End If
End Function

Private Function getInputBit6() As Boolean
        Dim bit6 As Byte = CByte(Input)

        bit6 = CByte(bit6 << 1)
        bit6 = CByte(bit6 >> 7)

        If bit6 = 1 Then
            Return True
        Else
            Return False
        End If
End Function

Private Function getInputBit7() As Boolean
        Dim bit7 As Byte = CByte(Input)

        bit7 = CByte(bit7 >> 7)

        If bit7 = 1 Then
            Return True
        Else
            Return False
        End If
End Function
```

```vbnet
    Private Function getInputBitC0() As Boolean
        Dim bit0 As Byte = CByte(InputC)

        bit0 = CByte(bit0 << 7)
        bit0 = CByte(bit0 >> 7)

        If bit0 = 1 Then
            Return True
        Else
            Return False
        End If
    End Function
    Private Function getInputBitC1() As Boolean
        Dim bit1 As Byte = CByte(InputC)

        bit1 = CByte(bit1 << 6)
        bit1 = CByte(bit1 >> 7)

        If bit1 = 1 Then
            Return True
        Else
            Return False
        End If
    End Function
    Private Function getInputBitC2() As Boolean
        Dim bit2 As Byte = CByte(InputC)

        bit2 = CByte(bit2 << 5)
        bit2 = CByte(bit2 >> 7)

        If bit2 = 1 Then
            Return True
        Else
            Return False
        End If
    End Function

    Private Function getInputBitC3() As Boolean
        Dim bit3 As Byte = CByte(InputC)

        bit3 = CByte(bit3 << 4)
        bit3 = CByte(bit3 >> 7)

        If bit3 = 1 Then
            Return True
        Else
            Return False
        End If
    End Function
#End Region

#Region "Get Output Bits"

    Private Function getOutputBit0() As Boolean
        Dim bit0 As Byte = CByte(Output)

        bit0 = CByte(bit0 << 7)
```

308

```
    bit0 = CByte(bit0 >> 7)

    If bit0 = 1 Then
        Return True
    Else
        Return False
    End If
End Function
Private Function getOutputBit1() As Boolean
    Dim bit1 As Byte = CByte(Output)

    bit1 = CByte(bit1 << 6)
    bit1 = CByte(bit1 >> 7)

    If bit1 = 1 Then
        Return True
    Else
        Return False
    End If
End Function
Private Function getOutputBit2() As Boolean
    Dim bit2 As Byte = CByte(Output)

    bit2 = CByte(bit2 << 5)
    bit2 = CByte(bit2 >> 7)

    If bit2 = 1 Then
        Return True
    Else
        Return False
    End If
End Function

Private Function getOutputBit3() As Boolean
    Dim bit3 As Byte = CByte(Output)

    bit3 = CByte(bit3 << 4)
    bit3 = CByte(bit3 >> 7)

    If bit3 = 1 Then
        Return True
    Else
        Return False
    End If
End Function

Private Function getOutputBit4() As Boolean
    Dim bit4 As Byte = CByte(Output)

    bit4 = CByte(bit4 << 3)
    bit4 = CByte(bit4 >> 7)

    If bit4 = 1 Then
        Return True
    Else
        Return False
    End If
```

309

```vbnet
    End Function

    Private Function getOutputBit5() As Boolean
        Dim bit5 As Byte = CByte(Output)

        bit5 = CByte(bit5 << 2)
        bit5 = CByte(bit5 >> 7)

        If bit5 = 1 Then
            Return True
        Else
            Return False
        End If
End Function

    Private Function getOutputBit6() As Boolean
        Dim bit6 As Byte = CByte(Output)

        bit6 = CByte(bit6 << 1)
        bit6 = CByte(bit6 >> 7)

        If bit6 = 1 Then
            Return True
        Else
            Return False
        End If
End Function

    Private Function getOutputBit7() As Boolean
        Dim bit7 As Byte = CByte(Output)

        bit7 = CByte(bit7 >> 7)

        If bit7 = 1 Then
            Return True
        Else
            Return False
        End If
End Function

    Private Function getOutputBitC0() As Boolean
        Dim bit0 As Byte = CByte(OutputC)

        bit0 = CByte(bit0 << 7)
        bit0 = CByte(bit0 >> 7)

        If bit0 = 1 Then
            Return True
        Else
            Return False
        End If
End Function
    Private Function getOutputBitC1() As Boolean
        Dim bit1 As Byte = CByte(OutputC)

        bit1 = CByte(bit1 << 6)
        bit1 = CByte(bit1 >> 7)
```

310

```
        If bit1 = 1 Then
            Return True
        Else
            Return False
        End If
    End Function
    Private Function getOutputBitC2() As Boolean
        Dim bit2 As Byte = CByte(OutputC)

        bit2 = CByte(bit2 << 5)
        bit2 = CByte(bit2 >> 7)

        If bit2 = 1 Then
            Return True
        Else
            Return False
        End If
    End Function

    Private Function getOutputBitC3() As Boolean
        Dim bit3 As Byte = CByte(OutputC)

        bit3 = CByte(bit3 << 4)
        bit3 = CByte(bit3 >> 7)

        If bit3 = 1 Then
            Return True
        Else
            Return False
        End If
    End Function
#End Region

#Region "Read Bus"

    Private Sub buttonReadDBus_Click(ByVal sender As Object, ByVal e As wrap
                                EventArgs) Handles buttonReadDBus.Click
        SM.bitBang_GetBitMode(ftHandle, Input)

        If D0_IO_State = State_In Then
            If getInputBit0() Then
                LED0.image = CInt(Fix(LED.LED22.LEDColor.RedOff))
            Else
                LED0.image = CInt(Fix(LED.LED22.LEDColor.RedOn))
            End If
        End If

        If D1_IO_State = State_In Then
            If getInputBit1() Then
                LED1.image = CInt(Fix(LED.LED22.LEDColor.RedOff))
            Else
                LED1.image = CInt(Fix(LED.LED22.LEDColor.RedOn))
            End If
        End If

        If D2_IO_State = State_In Then
```

```
        If getInputBit2() Then
            LED2.image = CInt(Fix(LED.LED22.LEDColor.RedOff))
        Else
            LED2.image = CInt(Fix(LED.LED22.LEDColor.RedOn))
        End If
    End If

    If D3_IO_State = State_In Then
        If getInputBit3() Then
            LED3.image = CInt(Fix(LED.LED22.LEDColor.RedOff))
        Else
            LED3.image = CInt(Fix(LED.LED22.LEDColor.RedOn))
        End If
    End If

    If D4_IO_State = State_In Then
        If getInputBit4() Then
            LED4.image = CInt(Fix(LED.LED22.LEDColor.RedOff))
        Else
            LED4.image = CInt(Fix(LED.LED22.LEDColor.RedOn))
        End If
    End If

    If D5_IO_State = State_In Then
        If getInputBit5() Then
            LED5.image = CInt(Fix(LED.LED22.LEDColor.RedOff))
        Else
            LED5.image = CInt(Fix(LED.LED22.LEDColor.RedOn))
        End If
    End If

    If D6_IO_State = State_In Then
        If getInputBit6() Then
            LED6.image = CInt(Fix(LED.LED22.LEDColor.RedOff))
        Else
            LED6.image = CInt(Fix(LED.LED22.LEDColor.RedOn))
        End If
    End If

    If D7_IO_State = State_In Then
        If getInputBit7() Then
            LED7.image = CInt(Fix(LED.LED22.LEDColor.RedOff))
        Else
            LED7.image = CInt(Fix(LED.LED22.LEDColor.RedOn))
        End If
    End If
End Sub

Private Sub buttonReadCBus_Click(ByVal sender As Object, ByVal e As wrap
                                EventArgs) Handles buttonReadCBus.Click
    ' Set CBUS pins to I/O state
    Dim temp As Byte = 0

    If C0_IO_State = State_Out Then
        temp += Convert.ToByte(16)
    End If
```

```
        If C1_IO_State = State_Out Then
            temp += Convert.ToByte(32)
        End If

        If C0_IO_State = State_Out Then
            temp += Convert.ToByte(64)
        End If

        If C0_IO_State = State_Out Then
            temp += Convert.ToByte(128)
        End If

        ' Set to input on CBUS pins
        SM.bitBang_SetBitMode(ftHandle, temp, &H20)

        ' Read the input
        SM.bitBang_GetBitMode(ftHandle, InputC)

        If C0_IO_State = State_In Then
            If getInputBitC0() Then
                LEDC0.image = CInt(Fix(LED.LED22.LEDColor.RedOff))
            Else
                LEDC0.image = CInt(Fix(LED.LED22.LEDColor.RedOn))
            End If
        End If

        If C1_IO_State = State_In Then
            If getInputBitC1() Then
                LEDC1.image = CInt(Fix(LED.LED22.LEDColor.RedOff))
            Else
                LEDC1.image = CInt(Fix(LED.LED22.LEDColor.RedOn))
            End If
        End If

        If C2_IO_State = State_In Then
            If getInputBitC2() Then
                LEDC2.image = CInt(Fix(LED.LED22.LEDColor.RedOff))
            Else
                LEDC2.image = CInt(Fix(LED.LED22.LEDColor.RedOn))
            End If
        End If

        If C3_IO_State = State_In Then
            If getInputBitC3() Then
                LEDC3.image = CInt(Fix(LED.LED22.LEDColor.RedOff))
            Else
                LEDC3.image = CInt(Fix(LED.LED22.LEDColor.RedOn))
            End If
        End If
    End Sub

#End Region

#Region "Bit-bang Output"

    Private Sub bitBangOutD(ByVal Out As Byte)
        SM.bitBang_SetBitMode(ftHandle, Out, &H1)
```

```
    End Sub

    Private Sub bitBangOutC(ByVal Out As Byte)
        SM.bitBang_SetBitMode(ftHandle, Out, &H20)
    End Sub

#End Region

End Class
End Namespace
```

Chapter 18: Bit-Banging – Hardware Experiments

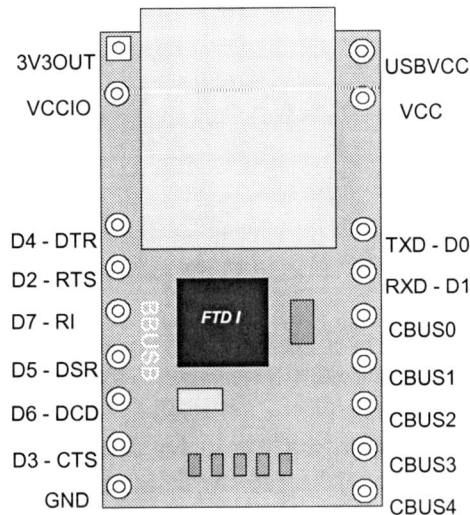

```
        3V3OUT ◎              ◎ USBVCC
         VCCIO ◎              ◎ VCC


       D4 - DTR ◎             ◎ TXD - D0
       D2 - RTS ◎             ◎ RXD - D1
        D7 - RI ◎    FTD I    ◎ CBUS0
       D5 - DSR ◎             ◎ CBUS1
       D6 - DCD ◎             ◎ CBUS2
       D3 - CTS ◎             ◎ CBUS3
           GND ◎              ◎ CBUS4
```

Despite the markings on the BBUSB, those pins lead a double life as shown above. The D Bus pins all have modem pin alias that they use when sneaking around in the underworld of serial communications, but for these experiments, we will use the D Bus names D0 to D7. Note that the pins are scattered about in no logical order. This wasn't done just to confuse you. (Really.) And do remember the discussion in the last chapter about 'Funky Logic', now is when the funk splats on the wall, so be prepared for a mess.

Output

We will test bit-banged output using LEDs that have their anodes tied to Vcc via 2.2k ohm resistors and their cathodes tied to a FT232R pin. When the pin is high, no current flows and the LED is off, when the pin is low, current flows and the LED is on. The fun starts when we try to remember true/false logic of which bit state is low and which is high since it differs for the D Bus and the C Bus. The D Bus On state is low and the C Bus On bit state is high.

Output on the D Bus

On a breadboard, place a BBUSB, 8-positon DIP switch, 8 LEDs, and 8 2.2k ohm resistors as shown:

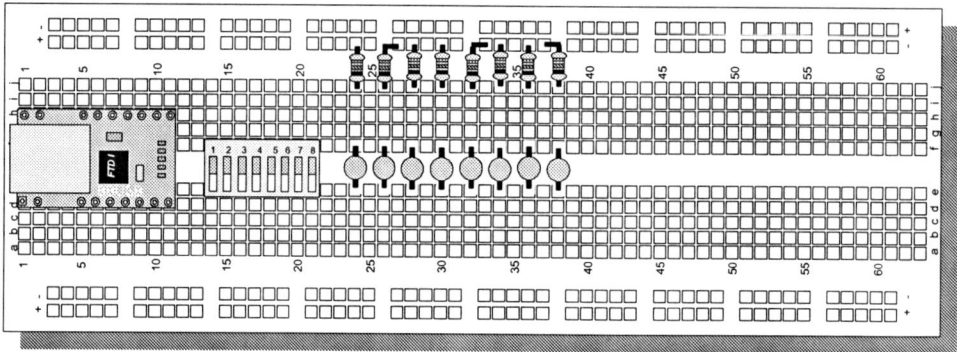

Wire the BBUSB for 5 volts as shown in an earlier chapter, then wire up the switch, LEDs, and resistors according to the following schematic:

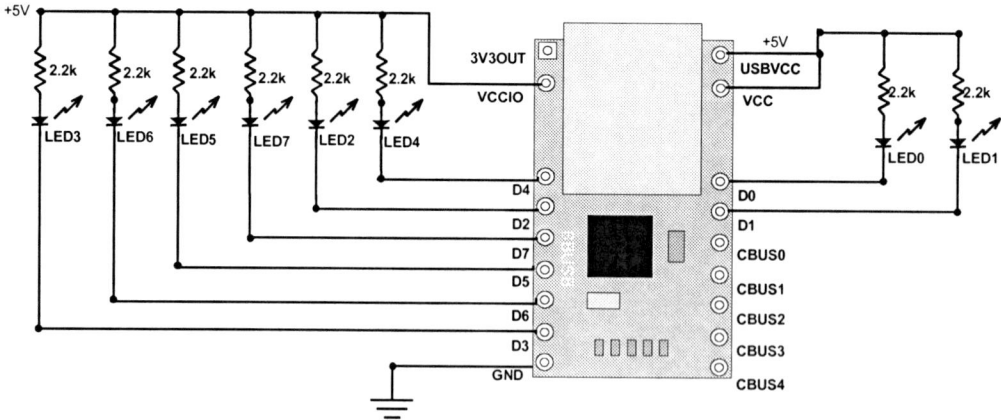

Which should look something like the following:

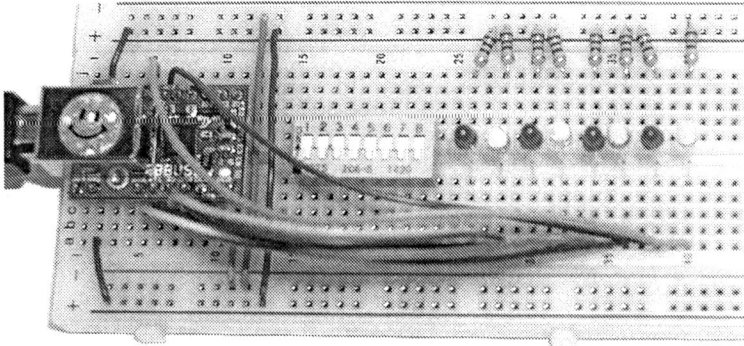

Open the Bit-bang Test program and select the BBUSB. Now, if you've done everything right (and if you are like me you haven't) when you flip the virtual switches as shown below you will output 0xAA which will then light up the LEDs in a 0x55 pattern (extra credit if you remember why.)

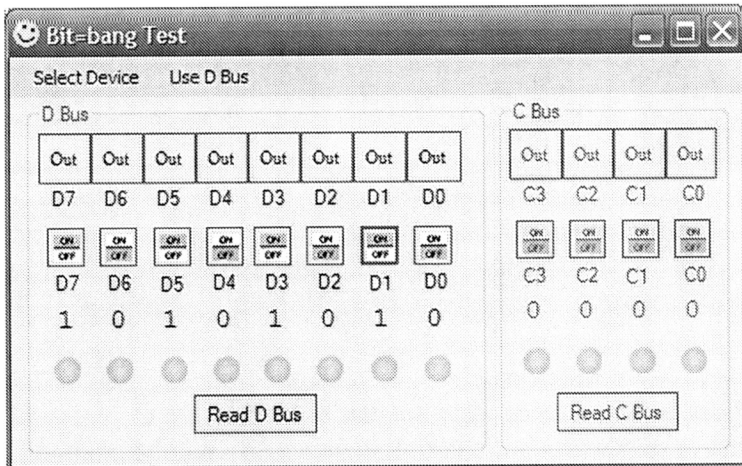

Output on the C Bus

Rewire to the following schematic:

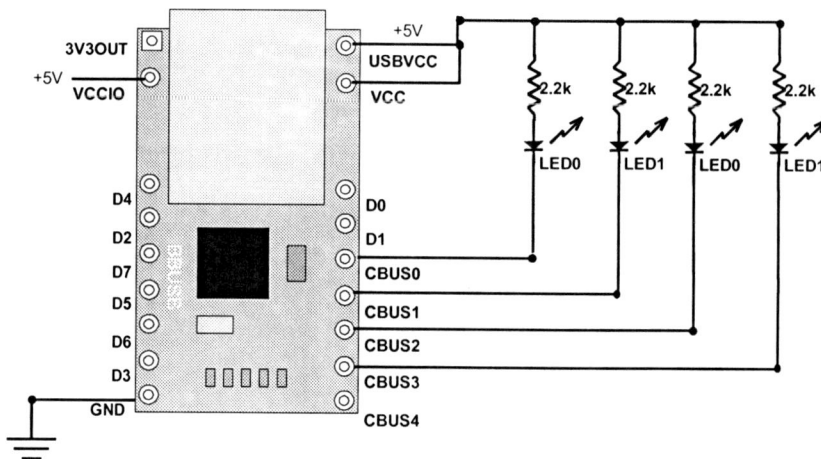

Which should look like:

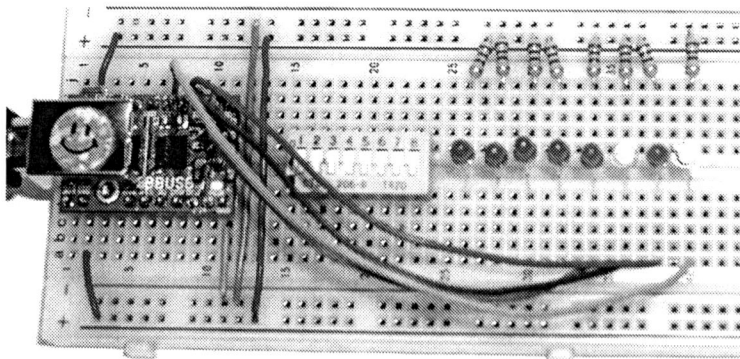

Toggle the 'Use D Bus' menu item so that it reads 'Use C Bus' and the D Bus groupBox will be disabled while the C Bus groupBox will be enabled.

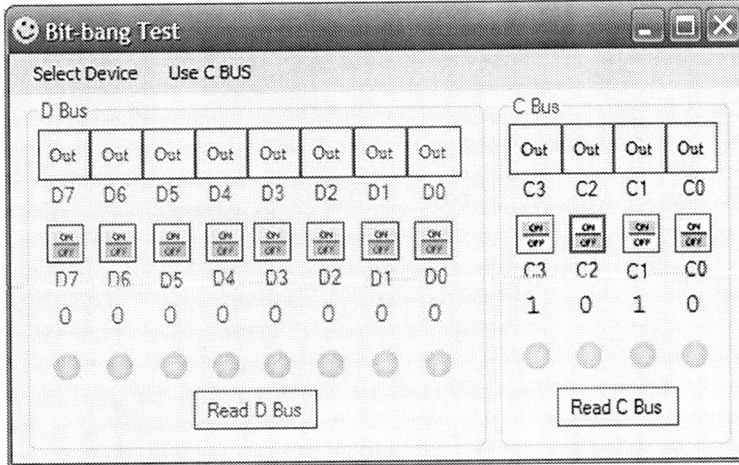

Input

Before beginning this, note that the 8-position DIP switch is numbered left to right 1, 2, 3, 4, 5, 6, 7, 8 but we will ignore those numbers and think of it as a binary sequence with the least bit on the right and thus numbered 7, 6, 5, 4, 3, 2, 1, 0 this will further our confusion making this experiment even more like the real world.

We will wire the pins to a 2.2k ohm resistor to ground and to the switch that when closed will connect the pin directly to ground.

Input on the D Bus

Rewire the breadboard according to the following schematic:

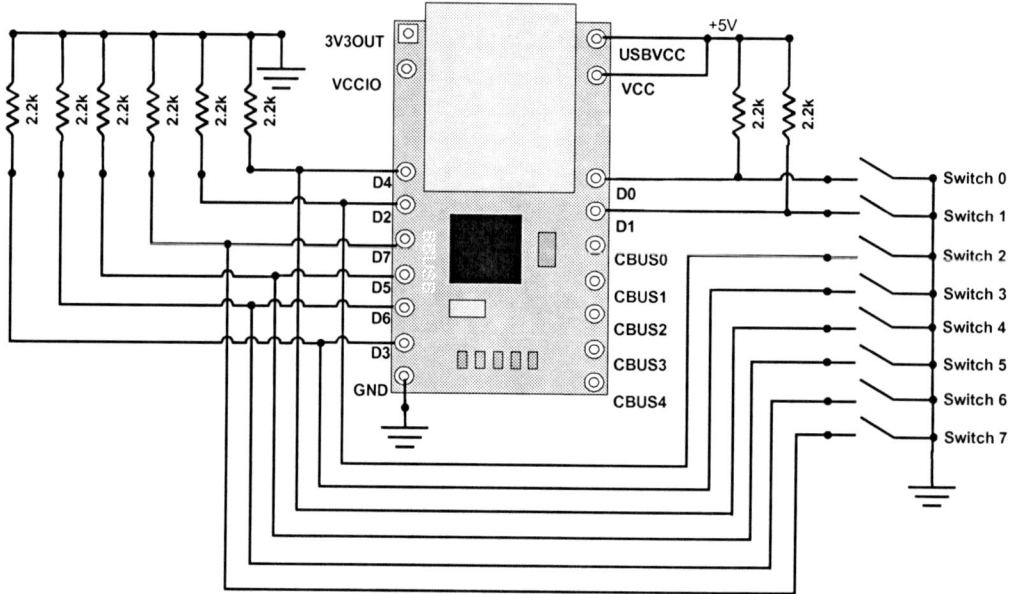

Which should look something like:

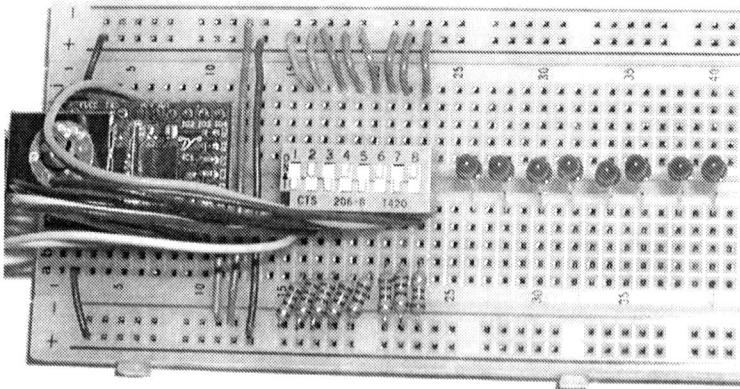

In the Bit-bang Test program click on all the buttons on the top row of the D Bus groupBox to convert each pin to an input.

320

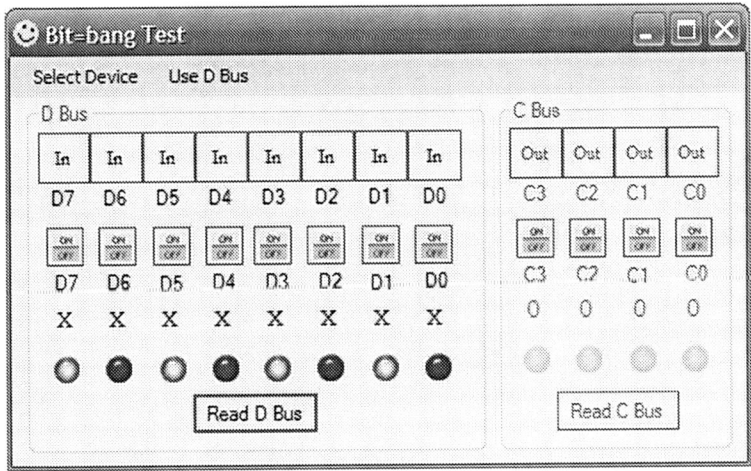

Input on the C Bus

By now you know the drill, so wire up things for the C Bus and run the test.

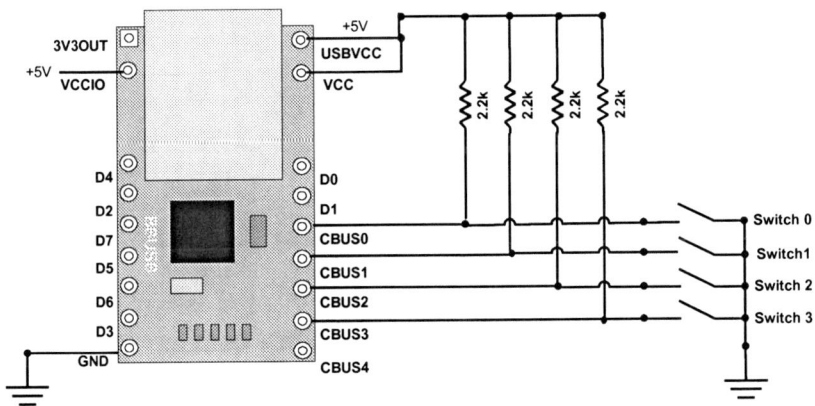

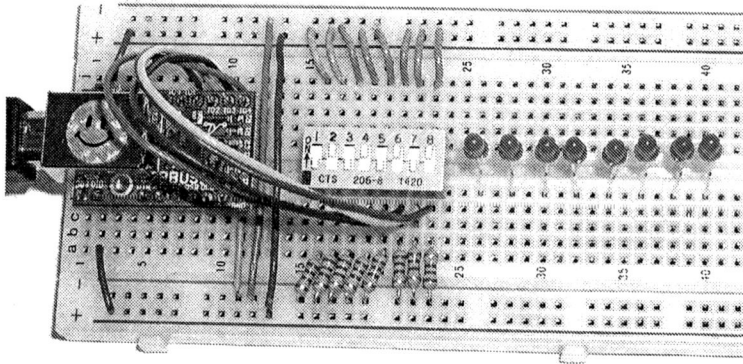

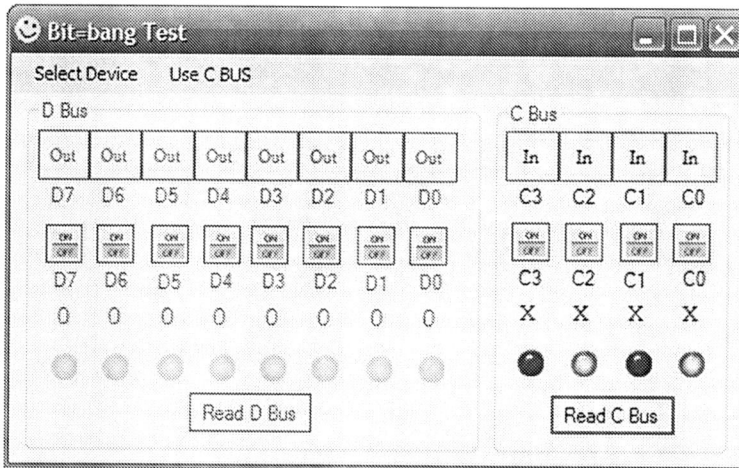

Well, all that was cool, but how about we use all this for something really useful, like a USB based very small scrolling message sign – coming right up.

Chapter 19: Bit-Banging – 7-Segment LED

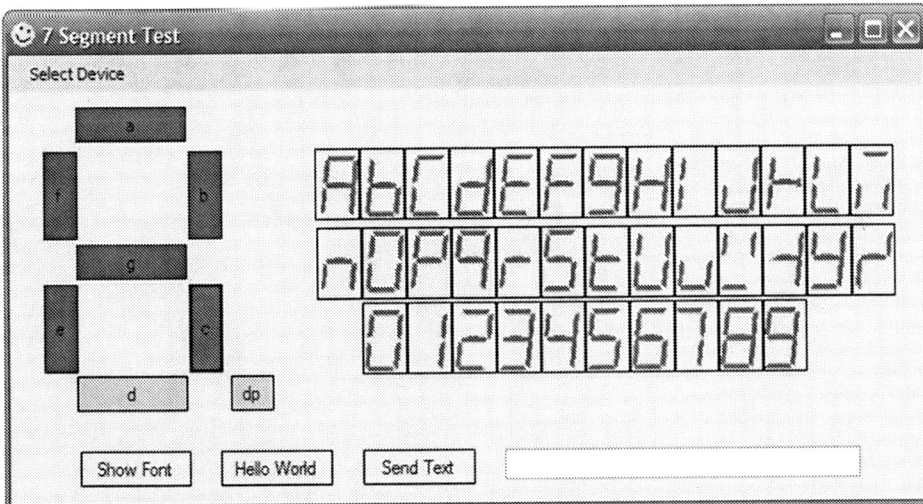

Our code will also allow us to set or clear each segment, select a character to show from a font matrix, show the whole font one character at a time, and output the classic 'HELLO WORLD' at the press of a button. And we will build in a feature that will allow us to enter a string of characters up to 64 characters and have them scroll on the 7-Seg LED by flashing each character in sequence. Some folks think you need to show at least 6 characters or so at one time and to show a longer message, you need to scroll the characters, and while that is certainly easier to read, using one 7-Seg LED will get across the message if the reader pays attention.

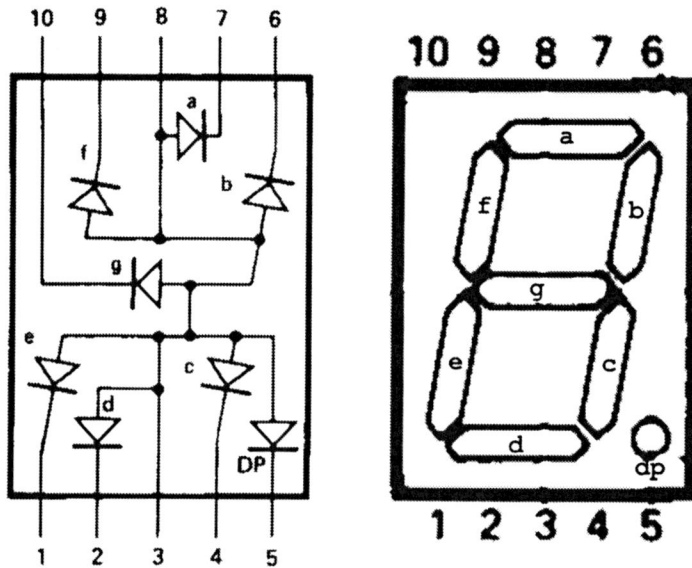

Note that although this is a 7-Segment LED, it actually has 8-Segments when you include the decimal point, so one byte can be used to code each segment on or off.

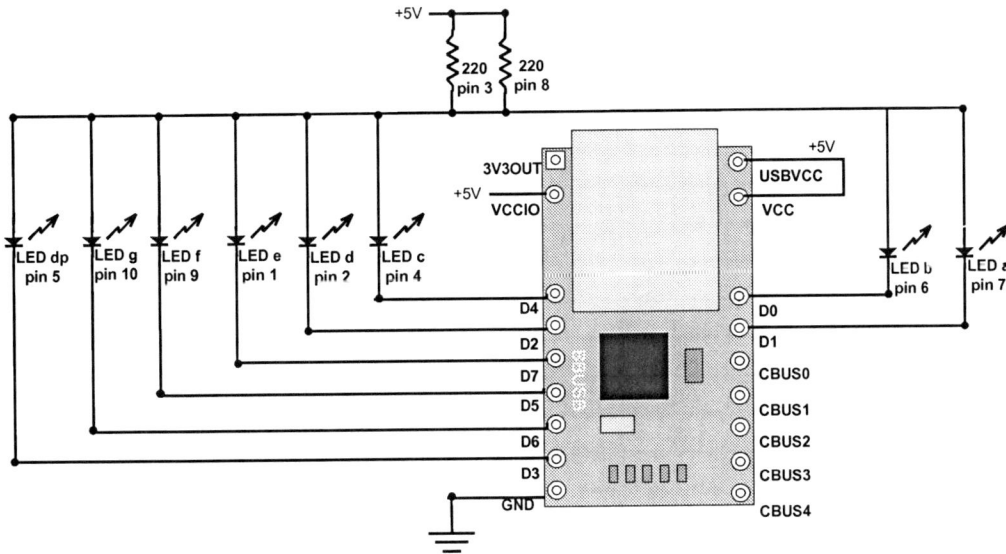

The wiring diagram looks much like the one for output to the 8 LEDs in the last chapter, and it is with the main exception that the LEDs have two common resistors between pin 3 and +5 and pin 8 and +5.

Character Codes for 7-Segment LED

The following table shows the byte value that when applied to the segments causes them to light up in a pattern for each character in our font. Of the 256 possible values only 36 are actually used.

Dp	g	f	e	d	c	b	a		
7	6	5	4	3	2	1	0		
0	1	1	1	0	1	1	1	A	0x77
0	1	1	1	1	1	0	0	B	0x7C
0	0	1	1	1	0	0	1	C	0x39
0	1	0	1	1	1	1	0	D	0x5E
0	1	1	1	1	0	0	1	E	0x79
0	1	1	1	0	0	0	1	F	0x71
0	1	1	0	1	1	1	1	G	0x6F

0	1	1	1	0	1	1	0	**H**	0x76
0	0	1	1	0	0	0	0	**I**	0x30
0	0	0	1	1	1	1	0	**J**	0x1E
0	1	1	1	0	0	0	0	**K**	0x70
0	0	1	1	1	0	0	0	**L**	0x38
0	0	0	1	0	1	0	1	**M**	0x15
0	1	0	1	0	1	0	0	**N**	0x54
0	0	1	1	1	1	1	1	**O**	0x3F
0	1	1	1	0	0	1	1	**P**	0x73
0	1	1	0	0	1	1	1	**Q**	0x67
0	1	0	1	0	0	0	0	**R**	0x50
0	1	1	0	1	1	0	1	**S**	0x6D
0	1	1	1	1	0	0	0	**T**	0x78
0	0	1	1	1	1	1	0	**U**	0x3E
0	0	0	1	1	1	0	0	**V**	0x1C
0	0	1	0	1	0	1	0	**W**	0x2A
0	1	0	0	0	1	1	0	**X**	0x46
0	1	1	0	1	1	1	0	**Y**	0x6E
0	1	0	1	0	0	1	0	**Z**	0x52
0	0	1	1	1	1	1	1	**0**	0x3F
0	0	0	0	0	1	1	0	**1**	0x06
0	1	0	1	1	0	1	1	**2**	0x5B
0	1	0	0	1	1	1	1	**3**	0x4F
0	1	1	0	0	1	1	0	**4**	0x66
0	1	1	0	1	1	0	1	**5**	0x6D
0	1	1	1	1	1	0	1	**6**	0x7D
0	0	0	0	0	1	1	1	**7**	0x07
0	1	1	1	1	1	1	1	**8**	0x7F
0	1	1	0	1	1	1	1	**9**	0x6F

As in the last chapter, we will assume you have developed sufficient expertise that you can look at the form and the code and write this program with out additional kibitzing.

7-Segment LED Tester in C#

```csharp
using System;
using System.Collections.Generic;
using System.ComponentModel;
using System.Data;
using System.Drawing;
using System.Text;
using System.Windows.Forms;

using SMD2XX;
using SelectDevice;

namespace Segment_Test
{

    public partial class Form1 : Form
    {

        #region intialization
        FT_STATUS ftStatus = 0;
        private UInt32 handle = 0;

        SM_D2XX SM = new SM_D2XX();

        Select_Device dev = new Select_Device();

        private byte Output = 0;
        public Form1()
        {
            InitializeComponent();
        }
        #endregion

        #region Segment Buttons
        private void buttona_Click(object sender, EventArgs e)
        {
            if (buttona.BackColor == Color.LightGray)
            {
                buttona.BackColor = Color.Red;
                Output += 0x01;
            }
            else
            {
                buttona.BackColor = Color.LightGray;
                if (Output >= 0x01) Output -= 0x01;
            }

            bitBangOutD(Output);
        }

        private void buttonb_Click(object sender, EventArgs e)
        {
```

327

```
        if (buttonb.BackColor == Color.LightGray)
        {
            buttonb.BackColor = Color.Red;
            Output += 0x02;
        }
        else
        {
            buttonb.BackColor = Color.LightGray;
            if (Output >= 0x02) Output -= 0x02;
        }

        bitBangOutD(Output);
}

private void buttonc_Click(object sender, EventArgs e)
{
    if (buttonc.BackColor == Color.LightGray)
    {
        buttonc.BackColor = Color.Red;
        Output += 0x04;
    }
    else
    {
        buttonc.BackColor = Color.LightGray;
        if (Output >= 0x04) Output -= 0x04;
    }

    bitBangOutD(Output);
}

private void buttond_Click(object sender, EventArgs e)
{
    if (buttond.BackColor == Color.LightGray)
    {
        buttond.BackColor = Color.Red;
        Output += 0x08;
    }
    else
    {
        buttond.BackColor = Color.LightGray;
        if (Output >= 0x08) Output -= 0x08;
    }

    bitBangOutD(Output);
}

private void buttone_Click(object sender, EventArgs e)
{
    if (buttone.BackColor == Color.LightGray)
    {
        buttone.BackColor = Color.Red;
        Output += 0x10;
    }
    else
    {
        buttone.BackColor = Color.LightGray;
        if (Output >= 0x10) Output -= 0x10;
```

```
        }

    bitBangOutD(Output);
}

private void buttonf_Click(object sender, EventArgs e)
{
    if (buttonf.BackColor == Color.LightGray)
    {
        buttonf.BackColor = Color.Red;
        Output += 0x20;
    }
    else
    {
        buttonf.BackColor = Color.LightGray;
        if (Output >= 0x20) Output -= 0x20;
    }

    bitBangOutD(Output);
}

private void buttong_Click(object sender, EventArgs e)
{
    if (buttong.BackColor == Color.LightGray)
    {
        buttong.BackColor = Color.Red;
        Output += 0x40;
    }
    else
    {
        buttong.BackColor = Color.LightGray;
        if (Output >= 0x40) Output -= 0x40;
    }

    bitBangOutD(Output);
}

private void buttondp_Click(object sender, EventArgs e)
{
    if (buttondp.BackColor == Color.LightGray)
    {
        buttondp.BackColor = Color.Red;
        Output += 0x80;
    }
    else
    {
        buttondp.BackColor = Color.LightGray;
        if (Output >= 0x80) Output -= 0x80;
    }

    bitBangOutD(Output);
}
#endregion

#region Select and Open a Device

private void selectDeviceToolStripMenuItem_Click_1( wrap
```

329

```
                                         object sender, EventArgs e)
    {
        dev.ShowDialog();

        switch (dev.OpenBy)
        {
            case (uint)OPENBY.SERIAL_NUMBER: // use OpenEX
                openBySerialNumber(dev.SerialNumber);
                break;
            case (uint)OPENBY.DESCRIPTION: // use OpenEX
                openByDescription(dev.Description);
                break;
            case (uint)OPENBY.LOCATIONID: // use OpenEX
                openByLocationID(dev.LocID);
                break;
            default:
                MessageBox.Show("ERROR - OpenBy = " + dev.OpenBy.ToString());
                break;
        }
    }

    // open by serial number
    private void openBySerialNumber(string SN)
    {
        ftStatus = SM.openSerialNumber(SN, ref handle);
        if (ftStatus != FT_STATUS.FT_OK)
        {
            MessageBox.Show("Error: buttonGet_Click failed to open device");
        }
    }

    // open by description
    private void openByDescription(string description)
    {
        ftStatus = SM.openDescription(description, ref handle);
        if (ftStatus != FT_STATUS.FT_OK)
        {
            MessageBox.Show("Error: buttonGet_Click failed to open port");
        }
    }

    // open by location
    private void openByLocationID(UInt32 locID)
    {
        ftStatus = SM.openLocationID(locID, ref handle);
        if (ftStatus != FT_STATUS.FT_OK)
        {
            MessageBox.Show("Error: buttonGet_Click failed to open port");
        }
    }

    // Assumes device is open
    private void closeDevice()
    {
        SM.closeDevice(handle);
    }
```

330

```
#endregion

#region Bit-bang Output

private void bitBangOutD(byte Out)
{
    SM.bitBang_SetBitMode(handle, Out, 0x01);
}

#endregion

byte[] font = new byte[37] {0x77, 0x7C, 0x39, 0x5E, 0x79, 0x71,
                            0x6F, 0x76, 0x30, 0x1E, 0x70, 0x38,
                            0x15, 0x54, 0x3F, 0x73, 0x67, 0x50,
                            0x6D, 0x78, 0x3E, 0x1C, 0x2A, 0x46,
                            0x6E, 0x52, 0x3F, 0x06, 0x5B, 0x4F,
                            0x66, 0x6D, 0x7D, 0x07, 0x7F, 0x6F,
                            0x08};

#region Font Buttons

private byte A = 0x77;
private byte B = 0x7C;
private byte C = 0x39;
private byte D = 0x5E;
private byte E = 0x79;
private byte F = 0x71;
private byte G = 0x6F;
private byte H = 0x76;
private byte I = 0x30;
private byte J = 0x1E;
private byte K = 0x70;
private byte L = 0x38;
private byte M = 0x15;
private byte N = 0x54;
private byte O = 0x3F;
private byte P = 0x73;
private byte Q = 0x67;
private byte R = 0x50;
private byte S = 0x6D;
private byte T = 0x78;
private byte U = 0x3E;
private byte V = 0x1C;
private byte W = 0x2A;
private byte X = 0x46;
private byte Y = 0x6E;
private byte Z = 0x52;
private byte F0 = 0x3F;
private byte F1 = 0x06;
private byte F2 = 0x5B;
private byte F3 = 0x4F;
private byte F4 = 0x66;
private byte F5 = 0x6D;
private byte F6 = 0x7D;
private byte F7 = 0x07;
private byte F8 = 0x7F;
private byte F9 = 0x6F;
```

```
private byte SP = 0x08; // show space as segment d
private byte vd = 0x00; // show no segments

private void buttonFontA_Click(object sender, EventArgs e)
{
    bitBangOutD(A);
}

private void buttonFontB_Click(object sender, EventArgs e)
{
    bitBangOutD(B);
}

private void buttonFontC_Click(object sender, EventArgs e)
{
    bitBangOutD(C);
}

private void buttonFontD_Click(object sender, EventArgs e)
{
    bitBangOutD(D);
}

private void buttonFontE_Click(object sender, EventArgs e)
{
    bitBangOutD(E);
}

private void buttonFontF_Click(object sender, EventArgs e)
{
    bitBangOutD(F);
}

private void buttonFontG_Click(object sender, EventArgs e)
{
    bitBangOutD(G);
}

private void buttonFontH_Click(object sender, EventArgs e)
{
    bitBangOutD(H);
}

private void buttonFontI_Click(object sender, EventArgs e)
{
    bitBangOutD(I);
}

private void buttonFontJ_Click(object sender, EventArgs e)
{
    bitBangOutD(J);
}

private void buttonFontK_Click(object sender, EventArgs e)
{
    bitBangOutD(K);
}
```

```
private void buttonFontL_Click(object sender, EventArgs e)
{
    bitBangOutD(L);
}

private void buttonFontM_Click(object sender, EventArgs e)
{
    bitBangOutD(M);
}

private void buttonFontN_Click(object sender, EventArgs e)
{
    bitBangOutD(N);
}

private void buttonFontO_Click(object sender, EventArgs e)
{
    bitBangOutD(O);
}

private void buttonFontP_Click(object sender, EventArgs e)
{
    bitBangOutD(P);
}

private void buttonFontQ_Click(object sender, EventArgs e)
{
    bitBangOutD(Q);
}

private void buttonFontR_Click(object sender, EventArgs e)
{
    bitBangOutD(R);
}

private void buttonFontS_Click(object sender, EventArgs e)
{
    bitBangOutD(S);
}

private void buttonFontT_Click(object sender, EventArgs e)
{
    bitBangOutD(T);
}

private void buttonFontU_Click(object sender, EventArgs e)
{
    bitBangOutD(U);
}

private void buttonFontV_Click(object sender, EventArgs e)
{
    bitBangOutD(V);
}

private void buttonFontW_Click(object sender, EventArgs e)
```

333

```
    {
        bitBangOutD(W);
    }

    private void buttonFontX_Click(object sender, EventArgs e)
    {
        bitBangOutD(X);
    }

    private void buttonFontY_Click(object sender, EventArgs e)
    {
        bitBangOutD(Y);
    }

    private void buttonFontZ_Click(object sender, EventArgs e)
    {
        bitBangOutD(Z);
    }

    private void buttonFont0_Click(object sender, EventArgs e)
    {
        bitBangOutD(F0);
    }

    private void buttonFont1_Click(object sender, EventArgs e)
    {
        bitBangOutD(F1);
    }

    private void buttonFont2_Click(object sender, EventArgs e)
    {
        bitBangOutD(F2);
    }

    private void buttonFont3_Click(object sender, EventArgs e)
    {
        bitBangOutD(F3);
    }

    private void buttonFont4_Click(object sender, EventArgs e)
    {
        bitBangOutD(F4);
    }

    private void buttonFont5_Click(object sender, EventArgs e)
    {
        bitBangOutD(F5);
    }

    private void buttonFont6_Click(object sender, EventArgs e)
    {
        bitBangOutD(F6);
    }

    private void buttonFont7_Click(object sender, EventArgs e)
    {
        bitBangOutD(F7);
```

```
    }

    private void buttonFont8_Click(object sender, EventArgs e)
    {
        bitBangOutD(F8);
    }

    private void buttonFont9_Click(object sender, EventArgs e)
    {
        bitBangOutD(F9);
    }

    #endregion

    #region Tests

    private byte count = 0;
    private void timer1_Tick(object sender, EventArgs e)
    {
        bitBangOutD(font[count++]);
        if (count >= 36 ) count = 0;
    }

    private void buttonShowFont_Click(object sender, EventArgs e)
    {
        if (timer1.Enabled) { timer1.Enabled = false; wrap
                              buttonShowFont.Text = "Show Font"; }
        else { timer1.Enabled = true; buttonShowFont.Text = "Stop Font"; }
    }

    int outCount = 0;
    byte[] outStr = new byte[128]; // 64 characters = 64 voids

    private bool hello = true;
    private void buttonHello_Click(object sender, EventArgs e)
    {
        if (hello)
        {
            hello = false;
            buttonHello.Text = "Stop Hello";
            sendtStringTo7SegOutput("Hello World");
        }
        else
        {
            timer2.Enabled = false;
            hello = true;
            buttonHello.Text = "Hello World";
        }
    }

    private bool sendTxt = true;
    private void buttonSendText_Click(object sender, EventArgs e)
    {
        if (sendTxt)
        {
            sendTxt = false;
            buttonSendText.Text = "Stop Text";
```

335

```
            sendtStringTo7SegOutput(textBoxSendText.Text);
        }
        else
        {
            timer2.Enabled = false;
            sendTxt = true;
            buttonSendText.Text = "Send Text";
        }
    }

    private void sendtStringTo7SegOutput(string str)
    {
        timer2.Enabled = false;
        timerCount = 0;
        outCount = 0;
        int temp = 0;
        foreach (byte s in outStr) outStr[temp++] = 0;

        // convert string to upper case
        str = str.ToUpper();

        // put it in an array
        char[] charStr = str.ToCharArray();

        byte b = 0;
        int strCount = 0;
        foreach (char c in charStr)
        {
            if (++outCount > 64)
            {
                MessageBox.Show("Out string cannot have > 64 characters");
                break;
            }

            b = Convert.ToByte(c);

            if (b == 32) // 32 is ASCII code for a space character
            {
                outStr[strCount++] = 0x08; // substitute d segment wrap
                                          // for space character: 32
                outStr[strCount++] = 0x00; // add a void to demark letters
                outCount++; // increase count for added voids
            }
            else
            {
                if ( (b > 64) && (b < 91))//filter for capital letters only
                {
                    b -= 65; // it is a character
                    outStr[strCount++] += font[b];
                    outStr[strCount++] = 0x00; // add a void to demark letters
                    outCount++; // increase count for added voids
                }
                else if ((b > 47) && (b < 58)) // filter for numerals
                {
                    b -= (48 - 26); // it is a number - numbers start wrap
                                   // a 26 in font array
                    outStr[strCount++] += font[b];
```

```
                        outStr[strCount++] = 0x00; // add a void to demark letters
                        outCount++; // increase count for added voids
                    }
                }
            }
            timer2.Enabled = true;
        }

        int timerCount = 0;
        private void timer2_Tick(object sender, EventArgs e)
        {
            bitBangOutD(outStr[timerCount++]);
            if(timerCount > outCount) timerCount = 0;
        }

        private void buttonstopText_Click(object sender, EventArgs e)
        {
            int temp = 0;
            foreach( byte b in outStr) outStr[temp++] = 0;
            timer2.Enabled = false;
        }

        #endregion
    }
}
```

7-Segment Tester in VB

```
Imports Microsoft.VisualBasic
Imports System
Imports System.Collections.Generic
Imports System.ComponentModel
Imports System.Data
Imports System.Drawing
Imports System.Text
Imports System.Windows.Forms

Imports SMD2XX
Imports SelectDevice

Namespace Segment_Test

    Partial Public Class Form1
        Inherits Form

#Region "intialization"
        Private ftStatus As FT_STATUS = 0
        Private ftHandle As UInt32 = 0

        Private SM As SM_D2XX = New SM_D2XX()

        Private dev As Select_Device = New Select_Device()

        Private Output As Byte = 0
```

337

```
        Public Sub New()
            InitializeComponent()
        End Sub
#End Region

#Region "Segment Buttons"
        Private Sub buttona_Click(ByVal sender As Object, wrap
                            ByVal e As EventArgs) Handles buttona.Click
            If buttona.BackColor = Color.LightGray Then
                buttona.BackColor = Color.Red
                Output += &H1
            Else
                buttona.BackColor = Color.LightGray
                If Output >= &H1 Then
                    Output -= &H1
                End If
            End If

            bitBangOutD(Output)
        End Sub

        Private Sub buttonb_Click(ByVal sender As Object, wrap
                            ByVal e As EventArgs) Handles buttonb.Click
            If buttonb.BackColor = Color.LightGray Then
                buttonb.BackColor = Color.Red
                Output += &H2
            Else
                buttonb.BackColor = Color.LightGray
                If Output >= &H2 Then
                    Output -= &H2
                End If
            End If

            bitBangOutD(Output)
        End Sub

        Private Sub buttonc_Click(ByVal sender As Object, wrap
                            ByVal e As EventArgs) Handles buttonc.Click
            If buttonc.BackColor = Color.LightGray Then
                buttonc.BackColor = Color.Red
                Output += &H4
            Else
                buttonc.BackColor = Color.LightGray
                If Output >= &H4 Then
                    Output -= &H4
                End If
            End If

            bitBangOutD(Output)
        End Sub

        Private Sub buttond_Click(ByVal sender As Object, wrap
                            ByVal e As EventArgs) Handles buttond.Click
            If buttond.BackColor = Color.LightGray Then
                buttond.BackColor = Color.Red
                Output += &H8
            Else
```

```
            buttond.BackColor = Color.LightGray
            If Output >= &H8 Then
                Output -= &H8
            End If
        End If

        bitBangOutD(Output)
    End Sub

    Private Sub buttone_Click(ByVal sender As Object, wrap
                        ByVal e As EventArgs) Handles buttone.Click
        If buttone.BackColor = Color.LightGray Then
            buttone.BackColor = Color.Red
            Output += &H10
        Else
            buttone.BackColor = Color.LightGray
            If Output >= &H10 Then
                Output -= &H10
            End If
        End If

        bitBangOutD(Output)
    End Sub

    Private Sub buttonf_Click(ByVal sender As Object, wrap
                        ByVal e As EventArgs) Handles buttonf.Click
        If buttonf.BackColor = Color.LightGray Then
            buttonf.BackColor = Color.Red
            Output += &H20
        Else
            buttonf.BackColor = Color.LightGray
            If Output >= &H20 Then
                Output -= &H20
            End If
        End If

        bitBangOutD(Output)
    End Sub

    Private Sub buttong_Click(ByVal sender As Object, wrap
                        ByVal e As EventArgs) Handles buttong.Click
        If buttong.BackColor = Color.LightGray Then
            buttong.BackColor = Color.Red
            Output += &H40
        Else
            buttong.BackColor = Color.LightGray
            If Output >= &H40 Then
                Output -= &H40
            End If
        End If

        bitBangOutD(Output)
    End Sub

    Private Sub buttondp_Click(ByVal sender As Object, wrap
                        ByVal e As EventArgs) Handles buttondp.Click
        If buttondp.BackColor = Color.LightGray Then
```

```
                buttondp.BackColor = Color.Red
                Output += &H80
            Else
                buttondp.BackColor = Color.LightGray
                If Output >= &H80 Then
                    Output -= &H80
                End If
            End If

            bitBangOutD(Output)
        End Sub
#End Region

#Region "Select and Open a Device"

        Private Sub selectDeviceToolStripMenuItem_Click_1(ByVal sender wrap
                        As Object, ByVal e As EventArgs) Handles wrap
                        selectDeviceToolStripMenuItem.Click
            dev.ShowDialog()

            Select Case dev.OpenBy
                Case CUInt(OPEN_BY.SERIAL_NUMBER) ' use OpenEX
                    openBySerialNumber(dev.SerialNumber)
                Case CUInt(OPEN_BY.DESCRIPTION) ' use OpenEX
                    openByDescription(dev.Description)
                Case CUInt(OPEN_BY.LOCATIONID) ' use OpenEX
                    openByLocationID(dev.LocID)
                Case Else
                    MessageBox.Show("ERROR - OpenBy = " & dev.OpenBy.ToString())
            End Select
        End Sub

        ' open by serial number
        Private Sub openBySerialNumber(ByVal SN As String)
            ftStatus = SM.openSerialNumber(SN, ftHandle)
            If ftStatus <> FT_STATUS.FT_OK Then
                MessageBox.Show("Error: buttonGet_Click failed to open device")
            End If
        End Sub

        ' open by description
        Private Sub openByDescription(ByVal description As String)
            ftStatus = SM.openDescription(description, ftHandle)
            If ftStatus <> FT_STATUS.FT_OK Then
                MessageBox.Show("Error: buttonGet_Click failed to open port")
            End If
        End Sub

        ' open by location
        Private Sub openByLocationID(ByVal locID As UInt32)
            ftStatus = SM.openLocationID(locID, ftHandle)
            If ftStatus <> FT_STATUS.FT_OK Then
                MessageBox.Show("Error: buttonGet_Click failed to open port")
            End If
        End Sub

        ' Assumes device is open
```

```
            Private Sub closeDevice()
                SM.closeDevice(ftHandle)
            End Sub

#End Region

#Region "Bit-bang Output"

            Private Sub bitBangOutD(ByVal Out As Byte)
                SM.bitBang_SetBitMode(ftHandle, Out, &H1)
            End Sub

#End Region

        Private myFont As Byte() = New Byte(36) {&H77, &H7C, &H39, &H5E, &H79,
&H71, &H6F, &H76, &H30, &H1E, &H70, &H38, &H15, &H54, &H3F, &H73, &H67, &H50,
&H6D, &H78, &H3E, &H1C, &H2A, &H46, &H6E, &H52, &H3F, &H6, &H5B, &H4F, &H66, &H6D,
&H7D, &H7, &H7F, &H6F, &H8}

#Region "Font Buttons"

            Private A As Byte = &H77
            Private B As Byte = &H7C
            Private C As Byte = &H39
            Private D As Byte = &H5E
            Private E As Byte = &H79
            Private F As Byte = &H71
            Private G As Byte = &H6F
            Private H As Byte = &H76
            Private I As Byte = &H30
            Private J As Byte = &H1E
            Private K As Byte = &H70
            Private L As Byte = &H38
            Private M As Byte = &H15
            Private N As Byte = &H54
            Private O As Byte = &H3F
            Private P As Byte = &H73
            Private Q As Byte = &H67
            Private R As Byte = &H50
            Private S As Byte = &H6D
            Private T As Byte = &H78
            Private U As Byte = &H3E
            Private V As Byte = &H1C
            Private W As Byte = &H2A
            Private X As Byte = &H46
            Private Y As Byte = &H6E
            Private Z As Byte = &H52
            Private F0 As Byte = &H3F
            Private F1 As Byte = &H6
            Private F2 As Byte = &H5B
            Private F3 As Byte = &H4F
            Private F4 As Byte = &H66
            Private F5 As Byte = &H6D
            Private F6 As Byte = &H7D
            Private F7 As Byte = &H7
            Private F8 As Byte = &H7F
            Private F9 As Byte = &H6F
```

341

```
'private byte SP = 0x08; // show space as segment d
'private byte vd = 0x00; // show no segments

        Private Sub buttonFontA_Click(ByVal sender As Object, wrap
ByVal e As EventArgs) Handles buttonFontA.Click
            bitBangOutD(A)
        End Sub

        Private Sub buttonFontB_Click(ByVal sender As Object, wrap
                        ByVal e As EventArgs) Handles buttonFontB.Click
            bitBangOutD(B)
        End Sub

        Private Sub buttonFontC_Click(ByVal sender As Object, wrap
                        ByVal e As EventArgs) Handles buttonFontC.Click
            bitBangOutD(C)
        End Sub

        Private Sub buttonFontD_Click(ByVal sender As Object, wrap
                        ByVal e As EventArgs) Handles buttonFontD.Click
            bitBangOutD(D)
        End Sub

        Private Sub buttonFontE_Click(ByVal sender As Object, wrap
                        ByVal e As EventArgs) Handles buttonFontE.Click
            bitBangOutD(Me.E)
        End Sub

        Private Sub buttonFontF_Click(ByVal sender As Object, wrap
                        ByVal e As EventArgs) Handles buttonFontF.Click
            bitBangOutD(F)
        End Sub

        Private Sub buttonFontG_Click(ByVal sender As Object, wrap
                        ByVal e As EventArgs) Handles buttonFontG.Click
            bitBangOutD(G)
        End Sub

        Private Sub buttonFontH_Click(ByVal sender As Object, wrap
                        ByVal e As EventArgs) Handles buttonFontH.Click
            bitBangOutD(H)
        End Sub

        Private Sub buttonFontI_Click(ByVal sender As Object, wrap
                        ByVal e As EventArgs) Handles buttonFontI.Click
            bitBangOutD(I)
        End Sub

        Private Sub buttonFontJ_Click(ByVal sender As Object, wrap
                        ByVal e As EventArgs) Handles buttonFontJ.Click
            bitBangOutD(J)
        End Sub

        Private Sub buttonFontK_Click(ByVal sender As Object, wrap
                        ByVal e As EventArgs) Handles buttonFontK.Click
            bitBangOutD(K)
        End Sub
```

```
Private Sub buttonFontL_Click(ByVal sender As Object, wrap
                    ByVal e As EventArgs) Handles buttonFontL.Click
    bitBangOutD(L)
End Sub

Private Sub buttonFontM_Click(ByVal sender As Object, wrap
                    ByVal e As EventArgs) Handles buttonFontM.Click
    bitBangOutD(M)
End Sub

Private Sub buttonFontN_Click(ByVal sender As Object, wrap
                    ByVal e As EventArgs) Handles buttonFontN.Click
    bitBangOutD(N)
End Sub

Private Sub buttonFontO_Click(ByVal sender As Object, wrap
                    ByVal e As EventArgs) Handles buttonFontO.Click
    bitBangOutD(O)
End Sub

Private Sub buttonFontP_Click(ByVal sender As Object, wrap
                    ByVal e As EventArgs) Handles buttonFontP.Click
    bitBangOutD(P)
End Sub

Private Sub buttonFontQ_Click(ByVal sender As Object, wrap
                    ByVal e As EventArgs) Handles buttonFontQ.Click
    bitBangOutD(Q)
End Sub

Private Sub buttonFontR_Click(ByVal sender As Object, wrap
                    ByVal e As EventArgs) Handles buttonFontR.Click
    bitBangOutD(R)
End Sub

Private Sub buttonFontS_Click(ByVal sender As Object, wrap
                    ByVal e As EventArgs) Handles buttonFontS.Click
    bitBangOutD(S)
End Sub

Private Sub buttonFontT_Click(ByVal sender As Object, wrap
                    ByVal e As EventArgs) Handles buttonFontT.Click
    bitBangOutD(T)
End Sub

Private Sub buttonFontU_Click(ByVal sender As Object, wrap
                    ByVal e As EventArgs) Handles buttonFontU.Click
    bitBangOutD(U)
End Sub

Private Sub buttonFontV_Click(ByVal sender As Object, wrap
                    ByVal e As EventArgs) Handles buttonFontV.Click
    bitBangOutD(V)
End Sub

Private Sub buttonFontW_Click(ByVal sender As Object, wrap
```

```
                              ByVal e As EventArgs) Handles buttonFontW.Click
        bitBangOutD(W)
End Sub

    Private Sub buttonFontX_Click(ByVal sender As Object, wrap
                              ByVal e As EventArgs) Handles buttonFontX.Click
        bitBangOutD(X)
End Sub

    Private Sub buttonFontY_Click(ByVal sender As Object, wrap
                              ByVal e As EventArgs) Handles buttonFontY.Click
        bitBangOutD(Y)
End Sub

    Private Sub buttonFontZ_Click(ByVal sender As Object, wrap
                              ByVal e As EventArgs) Handles buttonFontZ.Click
        bitBangOutD(Z)
End Sub

    Private Sub buttonFont0_Click(ByVal sender As Object, wrap
                              ByVal e As EventArgs) Handles buttonFont0.Click
        bitBangOutD(F0)
End Sub

    Private Sub buttonFont1_Click(ByVal sender As Object, wrap
                              ByVal e As EventArgs) Handles buttonFont1.Click
        bitBangOutD(F1)
End Sub

    Private Sub buttonFont2_Click(ByVal sender As Object, wrap
                              ByVal e As EventArgs) Handles buttonFont2.Click
        bitBangOutD(F2)
End Sub

    Private Sub buttonFont3_Click(ByVal sender As Object, wrap
                              ByVal e As EventArgs) Handles buttonFont3.Click
        bitBangOutD(F3)
End Sub

    Private Sub buttonFont4_Click(ByVal sender As Object, wrap
                              ByVal e As EventArgs) Handles buttonFont4.Click
        bitBangOutD(F4)
End Sub

    Private Sub buttonFont5_Click(ByVal sender As Object, wrap
                              ByVal e As EventArgs) Handles buttonFont5.Click
        bitBangOutD(F5)
End Sub

    Private Sub buttonFont6_Click(ByVal sender As Object, wrap
                              ByVal e As EventArgs) Handles buttonFont6.Click
        bitBangOutD(F6)
End Sub

    Private Sub buttonFont7_Click(ByVal sender As Object, wrap
                              ByVal e As EventArgs) Handles buttonFont7.Click
        bitBangOutD(F7)
```

```
        End Sub

        Private Sub buttonFont8_Click(ByVal sender As Object, wrap
                            ByVal e As EventArgs) Handles buttonFont8.Click
            bitBangOutD(F8)
        End Sub

        Private Sub buttonFont9_Click(ByVal sender As Object, wrap
                            ByVal e As EventArgs) Handles buttonFont9.Click
            bitBangOutD(F9)
        End Sub

#End Region

#Region "Tests"

        Private count As Byte = 0
        Private Sub timer1_Tick(ByVal sender As Object, wrap
                                ByVal e As EventArgs) Handles timer1.Tick
            bitBangOutD(myFont(count))
            count += Convert.ToByte(1)
            If count >= 36 Then
                count = 0
            End If
        End Sub

        Private Sub buttonShowFont_Click(ByVal sender As Object, wrap
                            ByVal e As EventArgs) Handles buttonShowFont.Click
            If timer1.Enabled Then
                timer1.Enabled = False
                buttonShowFont.Text = "Show Font"
            Else
                timer1.Enabled = True
                buttonShowFont.Text = "Stop Font"
            End If
        End Sub

        Private outCount As Integer = 0
        Private outStr As Byte() = New Byte(127) {} ' 64 characters = 64 voids

        Private hello As Boolean = True
        Private Sub buttonHello_Click(ByVal sender As Object, wrap
                            ByVal e As EventArgs) Handles buttonHello.Click
            If hello Then
                hello = False
                buttonHello.Text = "Stop Hello"
                sendtStringTo7SegOutput("Hello World")
            Else
                timer2.Enabled = False
                hello = True
                buttonHello.Text = "Hello World"
            End If
        End Sub

        Private sendTxt As Boolean = True
        Private Sub buttonSendText_Click(ByVal sender As Object, wrap
                            ByVal e As EventArgs) Handles buttonSendText.Click
```

345

```
        If sendTxt Then
            sendTxt = False
            buttonSendText.Text = "Stop Text"
            sendtStringTo7SegOutput(textBoxSendText.Text)
        Else
            timer2.Enabled = False
            sendTxt = True
            buttonSendText.Text = "Send Text"
        End If
    End Sub

    Private Sub sendtStringTo7SegOutput(ByVal str As String)
        timer2.Enabled = False
        timerCount = 0
        outCount = 0
        Dim temp As Integer = 0
        For Each s As Byte In outStr
            outStr(temp) = 0
            temp += 1
        Next s

        ' convert string to upper case
        str = str.ToUpper()

        ' put it in an array
        Dim charStr As Char() = str.ToCharArray()

        Dim b As Byte = 0
        Dim strCount As Integer = 0
        For Each c As Char In charStr
            outCount += 1
            If outCount > 64 Then
                MessageBox.Show("Out string cannot have > 64 characters")
                Exit For
            End If

            b = Convert.ToByte(c)

            If b = 32 Then ' 32 is ASCII code for a space character
                outStr(strCount) = &H8
                strCount += 1
                outStr(strCount) = &H0
                strCount += 1
                outCount += 1 ' increase count for added voids
            Else
                If (b > 64) AndAlso (b < 91) Then 'filter for wrap
                                                  capital letters only
                    b -= Convert.ToByte(65) ' it is a character
                    outStr(strCount) += myFont(b)
                    strCount += 1
                    outStr(strCount) = &H0
                    strCount += 1
                    outCount += 1 ' increase count for added voids
                ElseIf (b > 47) AndAlso (b < 58) Then ' filter for numerals
                    b -= Convert.ToByte((48 - 26)) ' it is a wrap
                                    number - numbers start a 26 in font array
                    outStr(strCount) += myFont(b)
```

346

```
                    strCount += 1
                    outStr(strCount) = &H0
                    strCount += 1
                    outCount += 1 ' increase count for added voids
                End If
            End If
        Next c
        timer2.Enabled = True
    End Sub

    Private timerCount As Integer = 0
    Private Sub timer2_Tick(ByVal sender As Object, wrap
                            ByVal e As EventArgs) Handles timer2.Tick
        bitBangOutD(outStr(timerCount))
        timerCount += 1
        If timerCount > outCount Then
            timerCount = 0
        End If
    End Sub

    Private Sub buttonstopText_Click(ByVal sender As Object, wrap
                                        ByVal e As EventArgs)
        Dim temp As Integer = 0
        For Each b As Byte In outStr
            outStr(temp) = 0
            temp += 1
        Next b
        timer2.Enabled = False
    End Sub

#End Region
    End Class
End Namespace
```

We've looked at some fun hardware projects that show us how to do bit-banged I/O with the FT232R. In the next chapter we will look at the FTDIChip-ID™ which is supposed to provide a security feature, but maybe not.

Chapter 20: FTDIChip-ID™ Security Feature

Is Computer Security a delusion?

The FTDIChip-ID is a unique 32-bit number burned into the FT232R that can be read, but cannot be changed by the user. One would think this could be used for bulletproof security, but one who thinks such thoughts hasn't spent much time actually working with computer security. The FTDI website provides some examples that might lead a casual reader to suspect that one could use this feature for copy protecting software or for other security via a USB hardware dongle and one thinking this would be very deluded indeed. Hardware copy-protection dongles were defeated by the early 90's and you rarely see them anymore. You can develop some sort of scheme that will make it difficult for the average user to steal your software, but a decent hacker can defeat most schemes. Microsoft bragged about releasing an uncrackable media encryption and the crack was released one hour after the product was released (to be fair, the Russian who did it had access to the beta release months before the commercial release). Microsoft bragged about Vista and this time by spending a vast fortune on security, it took a week to be broken. Sony has special encryption features added to their DVDs so that it now takes a full 20 seconds longer to rip a Sony DVD than it does other DVDs. The point is not how cool and easy it is to steal anything sold as a bundle of bits, but that if Microsoft and Sony can't get it right – you have exactly zero chance.

To make security matters even worse, if you are using .NET Express, your executable can be decompiled back to something very similar to the original source code using an internet tool FOR FREE. I thought I'd be sneaky and hardcode a FTDIChip-ID number in a program, and then I ran it through a decompiler and seconds later, I was able to recover the source code and hardcoded number. .NET Express software is Open Source, no matter what you intend. If you pony up a few bucks and get the regular Visual Studio edition, you can get access to DotFuscator, which makes reverse engineering your software much more difficult – but still not bullet-proof as witness Microsoft's own efforts at protecting its stuff. If you don't have a huge customer base or one that has lots of hackers, you can probably get some protection using DotFuscator, just don't build a business model that requires that your code cannot be reverse engineered.

This is all very controversial and would take several large academic treatises to cover, so we will only show how to get the FTDIChip-ID and use it to select and open a device. How you use it is up to you.

Okay, after all that ranting I do have to acknowledge that I'm being over broad about computer security. Banking transactions and systems like PayPal, Amazon, and eBay are about the juiciest targets imaginable for a digital thief, and as far as we know none have been breached. But we aren't talking microcontrollers or even PCs here, we are talking about some massive systems and my guess is that anybody smart enough to breach one is also smart enough to know that he can make plenty of money doing legal things.

Using the FTDIChip-ID™

You must use the FTChipIDNet.dll located in \Software\Chapter 19 – FTDIChip-ID to get the FTDIChip-ID™ number from the FT232R.

- Modify the SelectDevice form by adding a ChipID comboBox

- Copy the 'Select and Open' software directory and rename it 'FTDIChipID Select and Open'.
- Copy the FTChipID.dll to this directory.
- Open the project and in the Solutions Explorer click 'Add Reference' and then open the Browse tab and browse to find the FTChipID.dll and click on it.
- Open SelectDevice.cs or .vb in the editor and add the comboBoxChipID.
- In C# add:

```
using FTChipID;
```

- In VB add:

```
Imports FTChipID
```

- Modify the Open By enumeration
- In C#:

```
// 1 opens by serial number using FT_OpenEX
// 2 opens by description using FT_OpenEX
// 3 opens by Location Id using FT_OpenEX
// 4 opens by device number using FT_Open
// 5 opens by chip ID number using FT_OpenEX
public enum OPENBY
{
    SERIAL_NUMBER = 1,
    DESCRIPTION,
    LOCATIONID,
    DEVICE_NUMBER,
    CHIPID
}
```

- In VB:

```
' 1 opens by serial number using FT_OpenEX
' 2 opens by description using FT_OpenEX
' 3 opens by Location Id using FT_OpenEX
' 4 opens by device number using FT_Open
' 5 opens by chip ID number using FT_OpenEX
Public Enum OPEN_BY
    SERIAL_NUMBER = 1
    DESCRIPTION
    LOCATIONID
    DEVICE_NUMBER
    CHIPID
End Enum
```

- To the `SelectAndOpenDevice_Load` function –
- In C# add:

```
comboBoxChipID.Items.Add(chipID_p.ToString("X"));

richTextBox1.Text += "\nChipID = 0x" + chipID_p.ToString("X") + "\n";
```

- In VB add:

```
comboBoxChipID.Items.Add(chipID_p.ToString("X"))

richTextBox1.Text += Constants.vbLf & "ChipID = 0x" & chipID_p.ToString("X") wrap
                                    + Constants.vbLf
```

- To the Properties region -
- In C# add:

```
private UInt32 chipID_p;
public UInt32 ChipID { get { return chipID_p; } set { chipID_p = value; } }
```

- In VB add:

```
Private chipID_p As Int32
Public Property ChipID() As Int32
    Get
        Return chipID_p
    End Get
    Set(ByVal value As Int32)
        chipID_p = value
    End Set
End Property
```

- Add a SelectedIndexChanged method to the comboBoxChipId
- In C# add:

```
private void comboBoxChipID_SelectedIndexChanged(object sender, EventArgs e)
{
    openBy_p = (UInt32)OPENBY.CHIPID;
    chipID_p = UInt32.Parse(comboBoxChipID.SelectedItem.ToString(), wrap

        System.Globalization.NumberStyles.AllowHexSpecifier);
    index_p = (uint)comboBoxChipID.SelectedIndex;
    Close();
}
```

- In VB add:

```
Private Sub comboBoxChipID_SelectedIndexChanged(ByVal sender As Object, wrap
            ByVal e As EventArgs) Handles comboBoxChipID.SelectedIndexChanged
    openBy_p = CUInt(OPEN_BY.CHIPID)
    Dim temp As Integer
    temp = Int32.Parse(comboBoxChipID.SelectedItem.ToString(), wrap
                        System.Globalization.NumberStyles.AllowHexSpecifier)
    chipID_p = Convert.ToInt32(temp)
    index_p = CUInt(comboBoxChipID.SelectedIndex)
    Close()
End Sub
```

- To the Form1 code –
- In C# add:

```
// open by FTDIChip-ID
private void openByChipID(UInt32 ChipID)
{
    // some of this is redundant with what you can do in SelectDevice
    // but we will do it this way so that we can us this code in other
    // applications without the SelectDevices form available - such as
    // a security demo with a hardcoded ChipID

    // get the number of devices
    ftStatus = SM.createDeviceInfoList();
    if (ftStatus != FT_STATUS.FT_OK)
    {
        MessageBox.Show("Error: openChipID FT_CreateDeviceInfoList failed.");
        return;
```

```
    }

    // scan devices for ChipID
    UInt32 n = 0;
    for (; n < SM.NumDevs; n++)
    {
        // use ChipID to get device number
        int temp = 0;
        FTChipID.ChipID.GetDeviceChipID((int)n, ref temp);
        if (temp == (int)ChipID)
        {
            break;
        }
    }

    // if ChipID found, open that device
    ftStatus = SM.openChipID(n, ref handle);
    if (ftStatus != FT_STATUS.FT_OK)
    {
        MessageBox.Show("Error: openByChipID SM.openByChipID failed to wrap
                                                    open port");
    }
}
```

- **In VB add:**

```
' open by FTDIChip-ID
Private Sub openByChipID(ByVal ChipID As Int32)
    ' some of this is redundant with what you can do in SelectDevice
    ' but we will do it this way so that we can us this code in other
    ' applications without the SelectDevices form available - such as
    ' a security demo with a hardcoded ChipID

    ' get the number of devices
    ftStatus = SM.createDeviceInfoList()
    If ftStatus <> FT_STATUS.FT_OK Then
        MessageBox.Show("Error: openChipID FT_CreateDeviceInfoList failed.")
        Return
    End If

    ' scan devices for ChipID
    Dim n As UInt32 = 0
    Do While n < SM.NumDevs
        ' use ChipID to get device number
        Dim temp As Integer = 0
        FTChipID.ChipID.GetDeviceChipID(System.Convert.ToInt32(n), temp)
        If temp = System.Convert.ToInt32(ChipID) Then
            Exit Do
        End If
        n += 1
    Loop

    ' if ChipID found, open that device
    ftStatus = SM.openChipID(n, ftHandle)
    If ftStatus <> FT_STATUS.FT_OK Then
        MessageBox.Show("Error: openByChipID SM.openByChipID failed to open port")
    End If
End Sub
```

353

- **To the** `buttonGetDevInfo_Click` event handler switch statement-
- **In C# add:**

```
case (uint)OPENBY.CHIPID: // use OpenEX
    openByChipID(dev.ChipID);
    break;
```

- **In VB add:**

```
Case CUInt(OPEN_BY.CHIPID) ' use OpenEX
    openByChipID(dev.ChipID)
```

This software is used exactly like the 'Select and Open Test' software except you can now select by the FTDIChip-ID™ in the SelectDevice form as shown:

Clicking on FABEF5C9 will open the device whose FTDIChip-ID™ matches that number.

So is this useful for security? Maybe for the usual user, but as stated above, don't build your business on code that can't be reverse engineered since it all can.

In the next chapter we will develop software to duplicate the functions of FTDI's MPROG programming software.

Chapter 20: FTDIChip-ID™ Security Feature???

Chapter 21: FT232R Programmer User Manual

FT232R Programmer Introduction

FTDI supplies MPROG to program their devices. This is a perfectly good piece of software, but they do not provide the source code, so I decided to clone their program as much as possible and provide the source code in C# and Visual Basic – a great way to learn the D2XX functions. This chapter shows how to use the FT232R Programmer and the next chapter presents the source code.

FT232R Programmer Basics

Modes of Operation

The FT232R Programmer opens in the Edit Mode and may be switched between this mode and Program Mode by clicking the radio buttons in the Mode box:

Edit Mode:

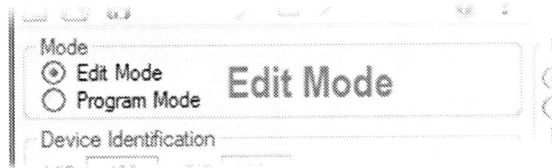

The Edit Mode is used to edit the settings of an EEPROM template file.

Program Mode:

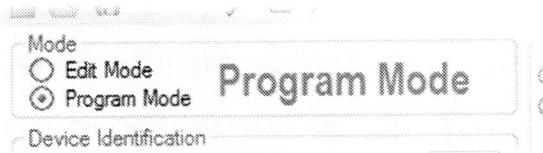

The Program Mode is used to write settings to a device or to erase it.

Edit Mode Functions

Create a New EEPROM Template

You can create a new EEPROM template by either clicking the New item in the File Menu, or clicking on the 'Create New Programming File' button on the toolbar:

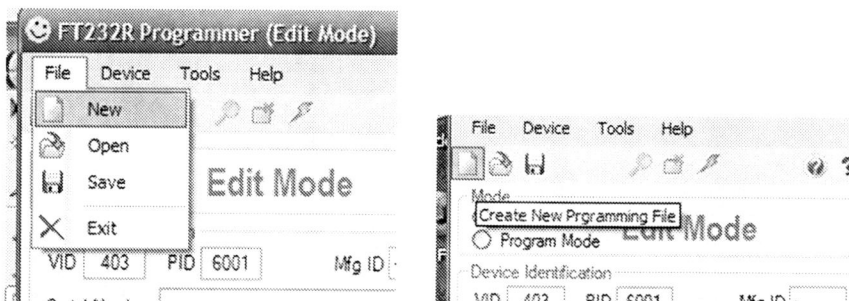

This action loads the settings with uninitialized values:

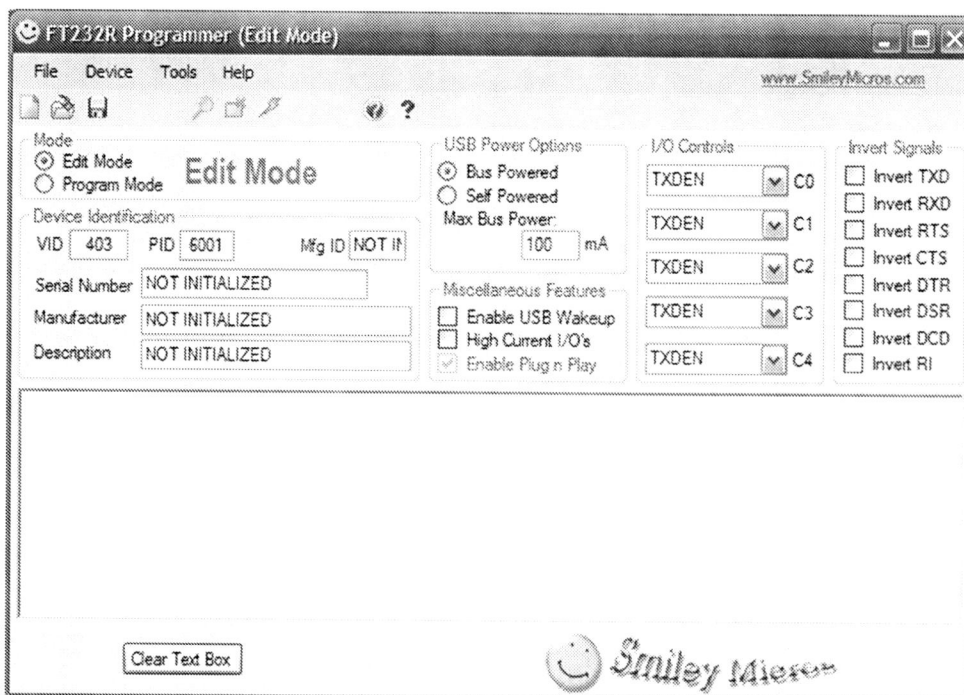

The user can enter values in the various textboxes or can set states by selecting items in comboBoxes or by clicking radio buttons or check boxes.

Modify an Existing EEPROM Template

Open an existing EEPROM template by clicking either the Open item in the File Menu or the 'Open Existing Programming File' button on the toolbar.

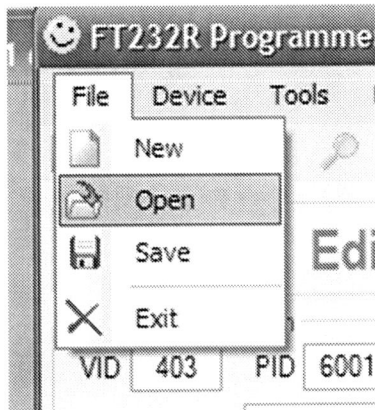

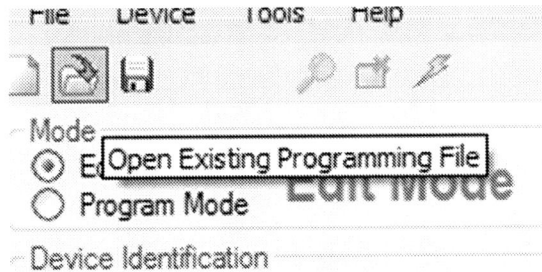

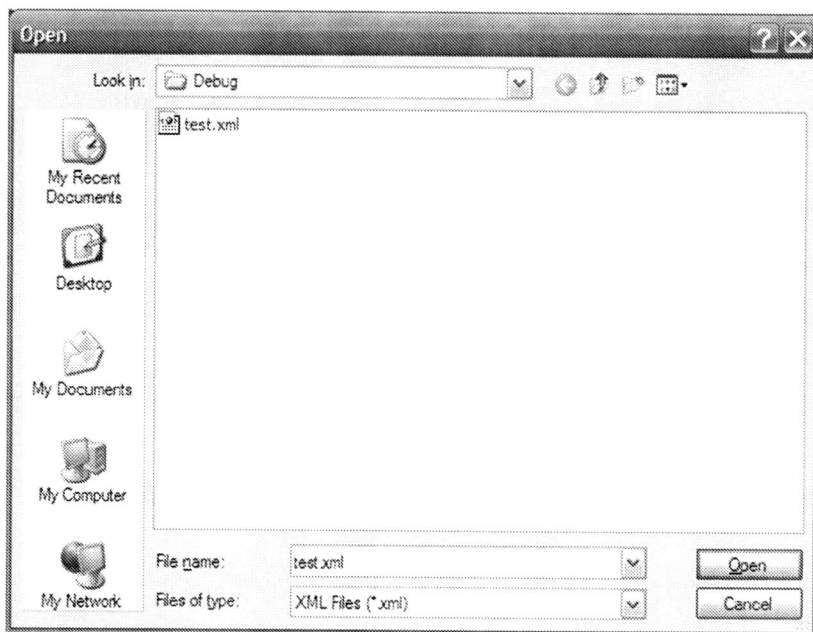

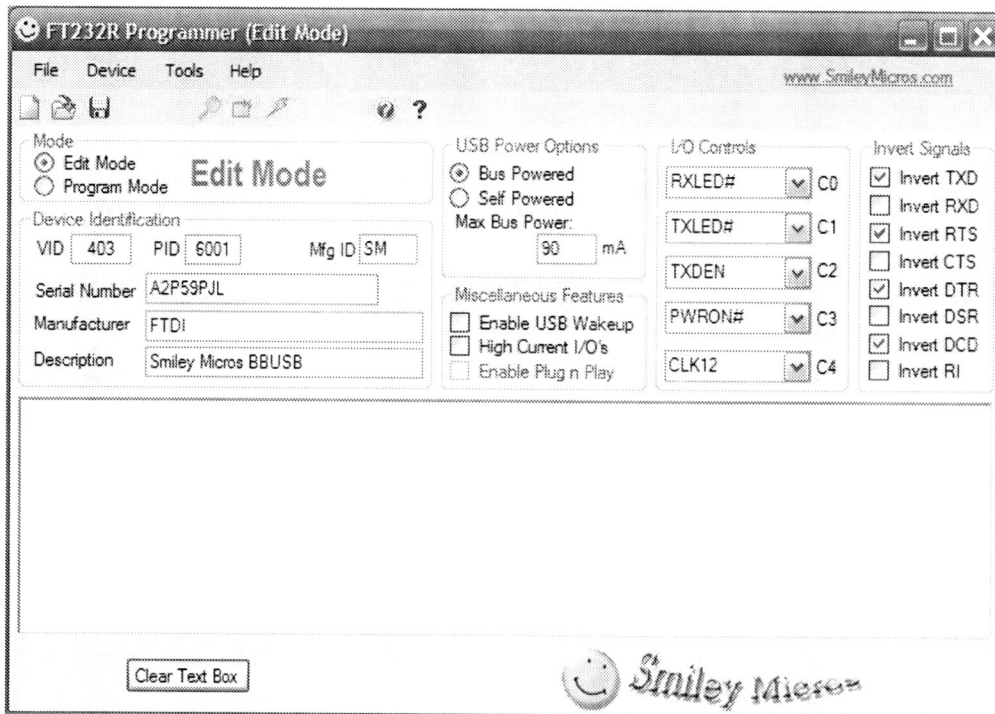

Text.xml file:

You may want to copy the Test.xml file to make changes to the template using Notepad, but remember the warnings in the chapters on XML – mainly if you make the slightest error, your XML file will fail and you won't get any hints as to why. You will see shortly how to alter the various settings and save the resulting XML file to a new template. That is the recommended method for handling templates.

```xml
<?xml version="1.0" encoding="utf-8"?>
<XMLData                 xmlns:xsi="http://www.w3.org/2001/XMLSchema-instance"
xmlns:xsd="http://www.w3.org/2001/XMLSchema">
  <VendorId>1027</VendorId>
  <ProductId>24577</ProductId>
  <Manufacturer>FTDI</Manufacturer>
  <ManufacturerID>SM</ManufacturerID>
  <Description>Smiley Micros BBUSB</Description>
  <SerialNumber>A2P59PJL</SerialNumber>
  <MaxPower>90</MaxPower>
  <PnP>false</PnP>
  <SelfPowered>false</SelfPowered>
  <RemoteWakeup>false</RemoteWakeup>
  <Rev4>0</Rev4>
  <IsoIn>0</IsoIn>
  <IsoOut>0</IsoOut>
  <PullDownEnable>0</PullDownEnable>
  <SerNumEnable>0</SerNumEnable>
  <USBVersionEnable>0</USBVersionEnable>
  <USBVersion>0</USBVersion>
  <UsbExtOsc>0</UsbExtOsc>
  <HighDriveIOs>false</HighDriveIOs>
  <EndpointSize>0</EndpointSize>
  <PullDownEnableR>0</PullDownEnableR>
  <SerNumEnableR>0</SerNumEnableR>
  <InvertTXD>true</InvertTXD>
  <InvertRXD>false</InvertRXD>
  <InvertRTS>true</InvertRTS>
  <InvertCTS>false</InvertCTS>
  <InvertDTR>true</InvertDTR>
  <InvertDSR>false</InvertDSR>
  <InvertDCD>true</InvertDCD>
  <InvertRI>false</InvertRI>
  <Cbus0>2</Cbus0>
  <Cbus1>3</Cbus1>
  <Cbus2>0</Cbus2>
  <Cbus3>1</Cbus3>
  <Cbus4>8</Cbus4>
  <RIsVCP>0</RIsVCP>
</XMLData>
```

Device EEPROM Parameters

The various FT232R Programming settings conform to the EEPROM parameters and are settable by the template parameters that can be saved and loaded as XML files.

Device Identification:

VID and PID

We recommend that for personal experimental use, that you use the FTDI VID of 0x0403 and PID of 0x6001 that correspond to the default installation driver INF files. Changing either of these numbers will require you to alter the INF files and reinstall the drivers for your device.

TOP LINE: DON'T MESS WITH THE VID AND PID UNTIL YOU'VE READ THE SECTION ON THE INF FILES. You can set your own VID (Vendor IDentification) number and PID (Product IDentification) number by the simple process of changing the value in the VID and PID boxes and then programming the device. And after doing this you will discover that your device no longer works! The reason is that Windows looks at the VID and PID of a device to decide what drivers to load for it. Windows gets the VID and PID information from the USB INF files and since you haven't changed the VID and PID in that file, it has no way of recognizing your device and won't open it. And to make matters worse, once you have programmed the new VID and PID, you can't reprogram it until you change the INF and INI file so that Windows will open it and make it accessible to the programmer. **BOTTOM LINE: DON'T MESS WITH THE VID AND PID UNTIL YOU'VE READ THE SECTION ON THE INF FILES.**

You can use FTDI's VID and they will give you your own unique PID if you contact them at: support2@ftdichip.com .

Serial Number
Each device plugged in that has identical VID/PID must have a unique serial number or only the first found device will be opened.

Manufacturer
Keep this as short as possible to provide minimal relevant information.

Description
Keep this as short as possible to provide minimal relevant information.

USB Power Options:

You can select either Bus Powered, if you want to use the USB bus power, or Self Powered if you want to provide your own power. You can also request that the USB bus provide you with a maximum bus power, above shows 90 mA, and the USB may OR MAY NOT provide you with that amount of power. This will depend on other devices on the bus and additional factors, some of which were discussed in an earlier chapter.

When first plugged in a USB device can consume no more than 100 mA. The device must wait until it is fully enumerated by Windows (its drivers are loaded) before attempting to use more than 100 mA. Using more than 100 mA should be negotiated between the device and the Windows driver. You can use the

PWREN# mode of a CBUS pin to control peripheral power use to prevent using more than 100 mA before enumeration

Devices that use under 100 mA are considered low power devices and do not require any special considerations. High power devices which use 101 to 500 mA from the USB bus can be plugged into any USB host, however bus powered hubs can only supply 100 mA per port, so if you need more power from a hub, you must use a self-powered hub.

Self-powered USB devices supply their own power and do not use USB bus power so enter 0 in the Max Bus Power textbox.

I/O Controls:

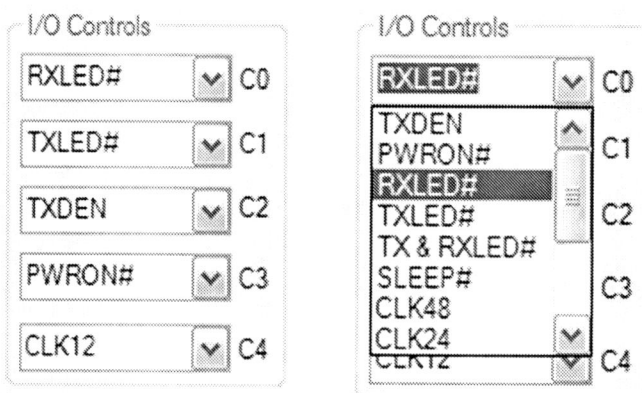

The I/O Controls comboBoxes allow you to select configurations for the CBUS output. C0 to C3 are mostly the same, except for the last item on each, and C4 is somewhat different lacking several of the other CBUS type functions. Below are the options selectable for each.

Table for various CBUS pin modes:

CBUS0	CBUS1	CBUS2	CBUS3	CBUS4
"TXDEN"	"TXDEN"	"TXDEN"	"TXDEN"	"TXDEN"
"PWRON#"	"PWRON#"	"PWRON#"	"PWRON#"	"PWRON#"
"RXLED#"	"RXLED#"	"RXLED#"	"RXLED#"	"RXLED#"
"TXLED#"	"TXLED#"	"TXLED#"	"TXLED#"	"TXLED#"
"TX & RXLED#"	"TX & RXLED#"	"TX & RXLED#"	"TX & RXLED#"	"TX & RXLED#"

"SLEEP#"	"SLEEP#"	"SLEEP#"	"SLEEP#"	"SLEEP#"
"CLK48"	"CLK48"	"CLK48"	"CLK48"	"CLK48"
"CLK24"	"CLK24"	"CLK24"	"CLK24"	"CLK24"
"CLK12"	"CLK12"	"CLK12"	"CLK12"	"CLK12"
"CLK6"	"CLK6"	"CLK6"	"CLK6"	"CLK6"
"I/O Mode"	"I/O Mode"	"I/O Mode"	"I/O Mode"	
"BitBang WRn"	"BitBang WRn"	"BitBang WRn"	"BitBang WRn"	
"BitBang RDn"	"BitBang RDn"	"BitBang RDn"	"BitBang RDn"	
"RXF#"	"TXE#"	"RD#"	"WR#"	

- "TXDEN" – Enable RS485 transmit data
- "PWRON#" – Remains high until USB device is enabled, then goes low. Goes high during USB suspend
- "RXLED#" – Drive an LED to indicate USB traffic by pulsing low when data is being received.
- "TXLED#" – Drive an LED to indicate USB traffic by pulsing low when data is being transmitted.
- "TX & RXLED#" – Drive an LED to indicate USB traffic by pulsing low when data is being transmitted or received.
- "SLEEP#" – Set low during USB suspend mode. Use to power down external devices such as an RS232 level converter.
- "CLK48" – Output 48 MHz clock.
- "CLK24" – Output 24 MHz clock.
- "CLK12" – Output 12 MHz clock.
- "CLK6" – Output 6 MHz clock.
- "I/O Mode" – Pin is used for bit banged general purpose input or output.
- "BitBang WRn" – Write strobe output for synchronous and asynchronous bit bang mode.
- "BitBang RDn" – Read strobe output for synchronous and asynchronous bit bang mode.
- "RXF#" – Goes low to indicate that byte wide data is available for a peripheral to read out, remains low until all data is read.
- "TXE#" – Set low when a peripheral may write byte wide data to the device.
- "RD#" – Asynchronous bit bang read strobe.
- "WR#" – Asynchronous bit bang write strobe.

Invert Signals:

Invert Signals
- ☑ Invert TXD
- ☐ Invert RXD
- ☑ Invert RTS
- ☐ Invert CTS
- ☑ Invert DTR
- ☐ Invert DSR
- ☑ Invert DCD
- ☐ Invert RI

Each UART signal may be individually inverted by checking the relevant box.

Miscellaneous Features:

Miscellaneous Features
- ☐ Enable USB Wakeup
- ☐ High Current I/O's
- ☐ Enable Plug n Play

Checking these boxes allows use of miscellaneous features. High Current I/Os set the pins to provide 12 mA instead of the default 4 mA. The 'Enable Plug and Play' checkbox is not implemented.

Program Mode Functions

Program Device

Check the 'Program Mode' radio button in the Mode box. You can program a device with data that you enter directly into the various entry fields on the form, or you can open a template with previously saved EEPROM data that will fill out the form for you. Further, you can change any item on the form and then save it as a template for future use. And you can read a device and then save the readings as a template.

Scan for Devices

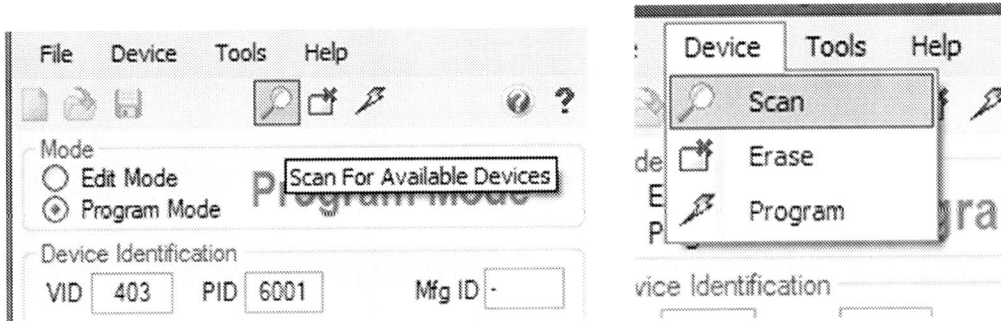

Click the 'Program Mode' radio button and then in the toolbar select the Scan tool 'Scan For Available devices' or from the Device Menu select Scan.

This will open the Select Device form, from which you select a device:

Read and Parse

From the Tool Menu select Read and Parse:

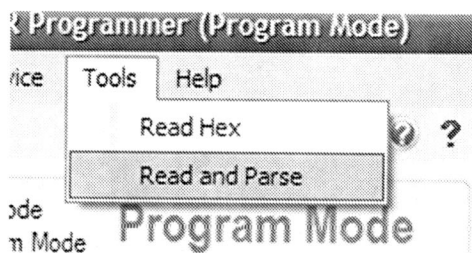

This will read the EEPROM data from the selected device and display it in the various editable boxes:

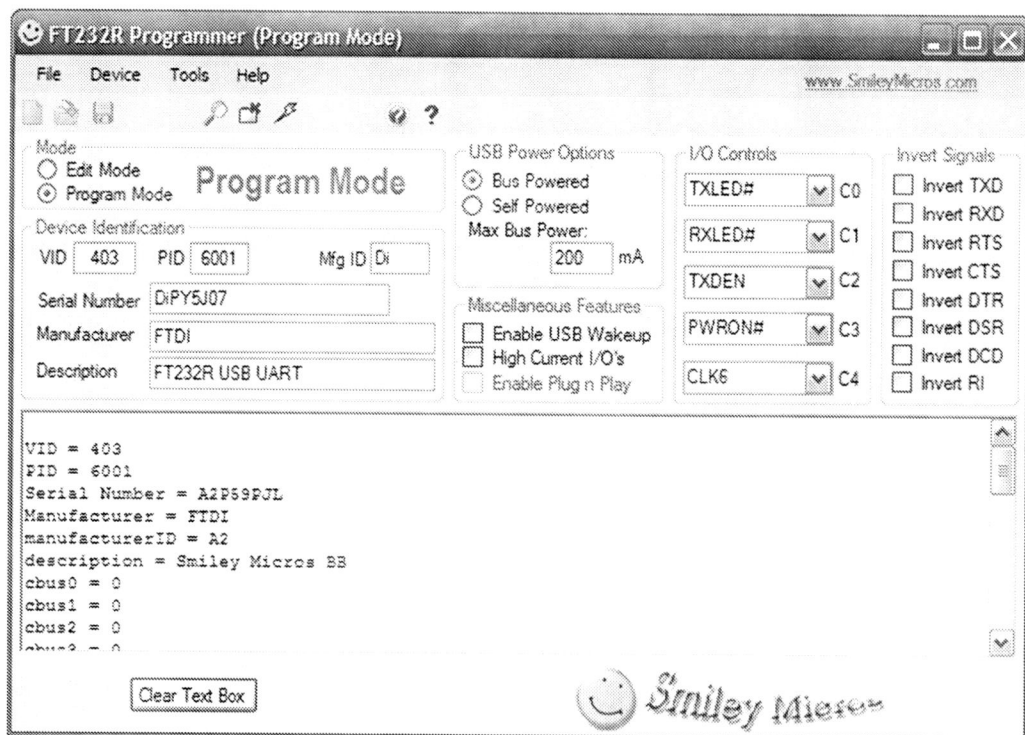

Read Hex

You can show the EEPROM data as a memory dump in the richTextBox by clicking the Tools Menu Read Hex item:

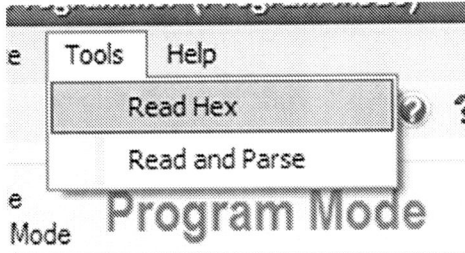

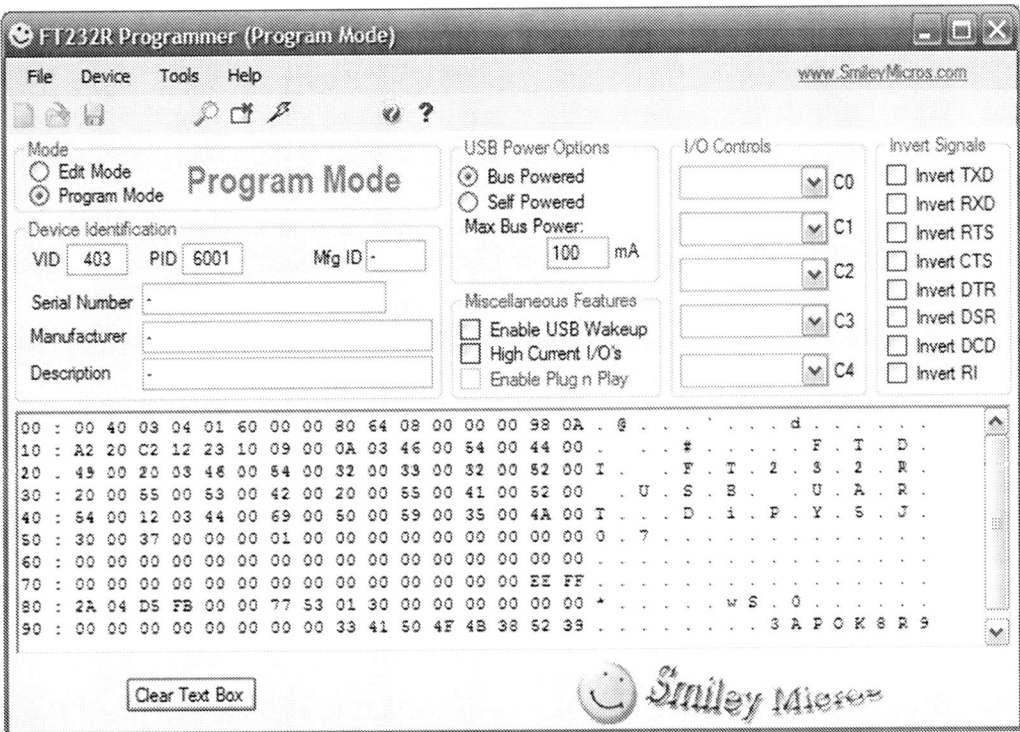

You will note that some of the data saved using D2XX functions puts a single byte in a two-byte word. You also see this with MPROG and I don't know why they choose to use their EEPROM memory this way. The User Area data is all saved as contiguous bytes.

Erase Device

For some odd reason this doesn't work in either this program or in the MPROG software. It is all written as it is supposed to be, calls the EraseEE function from the D2XX and returns with no error, but the data is still there. Must be some undocumented feature of the FT232R.

Customising FTDI's CDM Drivers

You can set your own VID (Vendor IDentification) number and PID (Product IDentification) number by the simple process of changing the value in the VID and PID boxes and then programming the device. And after doing this you will discover that your device no longer works! The reason is that Windows looks at the VID and PID of a device to decide what drivers to load for it. Windows gets the VID and PID information from the USB INF files and since you haven't changed the VID and PID in that file, it has no way of recognizing your device and won't open it. And to make matters worse, once you have programmed the new VID and PID, you can't reprogram it until you change the INF and INI file so that Windows will open it and make it accessible to the programmer.

The version of FTDIBUS.INF that is made available with the downloads on SmileyMicros.com has been modified to include lines that will allow you to accidentally set the VID or PID to 0x0000 and still open the device. This will come in handy when you make the same mistake I made a dozen times during development, especially when experimenting with the D2XX erase functions which seem to be a bit flaky for the FT232R.

Changing the FTDIBUS.INF File

Let's say that you purchase your own Vendor ID 0x1234 and decide that your first product ID will be 0x4321. You can open FTDIBUS.INF in Notepad and add lines in the [FtdiHw] and [ControlFlages] sections. You may also want to add a product description "HotShot Products Unlimited" to the [Strings] section. Make sure you keep a backup of the original that you haven't tampered with and don't change any other values. Add the VID_1234&PID_4321 lines below:

```
[FtdiHw]
%USB\VID_0403&PID_6001.DeviceDesc%=FtdiBus,USB\VID_0403&PID_6001
%USB\VID_0403&PID_0000.DeviceDesc%=FtdiBus,USB\VID_0403&PID_0000
%USB\VID_0000&PID_0000.DeviceDesc%=FtdiBus,USB\VID_0000&PID_0000
%USB\VID_0403&PID_6010&MI_00.DeviceDesc%=FtdiBus,USB\VID_0403&PID_6010&MI_00
%USB\VID_0403&PID_6010&MI_01.DeviceDesc%=FtdiBus,USB\VID_0403&PID_6010&MI_01
%USB\VID_1234&PID_4321.DeviceDesc%=FtdiBus,USB\VID_1234&PID_4321


[Strings]
Ftdi="FTDI"
DESC="CDM Driver Package"
DriversDisk="FTDI USB Drivers Disk"
USB\VID_0403&PID_6001.DeviceDesc="USB Serial Converter"
USB\VID_0403&PID_0000.DeviceDesc="Fix PID set to 0000"
USB\VID_0000&PID_0000.DeviceDesc="Fix VID and PID set to 0000"
USB\VID_0403&PID_6010&MI_00.DeviceDesc="USB Serial Converter A"
USB\VID_0403&PID_6010&MI_01.DeviceDesc="USB Serial Converter B"
USB\VID_1234&PID_4321.DeviceDesc="HotShot Products Unlimited"
WINUN="Software\Microsoft\Windows\CurrentVersion\Uninstall"
SvcDesc="USB Serial Converter Driver"

ClassName="USB"
```

Changing the FTDIPORT.INF File

If you will be using the device as a Virtual COM Port (serial port) follow the above instructions and modify the FTDIPORT.INF accordingly.

Chapter 22: FT232R Programmer Source Code

The last chapter showed you how to use the FT232R Programmer so you should now know where to put all the components on the form. You will need to add modules discussed elsewhere to the Solutions as shown below for C# and VB:

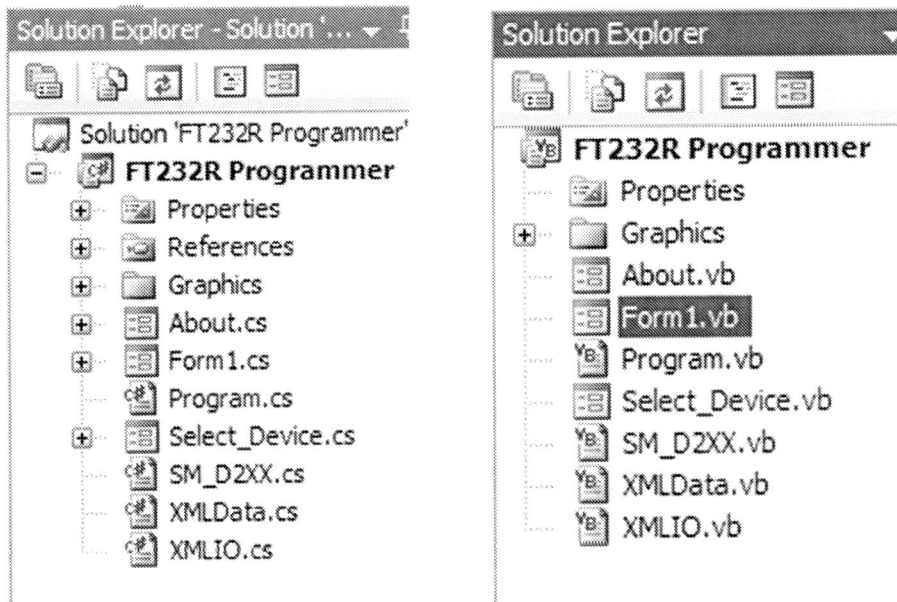

Again you should be familiar enough with C# or VB programming that you can reconstruct the form GUI design and that you can find and load previously discussed modules, we will only show the source code for Form1 in C# and in VB.

C# Source Code for Form1:

```csharp
using System;
using System.Collections.Generic;
using System.ComponentModel;
using System.Data;
using System.Drawing;
using System.Text;
using System.Windows.Forms;

using SMD2XX;
using SelectDevice;
using XML_Data;

namespace FT232R_Programmer
{
public partial class Form1 : Form
{
    FT_STATUS ftStatus = 0;
    private UInt32 ftHandle = 0;

    private string VersionDate = "Version 1.0 - 6/7/07";
    private uint SelectedDevice = 0;

    SM_D2XX SM = new SM_D2XX();

    Select_Device dev = new Select_Device();

    // Create an instance of the XMLData class
    private XMLData xMLData = new XMLData();

    // Create an instance of the TerminalXMLIO class to read the terminal data
    private XMLIO xMLIO = new XMLIO();

    public Form1()
    {
        InitializeComponent();

        editMode();
    }

    #region Menu and Toolbar
    private void newToolStripMenuItem_Click(object sender, EventArgs e)
    {
        New();
    }
    private void toolStripButtonNew_Click(object sender, EventArgs e)
    {
        New();
    }

    private void openToolStripMenuItem_Click(object sender, EventArgs e)
    {
        Open();
    }
```

```
private void toolStripButtonOpen_Click(object sender, EventArgs e)
{
    Open();
}

private void saveToolStripMenuItem_Click(object sender, EventArgs e)
{
    Save();
}
private void toolStripButtonSave_Click(object sender, EventArgs e)
{
    Save();
}

private void exitToolStripMenuItem_Click(object sender, EventArgs e)
{
    this.Close();
}

private void scanToolStripMenuItem_Click(object sender, EventArgs e)
{
    Scan();
}
private void toolStripButtonScan_Click(object sender, EventArgs e)
{
    Scan();
}

private void eraseToolStripMenuItem_Click(object sender, EventArgs e)
{
    Erase();
}
private void toolStripButtonErase_Click(object sender, EventArgs e)
{
    Erase();
}
private void Erase()
{
    this.Cursor = Cursors.WaitCursor;

    string temp = richTextBox1.Text;

    if (SM.eraseEEPROM(ftHandle))
    {
        SM.cyclePort(ftHandle);
        richTextBox1.Text = "Device was erased successfully\n";
    }
    else richTextBox1.Text = "Device was NOT erased successfully\n";

    richTextBox1.Text += temp;

    this.Cursor = Cursors.Default;
}

private void programToolStripMenuItem_Click(object sender, EventArgs e)
{
    Program();
```

375

```
    }
    private void toolStripButtonProgram_Click(object sender, EventArgs e)
    {
        Program();
    }

    private void readHexToolStripMenuItem_Click(object sender, EventArgs e)
    {
        ReadHex();
    }
    private void ReadHex()
    {
        ReadEE();
    }

    private void readAndParseToolStripMenuItem_Click(object sender, EventArgs e)
    {
        ReadAndParse();
    }

    private void helpToolStripMenuItem1_Click(object sender, EventArgs e)
    {
        Help();
    }
    private void toolStripButtonHelp_Click(object sender, EventArgs e)
    {
        Help();
    }
    private void Help()
    {
        System.Diagnostics.Process.Start("FT232 Programmer.pdf");
    }
    private void aboutToolStripMenuItem_Click(object sender, EventArgs e)
    {
        About();
    }
    private void toolStripButtonAbout_Click(object sender, EventArgs e)
    {
        About();
    }
    private void About()
    {
        About about = new About();
        about.versionDate = VersionDate;
        about.Show();
    }

    private void buttonClear_Click(object sender, EventArgs e)
    {
        richTextBox1.Text = "";
    }

    #endregion

    #region Edit or Program Mode
    private void radioButtonEditMode_CheckedChanged(object sender, EventArgs e)
    {
```

```
    if (radioButtonEditMode.Checked == true)
    {
        editMode();
        labelMode.Text = "Edit Mode";
    }
    else
    {
        programMode();
        labelMode.Text = "Program Mode";
    }
}

private void radioButtonProgramMode_CheckedChanged(object sender, EventArgs e)
{
    if (radioButtonProgramMode.Checked == true)
    {
        programMode();
        labelMode.Text = "Program Mode";
    }
    else
    {
        editMode();
        labelMode.Text = "Edit Mode";
    }
}

private void editMode()
{
    this.Text = "FT232R Programmer (Edit Mode)";

    this.groupBoxMiscFeatures.Enabled = true;
    this.groupBoxUSBPower.Enabled = true;
    this.groupBoxInvertSignals.Enabled = true;
    this.groupBoxIOControls.Enabled = true;

    this.newToolStripMenuItem.Enabled = true;
    this.toolStripButtonNew.Enabled = true;

    this.openToolStripMenuItem.Enabled = true;
    this.toolStripButtonOpen.Enabled = true;

    this.saveToolStripMenuItem.Enabled = true;
    this.toolStripButtonSave.Enabled = true;

    this.scanToolStripMenuItem.Enabled = false;
    this.toolStripButtonScan.Enabled = false;

    this.eraseToolStripMenuItem.Enabled = false;
    this.toolStripButtonErase.Enabled = false;

    this.programToolStripMenuItem.Enabled = false;
    this.toolStripButtonProgram.Enabled = false;

    this.readHexToolStripMenuItem.Enabled = false;
    this.readAndParseToolStripMenuItem.Enabled = false;

}
```

377

```
private void programMode()
{
    this.Text = "FT232R Programmer (Program Mode)";

    this.groupBoxMiscFeatures.Enabled = true;
    this.groupBoxUSBPower.Enabled = true;
    this.groupBoxInvertSignals.Enabled = true;
    this.groupBoxIOControls.Enabled = true;

    this.toolStripButtonNew.Enabled = false;
    this.newToolStripMenuItem.Enabled = false;

    this.openToolStripMenuItem.Enabled = false;
    this.toolStripButtonOpen.Enabled = false;

    this.saveToolStripMenuItem.Enabled = false;
    this.toolStripButtonSave.Enabled = false;

    this.scanToolStripMenuItem.Enabled = true;
    this.toolStripButtonScan.Enabled = true;

    this.eraseToolStripMenuItem.Enabled = true;
    this.toolStripButtonErase.Enabled = true;

    this.programToolStripMenuItem.Enabled = true;
    this.toolStripButtonProgram.Enabled = true;

    this.readHexToolStripMenuItem.Enabled = true;
    this.readAndParseToolStripMenuItem.Enabled = true;


}
#endregion

#region Select and Open a Device

private void Scan()
{
    dev.ShowDialog();

    switch (dev.OpenBy)
    {
        case (uint)OPEN_BY.SERIAL_NUMBER:
            openBySerialNumber(dev.SerialNumber);
            break;
        case (uint)OPEN_BY.DESCRIPTION:
            openByDescription(dev.Description);
            break;
        case (uint)OPEN_BY.LOCATIONID:
            openByLocationID(dev.LocID);
            break;
        default:
            MessageBox.Show("ERROR - OpenBy = " + dev.OpenBy.ToString());
            break;
    }
}
```

```csharp
// open by serial number
private void openBySerialNumber(string SN)
{
    ftStatus = SM.openSerialNumber(SN, ref ftHandle);
    if (ftStatus != FT_STATUS.FT_OK)
    {
        MessageBox.Show("Error: openBySerialNumber failed to open device");
    }
}

// open by description
private void openByDescription(string description)
{
    ftStatus = SM.openDescription(description, ref ftHandle);
    if (ftStatus != FT_STATUS.FT_OK)
    {
        MessageBox.Show("Error: openByDescription failed to open port");
    }
}

// open by location
private void openByLocationID(UInt32 locID)
{
    ftStatus = SM.openLocationID(locID, ref ftHandle);
    if (ftStatus != FT_STATUS.FT_OK)
    {
        MessageBox.Show("Error: openByLocationID( failed to open port");
    }
}

// Assumes device is open
private void closeDevice()
{
    SM.closeDevice(ftHandle);
}

#endregion

#region ReadEE
private void ReadEE()
{
    byte[] data = new byte[16];//0xA0];
    UInt16 k = 0;
    try
    {
        for (UInt16 j = 0; j < 160 / 2; j += 8)
        {
            for (UInt16 i = 0; i < 8; i++)
            {
                k = (UInt16)(i + j);
                ushort val = SM.readEE(ftHandle, k);
                data[i * 2] = (byte)(val & 0x00ff);
                data[i * 2 + 1] = (byte)(val >> 8);
            }
            richTextBox1.Text += memoryDumpLine(data, (j * 2));            }
```

379

```
        }
        catch (Exception ex)
        {
            MessageBox.Show("ReadEE - " + ex.Message);
            return;
        }
    }

    private string memoryDumpLine(byte[] line, int address)
    {
        if (line.Length > 16) return "memoryDumpLine Error: line to long.";

        char[] lineChar = new char[16];

        convertByteArrayToCharArray(line, lineChar);

        StringBuilder lineString = new StringBuilder();

        for (int i = 0; i < 16; i++)
        {
            if (line[i] < 16) lineString.Append("0");//Add leading 0 if number < F
            lineString.Append(line[i].ToString("X") + " ");
        }

        for (int i = 0; i < 16; i++)
        {
            if (isASCIIPrintable(line[i]))
                lineString.Append(lineChar[i] + " ");
            else lineString.Append(". ");
        }

        if (address < 16) return "0" + address.ToString("X") + " : " wrap
                                        + lineString.ToString() + "\n";
        else return address.ToString("X") + " : " + lineString.ToString() + "\n";
    }

    public bool convertByteArrayToCharArray(byte[] byteArray, char[] charArray)
    {
        // Make sure the arrays are the same length
        if (byteArray.Length != charArray.Length) return false;

        Encoding ascii = Encoding.ASCII;
        ascii.GetChars(byteArray, 0, byteArray.Length, charArray, 0);

        return true;
    }
    public bool isASCIIPrintable(byte b)
    {
        if (b < 32) return false;
        if (b > 126) return false;
        return true;
    }

    #endregion

    #region ReadEX
    private void ReadAndParse()
```

```
{
    SM.readEEPROM(ftHandle);

    richTextBox1.Text += "\nVID = " + SM.VendorId.ToString("x");
    richTextBox1.Text += "\nPID = " + SM.ProductId.ToString("x");
    richTextBox1.Text += "\nSerial Number = " + SM.SerialNumber;
    richTextBox1.Text += "\nManufacturer = " + SM.Manufacturer;
    richTextBox1.Text += "\nmanufacturerID = " + SM.ManufacturerID;
    richTextBox1.Text += "\ndescription = " + SM.Description;

    richTextBox1.Text += "\ncbus0 = " + SM.Cbus0.ToString();
    richTextBox1.Text += "\ncbus1 = " + SM.Cbus1.ToString();
    richTextBox1.Text += "\ncbus2 = " + SM.Cbus2.ToString();
    richTextBox1.Text += "\ncbus3 = " + SM.Cbus3.ToString();
    richTextBox1.Text += "\ncbus4 = " + SM.Cbus4.ToString();

    richTextBox1.Text += "\nInvertCTS = " + SM.InvertCTS.ToString();
    richTextBox1.Text += "\nInvertDCD = " + SM.InvertDCD.ToString();
    richTextBox1.Text += "\nInvertDSR = " + SM.InvertDSR.ToString();
    richTextBox1.Text += "\nInvertDTR = " + SM.InvertDTR.ToString();
    richTextBox1.Text += "\nInvertRI = " + SM.InvertRI.ToString();
    richTextBox1.Text += "\nInvertRTS = " + SM.InvertRTS.ToString();
    richTextBox1.Text += "\nInvertRXD = " + SM.InvertRXD.ToString();
    richTextBox1.Text += "\nInvertTXD = " + SM.InvertTXD.ToString();


    textBoxManufacturer.Text = SM.Manufacturer;
    textBoxProductDescription.Text = SM.Description;
    textBoxSerialNumber.Text = SM.SerialNumber;
    textBoxVID.Text = SM.VendorId.ToString("X");
    textBoxPID.Text = SM.ProductId.ToString("X");
    textBoxMfgID.Text = SM.ManufacturerID.ToString();

    textBoxMaxBusPower.Text = SM.MaxPower.ToString();

    comboBoxCBus0.SelectedIndex = SM.Cbus0;
    comboBoxCBus1.SelectedIndex = SM.Cbus1;
    comboBoxCBus2.SelectedIndex = SM.Cbus2;
    comboBoxCBus3.SelectedIndex = SM.Cbus3;
    comboBoxCBus4.SelectedIndex = SM.Cbus4;

    if (SM.InvertCTS != 0) checkBoxInvertCTS.Checked = true;
    else checkBoxInvertCTS.Checked = false;

    if (SM.InvertDCD != 0) checkBoxInvertDCD.Checked = true;
    else checkBoxInvertDCD.Checked = false;

    if (SM.InvertDSR != 0) checkBoxInvertDSR.Checked = true;
    else checkBoxInvertDSR.Checked = false;

    if (SM.InvertDTR != 0) checkBoxInvertDTR.Checked = true;
    else checkBoxInvertDTR.Checked = false;

    if (SM.InvertRI != 0) checkBoxInvertRI.Checked = true;
    else checkBoxInvertRI.Checked = false;

    if (SM.InvertRTS != 0) checkBoxInvertRTS.Checked = true;
```

```
        else checkBoxInvertRTS.Checked = false;

        if (SM.InvertRXD != 0) checkBoxInvertRXD.Checked = true;
        else checkBoxInvertRXD.Checked = false;

        if (SM.InvertTXD != 0) checkBoxInvertTXD.Checked = true;
        else checkBoxInvertTXD.Checked = false;

    }
    #endregion

    #region www.smileymicros.com
    private void pictureBox1_DoubleClick(object sender, EventArgs e)
    {
        System.Diagnostics.Process.Start("www.smileymicros.com");
    }

    private void linkLabel1_LinkClicked(object sender, wrap
                                 LinkLabelLinkClickedEventArgs e)
    {
        System.Diagnostics.Process.Start("www.smileymicros.com");
    }

    private void pictureBox1_Click(object sender, EventArgs e)
    {
        System.Diagnostics.Process.Start("www.smileymicros.com");
    }
    #endregion

    private void New()
    {
        loadXMLData();
    }

    private void Open()
    {
        openFileDialog1.Filter = "XML Files (*.xml)|*.xml";
        openFileDialog1.Title = "Open";
        openFileDialog1.DefaultExt = ".xml";

        if (openFileDialog1.ShowDialog() == DialogResult.OK)
        {
            xMLData = xMLIO.XMLRead(openFileDialog1.FileName);
            loadXMLData();
        }
        else
        {
            MessageBox.Show("Error: openFileDialog DialogResult wrap
                            != OK\nLoading default values.");
        }
    }

    private void loadXMLData()
    {
        textBoxVID.Text = xMLData.VendorId.ToString("X");
        textBoxPID.Text = xMLData.ProductId.ToString("X");
```

```csharp
        textBoxMfgID.Text = xMLData.ManufacturerID;
        textBoxManufacturer.Text = xMLData.Manufacturer;
        textBoxProductDescription.Text = xMLData.Description;
        textBoxSerialNumber.Text = xMLData.SerialNumber;

        textBoxMaxBusPower.Text = xMLData.MaxPower.ToString();

        checkBoxEnablePlugAndPlay.Checked = xMLData.PnP;

        if (xMLData.SelfPowered) radioButtonSelfPowered.Checked = true;
        else radioButtonBusPowered.Checked = true;

        checkBoxEnableUSBRemoteWakeup.Checked = xMLData.RemoteWakeup;

        checkBoxHighCurrent.Checked = xMLData.HighDriveIOs;

        checkBoxInvertTXD.Checked = xMLData.InvertTXD;
        checkBoxInvertRXD.Checked = xMLData.InvertRXD;
        checkBoxInvertRTS.Checked = xMLData.InvertRTS;
        checkBoxInvertCTS.Checked = xMLData.InvertCTS;
        checkBoxInvertDTR.Checked = xMLData.InvertDTR;
        checkBoxInvertDCD.Checked = xMLData.InvertDCD;
        checkBoxInvertRI.Checked = xMLData.InvertRI;

        // Cbus Mux control
        comboBoxCBus0.SelectedIndex = (int)xMLData.Cbus0;
        comboBoxCBus1.SelectedIndex = (int)xMLData.Cbus1;
        comboBoxCBus2.SelectedIndex = (int)xMLData.Cbus2;
        comboBoxCBus3.SelectedIndex = (int)xMLData.Cbus3;
        comboBoxCBus4.SelectedIndex = (int)xMLData.Cbus4;
    }

private void Save()
{
    saveFileDialog1.Filter = "XML Files (*.xml)|*.xml";
    saveFileDialog1.Title = "Save";
    saveFileDialog1.DefaultExt = ".xml";

    if (saveFileDialog1.ShowDialog() == DialogResult.OK)
    {
        saveXMLData();
        xMLIO.XMLWrite(xMLData, saveFileDialog1.FileName);
    }
    else
    {
        MessageBox.Show("Error: saveFileDialog DialogResult wrap
                                != OK\nFile not saved.");
    }
}

private void saveXMLData()
{
    ushort temp = 0;

    try
    {
        temp = Convert.ToUInt16(textBoxVID.Text, 16);
```

```
    }
    catch (Exception ex)
    {
        MessageBox.Show("Error: saveXMLData wrap
            Convert.ToUInt16(textBoxVID.Text) error: " + ex.ToString());
        return;
    }
    if (temp == 0)
    {
        MessageBox.Show("FILE NOT SAVED\n\nSETTING wrap
                        VID TO 0 WILL KILL YOUR BBUSB!\n\nRTFM!");
        return;
    }
    xMLData.VendorId = temp;

    try
    {
        temp = Convert.ToUInt16(textBoxPID.Text, 16);
    }
    catch (Exception ex)
    {
        MessageBox.Show("Error: saveXMLData wrap
            Convert.ToUInt16(textBoxPID.Text) error: " + ex.ToString());
        return;
    }
    xMLData.ProductId = temp;

    xMLData.Manufacturer = textBoxManufacturer.Text;
    xMLData.Description = textBoxProductDescription.Text;
    xMLData.SerialNumber = textBoxSerialNumber.Text;
    xMLData.ManufacturerID = textBoxMfgID.Text;

    try
    {
        temp = Convert.ToUInt16(textBoxMaxBusPower.Text);
    }
    catch (Exception ex)
    {
        MessageBox.Show("Error: saveXMLData wrap
Convert.ToUInt16(textBoxMaxBusPower.Text) error: " + ex.ToString());
        return;
    }
    xMLData.MaxPower = temp;


    xMLData.PnP = checkBoxEnablePlugAndPlay.Checked;

    xMLData.SelfPowered = radioButtonSelfPowered.Checked;

    xMLData.RemoteWakeup = checkBoxEnableUSBRemoteWakeup.Checked;

    xMLData.HighDriveIOs = checkBoxHighCurrent.Checked;

    xMLData.InvertTXD = checkBoxInvertTXD.Checked;
    xMLData.InvertRXD = checkBoxInvertRXD.Checked;
    xMLData.InvertRTS = checkBoxInvertRTS.Checked;
    xMLData.InvertCTS = checkBoxInvertCTS.Checked;
```

384

```csharp
        xMLData.InvertDTR = checkBoxInvertDTR.Checked;
        xMLData.InvertDCD = checkBoxInvertDCD.Checked;
        xMLData.InvertRI = checkBoxInvertRI.Checked;


        // Cbus Mux control
        xMLData.Cbus0 = (byte)comboBoxCBus0.SelectedIndex;
        xMLData.Cbus1 = (byte)comboBoxCBus1.SelectedIndex;
        xMLData.Cbus2 = (byte)comboBoxCBus2.SelectedIndex;
        xMLData.Cbus3 = (byte)comboBoxCBus3.SelectedIndex;
        xMLData.Cbus4 = (byte)comboBoxCBus4.SelectedIndex;
    }

    private void Program()
    {
        this.Cursor = Cursors.WaitCursor;

        string temp = richTextBox1.Text;
        if (SM.programEEPROM(ftHandle))
        {
            SM.cyclePort(ftHandle);
            richTextBox1.Text = "Device was programmed successfully\n";
        }
        else richTextBox1.Text = "Device was NOT programmed successfully\n";
        richTextBox1.Text += temp;
        this.Cursor = Cursors.Default;
    }

    #region User Input

    private void textBoxVID_TextChanged(object sender, EventArgs e)
    {
        xMLData.VendorId = SM.VendorId = Convert.ToUInt16(textBoxVID.Text, 16);
    }

    private void textBoxPID_TextChanged(object sender, EventArgs e)
    {
        xMLData.ProductId = SM.ProductId = Convert.ToUInt16(textBoxPID.Text, 16);
    }

    private void textBoxSerialNumber_TextChanged(object sender, EventArgs e)
    {
        xMLData.SerialNumber = SM.SerialNumber = textBoxSerialNumber.Text;
    }

    private void textBoxManufacturer_TextChanged(object sender, EventArgs e)
    {
        xMLData.Manufacturer = SM.Manufacturer = textBoxManufacturer.Text;
    }

    private void textBoxProductDescription_TextChanged(object sender, EventArgs e)
    {
        xMLData.Description = SM.Description = textBoxProductDescription.Text;
    }

    private void textBoxMfgID_TextChanged(object sender, EventArgs e)
    {
```

```
    xMLData.ManufacturerID = SM.ManufacturerID = textBoxMfgID.Text;
}

private void textBoxMaxBusPower_TextChanged(object sender, EventArgs e)
{
    xMLData.MaxPower = SM.MaxPower = wrap
                Convert.ToUInt16(textBoxMaxBusPower.Text);
}

private void comboBoxCBus0_SelectedValueChanged(object sender, EventArgs e)
{
    xMLData.Cbus0 = SM.Cbus0 = (byte)comboBoxCBus0.SelectedIndex;
}

private void comboBoxCBus1_SelectedValueChanged(object sender, EventArgs e)
{
    xMLData.Cbus1 = SM.Cbus1 = (byte)comboBoxCBus1.SelectedIndex;
}

private void comboBoxCBus2_SelectedValueChanged(object sender, EventArgs e)
{
    xMLData.Cbus2 = SM.Cbus2 = (byte)comboBoxCBus2.SelectedIndex;
}

private void comboBoxCBus3_SelectedValueChanged(object sender, EventArgs e)
{
    xMLData.Cbus3 = SM.Cbus3 = (byte)comboBoxCBus3.SelectedIndex;
}

private void comboBoxCBus4_SelectedIndexChanged(object sender, EventArgs e)
{
    xMLData.Cbus4 = SM.Cbus4 = (byte)comboBoxCBus4.SelectedIndex;
}

private void checkBoxInvertTXD_CheckedChanged(object sender, EventArgs e)
{
    if (checkBoxInvertTXD.Checked)
    {
        xMLData.InvertTXD = true;
        SM.InvertTXD = 1;
    }
    else
    {
        xMLData.InvertTXD = false;
        SM.InvertTXD = 0;
    }
}

private void checkBoxInvertRXD_CheckedChanged(object sender, EventArgs e)
{
    if (checkBoxInvertRXD.Checked)
    {
        xMLData.InvertRXD = true;
        SM.InvertRXD = 1;
    }
    else
    {
```

```
            xMLData.InvertRXD = false;
            SM.InvertRXD = 0;
        }
    }

    private void checkBoxInvertRTS_CheckedChanged(object sender, EventArgs e)
    {
        if (checkBoxInvertRTS.Checked)
        {
            xMLData.InvertRTS = true;
            SM.InvertRTS = 1;
        }
        else
        {
            xMLData.InvertRTS = false;
            SM.InvertRTS = 0;
        }
    }

    private void checkBoxInvertCTS_CheckedChanged(object sender, EventArgs e)
    {
        if (checkBoxInvertCTS.Checked)
        {
            xMLData.InvertCTS = true;
            SM.InvertCTS = 1;
        }
        else
        {
            xMLData.InvertCTS = false;
            SM.InvertCTS = 0;
        }
    }

    private void checkBoxInvertDTR_CheckedChanged(object sender, EventArgs e)
    {
        if (checkBoxInvertDTR.Checked)
        {
            xMLData.InvertDTR = true;
            SM.InvertDTR = 1;
        }
        else
        {
            xMLData.InvertDTR = false;
            SM.InvertDTR = 0;
        }
    }

    private void checkBoxInvertDSR_CheckedChanged(object sender, EventArgs e)
    {
        if (checkBoxInvertDSR.Checked)
        {
            xMLData.InvertDSR = true;
            SM.InvertDSR = 1;
        }
        else
        {
            xMLData.InvertDSR = false;
```

```
            SM.InvertDSR = 0;
        }
    }

    private void checkBoxInvertDCD_CheckedChanged(object sender, EventArgs e)
    {
        if (checkBoxInvertDCD.Checked)
        {
            xMLData.InvertDCD = true;
            SM.InvertDCD = 1;
        }
        else
        {
            xMLData.InvertDCD = false;
            SM.InvertDCD = 0;
        }
    }

    private void checkBoxInvertRI_CheckedChanged(object sender, EventArgs e)
    {
        if (checkBoxInvertRI.Checked)
        {
            xMLData.InvertRI = true;
            SM.InvertRI = 1;
        }
        else
        {
            xMLData.InvertRI = false;
            SM.InvertRI = 0;
        }
    }

    private void checkBoxEnableUSBRemoteWakeup_CheckedChanged(object wrap
                                                    sender, EventArgs e)
    {
        if (checkBoxEnableUSBRemoteWakeup.Checked)
        {
            xMLData.RemoteWakeup = true;
            SM.RemoteWakeup = 1;
        }
        else
        {
            xMLData.RemoteWakeup = false;
            SM.RemoteWakeup = 0;
        }
    }

    private void checkBoxHighCurrent_CheckedChanged(object sender, EventArgs e)
    {
        if (checkBoxHighCurrent.Checked)
        {
            xMLData.HighDriveIOs = true;
            SM.HighDriveIOs = 1;
        }
        else
        {
            xMLData.HighDriveIOs = false;
```

```
                SM.HighDriveIOs = 0;
        }
}

private void radioButtonBusPowered_CheckedChanged(object sender, EventArgs e)
{
    if (radioButtonBusPowered.Checked)
    {
        xMLData.SelfPowered = false;
        SM.SelfPowered = 0;
    }
    else
    {
        xMLData.SelfPowered = true;
        SM.SelfPowered = 1;
    }
}

private void radioButtonSelfPowered_CheckedChanged(object sender, EventArgs e)
{
    if (radioButtonBusPowered.Checked)
    {
        xMLData.SelfPowered = true;
        SM.SelfPowered = 1;
    }
    else
    {
        xMLData.SelfPowered = false;
        SM.SelfPowered = 0;
    }
}

#endregion

#region Accessors

private string SerialNumber = "Not Initialized";
public string serialNumber
{
    get
    {
        return SerialNumber;
    }
}

private string Description = "Not Initialized";
public string description
{
    get
    {
        return Description;
    }
}

private string LocID = "Not Initialized";
public string locID
{
```

```
        get
        {
            return LocID;
        }
    }
    #endregion
}
}
```

Visual Basic Source Code for Form1:

```
Partial Public Class Form1
    Inherits Form
    Private ftStatus As FT_STATUS = 0
    Private ftHandle As UInt32 = 0

    Private VersionDate As String = "Version 1.0 - 6/7/07"
    Private SelectedDevice As UInteger = 0

    Private SM As SM_D2XX = New SM_D2XX()

    Private dev As Select_Device = New Select_Device()

    ' Create an instance of the XMLData class
    Private xMLData As XMLData = New XMLData()

    ' Create an instance of the TerminalXMLIO class to read the terminal data
    Private xMLIO As XMLIO = New XMLIO()

    Public Sub New()
        InitializeComponent()

        editMode()
    End Sub

#Region "Menu and Toolbar"
    Private Sub newToolStripMenuItem_Click(ByVal sender As Object, wrap
                    ByVal e As EventArgs) Handles newToolStripMenuItem.Click
        NewTemp()
    End Sub wrap
    Private Sub toolStripButtonNew_Click(ByVal sender As Object,
                    ByVal e As EventArgs) Handles toolStripButtonNew.Click
        NewTemp()
    End Sub

    Private Sub openToolStripMenuItem_Click(ByVal sender As Object, wrap
                    ByVal e As EventArgs) Handles openToolStripMenuItem.Click
        OpenTemp()
    End Sub
    Private Sub toolStripButtonOpen_Click(ByVal sender As Object, wrap
                    ByVal e As EventArgs) Handles toolStripButtonOpen.Click
        OpenTemp()
    End Sub

    Private Sub saveToolStripMenuItem_Click(ByVal sender As Object, wrap
                    ByVal e As EventArgs) Handles saveToolStripMenuItem.Click
        SaveTemp()
    End Sub
    Private Sub toolStripButtonSave_Click(ByVal sender As Object, wrap
                    ByVal e As EventArgs) Handles toolStripButtonSave.Click
        SaveTemp()
    End Sub
```

```
Private Sub exitToolStripMenuItem_Click(ByVal sender As Object, wrap
                ByVal e As EventArgs) Handles exitToolStripMenuItem.Click
    Me.Close()
End Sub

Private Sub scanToolStripMenuItem_Click(ByVal sender As Object, wrap
                ByVal e As EventArgs) Handles scanToolStripMenuItem.Click
    Scan()
End Sub
Private Sub toolStripButtonScan_Click(ByVal sender As Object, wrap
                ByVal e As EventArgs) Handles toolStripButtonScan.Click
    Scan()
End Sub

Private Sub eraseToolStripMenuItem_Click(ByVal sender As Object, wrap
                ByVal e As EventArgs) Handles eraseToolStripMenuItem.Click
    '[Erase]()
End Sub
Private Sub toolStripButtonErase_Click(ByVal sender As Object, wrap
                ByVal e As EventArgs) Handles toolStripButtonErase.Click
    '[Erase]()
End Sub
'Doesn't work right so commented out
'Private Sub [Erase]()
'   Me.Cursor = Cursors.WaitCursor

'Dim temp As String = richTextBox1.Text

'   If SM.eraseEEPROM(ftHandle) Then
'           SM.cyclePort(ftHandle)
'           richTextBox1.Text = "Device was erased successfully" &
                                                Constants.vbLf
'   Else
'           richTextBox1.Text = "Device was NOT erased successfully" &
                                                Constants.vbLf
'   End If

'   richTextBox1.Text += temp

'   Me.Cursor = Cursors.Default
'End Sub

Private Sub programToolStripMenuItem_Click(ByVal sender As Object, wrap
            ByVal e As EventArgs) Handles programToolStripMenuItem.Click
    Program()
End Sub
Private Sub toolStripButtonProgram_Click(ByVal sender As Object, wrap
            ByVal e As EventArgs) Handles toolStripButtonProgram.Click
    Program()
End Sub

Private Sub readHexToolStripMenuItem_Click(ByVal sender As Object, wrap
            ByVal e As EventArgs) Handles readHexToolStripMenuItem.Click
    ReadHex()
End Sub
Private Sub ReadHex()
    ReadEE()
```

```
    End Sub

    Private Sub readAndParseToolStripMenuItem_Click(ByVal sender As wrap
        Object, ByVal e As EventArgs) Handles readAndParseToolStripMenuItem.Click
        ReadAndParse()
    End Sub

    Private Sub helpToolStripMenuItem1_Click(ByVal sender As Object, wrap
                    ByVal e As EventArgs) Handles helpToolStripMenuItem1.Click
        Help()
    End Sub
    Private Sub toolStripButtonHelp_Click(ByVal sender As Object, wrap
                    ByVal e As EventArgs) Handles toolStripButtonHelp.Click
        Help()
    End Sub
    Private Sub Help()
        System.Diagnostics.Process.Start("FT232 Programmer.pdf")

    End Sub

    Private Sub aboutToolStripMenuItem_Click(ByVal sender As Object, wrap
                    ByVal e As EventArgs) Handles aboutToolStripMenuItem.Click
        About()
    End Sub
    Private Sub toolStripButtonAbout_Click(ByVal sender As Object, wrap
                    ByVal e As EventArgs) Handles toolStripButtonAbout.Click
        About()
    End Sub
    Private Sub About()
        Dim about_Renamed As About = New About()
        about_Renamed.versionDate = VersionDate
        about_Renamed.Show()
    End Sub

    Private Sub buttonClear_Click(ByVal sender As Object, ByVal e As wrap
                                        EventArgs) Handles buttonClear.Click
        richTextBox1.Text = ""
    End Sub

#End Region

#Region "Edit or Program Mode"
    Private Sub radioButtonEditMode_CheckedChanged(ByVal sender As Object, wrap
            ByVal e As EventArgs) Handles radioButtonEditMode.CheckedChanged
        If radioButtonEditMode.Checked = True Then
            editMode()
            labelMode.Text = "Edit Mode"
        Else
            programMode()
            labelMode.Text = "Program Mode"
        End If
    End Sub

    Private Sub radioButtonProgramMode_CheckedChanged(ByVal sender As wrap
Object, ByVal e As EventArgs) Handles radioButtonProgramMode.CheckedChanged
        If radioButtonProgramMode.Checked = True Then
            programMode()
```

```
            labelMode.Text = "Program Mode"
        Else
            editMode()
            labelMode.Text = "Edit Mode"
        End If
    End Sub

    Private Sub editMode()
        Me.Text = "FT232R Programmer (Edit Mode)"

        Me.groupBoxMiscFeatures.Enabled = True
        Me.groupBoxUSBPower.Enabled = True
        Me.groupBoxInvertSignals.Enabled = True
        Me.groupBoxIOControls.Enabled = True

        Me.newToolStripMenuItem.Enabled = True
        Me.toolStripButtonNew.Enabled = True

        Me.openToolStripMenuItem.Enabled = True
        Me.toolStripButtonOpen.Enabled = True

        Me.saveToolStripMenuItem.Enabled = True
        Me.toolStripButtonSave.Enabled = True

        Me.scanToolStripMenuItem.Enabled = False
        Me.toolStripButtonScan.Enabled = False

        Me.eraseToolStripMenuItem.Enabled = False
        Me.toolStripButtonErase.Enabled = False

        Me.programToolStripMenuItem.Enabled = False
        Me.toolStripButtonProgram.Enabled = False

        Me.readHexToolStripMenuItem.Enabled = False
        Me.readAndParseToolStripMenuItem.Enabled = False

    End Sub

    Private Sub programMode()
        Me.Text = "FT232R Programmer (Program Mode)"

        Me.groupBoxMiscFeatures.Enabled = True
        Me.groupBoxUSBPower.Enabled = True
        Me.groupBoxInvertSignals.Enabled = True
        Me.groupBoxIOControls.Enabled = True

        Me.toolStripButtonNew.Enabled = False
        Me.newToolStripMenuItem.Enabled = False

        Me.openToolStripMenuItem.Enabled = False
        Me.toolStripButtonOpen.Enabled = False

        Me.saveToolStripMenuItem.Enabled = False
        Me.toolStripButtonSave.Enabled = False

        Me.scanToolStripMenuItem.Enabled = True
        Me.toolStripButtonScan.Enabled = True
```

394

```vbnet
            Me.eraseToolStripMenuItem.Enabled = True
            Me.toolStripButtonErase.Enabled = True

            Me.programToolStripMenuItem.Enabled = True
            Me.toolStripButtonProgram.Enabled = True

            Me.readHexToolStripMenuItem.Enabled = True
            Me.readAndParseToolStripMenuItem.Enabled = True


    End Sub
#End Region

#Region "Select and Open a Device"

    Private Sub Scan()
        dev.ShowDialog()

        Select Case dev.OpenBy
            Case CUInt(OPEN_BY.SERIAL_NUMBER)
                openBySerialNumber(dev.SerialNumber)
            Case CUInt(OPEN_BY.DESCRIPTION)
                openByDescription(dev.Description)
            Case CUInt(OPEN_BY.LOCATIONID)
                openByLocationID(dev.LocID)
            Case Else
                MessageBox.Show("ERROR - OpenBy = " & dev.OpenBy.ToString())
        End Select
    End Sub

    ' open by serial number
    Private Sub openBySerialNumber(ByVal SN As String)
        ftStatus = SM.openSerialNumber(SN, ftHandle)
        If ftStatus <> FT_STATUS.FT_OK Then
            MessageBox.Show("Error: openBySerialNumber failed to open device")
        End If
    End Sub

    ' open by description
    Private Sub openByDescription(ByVal description As String)
        ftStatus = SM.openDescription(description, ftHandle)
        If ftStatus <> FT_STATUS.FT_OK Then
            MessageBox.Show("Error: openByDescription failed to open port")
        End If
    End Sub

    ' open by location
    Private Sub openByLocationID(ByVal locID As UInt32)
        ftStatus = SM.openLocationID(locID, ftHandle)
        If ftStatus <> FT_STATUS.FT_OK Then
            MessageBox.Show("Error: openByLocationID( failed to open port")
        End If
    End Sub

    ' Assumes device is open
    Private Sub closeDevice()
```

```vbnet
            SM.closeDevice(ftHandle)
        End Sub

#End Region

#Region "ReadEE"
    Private Sub ReadEE()
        Dim data As Byte() = New Byte(15) {} '0xA0];
        Dim k As UInt16 = 0
        Try
            For j As UInt16 = 0 To 160 / 2 - 1 Step 8
                For i As UInt16 = 0 To 7
                    k = CUShort(i + j)
                    Dim val As UShort = SM.ReadEE(ftHandle, k)
                    data(i * 2) = CByte(val And &HFF)
                    data(i * 2 + 1) = CByte(val >> 8)
                Next i
                richTextBox1.Text += memoryDumpLine(data, (j * 2))
            Next j
        Catch ex As Exception
            MessageBox.Show("ReadEE - " & ex.Message)
            Return
        End Try
    End Sub

    Private Function memoryDumpLine(ByVal line As Byte(), ByVal address wrap
                                            As Integer) As String
        If line.Length > 16 Then
            Return "memoryDumpLine Error: line to long."
        End If

        Dim lineChar As Char() = New Char(15) {}

        convertByteArrayToCharArray(line, lineChar)

        Dim lineString As StringBuilder = New StringBuilder()

        For i As Integer = 0 To 15
            If line(i) < 16 Then ' Add leading 0 if number < F
                lineString.Append("0")
            End If
            lineString.Append(line(i).ToString("X") & " ")
        Next i

        For i As Integer = 0 To 15
            If isASCIIPrintable(line(i)) Then
                lineString.Append(lineChar(i) & " ")
            Else
                lineString.Append(". ")
            End If
        Next i

        If address < 16 Then
            Return "0" & address.ToString("X") & " : " & wrap
                            lineString.ToString() & Constants.vbLf
        Else
            Return address.ToString("X") & " : " & lineString.ToString() wrap
```

```
                                                 & Constants.vbLf
        End If
    End Function

    Public Function convertByteArrayToCharArray(ByVal byteArray As Byte(),wrap
                                    ByVal charArray As Char()) As Boolean
        ' Make sure the arrays are the same length
        If byteArray.Length <> charArray.Length Then
            Return False
        End If

        Dim ascii As Encoding = Encoding.ASCII
        ascii.GetChars(byteArray, 0, byteArray.Length, charArray, 0)

        Return True

    End Function
    Public Function isASCIIPrintable(ByVal b As Byte) As Boolean
        If b < 32 Then
            Return False
        End If
        If b > 126 Then
            Return False
        End If
        Return True
    End Function

#End Region

#Region "ReadEX"
    Private Sub ReadAndParse()
        SM.readEEPROM(ftHandle)

        richTextBox1.Text += Constants.vbLf & "VID = " & SM.VendorId.ToString("x")
        richTextBox1.Text += Constants.vbLf & "PID = " wrap
                                    & SM.ProductId.ToString("x")
        richTextBox1.Text += Constants.vbLf & "Serial Number = " & SM.SerialNumber
        richTextBox1.Text += Constants.vbLf & "Manufacturer = " & SM.Manufacturer
        richTextBox1.Text += Constants.vbLf & "manufacturerID = " wrap
                                            & SM.ManufacturerID
        richTextBox1.Text += Constants.vbLf & "description = " & SM.Description

        richTextBox1.Text += Constants.vbLf & "cbus0 = " & SM.Cbus0.ToString()
        richTextBox1.Text += Constants.vbLf & "cbus1 = " & SM.Cbus1.ToString()
        richTextBox1.Text += Constants.vbLf & "cbus2 = " & SM.Cbus2.ToString()
        richTextBox1.Text += Constants.vbLf & "cbus3 = " & SM.Cbus3.ToString()
        richTextBox1.Text += Constants.vbLf & "cbus4 = " & SM.Cbus4.ToString()

        richTextBox1.Text += Constants.vbLf & "InvertCTS = " wrap
                                    & SM.InvertCTS.ToString()
        richTextBox1.Text += Constants.vbLf & "InvertDCD = " wrap
                                    & SM.InvertDCD.ToString()
        richTextBox1.Text += Constants.vbLf & "InvertDSR = " wrap
                                    & SM.InvertDSR.ToString()
        richTextBox1.Text += Constants.vbLf & "InvertDTR = " wrap
                                    & SM.InvertDTR.ToString()
        richTextBox1.Text += Constants.vbLf & "InvertRI = " wrap
```

```
                                        & SM.InvertRI.ToString()
        richTextBox1.Text += Constants.vbLf & "InvertRTS = " wrap
                                        & SM.InvertRTS.ToS wrap tring()
        richTextBox1.Text += Constants.vbLf & "InvertRXD = " wrap
                                        & SM.InvertRXD.ToString()
        richTextBox1.Text += Constants.vbLf & "InvertTXD = " wrap
                                        & SM.InvertTXD.ToString()


        textBoxManufacturer.Text = SM.Manufacturer
        textBoxProductDescription.Text = SM.Description
        textBoxSerialNumber.Text = SM.SerialNumber
        textBoxVID.Text = SM.VendorId.ToString("X")
        textBoxPID.Text = SM.ProductId.ToString("X")
        textBoxMfgID.Text = SM.ManufacturerID.ToString()

        textBoxMaxBusPower.Text = SM.MaxPower.ToString()

        comboBoxCBus0.SelectedIndex = SM.Cbus0
        comboBoxCBus1.SelectedIndex = SM.Cbus1
        comboBoxCBus2.SelectedIndex = SM.Cbus2
        comboBoxCBus3.SelectedIndex = SM.Cbus3
        comboBoxCBus4.SelectedIndex = SM.Cbus4

        If SM.InvertCTS <> 0 Then
            checkBoxInvertCTS.Checked = True
        Else
            checkBoxInvertCTS.Checked = False
        End If

        If SM.InvertDCD <> 0 Then
            checkBoxInvertDCD.Checked = True
        Else
            checkBoxInvertDCD.Checked = False
        End If

        If SM.InvertDSR <> 0 Then
            checkBoxInvertDSR.Checked = True
        Else
            checkBoxInvertDSR.Checked = False
        End If

        If SM.InvertDTR <> 0 Then
            checkBoxInvertDTR.Checked = True
        Else
            checkBoxInvertDTR.Checked = False
        End If

        If SM.InvertRI <> 0 Then
            checkBoxInvertRI.Checked = True
        Else
            checkBoxInvertRI.Checked = False
        End If

        If SM.InvertRTS <> 0 Then
            checkBoxInvertRTS.Checked = True
        Else
```

```vb
            checkBoxInvertRTS.Checked = False
        End If

        If SM.InvertRXD <> 0 Then
            checkBoxInvertRXD.Checked = True
        Else
            checkBoxInvertRXD.Checked = False
        End If

        If SM.InvertTXD <> 0 Then
            checkBoxInvertTXD.Checked = True
        Else
            checkBoxInvertTXD.Checked = False
        End If

    End Sub
#End Region

#Region "www.smileymicros.com"
    Private Sub pictureBox1_DoubleClick(ByVal sender As Object, wrap
                    ByVal e As EventArgs) Handles pictureBox1.DoubleClick
        System.Diagnostics.Process.Start("www.smileymicros.com")
    End Sub

    Private Sub linkLabel1_LinkClicked(ByVal sender As Object, wrap
        ByVal e As LinkLabelLinkClickedEventArgs) Handles linkLabel1.LinkClicked
        System.Diagnostics.Process.Start("www.smileymicros.com")
    End Sub

    Private Sub pictureBox1_Click(ByVal sender As Object, ByVal e As wrap
                    EventArgs) Handles pictureBox1.Click
        System.Diagnostics.Process.Start("www.smileymicros.com")
    End Sub
#End Region

    Private Sub NewTemp()
        loadXMLData()
    End Sub

    Private Sub OpenTemp()
        openFileDialog1.Filter = "XML Files (*.xml)|*.xml"
        openFileDialog1.Title = "Open"
        openFileDialog1.DefaultExt = ".xml"

        If openFileDialog1.ShowDialog() = wrap
                        System.Windows.Forms.DialogResult.OK Then
            xMLData = xMLIO.XMLRead(openFileDialog1.FileName)
            loadXMLData()
        Else
            MessageBox.Show("Error: openFileDialog DialogResult wrap
                        != OK" & Constants.vbLf & "Loading default values.")
        End If
    End Sub

    Private Sub loadXMLData()
        textBoxVID.Text = xMLData.VendorId.ToString("X")
        textBoxPID.Text = xMLData.ProductId.ToString("X")
```

399

```vb
        textBoxMfgID.Text = xMLData.ManufacturerID
        textBoxManufacturer.Text = xMLData.Manufacturer
        textBoxProductDescription.Text = xMLData.Description
        textBoxSerialNumber.Text = xMLData.SerialNumber

        textBoxMaxBusPower.Text = xMLData.MaxPower.ToString()

        checkBoxEnablePlugAndPlay.Checked = xMLData.PnP

        If xMLData.SelfPowered Then
            radioButtonSelfPowered.Checked = True
        Else
            radioButtonBusPowered.Checked = True
        End If

        checkBoxEnableUSBRemoteWakeup.Checked = xMLData.RemoteWakeup

        checkBoxHighCurrent.Checked = xMLData.HighDriveIOs

        checkBoxInvertTXD.Checked = xMLData.InvertTXD
        checkBoxInvertRXD.Checked = xMLData.InvertRXD
        checkBoxInvertRTS.Checked = xMLData.InvertRTS
        checkBoxInvertCTS.Checked = xMLData.InvertCTS
        checkBoxInvertDTR.Checked = xMLData.InvertDTR
        checkBoxInvertDCD.Checked = xMLData.InvertDCD
        checkBoxInvertRI.Checked = xMLData.InvertRI

        ' Cbus Mux control
        comboBoxCBus0.SelectedIndex = CInt(Fix(xMLData.Cbus0))
        comboBoxCBus1.SelectedIndex = CInt(Fix(xMLData.Cbus1))
        comboBoxCBus2.SelectedIndex = CInt(Fix(xMLData.Cbus2))
        comboBoxCBus3.SelectedIndex = CInt(Fix(xMLData.Cbus3))
        comboBoxCBus4.SelectedIndex = CInt(Fix(xMLData.Cbus4))
End Sub

Private Sub SaveTemp()
        saveFileDialog1.Filter = "XML Files (*.xml)|*.xml"
        saveFileDialog1.Title = "Save"
        saveFileDialog1.DefaultExt = ".xml"

        If saveFileDialog1.ShowDialog() = _
                                System.Windows.Forms.DialogResult.OK Then
            saveXMLData()
            xMLIO.XMLWrite(xMLData, saveFileDialog1.FileName)
        Else
            MessageBox.Show("Error: saveFileDialog DialogResult _
                            != OK" & Constants.vbLf & "File not saved.")
        End If
End Sub

Private Sub saveXMLData()
        Dim temp As UShort = 0

        Try
            temp = Convert.ToUInt16(textBoxVID.Text, 16)
        Catch ex As Exception
```

```
        MessageBox.Show("Error: saveXMLData wrap
                Convert.ToUInt16(textBoxVID.Text) error: " & ex.ToString())
    Return
End Try
If temp = 0 Then
    MessageBox.Show("FILE NOT SAVED" & wrap
                Constants.vbLf + Constants.vbLf & wrap
                "Must set VID and PID to something.")
    Return
End If
xMLData.VendorId = temp


Try
    temp = Convert.ToUInt16(textBoxPID.Text, 16)
Catch ex As Exception
    MessageBox.Show("Error: saveXMLData wrap
                Convert.ToUInt16(textBoxPID.Text) error: " & ex.ToString())
    Return
End Try
xMLData.ProductId = temp

xMLData.Manufacturer = textBoxManufacturer.Text
xMLData.Description = textBoxProductDescription.Text
xMLData.SerialNumber = textBoxSerialNumber.Text
xMLData.ManufacturerID = textBoxMfgID.Text

Try
    temp = Convert.ToUInt16(textBoxMaxBusPower.Text)
Catch ex As Exception
    MessageBox.Show("Error: saveXMLData wrap
        Convert.ToUInt16(textBoxMaxBusPower.Text) error: " & ex.ToString())
    Return
End Try
xMLData.MaxPower = temp


xMLData.PnP = checkBoxEnablePlugAndPlay.Checked

xMLData.SelfPowered = radioButtonSelfPowered.Checked

xMLData.RemoteWakeup = checkBoxEnableUSBRemoteWakeup.Checked

xMLData.HighDriveIOs = checkBoxHighCurrent.Checked

xMLData.InvertTXD = checkBoxInvertTXD.Checked
xMLData.InvertRXD = checkBoxInvertRXD.Checked
xMLData.InvertRTS = checkBoxInvertRTS.Checked
xMLData.InvertCTS = checkBoxInvertCTS.Checked
xMLData.InvertDTR = checkBoxInvertDTR.Checked
xMLData.InvertDCD = checkBoxInvertDCD.Checked
xMLData.InvertRI = checkBoxInvertRI.Checked


' Cbus Mux control
xMLData.Cbus0 = CByte(comboBoxCBus0.SelectedIndex)
xMLData.Cbus1 = CByte(comboBoxCBus1.SelectedIndex)
xMLData.Cbus2 = CByte(comboBoxCBus2.SelectedIndex)
```

```
        xMLData.Cbus3 = CByte(comboBoxCBus3.SelectedIndex)
        xMLData.Cbus4 = CByte(comboBoxCBus4.SelectedIndex)
    End Sub

    Private Sub Program()
        Me.Cursor = Cursors.WaitCursor

        Dim temp As String = richTextBox1.Text
        If SM.programEEPROM(ftHandle) Then
            SM.cyclePort(ftHandle)
            richTextBox1.Text = "Device was programmed successfully" wrap
                                                    & Constants.vbLf
        Else
            richTextBox1.Text = "Device was NOT programmed successfully" wrap
                                                    & Constants.vbLf
        End If
        richTextBox1.Text += temp
        Me.Cursor = Cursors.Default
    End Sub

#Region "User Input"

    Private Sub textBoxVID_TextChanged(ByVal sender As Object, wrap
                        ByVal e As EventArgs) Handles textBoxVID.TextChanged
        SM.VendorId = Convert.ToUInt16(textBoxVID.Text, 16)
        xMLData.VendorId = SM.VendorId
    End Sub

    Private Sub textBoxPID_TextChanged(ByVal sender As Object, wrap
                        ByVal e As EventArgs) Handles textBoxPID.TextChanged
        SM.ProductId = Convert.ToUInt16(textBoxPID.Text, 16)
        xMLData.ProductId = SM.ProductId
    End Sub

    Private Sub textBoxSerialNumber_TextChanged(ByVal sender As Object, wrap
            ByVal e As EventArgs) Handles textBoxSerialNumber.TextChanged
        SM.SerialNumber = textBoxSerialNumber.Text
        xMLData.SerialNumber = SM.SerialNumber
    End Sub

    Private Sub textBoxManufacturer_TextChanged(ByVal sender As Object, wrap
            ByVal e As EventArgs) Handles textBoxManufacturer.TextChanged
        SM.Manufacturer = textBoxManufacturer.Text
        xMLData.Manufacturer = SM.Manufacturer
    End Sub

    Private Sub textBoxProductDescription_TextChanged(ByVal sender As wrap
                        Object, ByVal e As EventArgs) Handles wrap
                        textBoxProductDescription.TextChanged
        SM.Description = textBoxProductDescription.Text
        xMLData.Description = SM.Description
    End Sub

    Private Sub textBoxMfgID_TextChanged(ByVal sender As Object, wrap
                    ByVal e As EventArgs) Handles textBoxMfgID.TextChanged
        SM.ManufacturerID = textBoxMfgID.Text
        xMLData.ManufacturerID = SM.ManufacturerID
```

```
End Sub

Private Sub textBoxMaxBusPower_TextChanged(ByVal sender As Object, wrap
        ByVal e As EventArgs) Handles textBoxMaxBusPower.TextChanged
    SM.MaxPower = Convert.ToUInt16(textBoxMaxBusPower.Text)
    xMLData.MaxPower = SM.MaxPower
End Sub

Private Sub comboBoxCBus0_SelectedValueChanged(ByVal sender As Object, wrap
        ByVal e As EventArgs) Handles comboBoxCBus0.SelectedValueChanged
    SM.Cbus0 = CByte(comboBoxCBus0.SelectedIndex)
    xMLData.Cbus0 = SM.Cbus0
End Sub

Private Sub comboBoxCBus1_SelectedValueChanged(ByVal sender As Object, wrap
        ByVal e As EventArgs) Handles comboBoxCBus1.SelectedValueChanged
    SM.Cbus1 = CByte(comboBoxCBus1.SelectedIndex)
    xMLData.Cbus1 = SM.Cbus1
End Sub

Private Sub comboBoxCBus2_SelectedValueChanged(ByVal sender As Object, wrap
        ByVal e As EventArgs) Handles comboBoxCBus2.SelectedValueChanged
    SM.Cbus2 = CByte(comboBoxCBus2.SelectedIndex)
    xMLData.Cbus2 = SM.Cbus2
End Sub

Private Sub comboBoxCBus3_SelectedValueChanged(ByVal sender As Object, wrap
        ByVal e As EventArgs) Handles comboBoxCBus3.SelectedValueChanged
    SM.Cbus3 = CByte(comboBoxCBus3.SelectedIndex)
    xMLData.Cbus3 = SM.Cbus3
End Sub

Private Sub comboBoxCBus4_SelectedIndexChanged(ByVal sender As Object, wrap
        ByVal e As EventArgs) Handles comboBoxCBus4.SelectedIndexChanged
    SM.Cbus4 = CByte(comboBoxCBus4.SelectedIndex)
    xMLData.Cbus4 = SM.Cbus4
End Sub

Private Sub checkBoxInvertTXD_CheckedChanged(ByVal sender As Object, wrap
        ByVal e As EventArgs) Handles checkBoxInvertTXD.CheckedChanged
    If checkBoxInvertTXD.Checked Then
        xMLData.InvertTXD = True
        SM.InvertTXD = 1
    Else
        xMLData.InvertTXD = False
        SM.InvertTXD = 0
    End If
End Sub

Private Sub checkBoxInvertRXD_CheckedChanged(ByVal sender As Object, wrap
        ByVal e As EventArgs) Handles checkBoxInvertRXD.CheckedChanged
    If checkBoxInvertRXD.Checked Then
        xMLData.InvertRXD = True
        SM.InvertRXD = 1
    Else
        xMLData.InvertRXD = False
        SM.InvertRXD = 0
```

```
        End If
End Sub

Private Sub checkBoxInvertRTS_CheckedChanged(ByVal sender As Object, wrap
        ByVal e As EventArgs) Handles checkBoxInvertRTS.CheckedChanged
    If checkBoxInvertRTS.Checked Then
        xMLData.InvertRTS = True
        SM.InvertRTS = 1
    Else
        xMLData.InvertRTS = False
        SM.InvertRTS = 0
    End If
End Sub

Private Sub checkBoxInvertCTS_CheckedChanged(ByVal sender As Object, wrap
        ByVal e As EventArgs) Handles checkBoxInvertCTS.CheckedChanged
    If checkBoxInvertCTS.Checked Then
        xMLData.InvertCTS = True
        SM.InvertCTS = 1
    Else
        xMLData.InvertCTS = False
        SM.InvertCTS = 0
    End If
End Sub

Private Sub checkBoxInvertDTR_CheckedChanged(ByVal sender As Object, wrap
        ByVal e As EventArgs) Handles checkBoxInvertDTR.CheckedChanged
    If checkBoxInvertDTR.Checked Then
        xMLData.InvertDTR = True
        SM.InvertDTR = 1
    Else
        xMLData.InvertDTR = False
        SM.InvertDTR = 0
    End If
End Sub

Private Sub checkBoxInvertDSR_CheckedChanged(ByVal sender As Object, wrap
        ByVal e As EventArgs) Handles checkBoxInvertDSR.CheckedChanged
    If checkBoxInvertDSR.Checked Then
        xMLData.InvertDSR = True
        SM.InvertDSR = 1
    Else
        xMLData.InvertDSR = False
        SM.InvertDSR = 0
    End If
End Sub

Private Sub checkBoxInvertDCD_CheckedChanged(ByVal sender As Object, wrap
        ByVal e As EventArgs) Handles checkBoxInvertDCD.CheckedChanged
    If checkBoxInvertDCD.Checked Then
        xMLData.InvertDCD = True
        SM.InvertDCD = 1
    Else
        xMLData.InvertDCD = False
        SM.InvertDCD = 0
    End If
End Sub
```

```
Private Sub checkBoxInvertRI_CheckedChanged(ByVal sender As Object, wrap
        ByVal e As EventArgs) Handles checkBoxInvertRI.CheckedChanged
    If checkBoxInvertRI.Checked Then
        xMLData.InvertRI = True
        SM.InvertRI = 1
    Else
        xMLData.InvertRI = False
        SM.InvertRI = 0
    End If
End Sub

Private Sub checkBoxEnableUSBRemoteWakeup_CheckedChanged(ByVal sender wrap
                    As Object, ByVal e As EventArgs) Handles wrap
                    checkBoxEnableUSBRemoteWakeup.CheckedChanged
    If checkBoxEnableUSBRemoteWakeup.Checked Then
        xMLData.RemoteWakeup = True
        SM.RemoteWakeup = 1
    Else
        xMLData.RemoteWakeup = False
        SM.RemoteWakeup = 0
    End If
End Sub

Private Sub checkBoxHighCurrent_CheckedChanged(ByVal sender As Object, wrap
        ByVal e As EventArgs) Handles checkBoxHighCurrent.CheckedChanged
    If checkBoxHighCurrent.Checked Then
        xMLData.HighDriveIOs = True
        SM.HighDriveIOs = 1
    Else
        xMLData.HighDriveIOs = False
        SM.HighDriveIOs = 0
    End If
End Sub

Private Sub radioButtonBusPowered_CheckedChanged(ByVal sender As Object, wrap
        ByVal e As EventArgs) Handles radioButtonBusPowered.CheckedChanged
    If radioButtonBusPowered.Checked Then
        xMLData.SelfPowered = False
        SM.SelfPowered = 0
    Else
        xMLData.SelfPowered = True
        SM.SelfPowered = 1
    End If
End Sub

Private Sub radioButtonSelfPowered_CheckedChanged(ByVal sender As wrap
                    Object, ByVal e As EventArgs) Handles wrap
                    radioButtonSelfPowered.CheckedChanged
    If radioButtonBusPowered.Checked Then
        xMLData.SelfPowered = True
        SM.SelfPowered = 1
    Else
        xMLData.SelfPowered = False
        SM.SelfPowered = 0
    End If
End Sub
```

405

```
#End Region

#Region "Accessors"

    Private SerialNumber_Renamed As String = "Not Initialized"
    Public ReadOnly Property serialNumber() As String
        Get
            Return SerialNumber_Renamed
        End Get
    End Property

    Private Description_Renamed As String = "Not Initialized"
    Public ReadOnly Property description() As String
        Get
            Return Description_Renamed
        End Get
    End Property

    Private LocID_Renamed As String = "Not Initialized"
    Public ReadOnly Property locID() As String
        Get
            Return LocID_Renamed
        End Get
    End Property
#End Region
End Class
```

Appendix 1: ASCII Table

Table 1: ASCII Table

```
Char  Dec   Hex | Char  Dec   Hex | Char  Dec   Hex | Char Dec    Hex
----------------------------------------------------------------------
(nul)   0  0x00 | (sp)   32  0x20 | @     64  0x40 |  `        96  0x60
(soh)   1  0x01 | !      33  0x21 | A     65  0x41 | a         97  0x61
(stx)   2  0x02 | "      34  0x22 | B     66  0x42 | b         98  0x62
(etx)   3  0x03 | #      35  0x23 | C     67  0x43 | c         99  0x63
(eot)   4  0x04 | $      36  0x24 | D     68  0x44 | d        100  0x64
(enq)   5  0x05 | %      37  0x25 | E     69  0x45 | e        101  0x65
(ack)   6  0x06 | &      38  0x26 | F     70  0x46 | f        102  0x66
(bel)   7  0x07 | '      39  0x27 | G     71  0x47 | g        103  0x67
(bs)    8  0x08 | (      40  0x28 | H     72  0x48 | h        104  0x68
(ht)    9  0x09 | )      41  0x29 | I     73  0x49 | i        105  0x69
(nl)   10  0x0a | *      42  0x2a | J     74  0x4a | j        106  0x6a
(vt)   11  0x0b | +      43  0x2b | K     75  0x4b | k        107  0x6b
(np)   12  0x0c | ,      44  0x2c | L     76  0x4c | l        108  0x6c
(cr)   13  0x0d | -      45  0x2d | M     77  0x4d | m        109  0x6d
(so)   14  0x0e | .      46  0x2e | N     78  0x4e | n        110  0x6e
(si)   15  0x0f | /      47  0x2f | O     79  0x4f | o        111  0x6f
(dle)  16  0x10 | 0      48  0x30 | P     80  0x50 | p        112  0x70
(dc1)  17  0x11 | 1      49  0x31 | Q     81  0x51 | q        113  0x71
(dc2)  18  0x12 | 2      50  0x32 | R     82  0x52 | r        114  0x72
(dc3)  19  0x13 | 3      51  0x33 | S     83  0x53 | s        115  0x73
(dc4)  20  0x14 | 4      52  0x34 | T     84  0x54 | t        116  0x74
(nak)  21  0x15 | 5      53  0x35 | U     85  0x55 | u        117  0x75
(syn)  22  0x16 | 6      54  0x36 | V     86  0x56 | v        118  0x76
(etb)  23  0x17 | 7      55  0x37 | W     87  0x57 | w        119  0x77
(can)  24  0x18 | 8      56  0x38 | X     88  0x58 | x        120  0x78
(em)   25  0x19 | 9      57  0x39 | Y     89  0x59 | y        121  0x79
(sub)  26  0x1a | :      58  0x3a | Z     90  0x5a | z        122  0x7a
(esc)  27  0x1b | ;      59  0x3b | [     91  0x5b | {        123  0x7b
(fs)   28  0x1c | <      60  0x3c | \     92  0x5c | |        124  0x7c
(gs)   29  0x1d | =      61  0x3d | ]     93  0x5d | }        125  0x7d
(rs)   30  0x1e | >      62  0x3e | ^     94  0x5e | ~        126  0x7e
(us)   31  0x1f | ?      63  0x3f | _     95  0x5f | (del)   127  0x7f
```

```
Name  Description  C Escape Sequence
nul   null byte         \0
bel   bell character    \a
bs    backspace         \b
ht    horizontal tab    \t
np    formfeed          \f
nl    newline           \n
cr    carriage return   \r
```

Appendix 2: Decimal, Hexadecimal, and Binary

Table 2: Decimal, Hexadecimal, and Binary Conversion

Dec	Hex	Bin	Dec	Hex	Bin	Dec	Hex	Bin	Dec	Hex	Bin
0	0	00000000	64	40	01000000	128	80	10000000	192	c0	11000000
1	1	00000001	65	41	01000001	129	81	10000001	193	c1	11000001
2	2	00000010	66	42	01000010	130	82	10000010	194	c2	11000010
3	3	00000011	67	43	01000011	131	83	10000011	195	c3	11000011
4	4	00000100	68	44	01000100	132	84	10000100	196	c4	11000100
5	5	00000101	69	45	01000101	133	85	10000101	197	c5	11000101
6	6	00000110	70	46	01000110	134	86	10000110	198	c6	11000110
7	7	00000111	71	47	01000111	135	87	10000111	199	c7	11000111
8	8	00001000	72	48	01001000	136	88	10001000	200	c8	11001000
9	9	00001001	73	49	01001001	137	89	10001001	201	c9	11001001
10	a	00001010	74	4a	01001010	138	8a	10001010	202	ca	11001010
11	b	00001011	75	4b	01001011	139	8b	10001011	203	cb	11001011
12	c	00001100	76	4c	01001100	140	8c	10001100	204	cc	11001100
13	d	00001101	77	4d	01001101	141	8d	10001101	205	cd	11001101
14	e	00001110	78	4e	01001110	142	8e	10001110	206	ce	11001110
15	f	00001111	79	4f	01001111	143	8f	10001111	207	cf	11001111
16	10	00010000	80	50	01010000	144	90	10010000	208	d0	11010000
17	11	00010001	81	51	01010001	145	91	10010001	209	d1	11010001
18	12	00010010	82	52	01010010	146	92	10010010	210	d2	11010010
19	13	00010011	83	53	01010011	147	93	10010011	211	d3	11010011
20	14	00010100	84	54	01010100	148	94	10010100	212	d4	11010100
21	15	00010101	85	55	01010101	149	95	10010101	213	d5	11010101
22	16	00010110	86	56	01010110	150	96	10010110	214	d6	11010110
23	17	00010111	87	57	01010111	151	97	10010111	215	d7	11010111
24	18	00011000	88	58	01011000	152	98	10011000	216	d8	11011000
25	19	00011001	89	59	01011001	153	99	10011001	217	d9	11011001
26	1a	00011010	90	5a	01011010	154	9a	10011010	218	da	11011010
27	1b	00011011	91	5b	01011011	155	9b	10011011	219	db	11011011
28	1c	00011100	92	5c	01011100	156	9c	10011100	220	dc	11011100
29	1d	00011101	93	5d	01011101	157	9d	10011101	221	dd	11011101
30	1e	00011110	94	5e	01011110	158	9e	10011110	222	de	11011110
31	1f	00011111	95	5f	01011111	159	9f	10011111	223	df	11011111
32	20	00100000	96	60	01100000	160	a0	10100000	224	e0	11100000
33	21	00100001	97	61	01100001	161	a1	10100001	225	e1	11100001
34	22	00100010	98	62	01100010	162	a2	10100010	226	e2	11100010
35	23	00100011	99	63	01100011	163	a3	10100011	227	e3	11100011
36	24	00100100	100	64	01100100	164	a4	10100100	228	e4	11100100
37	25	00100101	101	65	01100101	165	a5	10100101	229	e5	11100101
38	26	00100110	102	66	01100110	166	a6	10100110	230	e6	11100110
39	27	00100111	103	67	01100111	167	a7	10100111	231	e7	11100111
40	28	00101000	104	68	01101000	168	a8	10101000	232	e8	11101000
41	29	00101001	105	69	01101001	169	a9	10101001	233	e9	11101001
42	2a	00101010	106	6a	01101010	170	aa	10101010	234	ea	11101010
43	2b	00101011	107	6b	01101011	171	ab	10101011	235	eb	11101011
44	2c	00101100	108	6c	01101100	172	ac	10101100	236	ec	11101100

409

45	2d	00101101	109	6d	01101101	173	ad	10101101	237	ed	11101101
46	2e	00101110	110	6e	01101110	174	ae	10101110	238	ee	11101110
47	2f	00101111	111	6f	01101111	175	af	10101111	239	ef	11101111
48	30	00110000	112	70	01110000	176	b0	10110000	240	f0	11110000
49	31	00110001	113	71	01110001	177	b1	10110001	241	f1	11110001
50	32	00110010	114	72	01110010	178	b2	10110010	242	f2	11110010
51	33	00110011	115	73	01110011	179	b3	10110011	243	f3	11110011
52	34	00110100	116	74	01110100	180	b4	10110100	244	f4	11110100
53	35	00110101	117	75	01110101	181	b5	10110101	245	f5	11110101
54	36	00110110	118	76	01110110	182	b6	10110110	246	f6	11110110
55	37	00110111	119	77	01110111	183	b7	10110111	247	f7	11110111
56	38	00111000	120	78	01111000	184	b8	10111000	248	f8	11111000
57	39	00111001	121	79	01111001	185	b9	10111001	249	f9	11111001
58	3a	00111010	122	7a	01111010	186	ba	10111010	250	fa	11111010
59	3b	00111011	123	7b	01111011	187	bb	10111011	251	fb	11111011
60	3c	00111100	124	7c	01111100	188	bc	10111100	252	fc	11111100
61	3d	00111101	125	7d	01111101	189	bd	10111101	253	fd	11111101
62	3e	00111110	126	7e	01111110	190	be	10111110	254	fe	11111110
63	3f	00111111	127	7f	01111111	191	bf	10111111	255	ff	11111111

Index

411

Printed in the United States
116546LV00002B/79/A